CADDISFLIES

Gary LaFontaine

drawings by Harvey Eckert

The Lyons Press
Guilford, Connecticut
An imprint of The Globe Pequot Press

This book is dedicated to
ALFRED LaFONTAINE:
It is not necessary for a father
to understand the obsessions
of a son; it is enough
if he appreciates them.

The Lyons Press is an imprint of The Globe Pequot Press.

Library of Congress Catalog Card Number 83-61055

LaFontaine, Gary.
    Caddisflies.

        Bibliography: p. 336
        Includes index.
        1. Trout fishing. 2. Caddis-flies. 3. Fly fishing.
4. Fly tying. I. Title.
SH687.L317   799.1'755   81-10430
ISBN 0-941130-98-3   AACR2

Design and Production by Woods End Studio

Manufactured in the United States of America
First edition/Fifteenth printing

Contents

Acknowledgments

There is one question that friends have asked me repeatedly, "Why has it taken ten years to write this book?"

It was not the writing that took so long. If doing this book only involved filling five hundred or so pages with words, it would have been done in a matter of months—not years. The subject, however, proved to be so fascinating that it deserved much more than just a rehash of past literature or a smattering of untested opinions. Caddisflies were worth the research needed to identify and solve the fly-fishing problems that they created on streams and lakes. Finding the answers involved controlled experiments and a lot of study. It also involved the help of many generous people.

The people who make the greatest sacrifice during the development of a book are the author's family—and this was certainly true in my case. My wife Ardyce read and reread the original drafts and did a large portion of the typing and copying. My daughter Heather, a one-man gang when it came to collecting specimens, stalked streams with me all across the country. My brother Jay Gaudreau helped extensively with the photography. My father-in-law Jonas Johnson collected scientific papers for me. These people also provided a limitless amount of moral support.

Two people in particular gave so unstintingly of their time and skills that this book would have been impossible without them. Ken Thompson, with his professional abilities as an entomologist, and Graham Marsh, with his efforts in the original experiments, each put in over 1,000 hours apiece on the research for *Caddisflies*.

Professional entomologists without exception answered my requests for information with enthusiasm and thoroughness. Professors and graduate students who helped me by sending scientific papers, providing insect specimens, or identifying my collections were Chuck Hawkins, Steve Johnson, Don Alstad, Tim Hansen, Dr. R. L. Blickle, Dr. Stamford Smith, Dr. William Hilsenhoff, Dr. Donald Denning, Dr. A. Sheldon, Dr. Oliver Flint, Dr. George Edmunds, Dr. Glenn B. Wiggins, Dr. Richard Baumann, Dr. George Roemhild, Dr. Merlyn Brusven, Dr. Robert Newell, Dr. Vincent Resh, Russ Biggam, and Dr. J. V. Ward.

Dr. Norman Anderson has graciously supplied the photographs by Jon Spier (which originally appeared in Dr. Anderson's *The Distribution and Biology of the Oregon Trichoptera*).

Fly-fishing friends who contributed to this book by collecting samples of caddisflies from around the country, by searching for scientific papers, or by arranging meetings with entomologists were Kevin Toman, Fred Arbona, Jr., Ron Frederickson, Dave Engerbretson, Arnie Gidlow, Fred Reimherr, Bruce Solomon, John Gantner, Ron Cordes, Mike Lawson, Bill Blackburn, Rex Wheeler, Joe Mackicich, Cindy Mackicich, Tom Poole, Bob Anderson, Tory Stosich, Vern McArthur, Wayne Douglas, Dan Antonelli, Randy Ochse, Greg Taylor, and Howard Bresson.

The DuPont Company, through the efforts of Charles Booz, Howard Benner, and Ed Berling, provided a great deal of technical assistance for determining the physical properties of Sparkle Yarn (Antron).

Robert Dent of the Anaconda Company supplied the biological data on the rehabilitation of the upper Clark Fork River.

Howard West of the 3M Company aided many of my angling experiments by sending an endless supply of Scientific Angler lines (and also by providing sink-rate data on these lines).

Rich Anderson and Frank Johnson, owners of Streamside Anglers, arranged important contacts for me with other fly fisherman interested in caddisflies.

Don Pillotte of the Montana State University Photographic Services gave me much invaluable advice on close-up photography. Larry Bragg added his darkroom skills to the photographic effort.

Fellow angling writers Ernest Schwiebert, Larry Solomon, and Eric Leiser have generously shared their ideas about caddisflies with me during some long and enjoyable conversations.

Joan and Phil Wright provided me over the years with a number of valuable contacts.

A number of fly-fishing authors over the past few years have aided my efforts immeasurably by supporting my caddisfly "heresies" in their own writings. Their reports of success with my patterns and tactics have converted a growing web of fly fishermen to these ideas. These writers include Jack Dennis, Paul Dodds, Dan Abrams, Ken Parkany, Bob Saile, Charlie Myers, Bill Seeples, Andre Puyans, Eric Peper, and Bill Saunders.

Some of the material in this book has appeared previously in magazines. Pre-publishing parts from a book serves two purposes. The introduction of new ideas allows a writer to test how well his readership accepts such heresies. The appearance of innovations in published form also means that the ideas are in effect "patented" for the writer.

Parts of Chapter 3, mainly my original theories on the triggering characteristics of insects and the control these visual traits have on the selective feeding of trout, appeared in the May 1978 issue of *Sports Afield* in the article, "Creating the Effective Fly Pattern." Also, the fly-tying instructions for the various caddisfly patterns in Chapter 3 appeared in my regular column in *The Fly Tyer*.

"The Dynamics of Nymph Fishing," Part 1 of Chapter 5, introducing the concept of a subsurface buffer zone where drifting insects are concentrated, appeared in slightly different form in the March/April 1979 issue of *Fishing World*.

"Will the Real Caddisfly Pupa Please Stand Up?"—Part 1 of Chapter 6—my underwater observations of emerging caddisfly pupae, was in the 1980 *Scientific Anglers Fly Fishing Handbook* (under the title "The Misunderstood Caddis Pupa").

Chapter 9, "The Biology of Caddisflies," appeared as a four-part series in *The Fly Tyer* (Summer 1979, Fall 1979, Winter 1980, Spring 1980).

Some segments of Chapter 12, the Insect Listings, were also prepublished. Comments on night fishing and nighttime caddisflies appeared in my January 1979 *Field & Stream* article, "Trophy Trout." The facts about the caseless, free drift of two caddisfly genera (*Glossosoma* and *Dicosmoecus*) appeared in copyrighted form in the 1978 Angler's Agency catalog.

The Caddisfly Revolution

Throughout fly-fishing history caddisflies have been treated as if they were less important than mayflies. They have been the drab sisters, disparaged or ignored, in the literature. On the stream they have been a puzzle that anglers have chosen to neglect all too often. But for what reason? Certainly not because of the relative value of these insects to the trout. Nor has it been because of their relative value to fly fishermen on the trout stream.

There have been studies on both running and stillwater habitats that show the importance of caddisflies as a food source for trout. Even the well-known research by Paul Needham for *Trout Streams* (1938) demonstrates the important role caddisflies play in the diet of a trout:

Caddisfly adult

Comparison of Available Bottom Foods with Those Consumed by Trout*

Order	Available Aquatic Foods	Aquatic Foods Eaten by Trout
Mayfly nymphs	36.9%	30.1%
Caddisfly larvae and pupae	21.3	44.7
Stonefly nymphs	14.7	3.5
Fly larvae and pupae	13.8	15.8
Beetle larvae	7.6	2.8
Crayfish and scuds	3.7	1.1
Miscellaneous	1.9	1.9

*Needham, Paul R., *Trout Streams*. Ithaca, N.Y.: Comstock, 1938.

Mayfly adult

Through angling history mayflies have been favored by fly fishermen while caddisflies have been virtually ignored.

This research was limited in a number of ways. It was conducted on small, freestone streams. Most of the trout taken for stomach samples were tiny, about 6½ inches average and ranging in size from three inches to twelve inches. The collections were neither numerous enough nor structured enough to allow a valid breakdown.

A recent study on the Saluda River, a tailwater fishery in South Carolina, indicates that for bigger trout, ten to fifteen inches, caddisflies can constitute as much as forty-five percent of the total diet—significantly more than the second- and third-place two-winged flies and mayflies. On other types of water their importance can vary considerably from this figure, but they are a well-represented order in every trout habitat.[1]

Fly fishermen on the stream, of course, have to face specific situations and they need to know how selectively trout feed on individual species. Here, too, caddisflies are very important. There are three factors that lock fish into a rigid feeding pattern: high population densities of an insect species, accumulations of vulnerable individuals, and unique visual characteristics for the particular insect life stage. These factors working together, as often happens with caddisflies, inspire such strong selectivity that the insect cannot be ignored. General flies and tactics are not adequate for matching the activity of a major caddisfly species that triggers selective feeding.

In spite of the evidence showing that caddisflies are an important food supply on many trout streams, until the late 1970s not one major book dealt with the insect. This lack of attention seems like more than a slight imbalance.

Fly fishermen, of course, have been finding out for themselves just how important caddisflies are on the stream. It was becoming evident that dry-fly and wet-fly imitations of mayflies, the most popular pattern types, were not even solving the majority of feeding situations. There were soon demands at the fishing level for better flies and techniques to imitate the caddisflies, and the angling community began to place the different aquatic insects in a more balanced perspective, recognizing the importance of one without lessening the significance of another. No immediate body of literature on caddisflies sprang up to match the volumes on mayflies, but at least the problems were beginning to be explored in print.

Why have caddisflies been slighted? There are many reasons, one of which is that fly fishermen have seldom been able to catch fish when caddisflies are on the water. The consistent failure to solve the problems caused by selective feeding on caddisflies has diminished their practical value to anglers.

It has only been in the past sixty years that caddisflies have gained any notice at all in this country, but these scattered mentions in the literature have not helped **anglers. On the contrary, in areas of fly patterns, fishing tactics, and entomology this information has hopelessly misled fly fishermen. It has been these errors—some** repeated so often that they have become angling gospel—that have caused the problems with caddisflies. Anglers have been using the wrong flies with the wrong methods in the wrong places. No wonder, then, that they have been so willing to believe that caddisflies are not important to them.

Angling writers, unable to solve the problem, were faced with a dilemma: how to tell readers how to deal with something the writers could only guess about. The guesswork has contributed many fallacies to the lore of the insect.

Why are caddisflies such a fascinating challenge to fly fishermen? The other major trout-stream insects, mayflies and stoneflies, have been studied extensively by angling entomologists. Facing a hatch of mayflies, for example, fishermen have a comprehensive body of research to tell them which life stage to imitate, which fly to use, which presentation to use—not that success is guaranteed even then, but at least skill will be fairly rewarded if everything is done properly.

But fishermen facing a caddisfly hatch are in a quandary. They may have the skill to do everything right, but what is right? What if the very approaches offered in written angling instruction decrease their chances of success to almost nil?

Ten years ago this was the situation in which I found myself. I stood out on trout streams, flailing away with every prescribed technique, while fish blithely gorged themselves on caddisflies. And I was not the only one out there. Most of the other fly fishermen were faced with making the same decision: either ignore the caddisfly situation and catch little, or fish the caddisfly situation and catch little. It was definitely time for someone to declare, "Something is rotten!"

There are bright truths about caddisflies in some American fishing books, perceptive observations and careful studies that have uncovered valuable facts, but unfortunately these truths have been lost in the mass of misinformation. The fallacies have received much wider play than the scattered truths.

This is why there must be a revolution in the caddisfly knowledge of anglers, not just growth. Too much of what has become the established lore on this insect is wrong, and before fly fishermen can learn techniques to successfully cope with caddisflies they will have to abandon most of the time-honored myths.

What this book will do—

1. Introduce new and better patterns that impressionistically and effectively imitate the live insect.

2. Offer new and better tactics for fishing the larval, pupal, and adult flies.

3. Explain the indicators that signal either emergence or egg laying; and point out the different ways fish feed on each stage.

4. Present a comprehensive entomology of important caddisfly species, with emergence tables and distribution charts for the trout streams of North America.

Part One

Tying and Fishing Caddisfly Imitations

Anticipating a Caddisfly Hatch

Hatch—a magic word. What is hatching? Many fly fishermen travel hundreds of miles to fish a stream or lake when a particular insect is emerging. The appearance of a major mayfly, stonefly, or caddisfly becomes an event, even a ritual, that anglers in an area wait for each season.

The change from larva or nymph to adult (with an intermediate pupal stage for caddisflies) marks a period of abundance. It is almost as if nature deems that the bulk of a particular insect population is suddenly expendable. The insects that have been so well camouflaged expose themselves completely to the fish. Caution is possibly unnecessary at this point in the insect life cycle because, with the large number of eggs produced by each female, most of the immature survivors are not needed to replenish the stream. The emerging insects gather at specific levels in the current and create an immense food supply. For many species, forty to seventy percent of the fish predation for the entire life cycle occurs just prior to or during hatching.

A trout in a stream can gain as much as fifty percent of its yearly growth during two months of spring or early summer. The heavy hatches of these months provide an abundance of easy prey. The fish settle into a daily schedule and feed actively only when they can forage with the greatest efficiency. Often they lie semidormant except during the emergence periods. When they do begin to work a hatch the trout concentrate on the specific areas in the stream where the insects appear.

Is there any doubt why the emergence of a major insect is so important to fly fishermen? The activity is going to control not only what the fish feed on, but also where, when, and how they feed. Nearly every healthy trout stream contains insect species that reach high population densities and create these opportunities.

Resistance by anglers to the entomology of fly-fishing is baffling for two reasons: one, because entomology is so vital to angling success; and two, because it is so easy. It

Which pattern should be used? Which technique is most effective? Which part of the stream is best? These are questions the fly fisherman must answer before he begins casting. Some knowledge of aquatic insects can provide answers to these questions.

is the way for even a beginner to understand the movements and preferences of the fish.

Entomology and fly-fishing for trout are inseparably linked. Certain flies simulate food types other than insects, such as minnows, crustaceans, leeches, or land creatures, but insects are still the major food for the average-size trout. Too many fly fishermen choose to ignore entomology completely because they misunderstand the value of it. Perhaps they see the more complicated manifestations of angling entomology, such as the exact-imitation theories, and do not see the more basic functions of entomology.

As a fly-fishing friend once stated, "Entomology will let me know if the thorax of my fly should be reddish brown instead of olive brown, or if the hook on my fly should be a number twenty-eight instead of a number twenty-six, or if the wings on my fly should be forty-five degrees up instead of seventy-five degrees up; none of which I want to know." Such minor refinements of imitation, of course, can be critical during periods of selective feeding, but situations when the trout are that fussy are uncommon—less than ten percent of the feeding time in most streams—and even then the presentation of the fly is as important as the choice of fly.

The major benefit derived from even a basic study of entomology is not the ability to solve minor problems of imitation. The important advantage a fly fisherman gains with that knowledge is the ability to predict trout feeding patterns—and consequently the ability to suit his techniques to those patterns.

A sad fact of modern fly-fishing is that so much of the lore is geared to one insect, mayflies, that the typical angler has difficulty adapting his methods to the feeding that occurs during a caddisfly hatch. He is conditioned to fish his flies to simulate the typical habits of a mayfly, not a caddisfly.

The information that has been written about caddisflies, however, is not particularly accurate either. The typical angling description of an emerging pupa usually paints a picture of a super insect: "The pupa rips free of the cocoon and rises like a rocket through the water, popping through the surface and flying off immediately." Pity the poor trout trying to capture such an energetic creature. And pity the poor fisherman trying to imitate such insect behavior. This account of the emergence, fortunately, is an exaggeration.

The speed with which caddisflies, the swimming type, ascend to the surface varies with the species, but it is doubtful if any of them rise like a rocket and shoot out into the air. A few accounts by entomologists describe the struggles the emerging insect goes through. For example, Dr. Cornelius Betten, in *The Caddis Flies, or Trichoptera, of New York State*, in a section written in approximately 1915, states about a common Spotted Sedge (*Hydropsyche* sp.): "I did not find the larvae but observed the pupae transforming on the surface of the water alongside of the government breakwater . . ." and in another section, "The pupae were caught as they were coming up for emergence alongside the government breakwater, but these specimens had doubtless been carried some distance by the swift current since they left the rocks."

My studies of how trout feed on emerging pupae and my observations of the naturals also shed considerable doubt on the "rocket" concept of a caddisfly hatch. At least for those swimming emergers observed, including six important trout-stream families, my studies show that the ascent has definite periods of hesitation. It is the insect during these periods of hesitation that fly fishermen must imitate with their flies. They have to know where the pupae will pause and struggle before they can begin to fish a caddisfly hatch successfully.

What is the secret? Efficiency. The principle is simple; the actual attainment of it is not. Many anglers flail randomly, their fly occasionally crossing those areas where vulnerable insects concentrate, catching fish only when their fly is in a prime area. The expert, however, changes his tactics as the prime areas change, and keeps his fly for as long as possible in the productive zone.

The key to anticipating, or "ambushing," a caddisfly hatch requires breaking the common notion of what it is. Too many fishermen only recognize the peak of the action, the frantic surface feeding coinciding with the heaviest concentration of insects on or under the surface film, but these fishermen miss out on fishing before or after the peak—fishing that is sometimes even better.

The first time an angler encounters heavy insect activity, he cannot anticipate it. It is a blind situation—he is unprepared for the ensuing feeding spree. He fumbles in his fly box for some kind of a matching fly and casts to the rising trout with various techniques. If he fails to find the right combination with his hasty attempts, he probably ends up frustrated and fishless.

Even a regular on a stream, lacking an understanding of entomology, cannot fully master such a situation. He might have enough experience with a particular insect to use proper flies and tactics during the main hatch, his methods worked out by past trial and error, but he can still only take advantage of the activity he sees, the hour or so of actual surface feeding. He cannot take advantage of the subsurface activity he does not see.

The fly fisherman who understands the typical life cycle of stream caddisflies, however, knows the vulnerable subsurface stages. He discovers where, when, and how the concentrations occur during an emergence, which allows him to anticipate and prepare for the appearance of the insect. This knowledge also allows him to take full advantage of the predictable daily feeding schedule of the trout. Such an angler is not a member of a scientific cult, but simply a fly fisherman who is prepared to match his tactics and flies to the changing concentrations of insects. There are three areas in which caddisflies concentrate during a hatch.

The first area of concentration. Usually, hours before the main hatch, some caddisflies begin popping out. The first of these random emergers often reaches the surface safely because trout are not conditioned to the occurrence, but soon fish take notice of the hatch. Even when they do start feeding, however, the trout seldom rise to grab a natural from the surface.

The emerging insects, fully formed adults inside thin and flexible pupal skins, cut their way free of the cocoon. Most species do not begin to rise immediately, though. Before they can start swimming they must generate air bubbles inside the transparent pupal skin. They drift momentarily with the bottom currents, enough of them carried along to create a concentration of helpless prey.

This is the first hesitation in the emergence of caddisflies; and preliminary to the main hatch the fish seem content to stay on the bottom, plucking the freely drifting pupae. Trout can feed for hours on these forms without breaking the surface or chasing an active insect.

A stomach sample from a trout caught just before the main caddisfly hatch will often be jammed with hundreds of emergents. These stomach contents are usually a

*The first area of concentration:
Trout begin feeding on drifting
pupae near the bottom.*

complete surprise to the angler, but they demonstrate the extent and intensity of this unseen bottom feeding.

The tactic for matching this early hesitation of emerging caddisflies is seldom associated with the pupa. All kinds of techniques are recommended for a hatch, usually lifts, swings, or retrieves, which may be suitable at a different time, but when trout are keyed to the inert insect near the bottom the way to fish an imitation is dead drift with the standard upstream or across-stream nymph presentation. An occasional tightening of the line, kicking the fly into brief motion, followed quickly by a mend that drops it back into a drift can be added to the basic method.

Imagine, then, being able to fish successfully for hours before the main hatch and the visible surface feeding of trout. It is not difficult to capitalize on this opportunity if the angler will only take the time to learn the approximate emergence dates of the important caddisflies in the streams he fishes.

The second area of concentration. Once out of the silk-lined, stone or vegetable cocoon, drifting freely in the stream, the swimming caddisfly emergent begins inflating its surrounding skin with gas bubbles and beating with hair-fringed legs, both of these actions lifting the insect up through the water. At the surface the adult hesitates, pushing against the underside of the meniscus (surface film) and struggling to shed the pupal skin.

Most caddisflies do not ride on top of the water for great distances, but they do drift, some longer than others, hanging half in and half out of the surface film and invisible to all but the most careful observers. The emergent pulls out of the pupal skin with a series of wiggling motions. Once free, it takes off after a preliminary hop or two.

Ken Thompson, an aquatic biologist, puts the role of the surface film during emergence into perspective, "The meniscus, or surface film, poses an unbelievable barrier to insects trying to pass through it, either from above or from below. It is the result of the molecular bonding of water molecules, which have areas of positive and negative charge. Under the surface the charges are equal, but at the surface the molecules are 'unsatisfied' and under tension.

"A great amount of physical energy is required for an insect to break through the resultant surface tension (meniscus). An example, in human terms, would be the amount of energy needed for a full-grown person to escape if he were covered with three feet of dirt. Aquatic insects have evolved (through necessity) various ways to overcome this barrier. Swimming emergents swim to the surface and push against it. When the top part of the pupal thorax protrudes through the surface and splits open, a meniscus forms around it, thus creating an escape hole in the surface. As the pupal skin (nymphal skin in the case of mayflies and stoneflies) splits open, it is actually aided by the force of the surrounding meniscus, and the adult insect passes through

The second area of concentration: Trout break the surface with porpoiselike rolls, taking pupae from the underside of the meniscus.

the hole, never even touching the water. Once an insect is on the surface, its structural hairs and water resistant skin help to keep it floating high until it flies away."

During a major hatch this second period of hesitation creates a tremendous supply of helpless prey in the surface film. This is the stage that triggers the visible feeding. Trout break the surface with porpoising rolls, taking an insect and turning down. Occasionally a trout jumps into the air, its momentum carrying it out of the water.

The fish usually switch over very quickly, abandoning deep feeding, once the main hatch erupts because pupae hesitate and drift longer at the surface than they do near the bottom. The concentration of insects becomes much heavier in the meniscus, and once this happens the upper level is where fish can feed most efficiently.

A trout can feed in one of three ways when it begins taking pupae from just under the film: it can hold at the bottom and when it spots an ascending pupa it can follow the insect (seldom trying to grab it while it is swimming) and suck the pupa in as the insect begins struggling to shed the shuck; or the trout can hold at the bottom and watch for emergents already in the surface film and rise for the pupae as the insects pass over; or the trout can hold just under the surface and sip emergents drifting toward it. Which feeding mechanism a trout uses is determined by the quickness of the insects and the speed of the current. A trout only feeds the third way, holding under the surface, in the gentler flows. It feeds in either the first or second way in faster currents.

The peak feeding, with fish rolling and jumping all over the stream, should be a time when fly fishermen master the fish, but it can be a time of total failure and frustration. Too often anglers fail to realize that the insects are hesitating and concentrating under the film, not on it, and as a result they mistakenly assume that it is an occasion for dry flies.

Again, an effective tactic for fishing this stage of the hatch is one not usually associated with caddisflies. Especially when trout are holding just under the surface or rising to pupae already in the film, an emergent imitation designed to ride semidry generally outperforms any sunken fly fished with an active presentation. Used either dead drift or with a twitch and swim, the "damp" imitation stays in the surface film for the entire time, not just for a moment at the end of a swing or lift.

A technique that kicks the fly into a pulsing swim toward the top, the Leisenring lift, is generally effective when trout are rising all the way from the bottom to take emergents. A sinking pattern is cast upstream and allowed to drift near the bottom, but when it reaches a likely holding spot it is teased to life, hopefully in front of a trout. It is a method that demands skill in reading water if the angler is not casting to visible fish.

The feeding that occurs during this second concentration of pupae takes place in plain view, and a fly fisherman can figure out what to do when he sees the riseforms, but some anticipation of a particular hatch is still valuable. Possibly no other insect type inspires such strong selectivity in trout as a caddisfly pupa, mainly because the bright bubbles of air inside the pupal skin form such a visible characteristic. In this situation the proper method of presentation is not the overwhelming part of success that it is at other times. A fly fisherman cannot just pull out a general imitation and depend on his skill at mimicking the action of the natural. He needs both the proper presentation *and* the precise fly to consistently fool fish, and only a knowledge of local hatches can give him the chance to acquire or tie patterns beforehand that match a specific caddisfly.

The third area of concentration. When the peak hatch is over and the surface of the river is blank, most anglers quit fishing, or at least stop trying to match caddisflies but there is still an hour of so of very exciting action left. There is one more concentration of insects that pulls fish, often the largest, into specific areas of the stream.

During any hatch there is a low percentage of natural cripples. Seldom, if ever, are these cripples numerous enough to cause selective feeding during the main emergence period. They would have to make up a much higher proportion of the hatch to create such a response. When fish feed selectively they feed with a regular rhythm, and they cannot feed regularly on a component of the hatch that appears irregularly.

The purpose of selective feeding, a set of patterned responses to the stimulae of the insect, is efficient use of energy. By moving with rhythmical repetition a trout ingests as many calories as possible with the least expenditure of energy. The stronger the selectivity to a food item the more regular the feeding motion. There is no way a trout can determine if an insect partially out of its pupal skin, struggling to complete emergence, is in that condition temporarily or permanently. Certainly the cripples are eaten during the hatch along with the healthy insects, but considering them important at that time contradicts some basic principles that are controlling the trout.

Cripples are usually not important during the main hatch because they are not concentrated. During a heavy hatch, over a prolonged period of time, there are nevertheless quite a few of them, and if they could be gathered into a small area they would become a significant food source. Fortunately, for both trout and trout fishermen, that is exactly what happens after the hatch. Even after they drown, these crippled insects remain quite buoyant and are swept along with the current. Eventually many of them join with bits of flotsam or foam and collect in a backwater of the stream to become a great, swirling cafeteria for the fish.

It is after the main hatch that the leftover cripples become the center of attention. The trout abandon the regular feeding lanes and gather under the foam. In the gentle eddies they sip the inert insects, their snouts and backs breaking or bulging the white covering and leaving a momentary spot of clear water in the foam.

The best patterns for mimicking cripples are adult imitations that not only look like, but also act like, bedraggled, half-emerged caddisflies. They sprawl flat in the surface film, wings fanning out along the sides, and quiver with the slightest twitch. They recreate the last, feeble struggle of the natural because they are tied with soft materials.

The third area of concentration: In backwaters trout gather under the foam to take drowned emergents.

In backwaters that have a mixture of open and covered water an angler can see his fly floating if it is in a clear area and the casting and striking is quite normal. But in the foam, he has to slap it down hard enough to force it through the upper layer. The angler has to fish blind, striking when a bulge or gap occurs where the fly broke through.

Does the post-hatch feeding attract big fish? Graham Marsh rose an eight-pound rainbow three times on the lower Clark Fork River from a deep backwater. He watched the fish come slowly up out of the hole, but each time the drag on the line snatched the floating fly away just before it got there. Even with his considerable skill, Graham could not stretch out an extra half-second of free drift with the standard techniques he was using, but it was a glorious sight anyway watching that huge trout rise to a dry fly.

American fly fishermen have not begun to tap the potential of the caddisfly hatches popping out all around them, and they never will with general fly-fishing skills. They will need to understand the habits of the caddisflies in their home trout streams and the unique tactics for simulating the actions of those insects before they can work the full period of the hatch.

To benefit from the current revolution in caddisfly knowledge, fly fishermen will have to collect and identify the important groups, at least to generic level, that they encounter regularly. Then they will have to study the biological information in angling entomologies for these insects so that they can anticipate and properly fish the hatches.

Creating the Effective Pattern

My work in developing new flies has often led me back to the writings of Edward Ringwood Hewitt. His creative innovations in fly-tying have been a source of inspiration, a body of knowledge off of which to bounce my own ideas. He did not always succeed with his constant experiments, but even his failures were inspirational; they always stood on a reason, a theory.

Hewitt, patriarch of the Eastern angling establishment, was by all accounts dogmatic and argumentative, but his opinions were motivated by a need for understanding. In his final book, *A Trout and Salmon Fisherman for Seventy-Five Years*, he wrote, "Personally I shall not be satisfied to fish and not know the laws which govern the subject. I want to know, and I want the fish this knowledge enables me to catch."

During the first half of this century he was the leading innovator in American fly-fishing, originator of the Skating Spider, Bivisible, and Neversink Stone dry flies. A constant experimenter, he tested the gamut of hackling variations—flat to oversize—achieving results by altering the way the fly indented the surface film. He designed his dry-fly prototypes to fool trout, creating a light pattern on the meniscus that matched the actions of naturals. Then in his testing he studied the way visibly working fish responded to the flies.

Hewitt also tried to create subsurface artificials by copying natural nymphs and larvae. He and John Alden Knight originated a series of flat-body nymphs, carefully forming a base for the bodies with Plastic Wood. The patterns looked correct in shape, size, and color, and through the promotion of Hewitt and Knight they enjoyed a brief commercial popularity. But the flat-body nymphs, as much as it seemed they should work, were mediocre fish catchers, and they soon fell into disuse even in the Catskill region.

Hewitt's dry-fly creations are still sold through catalogs and fly shops, as valuable for fooling trout now as ever. His wet-fly experiments, on the other hand, are forgotten. The failure of his flat-body nymphs stands as an example of a fly-tier's dilemma: what you see is what you get with the dry fly, but what you see does not seem to matter with the wet fly.

Hewitt's experiments are a fair example of the pitfalls awaiting the creative fly tier, because Hewitt knew the requirements of any successful pattern. He listed factors governing the attractiveness of a fly in order of relative importance:

1. The light effects of the fly, above and below the surface
2. The way the fly is cast and manipulated, including where the fly is placed relative to the fish
3. Visibility of the leader to the fish
4. The size of the fly
5. The design of the fly
6. The color of the fly
7. Accuracy of imitation of natural insects.

Even by Hewitt's own criteria, flat-body nymphs were exact imitations satisfying the least important factor in this list. That stress on realistic representation overwhelmed more important effects.

The most important step in the creative process is the final judgment on a fly's effectiveness, and yet a fly tier cannot judge his wet-fly creations accurately through trial-and-error casting. There are too many variables. For example, Angler A catches six trout with a blue fly and Angler B catches two trout with a red fly. Does this prove that the blue fly is better? Angler A might have been quicker at detecting strikes, he might have been working different water, or he might have been fishing the fly with a different motion. A scorekeeper above the river surface has no way of monitoring such variables. The only way he could tell if the flies were presented correctly to an equal number of feeding fish would be by actually observing the action underwater.

Fortunately, it is possible by scuba diving in trout rivers to eliminate some of the frustration of not knowing, just as Hewitt wanted to know "the laws which govern the subject." With air tanks for breathing and lead belts for ballast it is relatively easy to become an unobtrusive observer in the trout's environment. Underwater it is possible to nestle just below pods of active fish and gather insights into feeding habits, movement schedules, and habitat preferences. And by studying the prey as well as the predator, a diver can pinpoint the problems of general imitation. He can serve as a scorekeeper by actually watching trout select or reject artificial flies.

I discovered that there was something my diving companions and I could not do, though. We could not list the factors of attractiveness for a fly pattern, not in a pat formula that would apply for creating all subsurface imitations. The hours of observation convinced me that we could neither verify Hewitt's rules nor formulate a set of our own.

When trout fed selectively, not only on aquatic insects but also on other forms of subsurface life, the various visible characteristics of the prey did not equally affect the process of selection. Motion, size, light effect, and color of the natural were each important, but different traits proved to be of greater importance on different forms. There was no set list because the formula for a successful imitation varied.

Every prey organism possessed one characteristic that tipped off vulnerability or availability, one characteristic that was visible at a greater distance than any of the other traits. When fish fed heavily on a single organism, locking into a stimulus-response pattern, they moved to intercept the prey when they recognized this identifying feature.

This triggering characteristic is always the most important factor in the attractiveness of the natural or in the imitation of the natural. If a pattern fails to simulate this main trait, a trout might accept the inadequate fake if the drift hit the fish on the nose, but the fish will not move far to pick it up. The fly that does not mimic the triggering characteristic still catches some trout when the feeding is selective, but the effective pattern fools more because it draws fish from a wider area as it passes in the water.

The creation of an effective imitation must be based on an understanding of the habits and appearance of the original in its environment, not on a picture or a description of the natural. Because the organism is alive and dynamic, the fly pattern, within the limits of the fly-tier's art, must simulate the factors that identify that organism as alive and dynamic, especially the triggering characteristic.

Effective imitations of the life stages of caddisflies were created only after comprehensive study. The triggering characteristic, often after long observation and initial mistakes, was segregated and copied in an imitation. The secondary characteristics, those traits that could still cause a refusal once the trout came nearer to the fly, were rated in importance and simulated.

These studies consisted of five basic phases. The natural was observed in either an aquarium or a fluvarium (a trough with running water). In a contained environment such as this, the habits of the insect were noted over a long period. The idiosyncrasies of the organism, the traits that most strongly distinguished it from other insects, were selectively isolated.

Then, in one of the most crucial stages, the reactions of the trout to the insect were studied in the natural environment. The rhythms and responses of the fish as it fed heavily on a particular species were carefully recorded. Later, this study would tell how well the actions of a trout toward the imitation matched the initial responses to naturals, providing the best measure of the effectiveness of the fly.

The fly-tying phase was an integral part of the testing. The fly-tying phase entailed making corrections in which it was necessary to kill many ideas that my colleagues and I considered brilliant, simply because the trout did not seem to agree. The parts of new patterns were continually altered until we felt they matched the perceptions of the fish.

The finished flies were then observed underwater in actual tests against conventional patterns. The diver recorded not only the takes and refusals but also the effective-attraction distance. These tests were repeated as often as possible with different scuba teams to verify our results as accurately as possible.

To complete the study, samples of an approved imitation were sent to angling experts all over the country for use on a variety of waters. After these evaluations of a fly, if it proved successful in the field for at least two years, it was released for commercial distribution.

The Larva Imitation

Why weren't the Hewitt flat-body nymphs effective? It took only a brief look at the patterns drifting underwater, the flies flip-flopping to alternately expose the dark back and light belly, to see how unnatural they appeared to the fish.

Aquatic nymphs and larvae are often washed off the rocks and debris of the bottom, carried along by the current until they can struggle back to a hold. The insects actually enter a state of shock when first swept away, drifting inert and helpless, but they usually do not revolve with the forces of the stream. They manage to maintain equilibrium, keeping the color of one side visible to the fish. Some mayfly nymphs, in this state of shock, ride belly-up in the current until ready to swim for the bottom, but even upside-down they drift in a stable position.

A properly weighted hook is still the basic answer for balancing the artificial nymph. A fly that has the correct proportion of lead wrap spread along the underside of the hook shank does not flip uncontrollably. It may wobble with the forces of the current when fished dead drift, the same as the insect, but it does not give itself away as an obvious fraud.

This drift stability is the first criterion for all nymph patterns. In the fly-tying instructions that follow the proper method of weighting the hook is explained.

There are two types of caddisfly larvae the fly fisherman must consider: the free-living, or *campodeiform* larva; and the case-building, or *eruciform* larva. The case builders, oddly, are seldom imitated by fly tiers, even though they are an important part of the trout's diet. At one time patterns were tried that had actual caddis cases cemented onto the hook shank. Although the material was the real case of the natural, these flies were imitating an aspect of the insect that was not alive; instead of emphasizing a larval trait that signified food to the fish, they were simulating an inanimate characteristic.

The only truly successful imitation developed of a cased caddis larva is the Strawman Nymph. This rough, deer-hair pattern, created by Paul Young to match stick cases, is an impressionistic design, and its effectiveness proves that it is possible to imitate the cased larva successfully.

The study of actual caddisfly larvae drifting with the current revealed a number of previously unknown characteristics. The main trait betraying the insect as live food was the movement of the larva in and out of the case. This wriggling motion exposed a contrasting band of body color between the head and case. This extension out of the case also changed the size of the total object.

These characteristics were important additions on new patterns. Tying the imitations larger and including a wrap of cotton chenille above the simulation of the case better imitated the extended insect. Two other impressionistic features—an upward bend of the hook shank above the case and extra-long, soft hackles—provides the dynamic look of a living organism.

There was still another problem. The case itself, though inanimate, was not an effective addition to an imitation if tied with inanimate materials. The solution to this is another impressionistic tying technique: a palmer of soft hackle feathers. The wrapping of the feathers, which are available in a full range of colors, leaves fibers sticking out that can be cut to any shape or size.

These new patterns produce well in general situations, but there is also a

The Hewitt nymphs failed because their two-color pattern, similar to a rotating barber pole, looked unnatural to fish.

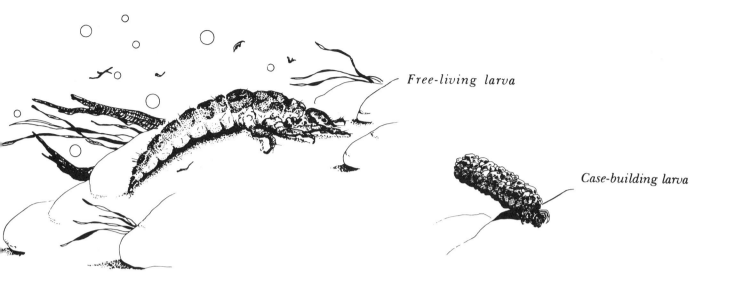

Two types of caddisfly larvae that fly fishermen must consider are those that do not build cases (campodeiform) and those that do (eruciform).

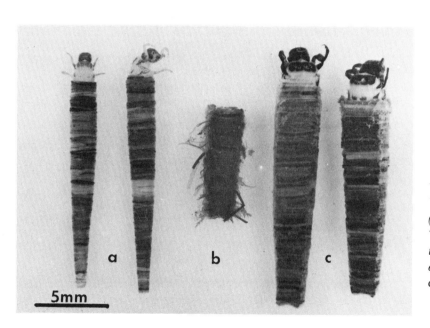

5mm

The larvae of both the (a) Little Western Weedy Water Sedge (Amiocentrus) and the (c) Grannom (Brachycentrus) drift freely. The movement of these larvae in and out of their cases exposes a light band of color. The empty case (b) of a rare genus, Eobrachycentrus, is also shown. Jon Spier

particular use for which they have proved invaluable. They are very effective when trout are rooting in the gravel. Rooting fish in shallow riffles are challenging quarry for the upstream-nymph fisherman, requiring a quiet approach and an accurate cast. These trout stir up the bottom, swim downstream, and turn around to await the loosened debris. They often key on the dominant type of cased caddisfly in the load because these are the first insects to sink out of the cloud of silt.

Case-Making Caddisfly Larva Imitations

1. LIGHT CASED CADDIS

HOOK:	Mustad 94840 (bent to shape)
THREAD:	brown nylon
WEIGHT:	lead wire (wrapped over rear portion of shank)
CASE:	pale speckled mallard breast feathers and lemon wood-duck feathers (wrapped together and clipped to shape)
INSECT BODY:	pale yellow cotton chenille (one wrap in front of case)
HACKLE:	dark brown and gray grouse feather fibers (a few long wisps tied underneath)

2. MEDIUM CASED CADDIS

HOOK:	Mustad 94840 (bent to shape)
THREAD:	brown nylon
WEIGHT:	lead wire (wrapped over rear portion of shank)
CASE:	lemon wood-duck feathers and dark brown and gray grouse feathers (wrapped together and clipped to shape)
INSECT BODY:	pale yellow cotton chenille (one wrap in front of case)
HACKLE:	dark brown and gray grouse feather fibers (a few long wisps tied underneath)

3. DARK CASED CADDIS

HOOK:	Mustad 94840 (bent to shape)
THREAD:	brown nylon
WEIGHT:	lead wire (wrapped over rear portion of shank)
CASE:	dark brown and gray grouse feathers (wrapped together and clipped to shape)
INSECT BODY:	pale yellow cotton chenille (one wrap in front of case)
HACKLE:	dark brown and gray grouse feather fibers (a few long wisps tied underneath)

A size 10 Dark Cased Caddis Photo Gary
LaFontaine

Tying instructions:

HOOK: Mustad 94840

                         1. Bend the front one-fifth of the hook shank up at a forty-five-degree angle.

WEIGHT: fine lead wire

                         2. Weight straight portion of the hook shank by tying in wire along the underside of the shank and wrapping the rest of the wire around the shank.

CASE: soft hackle feathers

                         3. Tie in two soft hackle feathers.

                         4. Wrap them, first one and then the other, but not so thickly that they completely obscure the lead wire and thread underneath (the case is impressionistically simulated better by gaps in the hackle fibers).

                         5. Trim to any desired shape (the shape of the imitation is determined by the shape of the natural's case).

INSECT BODY: cotton chenille

                         6. Tie in a piece of cotton chenille at the bent section of the hook.

                         7. Wrap one or two turns of cotton chenille up the shank.

HACKLE: soft hackle fibers

                         8. Tie in a few long wisps of soft hackle fibers, allowing them to sweep back and below the case. Whip-finish and cement head.

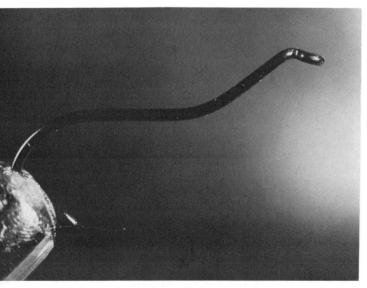

Step 1

The Cased Caddis **Gary LaFontaine**

Step 2

Step 3

Step 4

Step 5

Step 6 and

Step 8

Whip finish and cement he

Do case-making larvae ever abandon their cases? Most genera of case makers do not. But there are some primitive genera in which, for varying reasons, larvae quite regularly abandon their old cases and crawl or drift freely in the stream. This caseless period exposes these caddisflies to trout.

There is no need for special imitations to match this group of larvae. The patterns recommended next for those caddisflies that do not build cases during the larval stage are also suitable for the temporarily caseless ones. There might be slight differences in the body form of noncase makers and uncased case makers, but not enough to justify a separate set of flies. The Caddis Larva pattern in Yellow, Pink, and Pale Green varieties covers the coloration of the genera in this important group (see the following genera in the Insect Listing for more information on the case makers that abandon their cases: *Dicosmoecus, Glossosoma, Ptilostomis,* and *Phryganea*).

The caddisfly larvae that do not make cases, species that either roam freely or weave nets among the rocks, are just as important to nymph fishermen as the case makers. These insects are also apt to slip off the bottom and get lifted into the current, where they either drift away or dangle on a silky line. No matter which behavior occurs, they are exposed to fish once they are out of the rocks.

In most rich watersheds these larvae are important because they attain high densities in prime habitat. Many species of net-making caddisflies, for example, require a certain current velocity. So, in a riffle that is ideal for such a species, the concentration of these larvae make the resident trout predisposed to that size, shape, and color of nymph pattern.

The underwater studies of free-living caddisflies pinpointed another characteristic—a trait missing on all of my older imitations. At first this trait remained a mystery, but testing indicated that the standard flies lacked something. The missing factor became obvious after observation: along with color, size, and shape the other visible trait was the position of the body. For most of the caddisfly genera, a major characteristic was the curvilinear position assumed by the drifting larvae. The partial curl of the insect—confirming the value of using English bait hooks or sedge hooks for these imitations—was a selective trait for the fish.

My patterns tied to simulate the bent-over position encountered another complication. None of the flies matched the actual length of curled-up larvae because the sizes had been previously judged by measuring stretched-out specimens. The difference completely invalidated the original sizing system, making the original metric charts worthless.

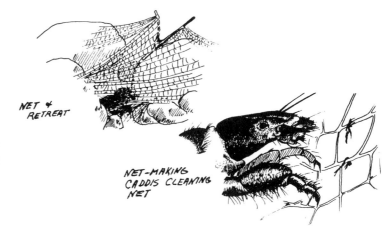

NET &
RETREAT

NET-MAKING
CADDIS CLEANING
NET

The larvae of net-making caddisflies are usually abundant in trout streams.

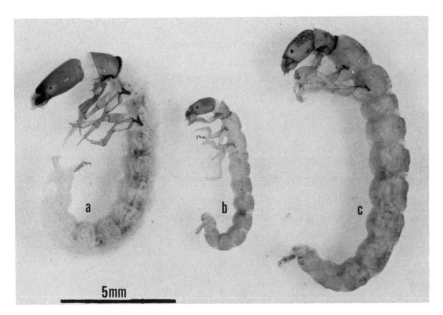

Larvae that do not build cases tend to curl up when they drift. The (a) Wormaldia, Little Autumn Stream Sedge; the (b) Psychomyia, Dinky Purple-Breasted Sedge; and the (c) Polycentropus, Brown Checkered Summer Sedge, are examples of such larvae. Jon Spier

5mm

The correct shape, size, color, and body position were each important factors for these imitations, with no single characteristic so overwhelming that it dominated the selection process.

One of the free-living caddisfly genera proved even more important as a model for imitation than the drab-colored, net-making larvae. For the Green Sedge, family Rhyacophilidae, all the traits were not equal in importance. The bright green color of the larva was a very strong triggering characteristic.

Comparative work with drab Spotted Sedge (*Hydropsyche*) and bright Green Sedge (*Rhyacophila*) larvae resulted in a tentative theory on subsurface imitation in general: *the stronger the main triggering characteristic of the natural, the more critical the need for a precise imitation.*

Observations of trout feeding on concentrations of drifting *Hydropsyche* larvae indicated a general preference, but not a strong stimulus-response selection process. The attraction area, the distance a fish moved to pick up a natural, was also limited to about a two-foot lateral range in slow water. Trout accepted mayfly nymphs almost as well as imitations of the larvae (roughly about a four to three ratio in favor of the *Hydropsyche* pattern).[1]

During feeding sessions on the Green Sedges (*Rhyacophila*), however, trout quickly locked into a very selective pattern. They recognized the bright color of the natural and aggressively plucked larvae from the drift. These fish preferred a proper imitation of the insect by a two to one ratio over a general mayfly nymph.

The brightness of the larva was not an easy trait to simulate. Natural fur, or even brightly dyed fur, failed to match the coloration. The insect possessed an iridescent greenness, a camouflage suited to the filamentous green algae (*Cladophora* sp.) of stream bottoms.

A modern synthetic, a common acrylic sold in hobby shops under the name Craft Fur, was the answer to the problem. This laboratory product possessed the proper gawdiness, the kind of brightness nature avoids in fur or hair, to simulate the color of the larva. In the form of dubbing it produced a realistic body for the new imitation.

A size 14 Bright-Green Caddis Larva
Gary LaFontaine

Free-Living Caddisfly Larva Imitations

1. YELLOW CADDIS LARVA

HOOK:	Partridge Sedge Hook or English bait hook
THREAD:	brown nylon
WEIGHT:	fine lead wire (optional)
BODY:	golden yellow fur (over rear two-thirds of hook)
THORAX:	brownish yellow fur
RIBBING:	light brown rooster quill (stripped)
HACKLE:	lemon wood-duck fibers (tied under)

2. OLIVE BROWN CADDIS LARVA

HOOK:	Partridge Sedge Hook or English bait hook
THREAD:	brown nylon
WEIGHT:	fine lead wire (optional)
BODY:	olive brown fur (over rear two-thirds of hook)
THORAX:	dark brown fur
HACKLE:	lemon wood-duck fibers (tied under)

3. BRIGHT GREEN CADDIS LARVA

HOOK:	Partridge Sedge Hook or English bait hook
THREAD:	brown nylon
WEIGHT:	fine lead wire (optional)
BODY:	one-half olive fur, one-half bright green acrylic fur (Craft Fur) (over rear two-thirds of hook)
THORAX:	dark olive brown fur
RIBBING:	light brown rooster quill (stripped)
HACKLE:	dark speckled grouse fibers (tied under)

4. PINK CADDIS LARVA

HOOK:	Partridge Sedge Hook or English bait hook
THREAD:	brown nylon
WEIGHT:	fine lead wire (optional)
BODY:	pale pink fur (over rear two-thirds of hook)
THORAX:	light brown fur
HACKLE:	lemon wood-duck fibers (tied under)

5. PALE GREEN CADDIS LARVA

HOOK:	Partridge Sedge Hook or English bait hook
THREAD:	brown nylon
WEIGHT:	fine lead wire (optional)
BODY:	pale green fur (over rear two-thirds of hook)
THORAX:	dark brown fur
HACKLE:	dark gray and brown grouse fibers (tied under)

Tying instructions:

HOOK:	Partridge Sedge Hook or English bait hook
WEIGHT:	fine lead wire (optional)
	1. Weight the hook shank by tying a piece of wire along each side of it.
RIBBING:	stripped rooster quill (some of the patterns do not have a rib)
	2. Tie in a stripped rooster quill at the bend of the hook and leave it hanging free for the moment.
BODY:	fur
	3. Dub a body of fur on rear two-thirds of the hook shank.
	4. Wrap the quill ribbing.
THORAX:	fur
	5. Dub a thorax of fur, heavier and differently colored than body.
HACKLE:	soft hackle fibers
	6. Tie in a few long wisps of soft hackle fibers underneath the body. Whip-finish and cement head.

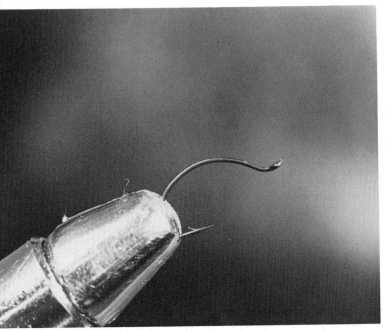

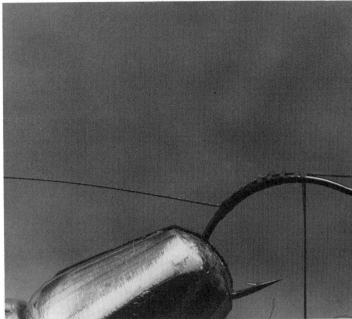

Partridge Sedge Hook Gary LaFontaine

Step 2

Step 3

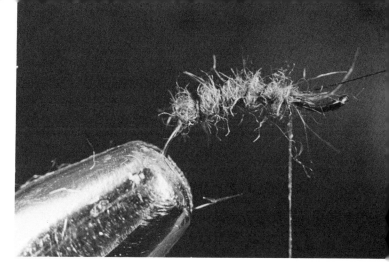

Step 4

Step 5

Step 6

The Pupa Imitation

My frustration was the catalyst for new ideas. My troubles with rising trout inspired a radical reappraisal of caddisfly lore and the subsequent abandonment of an old set of precepts. Something was terribly wrong with the old techniques and imitations. No matter how sensible they appeared to the angler, they certainly were not impressing the fish. Time and again, with the trout banging away on emerging caddisflies, the prescribed tactics triggered at best a few random strikes.

The standard method of fishing the pupa was the down-and-across cast, the sunken pattern being allowed to swing around as a belly of dragging line formed in the current. It was a repetitious and unskillful method of fly-fishing, but supposedly it mimicked the swimming dash of the natural pupa to the surface.

It was desperation caused by repeated failures trying to match the caddisfly pupa that initiated the scuba-diving experiments: first to see what the trout saw, and second to simulate that with a fly. Even the first dive under the surface was a revelation because finally it was possible at least to identify the problems if not to answer them immediately.

The scuba experiments that led to my new patterns and tactics took more than three years, from 1971 to 1974. Most of the testing took place in Montana rivers, mainly on the Big Hole and the Boulder, but follow-up verification was done by other divers in both the Far West and the East.

The observations revealed two flaws in the old system. The entire concept of how trout captured the emerging pupa was wrong, and the various patterns used to match the natural were poor. With the wrong fly presented in the wrong way, it was evident why fly fishermen were not catching fish effectively during caddisfly activity.

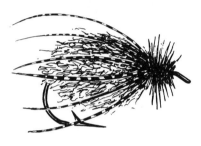

The general belief was that trout chased the ascending pupae and caught them halfway in the rise. Actually, trout very rarely fed on caddisfly pupae this way, and those fish that occasionally gave chase were usually small. So in spite of all those illustrations showing large trout with jaws agape in pursuit of the insect, the artificial fly swinging madly through the water was not really imitating the natural.

As described in the previous chapter, I found that there were two moments of hesitation in the rise of the pupa: first, it initially cuts its way free of the cocoon and the insect drifts with the bottom currents, often for as much as fifteen or twenty feet, before generating the gas to fill the sheath around the body; and second, after swimming to the surface, the pupa hangs on the underside of the meniscus as it struggles to split and shed the pupal shuck.

Two styles of pupa patterns are needed to imitate the e- merging natural— the Deep Sparkle Pupa (upper) and the Emergent Spar- kle Pupa (lower).

Trout concentrated almost exclusively on these two points of vulnerability. Why expend energy in a frantic chase when there were insects available for less effort? The fish would follow a rising pupa to the surface, making no attempt to snatch it, and would suck it in as it stopped at the film, or else the fish would hang on the bottom, sidling back and forth to pick motionless insects from the drift line.

The answers to imitating the pupa were two new fly designs to replace the old general pattern. A weighted version was tied for a deep presentation and an emergent version was tied for a semidry surface presentation.

But designing flies that would physically duplicate the actions of the natural was not enough, however, because the typical style of pupa imitation, even in deep and emergent variations, was still not right. It failed to mimic the most important visible trait of the natural.

When a caddisfly pupa emerges it fills a transparent sheath around its body with air bubbles. These globules of air shimmer and sparkle as they reflect sunlight, creating a highly visible triggering characteristic. This sparkle is the key to imitating the emergent caddisflies.

In this case, the light effect of the fly is the important factor. Trout quickly become super-selective to it, responding strongly to only that stimulus because it is so distinct. There is nothing else like it to confuse the fish. It is not at all like imitating a mayfly nymph, for example, where a color might be slightly off or a hook slightly too large. The sparkle of a caddisfly pupa underwater is unmistakable.

In some of the standard pupa patterns the problem of the air bubble is simply ignored. Many flies, for example, faithfully copy the color, size, and wingpads of certain pupae but make no attempt at all to simulate an air sack.

Silver tinsel, often promoted as the solution for matching the air bubble, is not the answer. Tinsel appears very unnatural on any insect imitation underwater. These flies performed so poorly in tests, worse even than drab wool patterns, that they rank with Hewitt's flat-body nymphs as examples of misguided imitation.

Air reflects and tinsel reflects; why shouldn't tinsel work? Light rays reflected from most shiny surfaces (for example, an air bubble) retain the color of the original light source: if the light is the golden yellow of late afternoon, the air bubble will be yellow. Metals are different, however, because they reflect selectively. The spectral composition of the original light source is changed to reproduce the surface color of the metal; even if the sunlight is yellow, silver tinsel still will reflect silver, copper tinsel will reflect copper, and gold tinsel will reflect gold.

Metallic substances were rejected after underwater testing, but although the need was apparent for a different material to simulate the shimmering air of the caddisfly pupa, there was no such material available. In two years of experiments, every natural and synthetic substitute I tried was rejected because each looked no more like an air bubble than the wrap of silver tinsel. During this two-year hiatus I was stuck, simply because I knew the problem so well. This understanding of the critical need for proper imitation eliminated any halfway solutions.

The discovery of a new type of synthetic, a nylon filament known as Antron made by Du Pont, provided fresh hope. The material had the two major qualifications: it was translucent and it reflected light. The filaments underwater looked perfect; by every laboratory measurement they simulated the air bubble exactly.

New patterns utilizing this Du Pont yarn were an immediate success with the fish. The flies still had to go through the five-phase testing to verify their effectiveness, but during the first underwater comparison with standard flies it was clear that the new imitations were very special. Antron, generically a three-sided (trilobal) nylon, was used on both the Deep and Emergent imitations.

How effective are the pupa patterns? It was easy to judge the usefulness of the Deep Pupa because there was a standard subsurface imitation to compare it to. By observing both types of flies in the same situations of selective feeding it was possible to determine the relative distances a fish would move to grab it (effective distance varies continually due to changes in water clarity and current speed).

I set a ratio figure, though, comparing the two styles of flies. By carefully watching the response of feeding fish I could see that in clear water the Sparkle Caddis Pupa drew the attention of trout three and a half feet away, while in the same situation a standard pupa drew the attention of fish no farther than a foot away. After

DuPont's Antron yarn produces the sparkling highlights needed in the (a) Deep Sparkle Pupa and the (b) Emergent Sparkle Pupa. Gary LaFontaine

verification of this study by other divers, I set the effectiveness ratio of three to one.

The Emergent Pupa, however, was not such an easy fly to study. Since it was the first of its kind there was nothing with which to compare it. It was easier to assume that since it was a success on the stream it was roughly three times better than a fly lacking the imitation of the air sack, rather than conduct a more extensive inquiry; but this lazy approach precipitated one of the great mysteries in my work.

The heroic fly-fishing achievements were there for the Emergent Pupa: twenty-eight browns on twenty-eight consecutive casts on the Beaverhead River in Montana; sixteen trout on sixteen consecutive casts and seventy trout altogether in one afternoon on the White River in Arkansas; twenty trout in a few hours on a morning when everyone was moaning about the poor fishing on the Henrys Fork in Idaho. Such incidents were not only with trout, either; I heard from Warren Phillips about the fly's effectiveness on bass on the Shenandoah, and from Malcolm Patterson, catching shad on the upper Connecticut.

So what? With the trilobal simulation of an air bubble it had to be effective. Successful incidents reported by my fly-fishing friends, among them Kevin Toman in California, Elmer Latham in Connecticut, Eric Peper in Minnesota, and Bruce Solomon in Utah, were not really indicative of any unknown fish-catching property; these men are such fine fly fishermen that they always catch trout. But letters and telephone calls from anglers, people who had used my flies after reading about them in my book *Challenge of the Trout* or in *The Caddis and the Angler* by Larry Solomon and Eric Leiser, kept repeating stories of great fishing with the Emergent Pupa.

It was easy to accept the fact that the Emergent was better than another semidry pattern as an imitation, the shimmer of the tri-lobal Antron accounting for its superiority. But this fly was doing more than any imitation could—trout feeding selectively typically stay in a territory with certain limits, but the Emergent was consistently drawing trout beyond these limits.

The feeding territory of a fish marks the farthest distance an imitative characteristic of a fly will draw attention. The fish will not travel beyond that territory for more natural food, so naturally it will not travel beyond that for an imitation of food. The only aspect of a fly that will draw a fish out of its territory is a strong attraction trait.

An inkling that there might be something other than imitation involved came from a telephone call from James Eisenmann, at the time the art director of *Sports Afield*. Jim, working with a photographer on an article on the Emergent Pupa, had a question. "Arie de Zanger, the photographer, is having a problem. He's never seen a fly like this. When he puts it in water, it gets covered with air bubbles. Is it supposed to do that?"

Was it? Did trilobal nylon have a special ability to cling to air bubbles? I honestly

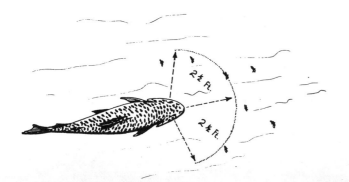

Once a fish establishes a feeding territory, only a strong attraction trait can draw it beyond its usual range.

did not know the answer. I quickly tested flies tied with the material along with other flies tied with different kinds of natural furs and synthetics, and found out that the assumption was true. As long as the Emergent Pupa stayed near the surface it carried a wreath of bubbles around it.

These living-room experiments were followed by a telephone call to Du Pont in Delaware. There, with Charles Booz and Howard Benner of Du Pont offering access to the scientific data of the corporation, the chemists provided the information that solved the mystery of the material's affinity to air bubbles.

Initially the characteristics of Antron, listed in a Du Pont bulletin as "a combination of unique luster, dry hand and improved print clarity" made it ideal for rug making. The way it reflected light made it especially useful for the purpose, trilobal fibers masking dirt accumulation in the rug. In 1973 Du Pont developed another member of the family, Antron III crepe yarn-type 877 A. This derivative synthetic filled the need in knitting for a fiber that resisted felting. The elimination of felting (the tendency of individual filaments to adhere to each other) kept a garment from clinging to the wearer.

This new characteristic, a laboratory miracle engineered by blending a polymeric conductive material with the Antron for static control, offered a unique filament for the fly tier. Unlike other natural or synthetic substances, the trilobal fibers resisted matting together in water. Each strand retained air space around itself, forming tiny traps to collect and hold the air bubbles in any liquid.

Once I learned that these clinging air bubbles were adding another dimension to the fly, I did the underwater observation that should have been done at the conception of the pattern. I not only studied its effect on trout feeding on natural pupae, but also its effect during general usage. I discovered a reason for its unexpected effectiveness.

The Emergent, hanging half in and half out of the water, kicks off a constant trail of air bubbles. In slow water especially, where there is no natural aeration to obscure the phenomenon, this stream of bubbles has an effect beyond imitation. The pattern becomes an ideal combination—an attractor and an imitator at the same time—actually making trout break a feeding rhythm to go after it. This attraction distance extends far beyond the feeding territory. In clear water a trout will move six to eight feet, abandoning an established lane to inspect the fly. With the Emergent, unlike many other attractor types, after a closer look the fish will not shy away.

Is it a miracle fly? It certainly has a unique duality: it not only works at the right moment to match the selective interest of the fish, it also works at other times by breaking the selective feeding cycle (a trout feeding on terrestrials or mayflies, for example). Few other flies can catch trout as well as it can, but scientific skepticism keeps me from tabbing it a miracle fly. It does not carry a guarantee of success. It is certainly, with the trail of air bubbles popping off of it, a superb pattern, and as an imitation of an emergent caddisfly pupa it is an indispensable fly.

I first introduced Du Pont's Antron yarn, known as Sparkle Yarn, as a fly-tying material in the February 1974 newsletter of the Connecticut Fly Fishermen's Association. At first I worked with the material only on pupal imitations, testing it both in the laboratory and on the trout stream, trying to determine the best possible way to use it.

When in the course of my research I made a telephone call to Charles Booz of the Du Pont Company, asking for some general information on Antron, I expected no more than a packet of publicity releases at best from this giant corporation, but the amount of cooperation I received from them was exemplary.

Du Pont's efforts provided some important answers for fly tiers. Their basic research, along with follow-up experiments, explained the physical properties of this material. Here are answers, based on scientific testing, to frequently asked questions about Sparkle Yarn.

What is Sparkle Yarn? For this discussion the term Sparkle Yarn will be limited to a type of nylon, Antron, made by DuPont. Antron is different from ordinary nylon because the filaments are three-sided, or trilobal. The properties of other synthetic yarns, sometimes inadvertently listed all together under the term Sparkle Yarn, will be described later.

What special properties of Sparkle Yarn are valuable to the fly tier? There are two main ones: the filaments reflect a high percentage of light and the filaments do not cling to each other.

Is it translucent? All nylon in the pure state is translucent. Opacity is controlled by adding titanium dioxide, which makes it white. Colored dyes are added later. The clear filaments in Sparkle Yarn, however, are pure, translucent nylon, with neither titanium dioxide nor dyes in them.

How does Sparkle Yarn reflect light? Do the filaments have flecks of metal in them? The theory of metal flecks is a recent explanation in fly-fishing literature, but it never has been correct. No foreign material makes the yarn sparkle. Trilobal nylon reflects light because each filament is triangular, or three-sided, rather than round like a standard nylon filament. The flat sides provide a much greater reflecting area than regular round filaments.

Does Sparkle Yarn reflect the same degree of light as an air bubble? In laboratory tests, physicist Paul Hale compared the light reflected off clear trilobal filaments to the light reflected off air bubbles. First the amount of light reflected back by each surface was measured with a reflectance meter. Then the color of the light reflected back by each surface was analyzed by a spectroscope. In each test the trilobal filaments produced virtually identical readings to those of an air bubble.

The fly tier must remember, of course, that Sparkle Yarn is a blend of clear and colored filaments. The emerging caddisfly pupa is not a pure air bubble either, but an insect that has body color. The yarn imitates the blend that the pupa shows to the fish.

The second physical property is that the filaments do not cling to each other. Why not? What advantage is this to the fly tier? Trilobal filaments were originally created for rugs. Both properties, the reflectance and the nonclinging characteristic of the fibers, help rugs retain a fresh look even after heavy use. The reflectance masks dirt accumulation and the noncling prevents the fibers from matting into unsightly clumps.

The chemists made their rug yarn so that it would not felt (or dub in fly-tying terms), which is a unique property. They accomplished this laboratory miracle by incorporating polymer antistatic control fibers in the structure of the filaments. This resistance to clinging means that in the water each strand remains separate rather than collapsing into a sodden mass, and every filament keeps an air space around itself. Mainly because of the nonclinging property of the yarn, the spread-out filaments attract and hold air bubbles better than any other material.

This is the feature that makes the Emergent Pupa, or any surface pattern using Antron, more than an imitation. All the air bubbles clustered around the fly turn it into an attractor as well as an imitator, often making it even better than just a perfect copy.

How do the filaments hold air bubbles? Many materials, flush on the water surface, will gather a few air bubbles, but none will attract or hold onto them as tenaciously as trilobal nylon does. There are four reasons for this:

One, more air bubbles are attracted initially because the filaments are not pressed against each other, leaving more free surface area on each strand. The air bubbles need surface area to cling to.

Two, with the individual filaments unclumped they naturally create spaces among themselves. These spaces trap any air bubbles, the filaments forming "cages" that hold the bubbles inside much more strongly than the ones on the outer surfaces.

Three, Ed Berling, a chemical engineer who heads the Industrial Fibers division for Du Pont, in one of his telephone calls gave another reason for the yarn's attraction to air: the filaments are coated with a water-resistant chemical, making it easier to wipe spills off a rug; this promotes the mechanical bonding of the air bubbles.

Four, Ken Parkany, who besides writing his fine *Afield and Astream* column for the *Hartford Courant*, is also an engineer, did some work on the reasons trilobal nylon holds onto air bubbles so strongly, and discovered that the bubbles can adhere much more firmly to the flat sides of the trilobal filaments than they can to the curving surfaces of regular round filaments.

Does Sparkle Yarn create the perfect imitation of an air bubble? The photograph of the Emergent Pupa in the color section answers this question easily enough. The fly is covered with air bubbles, but the clear filaments of trilobal nylon are also visible. Near the rear of the fly, however, where the bubbles and the filaments begin to go slightly out of focus, the air and the yarn become indistinguishable because the highlights reflected off them are identical.

The synthetic that I specifically recommend for my pupal patterns is Du Pont's trilobal nylon, or Antron, but there has been some confusion recently because other synthetics are also being marketed as Sparkle yarns under common names such as Dazzle, Twinkle, and Sparkle-Aire, and they look very similar to Antron. It is important for the fly tier to understand their physical properties.

Creslan. This material, introduced in *Challenge of the Trout*, is beautiful. It is a type of Orlon, a product made by American Cyanamid Corporation, that reflects light just like Antron. Its filaments also resist matting. The feeling of the yarn is fine and soft, almost like Angora fur, and it is a perfectly suitable substitute for Antron.

Acrilon. Acrilon is another type of bright filament material, made by Monsanto Corporation, and it is also highly reflective; however, it does not trap air bubbles as effectively as Antron or Creslan. It is suitable for underwater flies or whenever brightness is the only criterion.

One other synthetic that fly tiers should know about is marketed under the name Seal-Ex. Poul Jorgensen, the master of American fly-tying, markets this material as a substitute for seal fur. It became commercially available in 1975.

Fly tiers do not usually confuse Seal-Ex with Antron yarn. It is a dubbing produced from Kodel polyester yarn. The filaments are not clear, and not as translucent or as bright as Antron. It makes fine bodies for nymphs, but it is not suitable for imitating the shimmering air bubble of a caddisfly pupa.

Caddisfly Pupa Imitations

(There are four primary color variations and eleven secondary color variations for the pupal imitations—the Deep Sparkle Pupa and the Emergent Sparkle Pupa. The primary patterns cover approximately seventy percent of the situations an angler will encounter involving emerging caddisflies.)

Primary patterns:

1. BROWN AND YELLOW DEEP PUPA

HOOK:	Mustad 94840
WEIGHT:	lead or copper wire
UNDERBODY:	one-half russet or gold Sparkle Yarn and one-half brown fur (mixed and dubbed)
OVERBODY:	russet or gold Sparkle Yarn
HACKLE:	lemon wood-duck fibers (long wisps along the lower half of the sides)
HEAD:	brown marabou strands or brown fur

BROWN AND YELLOW EMERGENT PUPA

HOOK:	Mustad 94840
UNDERBODY:	one-half russet or gold Sparkle Yarn and one-half brown fur (mixed and dubbed)
OVERBODY:	russet or gold Sparkle Yarn
WING:	light speckled tips of deer body hair
HEAD:	brown marabou strands or brown fur

2. BROWN AND BRIGHT-GREEN DEEP PUPA

HOOK:	Mustad 94840
WEIGHT:	lead or copper wire
UNDERBODY:	one-third olive Sparkle Yarn and two-thirds bright green acrylic Craft fur (mixed and dubbed)
OVERBODY:	medium olive Sparkle Yarn
HACKLE:	dark grouse fibers (long wisps along the lower half of the sides)
HEAD:	brown marabou strands or brown fur

BROWN AND BRIGHT-GREEN EMERGENT PUPA

HOOK:	Mustad 94840
UNDERBODY:	one-third olive Sparkle Yarn and two-thirds bright green acrylic Craft fur (mixed and dubbed)
OVERBODY:	medium olive Sparkle Yarn
WING:	dark-brown speckled tips of deer body hair
HEAD:	brown marabou strands or brown fur

3. DARK GRAY DEEP PUPA

HOOK:	Mustad 94840
WEIGHT:	lead or copper wire
UNDERBODY:	one-half medium gray fur and one-half dark brown Sparkle Yarn (mixed and dubbed)
OVERBODY:	gray Sparkle Yarn
HACKLE:	dark gray hen-hackle fibers (long wisps along the lower half of the sides)
HEAD:	dark gray marabou fibers or dark gray fur

DARK GRAY EMERGENT PUPA

HOOK:	Mustad 94840
UNDERBODY:	one-half medium gray fur and one-half dark brown Sparkle Yarn (mixed and dubbed)
OVERBODY:	gray Sparkle Yarn
WING:	dark gray deer hair (preferably coastal deer)
HEAD:	dark gray marabou fibers or dark gray fur

4. GINGER DEEP PUPA

HOOK:	Mustad 94840
WEIGHT:	copper or lead wire
UNDERBODY:	one-half cream fur and one-half amber Sparkle Yarn (mixed and dubbed)
OVERBODY:	amber Sparkle Yarn
HACKLE:	lemon wood-duck fibers (long wisps along the lower half of the sides)
HEAD:	cream marabou fibers or cream fur

GINGER EMERGENT PUPA

HOOK:	Mustad 94840
UNDERBODY:	one-half cream fur and one-half amber Sparkle Yarn (mixed and dubbed)
OVERBODY:	amber Sparkle Yarn
WING:	light-brown deer hair
HEAD:	cream marabou fibers or cream fur

Secondary patterns:

5. BROWN DEEP PUPA

HOOK:	Mustad 94840
WEIGHT:	lead or copper wire
UNDERBODY:	one-half brown fur and one-half brown Sparkle Yarn (mixed and dubbed)
OVERBODY:	brown Sparkle Yarn
HACKLE:	dark grouse fibers (long wisps along the lower half of the sides)
HEAD:	brown marabou strands or brown fur

BROWN EMERGENT PUPA

HOOK:	Mustad 94840
UNDERBODY:	one-half brown fur and one-half brown Sparkle Yarn (mixed and dubbed)
OVERBODY:	brown Sparkle Yarn
WING:	brown deer body hair
HEAD:	brown marabou strands or brown fur

6. BLACK DEEP PUPA

HOOK:	Mustad 94840
WEIGHT:	copper or lead wire
UNDERBODY:	one-half dark-brown fur and one-half black Sparkle Yarn (mixed and dubbed)
OVERBODY:	black Sparkle Yarn
HACKLE:	dark brown hen hackle fibers (long wisps along the lower half of the sides)
HEAD:	black marabou strands or black fur

BLACK EMERGENT PUPA

HOOK:	Mustad 94840
UNDERBODY:	one-half dark-brown fur and one-half black Sparkle Yarn (mixed and dubbed)
OVERBODY:	black Sparkle Yarn
WING:	black deer hair
HEAD:	black marabou strands or black fur

7. GRAY AND YELLOW DEEP PUPA

HOOK:	Mustad 94840
WEIGHT:	lead or copper wire
UNDERBODY:	one-half pale-yellow fur and one-half gold Sparkle Yarn
OVERBODY:	yellow Sparkle Yarn
HACKLE:	light-gray snipe fibers (long wisps along the lower half of the sides)
HEAD:	dark-gray marabou strands or dark-gray fur

GRAY AND YELLOW EMERGENT PUPA

HOOK:	Mustad 94840
UNDERBODY:	one-half pale-yellow fur and one-half gold Sparkle Yarn (mixed and dubbed)
OVERBODY:	yellow Sparkle Yarn
WING:	gray speckled deer hair
HEAD:	dark-gray marabou strands or dark-gray fur

8. GRAY AND BROWN DEEP PUPA

HOOK: Mustad 94840

WEIGHT: copper or lead wire

UNDERBODY: one-half medium-brown fur and one-half medium-brown Sparkle Yarn (mixed and dubbed)

OVERBODY: brown Sparkle Yarn

HACKLE: light-gray partridge fibers (long wisps along the lower half of the sides)

HEAD: brown marabou strands or brown fur

GRAY AND BROWN EMERGENT PUPA

HOOK: Mustad 94840

UNDERBODY: one-half medium-brown fur and one-half medium-brown Sparkle Yarn (mixed and dubbed)

OVERBODY: brown Sparkle Yarn

WING: light-gray speckled deer hair

HEAD: brown marabou strands or brown fur

9. GRAY AND GREEN DEEP PUPA

HOOK: Mustad 94840

WEIGHT: copper or lead wire

UNDERBODY: one-half olive green Sparkle Yarn and one-half brown fur (mixed and dubbed)

OVERBODY: dark-olive green Sparkle Yarn

HACKLE: dark-gray partridge fibers (long wisps along the lower half of the sides)

HEAD: brown marabou fibers or brown fur

GRAY AND GREEN EMERGENT PUPA

HOOK: Mustad 94840

UNDERBODY: one-half olive green Sparkle Yarn and one-half brown fur (mixed and dubbed)

OVERBODY: dark-olive green Sparkle Yarn

WING: dark-gray speckled deer hair

HEAD: brown marabou fibers or brown fur

10. BROWN AND ORANGE DEEP PUPA

HOOK: Mustad 94840

WEIGHT: lead or copper wire

UNDERBODY: one-half rusty-orange fur and one-half orange Sparkle Yarn (mixed and dubbed)

OVERBODY: orange Sparkle Yarn

HACKLE: dark grouse fibers (long wisps along the lower half of the sides)

HEAD: cinnamon marabou strands or cinnamon fur

BROWN AND ORANGE EMERGENT PUPA

HOOK:	Mustad 94840
UNDERBODY:	one-half rusty-orange fur and one-half orange Sparkle Yarn (mixed and dubbed)
OVERBODY:	orange Sparkle Yarn
WING:	brown speckled deer hair
HEAD:	cinnamon marabou strands or cinnamon fur

11. BROWN AND DARK-BLUE DEEP PUPA

HOOK:	Mustad 94840
WEIGHT:	copper or lead wire
UNDERBODY:	one-half olive brown fur and one-half dark-blue Sparkle Yarn (mixed and dubbed)
OVERBODY:	light brown Sparkle Yarn
HACKLE:	lemon wood-duck fibers (long wisps along the sides)
HEAD:	dark-purple marabou fibers or dark-purple fur

BROWN AND DARK-BLUE EMERGENT PUPA

HOOK:	Mustad 94840
UNDERBODY:	one-half olive brown fur and one-half dark-blue Sparkle Yarn (mixed and dubbed)
OVERBODY:	light-brown Sparkle Yarn
WING:	brown deer hair and yellow deer hair (mixed into a single bunch)
HEAD:	dark-purple marabou fibers or dark purple fur

12. BLACK AND YELLOW DEEP PUPA

HOOK:	Mustad 94840
WEIGHT:	copper or lead wire
UNDERBODY:	one-half yellow fur and one-half yellow Sparkle Yarn (mixed and dubbed)
OVERBODY:	yellow Sparkle Yarn
HACKLE:	black hen-hackle fibers (long wisps along the sides)
HEAD:	black marabou fibers or black fur

BLACK AND YELLOW EMERGENT PUPA

HOOK:	Mustad 94840
UNDERBODY:	one-half yellow fur and one-half yellow Sparkle Yarn (mixed and dubbed)
OVERBODY:	yellow Sparkle Yarn
WING:	black deer hair
HEAD:	black marabou fibers or black fur

13. WHITE DEEP PUPA

HOOK:	Mustad 94840
WEIGHT:	copper or lead wire
UNDERBODY:	one-half cream fur and one-half white Sparkle Yarn (mixed and dubbed)
OVERBODY:	white Sparkle Yarn
HACKLE:	white hen-hackle fibers (long wisps along the sides)
HEAD:	white marabou fibers or white fur

WHITE EMERGENT PUPA

HOOK:	Mustad 94840
UNDERBODY:	one-half cream fur and one-half white Sparkle Yarn (mixed and dubbed)
OVERBODY:	white Sparkle Yarn
WING:	white deer hair
HEAD:	white marabou fibers or white fur

14. WHITE AND BRIGHT-GREEN DEEP PUPA

HOOK:	Mustad 94840
WEIGHT:	copper or lead wire
UNDERBODY:	one-half bright-green acrylic Craft fur and one-half green Sparkle Yarn (mixed and dubbed)
OVERBODY:	green Sparkle Yarn
HACKLE:	white hen hackle fibers (long wisps along the sides)
HEAD:	white marabou fibers or white fur

WHITE AND BRIGHT-GREEN EMERGENT PUPA

HOOK:	Mustad 94840
UNDERBODY:	one-half bright-green acrylic Craft fur and one-half green Sparkle Yarn (mixed and dubbed)
OVERBODY:	green Sparkle Yarn
WING:	white deer hair
HEAD:	white marabou fibers or white fur

15. TAN AND PALE-GREEN DEEP PUPA

HOOK:	Mustad 94840
WEIGHT:	copper or lead wire
UNDERBODY:	one-half green Sparkle Yarn and one-half cream fur (mixed and dubbed)
OVERBODY:	light-green Sparkle Yarn
HACKLE:	lemon wood-duck fibers (long wisps along the sides)
HEAD:	brown marabou fibers or brown fur

TAN AND PALE-GREEN EMERGENT PUPA

HOOK: Mustad 94840

UNDERBODY: one-half green Sparkle Yarn and one-half cream fur (mixed and dubbed)

OVERBODY: light-green Sparkle Yarn

WING: tan speckled tips of deer body hair

HEAD: brown marabou fibers or brown fur

Tying instructions for Deep Pupa:

HOOK: Mustad 94840

WEIGHT: copper wire or fine lead wire

1. Weight straight portion of the hook shank by tying in wire along the underside of the shank and wrapping the rest of the wire around the shank.

OVERBODY: Sparkle Yarn

2. Separate one ply from the four-ply yarn (and for very small flies even pull the single ply in half).

3. Completely fray one end of the yarn piece with a fine-toothed comb (either a No. 9 Ace comb or a mustache comb).

4. Spread the strands sparsely on top of the hook shank.

5. Tie down the strands at the bend of the hook.

6. Trim the stubs over shank (leave the frayed piece dangling off the rear of the hook for the moment).

7-11. Repeat the procedure. Tie down a second ply of yarn to the bottom side of the hook bend.

UNDERBODY: dubbing mix of one-half fur and one-half Sparkle Yarn

12. Dub the chopped blend onto the thread.

13. Wind the body three-fourths of the way up the shank.

14. Pick out the thin underbody to make it shaggy.

COMPLETING
THE OVERBODY: 15. Pull the top strands of Sparkle Yarn overbody forward.

16. Spread the strands evenly and sparsely over the top half of the underbody.

17. Tie down the strands in front of the underbody.

18-20. Repeat the procedure. Tie down the strands on the bottom of the shank.

The Deep Pupa Gary LaFontaine   *Step 1*   *Step 2*

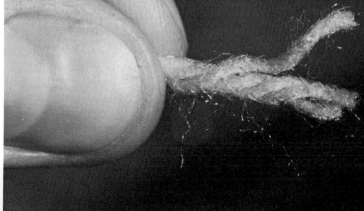

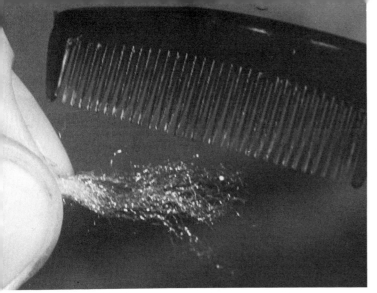

Step 3

Steps 4 and 5

Step 12

Step 13 and 14

Steps 15 and 16

Step 17

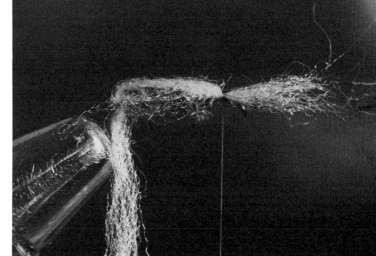

21. The overbody now covers the entire underbody in a sparse envelope—the key word is *sparse*. Before trimming the excess stubs in front of the tie off, take a dubbing needle and pull the overbody even looser.

22. Trim the stub.

HACKLE: soft hackle fibers

23. Tie in a few long wisps of soft hackle fibers, allowing them to sweep back along the lower half of the fly on each side.

HEAD: marabou strands

24. Tie in four or five strands of marabou.

25. Wrap the strands clockwise onto the thread (forming a rope).

26. Wind the covered thread to the eye. (Alternative for steps 24 through 26 [for commercial tiers]: dub a head of fur.) Whip-finish and cement thread.

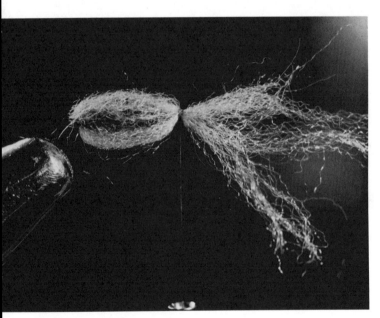

Repeat the procedure

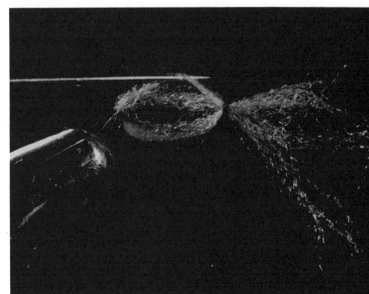

Step 21

Step 23

Step 24

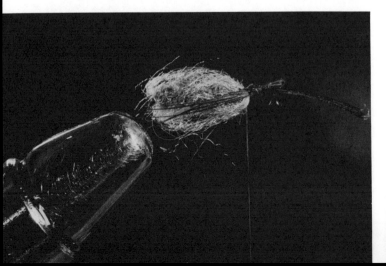

Step 25   Step 26

Tying instructions for Emergent Pupa:

HOOK: Mustad 94840

OVERBODY

AND

UNDERBODY: The materials and tying procedures for the overbody and under-
                 body on the Emergent Pupa are the same as they are on the Deep
                 Pupa. Steps 2 through 22 can be repeated for this version of the
                 Sparkle flies. No weight is used, so step 1 is eliminated.
                 23. With a scissors point, pull free some of the strands of the
                 overbody so that they dangle off the back. On the Emergent
                 imitation this represents the loosening sheath of the emerging
                 pupa.

WING: deer hair
                 24. Clip body hairs from a deer skin.
                 25. Level the tips in a hair tamper.
                 26. Tie a short wing on top of the hook with the hair.
                 27. Trim the stubs.

HEAD: marabou strands
                 28. Tie in four or five strands of marabou.
                 29. Wrap the strands clockwise onto the thread (forming a rope).
                 30. Wind the covered thread to the eye. Whip-finish and cement
                 thread.

The Simplified Sparkle patterns:

Fly-fishing friends have urged me to create a simplified version of the Sparkle
Pupa, an optional recipe minus the overbody, for easier and quicker tying. The first
prototypes early in 1974 were tied this way. These flies, with a basic body of dubbed
Antron or Creslan yarn, were—and still are—sold commercially by a few outlets as the
LaFontaine Sparkle Caddis Pupa. It might prevent some confusion, however, if these
were labeled as simplified versions.

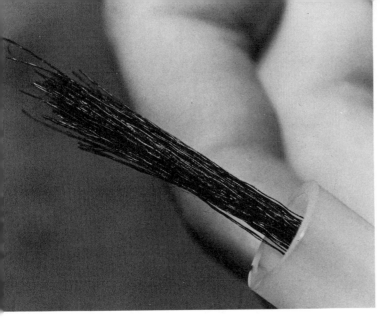

Step 25   *The Emergent Pupa* Gary LaFontaine

Step 26

Step 29

Step 30

DEEP PUPA

WEIGHT:	fine lead wire
BODY:	dubbed Sparkle Yarn
HACKLE:	soft hackle fibers
HEAD:	wrapped marabou

EMERGENT PUPA

BODY:	dubbed Sparkle Yarn
WING:	deer hair
HEAD:	wrapped marabou

*The Simplified Sparkle Pupa: (**a**) Deep and (**b**) Emergent* Gary LaFontaine

There is still the question of how effective this type is compared to the regular pattern. They are much better than any drab-bodied creations, but they are not quite as bright, nor do they trap air bubbles quite as well, as the overbody style. My preference for my own fishing is the regular type.

The Adult Imitation (Dry Fly)

The problems of creating an effective dry fly are entirely different from those of creating an underwater pattern; different even from the criteria of the Emergent Pupa, for example, because even that semidry imitation depends for much of its effectiveness on the portion that breaks through the film. The true surface fly, however, perching on top of the water, is subject to a different set of optical laws.

A trout's view of the surface is partially controlled by the meniscus, the rubbery interface between air and water created by molecular crowding. This film provides the tension that allows insects to float instead of sink, but it is not like a solid table top. It is an elastic sheet that bends under weight, each point of pressure by an insect indenting the film and forming a bump on the underside. Each of these bumps, in turn, acts as a lens to intensify light into a bright dot, these dots forming a light pattern that is unique to that insect type.

This light pattern, visible to the fish before the insect even enters the field of vision, presents the first problem in creating an effective dry fly. Before shape, size, or color can even be considered, the pressure points the fly pushes into the surface should usually approximate the imprint made by the natural.

In the case of the active caddisfly adult, in fact, the light pattern is sometimes the only problem the adult imitation must solve to be realistic. This is typically true, for example, when ovipositing females hop and skitter over the surface. If an insect or a fly is outside visual range (the trout's window) spreading a flash of light with every bounce and kick, the fish rushes toward the light pattern and never examines the finer details of the adult caddisfly. The major point emphasized by all the hours of observing trout feed on the surface is clear and simple: the light effect of the insect, whenever it is a prominent trigger for a strike, is so overwhelming that it is usually the only important characteristic.

Imagine the consequences for the fly tier—body, wings, hackle, tail: none of them very important in themselves on imitations of active insects. They are a factor in the success of the fly mostly in the way they create those points of pressure on the meniscus.

This fact had to be the starting point for the new imitations of the egg-laying caddisfly female. Observations of both flies and naturals—a diver acting as a surrogate trout—had to consider the insect or imitation when it was beyond the window of vision and leave the actual object creating the fuss out of sight.

It is important to reexamine Hewitt's list of factors to understand the criteria for a caddisfly pattern. Was Hewitt correct, at least in the case of the dry fly, in listing the light effect as the most important characteristic all the time?

No, the light effect is not always the number-one trait to imitate. Very small insects, for example, possess so little weight that they create either no pattern on the bottom of the meniscus or else an insignificant pattern. And yet these insects, including terrestrials and minute mayflies, can be major items in a trout's diet. Similarly, in fast water there is no significant light pattern because the mirror appearance of the meniscus underside is broken. An insect in rough water is snatched with a rush because it enters and leaves the trout's window so quickly.

Even with larger mayflies and terrestrials on quiet water, the light pattern is not the overwhelming characteristic it is with some caddisflies. A trout, holding in a specific line of drift, does not make a complete commitment to strike on the light pattern alone. Because the insect involved is relatively sedate as it floats, a fish holds a steady position and lets the flow act as a conveyor belt. The insect enters the window gradually, and the decision to accept or reject the object is also made gradually.

With the inactive natural or dry fly, the fish does not see the entire object during the approaching drift. Instead, the features become visible one by one as it floats nearer. It fools a fish if the important characteristics appear in the proper sequence.

There are caddisfly species that are also relatively inactive, flopping to the water and struggling feebly if at all after dropping the egg ball. These adults, subject to the same process of gradual acceptance, are taken by trout with a calm rise.

Accompanying illustrations show the differences in the relative traits of both a caddisfly and a mayfly, even if both of them are drifting quietly with the current.

The observation of feeding trout revealed a psychological quirk about the acceptance or refusal of a sedate imitation—possibly an explanation of why an angler's frauds work at all. It appears that the mind of the fish only looks for characteristics that are supposed to be there in the prescribed sequence, looking for what is right and ignoring what is wrong as each feature becomes visible. How else can fly fishermen explain that fortunate inability to recognize a hook?

But Hewitt was right about the light effect of many caddisfly species. The reason this trait is so overwhelming is that trout actually feed differently on active insects. And many egg-laying females, of course, do not drift quietly; they skip, hop, and run across the surface.

Usually a fish feeding on very active surface insects does not establish a holding position or a rise rhythm. It cruises, moving quickly to take the downed caddisflies. The trout recognizes the light pattern of the struggling insect and hurries toward the spot, its window to the surface never in focus because of its motion. The constant

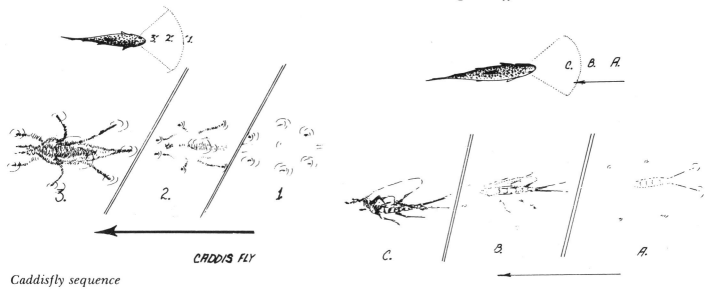

Caddisfly sequence

CADDIS FLY

Mayfly sequence

movement of the fish distorts and diminishes the visible characteristics of anything on the water.

Some insect species flutter and some do not. Dry flies are either consciously or unconsciously designed to imitate one or the other. Silhouette, color, and size are secondary features to this basic premise. A fly can sit high off the surface, held up by hackle and tail, and whether fished actively or not, suggest an insect about to take to the air. A fly can sit flush in the film, hook and body actually pressing through the meniscus, and suggest an insect helplessly trapped in the water. One fly cannot, of course, do both. Or can it?

The research to develop new dry-fly imitations began with observations of the naturals, species separated into strictly active or passive categories. This system of imitation died suddenly, though, when it became clear that some caddisflies belong in both categories. In many species the females split into both active and passive, some hopping all over and some collapsing quickly—actions apparently dependent on how well the individual survived the egg-laying ordeal.

During heavy mating and egg-laying flights of the Grannom (*Brachycentrus* sp.), for example, trout gorged on both types of females, one fish sipping dying insects and another cruising after struggling ones. Every trout fed selectively, but the division of the working fish made any fly, high-riding or flush, half worthless.

This split happened not only with caddisflies that lay their eggs on the surface but also with the diving types. After pasting the eggs to the bottom and swimming back to the meniscus, some of these adults pierced the film and flopped exhausted on top while others drowned on the underside.

The plan to type each species as active or passive was abandoned. The need was obvious for a dual caddisfly imitation: a fly that could settle flat on the water one moment, wing edges and body creating parallel pressure lines along the entire length of the shank, and the next moment could skate over the top, wing tips and other

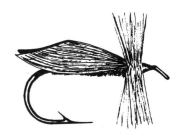

Older dry-fly imitations of caddisfly adults, such as the Halford caddis above, only work some of the time. Fly fishermen need a pattern that is consistently reliable.

Many egg-laying caddisflies bounce over the surface of the water.

protrusions flashing points of light.

The observation started with dying females because the visible characteristics were much more crucial with the sedate caddisfly. The studies of insects flush on the water verified the need for a full imprint with the fly. They also strongly indicated that a sharp V of the wings, the edges folded close to the body sides, detracted from the imitation. The sprawling wings of the spent natural demanded very flat edges extending out from each side of the fly body.

This discovery seemed to apply generally to all of the dry-fly experiments. It was the width of the silhouette, more so than the length, that was such a strong trait. On flat water in the evenings, with both fly and natural outlined against the sky, the lateral spread of the caddisfly wing was the feature keyed on by selective trout.

A proper design for a fly flat on the water, however, left the hook breaking the film. This did not ruin the effectiveness of the flush imitation, but the hook acted as an anchor. It prevented the flush pattern from skating, the fly unable to slide across the surface creating the points of light that would simulate the bouncing adult.

For very active caddisflies nothing except those light dots, stretched into streaks by motion, were really important. To mimic the intermittent fuss of a nearly dead female, though, the realistic characteristics were crucial to the fly's overall success.

The odd thing about the adult's action in taking off was that it was a running motion across the water, sometimes followed by a flutter of the wings. When the wings were folded down, the back edges acted like runners on a sleigh, the water-repellent hairs creating hydrofoils. This imprint on the surface is unique to caddisflies.

The spent adult caddisfly, seen from below, creates a distinct impression on the surface of the stream. To be effective, the wing edges of a matching dry fly must recreate the same impression.

The wing edges of a skating pattern also had to create these lines alongside the body. Each twitch and tug had to leave the twin streaks of light. The fly had to mimic the other light dots made by the natural—the intermittent pressure of the body and the light sparks of the hitting feet—but these were not as important as the streaks.

I was still faced with the same dilemma: a fly could be tied on a regular hook to imitate either a flush or active caddisfly, but not both. So I started experimenting with other styles of hooks—Fly Body, Parachute, and Keel Fly— but none of these was exactly right. The Keel Fly hook, however, did indicate that the solution had to be an upside-down hook style. The Keel Fly itself failed for my purposes because of the exaggerated belly hanging underneath, which is unnecessary for a dry fly. The upside-down landing of the dry fly depends on aerodynamics, not on a keel effect (which only works underwater).

An imitation tied on an upside-down hook could be effective for all types of adult caddisflies, the fly not only resting on the wing edges and body, but also skating on them. Without the hook to interfere, one fly could simulate the important characteristics whether drifting drag free or moving.

My experiments with home-machined hooks indicated that the style that worked best featured a nearly straight shank, the eye jutting upward and the bend lifting in an exaggerated curve. This design landed correctly every time on the water. It also placed

The new Dancing Caddis dry fly resting on a mirror. Gary LaFontaine

the barb above the wing of the fly, preventing missed strikes. (I later found that the commercially available Swedish Dry Fly Hook serves the purpose as well as my handcrafted hooks.)

The new fly proved very effective with both dead-drift and twitch presentations, eliminating most of the frustrating refusals by choosy trout. In specific instances it worked as well as flush imitations on fish that were feeding selectively on passive females, and it also worked as well as high-riding imitations on fish that were feeding selectively on active females.

My fly-fishing partners from Deer Lodge, Montana, saved the new dry imitation for an especially critical test—the massive return flights of the Spotted Sedge (*Hydropsyche occidentalis*) on the Clark Fork River. A number of factors—a spring-fed river, a brown-trout fishery, a heavy fall of insects—combined to create one of the most difficult fly-fishing situations in the country, characterized by the split pattern of feeding. This was precisely the type of hatch, however, that the fly was designed to master. It succeeded beautifully. The fly worked so well that the secret of the fly soon got out.

How good is the new fly? In no way is it meant to be the universal dry fly, because there are still some situations that demand even lower-floating imitations, flush patterns that actually sprawl awash in the film, or higher-riding imitations, skating patterns that bounce only on hackle tips. The Dancing Caddis, however, is certainly a very consistent all-around producer for selective trout.

Primary patterns:

1. BROWN AND YELLOW DANCING CADDIS

HOOK:	Swedish Dry Fly Hook
BODY:	yellow fur (with a brownish tinge)
WING:	speckled brown deer hair
HACKLE:	light-brown rooster hackle

2. BROWN AND GREEN DANCING CADDIS

HOOK:	Swedish Dry Fly Hook
BODY:	olive brown fur
WING:	speckled brown deer hair
HACKLE:	cree rooster hackle

3. DARK GRAY DANCING CADDIS

HOOK:	Swedish Dry Fly Hook
BODY:	one-half medium-gray fur and one-half dark-brown fur (mixed)
WING:	dark-gray deer hair
HACKLE:	bronze blue dun rooster hackle

4. GINGER DANCING CADDIS

HOOK:	Swedish Dry Fly Hook
BODY:	dark-cream fur
WING:	light-brown deer hair
HACKLE:	ginger rooster hackle

Secondary patterns:

5. BROWN DANCING CADDIS

HOOK:	Swedish Dry Fly Hook
BODY:	medium-brown fur
WING:	speckled brown deer hair
HACKLE:	brown rooster hackle

6. BLACK DANCING CADDIS

HOOK:	Swedish Dry Fly Hook
BODY:	very dark brown fur
WING:	black deer hair
HACKLE:	very dark brown rooster hackle

A size 14 Dancing Caddis Gary LaFontaine

7. GRAY AND YELLOW DANCING CADDIS

HOOK:	Swedish Dry Fly Hook
BODY:	pale-yellow fur
WING:	speckled light-gray deer hair
HACKLE:	dark-blue dun rooster hackle

8. GRAY AND BROWN DANCING CADDIS

HOOK:	Swedish Dry Fly Hook
BODY:	brown fur (with a dusky, grayish tinge)
WING:	speckled light-gray deer hair
HACKLE:	medium-brown rooster hackle

9. GRAY AND GREEN DANCING CADDIS

HOOK:	Swedish Dry Fly Hook
BODY:	olive brown fur
WING:	speckled dark-gray deer hair
HACKLE:	olive brown rooster hackle

10. BROWN AND ORANGE DANCING CADDIS

HOOK:	Swedish Dry Fly Hook
BODY:	rusty orange fur
WING:	speckled brown deer hair
HACKLE:	dark-ginger rooster hackle

11. BROWN AND DARK-BLUE DANCING CADDIS

HOOK:	Swedish Dry Fly Hook
BODY:	one-half dark-blue Sparkle Yarn and one-half olive brown fur (premixed into a dubbing)
WING:	brown deer hair and light-yellow deer hair (mixed into a single bunch before fastening it onto the hook)
HACKLE:	dark-purple rooster hackle

12. BLACK AND YELLOW DANCING CADDIS

HOOK:	Swedish Dry Fly Hook
BODY:	yellow fur
WING:	black deer hair
HACKLE:	black rooster hackle

13. WHITE DANCING CADDIS

HOOK:	Swedish Dry Fly Hook
BODY:	pale-cream fur
WING:	white deer hair
HACKLE:	white rooster hackle

14. WHITE AND GREEN DANCING CADDIS

HOOK:	Swedish Dry Fly Hook
BODY:	chartreuse fur
WING:	white deer hair
HACKLE:	white rooster hackle

15. TAN AND PALE-GREEN DANCING CADDIS

HOOK:	Swedish Dry Fly Hook
BODY:	one-half green fur and one-half cream fur (mixed and dubbed)
WING:	tan speckled deer hair
HACKLE:	light-brown rooster hackle

Tying instructions:

HOOK: Swedish Dry Fly Hook[3]
The tying design has been adapted to an effective upright hook, the Swedish Dry Fly Hook (patented by Nils Ericksson and Gunnar Johnson). This style achieves the same results obtained in the original handmade hooks, offering the aerodynamics and hooking ability in a readily available product.

BODY: dubbed fur
1. Remove any guardhairs from the dubbing mixture and spread it thinly on the thread.
2. Wrap a thin body. Wind from the bend up to the post in the shank, and then wind dubbing up that post.

WING: soft deer body hair
3. Stack the hair, evening the tips.
4. Point the tips to the rear, so that they extend as far as the bend of the hook. Bind the deer hair on top of the post.
5. Wrap the thread around the post notch, driving the wing downward, until the tips of the hair are bunched and angled under the hook point.
6. Trim the top of the wing so that the hairs are sparse in the middle. This area, under the hook point, must be clear for best hooking results.
7. Trim the hair butts on top of the post close to the shank.

HACKLE: rooster hackle (fibers matched to hook size as normal)
8. Tie down the hackle stem at the top of the post.
9. Wrap the hackle in the notch, through the deer-hair butts, with the dull side facing forward.
10. Trim the hackle fibers flat on the bottom. Whip-finish and cement head thread.

Floater series (Dancing Caddis)

Fly-fishing from a drifting boat, a method used extensively on western rivers, requires fairly unique tactics. It is possibly the ultimate test of reading water, both for

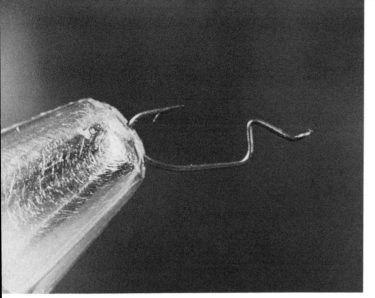

The Dancing Caddis Gary LaFontaine

Step 2

Step 3

Step 4

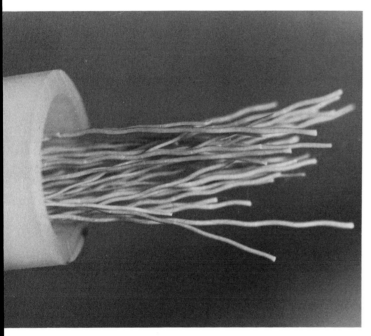

Step 5

Step 6

Step 7

Step 8

Step 9

Whip finish and cement head thread

rower and angler, because the holding spots pass so quickly, making the why, where, and how decisions immediate. There is usually only one chance at each spot.

The fly selected for this endeavor is typically a dry fly, an attractor type rather than an exact imitation. On most rivers favorite patterns are usually very bouyant and visible, often with white wings, so that the fisherman can see them in all types of water. The Floater Series is simply the basic Dancing Caddis in various body colors, but always with a white deer-hair wing.

Why alter the design of an exact imitation pattern for floating? What advantage does this type have over standard flies?

Bill Levine and I, during a float down the Madison River, first talked about adapting the Dancing Caddis for drift fishing. Bill estimated that he was hooking approximately three fish for every ten strikes using ordinary flies. Part of his hooking problem was caused by his overly quick reaction to the take, and we wondered if the Dancing Caddis might make a difference in his hooking percentage. He tried the first "Floater" prototype for twenty minutes and reported, "I never missed a fish."

Although there have not been any vigorously controlled tests, there have been enough experiences with the pattern from a boat to show that it is an incredibly fine hooker. In a drifting craft, where the movement, the excess of slack line, and the unnatural position of the fisherman all work to hamper the average angler's striking ability, the inverted style of the Dancing Caddis can sometimes double the hooking percentage.

Ironically, one of the early concerns before actually fishing this pattern type was whether or not it would set solidly with the strike, but it usually hooks a trout in the upper lip. On occasions, when the fish are striking quickly and lightly rather than with a wholehearted gulp, the Dancing Caddis seems to have an especially big advantage. The standard dry fly often slips out of the fish's mouth, or just catches the soft tissue near the lower jaw, but the upright hook sinks in many times even without an active strike by the fisherman.

FLOATER'S DANCING CADDIS SERIES:

HOOK:	Swedish Dry Fly Hook
BODY:	fur in either brown, cream, or gray, or peacock herl (an irridescent green)
WING:	always white deer hair
HACKLE:	always cree rooster hackle[4]

Caddisfly Adult Imitations (Wet Fly)

Sid Gordon, in his book *How to Fish From Top To Bottom* (1955), recognized the importance of diving, egg-laying females. He recorded an incident on the Brule River in Wisconsin: "As it pierced the water film, an almost unbelieveable change came over that drab fly. It suddenly seemed to be encased in a bright gleaming bubble, so bright that it looked like a shining ball of quicksilver. Fast moving legs propelled the bubble, angling it down toward the bottom of the clear water.

"There the bubble crawled nervously over a rubble stone and stopped. What was that fly doing there? I watched the bright, silvery insect for a moment or two, then reached down to seize it, but the fly let go its hold upon the rock and drifted away."

The large bubble clinging to the rough body and hairs of the adult caddisfly provides oxygen. The female stays underwater long enough to lay her eggs, and in many instances she returns safely to the surface. With this type of breathing, known as plastron respiration, the bubble does not diminish in size, the slow exchange of oxygen for carbon dioxide occurring within the encompassing dome, so that it is just as prominent on the swim up as it was on the swim down.

The females of many caddisfly species dive or crawl to the streambed to lay their eggs under-water.

*The common Green Sedge (*Rhyacophila carolina*) is one type of caddisfly that dives underwater to lay eggs. As soon as the female pierces the surface, her wings and body collect a silvery coating of air.* Ken Thompson

Both the brightness and the action of the diving female are distinct enough to make a wet-fly imitation necessary. In some situations a subsurface pattern replaces the dry-fly pattern; in others it is interchangeable with it. With one of my favorite techniques, a two- or three-fly dropper rig, it is possible to fish both a dry fly and a wet fly at the same time.

The main problem in creating an imitation of the adult is that the bubble surrounds most of the insect. It is not compressed inside a transparent sheath, squashed into many tiny bubbles, as in the instance of the pupa. The brightness is an overlaying shell, the insect clearly visible inside rather than just a splotchy combination of color and reflection. Around the wings, the wall of the bubble is plastered snugly, but it bulges so far away from the body that the insect looks like a silver sausage with legs sticking out.

The regular, commercial Sparkle Yarn, with a mix of clear and dyed filaments, might be ideal for pupal imitations, but it is not bright enough to imitate the overcoat of the diving adult. The pure Antron filaments, hanging free over the back, reflect more light. They are much more suitable for some parts of the wet-fly patterns.

I am sure that if Sid Gordon had lived long enough to see modern synthetics such as Antron and Creslan he would have immediately recognized their potential and would have used them creatively to solve his diving-caddisfly mystery. I know that his writings, identifying the problem clearly, influenced me so strongly that my goal became to find a material to simulate an air bubble.

Primary patterns:

1. BROWN AND YELLOW DIVING CADDIS

HOOK:	Mustad 7957-B
BODY:	rusty yellow Sparkle Yarn
UNDERWING:	speckled brown grouse fibers
OVERWING:	clear Antron or Creslan filaments
HACKLE:	light-brown rooster hackle

2. BROWN AND GREEN DIVING CADDIS

HOOK: Mustad 7957-B
BODY: olive green Sparkle Yarn
UNDERWING: dark-brown grouse fibers
OVERWING: clear Antron or Creslan filaments
HACKLE: brown rooster hackle

3. DARK-GRAY DIVING CADDIS

HOOK: Mustad 7957-B
BODY: one-half medium-gray Sparkle Yarn and one-half dark-brown
                Sparkle Yarn (blended into a dubbing mix)
UNDERWING: dark-gray duck quill fibers (frayed apart with a dubbing needle
                and rolled into a wing)
OVERWING: clear Antron or Creslan filaments
HACKLE: bronze blue dun rooster hackle

4. GINGER DIVING CADDIS

HOOK: Mustad 7957-B
BODY: amber Sparkle Yarn
UNDERWING: lemon wood-duck fibers
OVERWING: clear Antron or Creslan filaments
HACKLE: ginger rooster hackle

Secondary patterns:

5. BROWN DIVING CADDIS

HOOK: Mustad 7957-B
BODY: brown Sparkle Yarn
UNDERWING: dark-brown grouse fibers
OVERWING: clear Antron or Creslan filaments
HACKLE: brown rooster hackle

A size 14 Brown-and-Yellow Diving Caddis
Gary LaFontaine

6. BLACK DIVING CADDIS

HOOK:	Mustad 7957-B
BODY:	black Sparkle Yarn
UNDERWING:	black hen-hackle fibers
OVERWING:	clear Antron or Creslan filaments
HACKLE:	dark-brown rooster hackle

7. GRAY AND YELLOW DIVING CADDIS

HOOK:	Mustad 7957-B
BODY:	medium-yellow Sparkle Yarn
UNDERWING:	light-gray partridge fibers
OVERWING:	clear Antron or Creslan filaments
HACKLE:	dark-blue dun rooster hackle

8. GRAY AND BROWN DIVING CADDIS

HOOK:	Mustad 7957-B
BODY:	dark-brown Sparkle Yarn
UNDERWING:	light-gray partridge fibers
OVERWING:	clear Antron or Creslan filaments
HACKLE:	medium-brown rooster hackle

9. GRAY AND GREEN DIVING CADDIS

HOOK:	Mustad 7957-B
BODY:	two-thirds olive green Sparkle Yarn and one-third medium Sparkle Yarn (blended into a dubbing mix)
UNDERWING:	dark-gray partridge fibers
OVERWING:	clear Antron or Creslan filaments
HACKLE:	olive brown rooster hackle

10. BROWN AND ORANGE DIVING CADDIS

HOOK:	Mustad 7957-B
BODY:	rusty orange Sparkle Yarn
UNDERWING:	dark-brown grouse fibers
OVERWING:	clear Antron or Creslan filaments
HACKLE:	dark-ginger rooster hackle

11. BROWN AND DARK-BLUE DIVING CADDIS

HOOK:	Mustad 7957-B
BODY:	one-half dark-blue Sparkle Yarn and one-half olive brown Sparkle Yarn (blended into a dubbing mix)
UNDERWING:	brown hen-hackle fibers and yellow hen-hackle fibers (mixed into a single bunch)
OVERWING:	clear Antron or Creslan filaments
HACKLE:	dark-purple rooster hackle

Is tri-lobal nylon, Sparkle Yarn, perfect for simulating the air bubbles encased within the pupal sheath of the emerging caddisfly? Near the rear of this Black Emergent Pupa, where the air bubbles and the clear filaments of tri-lobal begin to go slightly out of focus, the air and the yarn become indistinguishable because the highlights reflected off them are identical. *Photo by Arie DeZanger*

The insect that cuts free of the pupal cocoon and swims or crawls to the surface is actually a fully formed adult sheathed in a loose, filmy skin. Every part of the emerging pupa—head, wings, legs, body—is enclosed within this skin. In this living pupa , the skin is swelling at the thorax of the insect. If this emergent was still submerged, the greater pressure of the water would force this air back until bubbles completely surrounded the insect.

Photo by John Gantner

Cased Caddis Larva pattern

Caddis Larva pattern

Deep Sparkle Pupa

Emergent Sparkle Pupa

Dancing Caddis

Diving Caddis

Psilotreta labida

Helicopsyche borealis

Ironoquia parvula

Hydatophylax argus

Rhyacophila fuscula

Hydropsyche morosa

Ptilostomis ocellifera

Limnephilus indivisus

Pycnopsyche guttifer

Platycentropus radiatus

Phryganea sayi

Banksiola crotchi

All photographs of adult natural insects are by Ken Thompson.

All photographs of the fly patterns are by Gary LaFontaine.

12. BLACK AND YELLOW DIVING CADDIS

HOOK: Mustad 7957-B
BODY: yellow Sparkle Yarn
UNDERWING: black hen-hackle fibers
OVERWING: clear Antron or Creslan filaments
HACKLE: black rooster hackle

13. WHITE DIVING CADDIS

HOOK: Mustad 7957-B
BODY: pale-cream Sparkle Yarn
UNDERWING: white hen-hackle fibers
OVERWING: clear Antron or Creslan filaments
HACKLE: white rooster hackle

14. WHITE AND BRIGHT-GREEN DIVING CADDIS

HOOK: Mustad 7957-B
BODY: one-half bright-green acrylic fur and one-half green Sparkle Yarn (blended into a dubbing mix)
UNDERWING: white hen-hackle fibers
OVERWING: clear Antron or Creslan filaments
HACKLE: white rooster hackle

15. TAN AND PALE-GREEN DIVING CADDIS

HOOK: Mustad 7957-B
BODY: one-half green Sparkle Yarn and one-half cream Sparkle Yarn (blended into a dubbing mix)
UNDERWING: lemon wood-duck fibers
OVERWING: clear Antron or Creslan filaments
HACKLE: light-brown rooster hackle

Tying instructions:

HOOK: Mustad 7957-B (a standard wet-fly hook)
BODY: Sparkle Yarn (the regular blend of clear and dyed filaments)
  1. Spread the chopped-up dubbing blend onto a thread.
  2. Wrap a thin body three-quarters of the way up the shank.
UNDERWING: soft hackle fibers
  3. Roll soft hackle fibers into a wing configuration.
  4. Tie down the underwing at the front of the body (the tips of the fibers extending to the bend of the hook).
  5. Trim the stubs.
OVERWING: clear Antron or Creslan filaments
  6. Tie down twenty to thirty filaments over the underwing.
  7. Trim the stubs.

The Diving Caddis Gary LaFontaine   *Step 1*

Step 2

Step 4

Step 6

Step 8

Steps 9 and 10

HACKLE: rooster hackle

8. Tie in a rooster hackle.

9. Wind one turn of stiff hackle (forming a sparse collar).

10. Wrap backward with the thread until the collar of hackle is forced back. The stiff rooster-hackle fibers stand out from the body and add vibrancy to the moving wet fly. Whip-finish and cement the head thread.

Ideas on Attraction

After reading my comments on attractor flies in *Challenge of the Trout*, many anglers wrote and asked me to postulate a Theory of Attraction, in tandem with my Theory of Imitation, for choosing the right fly at the right time. But, I have no Theory of Attraction simply because the basic studies have not been done. However, in scientific terms, I do have hypotheses, ideas that will have to be tested, at least on attraction in fast water.

Here they are:

1. Trout actually feed just as selectively in fast water as they do in slow water. The process of selecting or rejecting passing items in fast water, however, is not visual because there is not enough time for the food objects to be studied as there is in slow water. In fast water the trout grab anything they see that remotely resembles food, and use the taste buds in the mouth to decide whether or not it is edible. They are still exhibiting a stimulus/response feeding pattern, but the rejection does not come until after the item, either natural or imitation, is inside the mouth.

Fast water is a great equalizer of flies, both of subsurface and surface patterns. Without rapid water sections on our trout streams the huge variety of flies available would shrink drastically. Complete styles of fly tying would disappear; but they do not because in fast water almost any fly can catch some trout.

What happens in fast water? A fish cannot see an imitation or a natural coming, the object lost in the turbulence, so there is no chance for it to sort out the visual characteristics one by one. Actually, a fish probably does not make any distinction between objects at all because they enter and leave its area so quickly. It only recognizes that something is passing and inhales whatever it is; the fish sorting with its taste buds rather than with its eyes, and as a result snatching twigs, leaves, or pine needles—and even poor imitations that will not work anywhere else.

2. When trout are not feeding on something specific in fast water they are apt to snatch anything they can see, so the fly they can spot at the greatest distance is usually going to be the best attractor. Imitating a natural insect, and the protective coloration that hides it from the fish, may actually diminish the angler's chances.

3. The way to take advantage of random feeding in fast water is by using a highly visible fly. The factors that determine visibility—brightness and color—cannot be considered independently, however. The contrast between the colors and brightness in the fly and the contrast between the fly and the background, is also important.

On a day with blue sky for a background it would be hard to improve on a Royal Wulff or a Royal Trude as the ultimate, dry-fly attractor. If the water is fast, but smooth on the surface, the Royal Wulff might work better because the upright wings would be visible above the water line. If the water is fast but choppy, where nothing above the surface would be visible from below, the Royal Trude might work better because the flat wings would create a more distinctive silhouette.

What about underwater flies? As long as the water was not saturated with natural air bubbles the brightness of the fly would be an important trait. With contrasting colors in the materials, maybe red and white, either the Deep or Emergent Pupa patterns would be strong attractors. If the water was turbulent, however, dark solid colors might stand out better against the shiny bubbles. A pattern like the Bright Green Caddis Larva, maybe a size or two larger than normal, would be a good choice for choppy riffles.

These are just a few thoughts. An entire theory, with pattern recommendations for all ranges of water clarity, sky color, current velocities, and habitat type, might require years of experimentation to determine the influences of all factors of attraction.

—a last word from an avowed impressionist

Many fly tyers have apparently failed to learn from past mistakes. They have created any number of exquisite frauds, realistic in every detail, some so perfect that they capture the verisimilitude of any embalmed specimen. But do they catch fish? Poorly.

The crux is that a fly tyer must be more of an artist than a craftsman. Just as in painting, the technical perfectionist draws a precise (if plasticized) representation of the features of the face. The artist, on the other hand, with a few quick strokes captures the essence of what makes the person alive.

The fly tyer likewise must free imagination from a realistic imitation to create effective fly patterns instead of just precise replicas. He must simulate not only the general form, but also the qualities that identify an insect as a living organism.

3

Other Effective Caddisfly Imitations

The extensive observations of both natural insects and feeding fish produced my imitations for the various stages of caddisflies. The same observations and careful tests, however, also pinpointed angling situations where the standard favorites were very effective.

A pattern becomes accepted by producing over a period of time. This success is not guaranteed; any fly can fail miserably at moments simply because the situation is wrong for it, but the triumphs are frequent enough to give anglers confidence in its fish-catching abilities. This confidence spreads to other fishermen in two ways; by word-of-mouth recommendations and by accounts in books, magazines, and newspapers. Together such publicity can establish the reputation of a new pattern very quickly.

This widespread recognition, however, often leads to general rather than specific usage of the pattern. As more and more fishermen try the fly, adding it to their on-stream assortment, it is also used more and more randomly. Too often the popularity of the fly then obscures the reasons it was originally conceived. Instead of being fished in situations where it would be most effective, it is tried in a hit-or-miss fashion; it is fished in such a scattergun way it loses some of its value.

Thus, the secret of assembling and maintaining a stock of flies designed to meet as many angling problems as possible is to remember the concept behind each one. This does not deny that some flies have powers of imitation or attraction beyond the narrow limits of matching a particular insect. Recognizing that the use of a pattern is linked to one type of situation, however, guarantees that at the right moment for the fly it will not be left sitting in the box.

In no way is this chapter meant to be a "cookbook" of known caddisfly patterns. This listing singles out flies that have proven to be exceptionally effective in specific instances.

69

Larval Imitations

Strawman Nymph (originated by Paul Young)

This is one of the earliest and most effective imitations of a cased caddisfly larva. It was created by Paul Young specifically to match the stick cases of an unidentified species he found in the cold, slow-moving trout streams of the upper Midwest, but it also turned out to be a good imitation for the larvae of other genera elsewhere in the country (see Chapter 11, Insect Listing, genus *Platycentropus*, for my guess at which species he was imitating).

This pattern is practically indispensable in early spring, when high water swirls into the back eddies and washes the big stick larvae free of the debris. The tactic for the angler to use then is one of the simplest, the hand-twist retrieve, because it can work the fly at a crawl through the deeper water. This tactic once fooled a three-pound brown trout in the Salmon River in Connecticut on Opening Day for me.

HOOK:	Mustad 9671, 2XL, sizes 4, 6, 8
WEIGHT:	fine lead wire (weighting optional)
BODY:	natural deer hair (spun very thinly; clipped roughly in a taper from tail to head)
RIBBING:	pale-yellow floss (worked through the fibers)

South Platte Brassie (originated by Gene Lynch)

Can the popular Colorado nymph, the Brassie, be an insect imitation? There are no nymphs or larvae that a Brassie looks like because the metallic glitter of the copper-wire body is unnaturally bright. The fly is usually fished dead drift, rather than with an active retrieve, so it probably does not simulate a flashy minnow. Nevertheless this pattern catches a lot of trout.

No fly ever baffled me as much as this one. It failed pathetically at times when any fly could fool fish, but then there were moments when it was incredibly effective. It had no apparent reason for working and none for not working. It was a pattern without a theory of imitation to indicate when to use it.

One day while scuba diving in the Clark Fork River, I thought for a moment that someone was fishing a Brassie near my position. Then I began to see more of the metallic reddish objects, and watched trout begin feeding on them. I captured a few of these drifting insects.

The glitter was caused by minerals such as mica, schist, garnet, and feldspar in the stone cases of the caddisfly larvae. The immature caddisflies were later identified to generic level as *Oligophlebodes* sp. (Little Western Dark Sedge), a common insect in gravel-bottomed trout streams of the West. This provided the first plausible clue to the Brassie's effectiveness.

There are caddisfly larvae with rough stone cases, ranging in size from five to forty millimeters, in most trout streams. They might be the tiny microcaddis, genus *Hydroptila*, important in many spring creeks, or the Giant Orange Sedges, genus *Dicosmoecus*, inhabiting the swiftest areas of large rivers, but if the larvae have stone cases of reddish yellow or metallic minerals the Brassie can match them all.

HOOK: Mustad 3906, sizes 6-20
BODY: copper wire (wrap white floss under the wire as a tapered base; use
           26-gauge wire for sizes 6 and 8, 28-gauge wire for sizes 10 and 12,
           30-gauge wire for sizes 14 and 16, 34-gauge wire for sizes 18 and 20)
HEAD: dubbed gray fur (guardhairs left in)

Pupal Imitations

At this time there are no pupal imitations other than the Sparkle patterns that
can effectively match the swimming emergers. Both drab-bodied and tinsel-bodied
types are unnatural and fail to create the illusion of air bubbles inside the loosening
sheath of the insect.

Strawman Nymph Gary LaFontaine

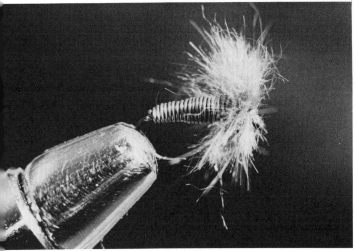

South Platte Brassie Gary LaFontaine

*The smaller sizes of the Brassie match the stone cases of
the* Hydroptila *larvae. Sand grain cases are shown
above on the left and right. An uncased larva is shown
in the center.* Ken Thompson

The drab-bodied, Sens types appear underwater as if they should be fair imitations of the crawling emergers, which do not generate quite as many air bubbles as the swimmers, but even in these situations they do not produce as well as more reflective flies.

Adult Imitations

Henryville (originator unknown)

Hiram Brobst discovered this fly in an old English angling book, but there was no identification with the illustration. He resurrected it as a popular fly in the Pennsylvania Poconos. In the 1920s and 1930s it became such a standard on Brodheads Creek that it was named after a section of that stream.

HOOK:	Mustad 94840, sizes 14-22
BODY:	green floss
PALMERED BODY HACKLE:	grizzly rooster hackle (trimmed on top)
UNDERWING:	wood-duck fibers (sparse)
OVERWING:	matched slips of slate-duck quill (flat over back)
HEAD HACKLE:	dark-ginger rooster hackle

The original body color of the Henryville was red, but Ernest Schwiebert tied the pattern with a green body to better match the abundant Green Sedges (*Rhyacophila* sp.) of the Brodheads. This became the accepted version, the new fly also matching other important genera with green coloration.

The uniqueness of the Henryville is that it suggests motion even when it is drifting dead with the current. It rides high for a dry fly, the palmered hackle lifting the wings off the surface, giving it the appearance of a caddisfly adult about to fly off.

It is a good imitation to use whenever green-bodied females are laying eggs, even as a match for those species that dive under the surface, but it is especially effective when the females stay on the water. Then, with insects flopping and struggling on top to drop the ball of eggs rather than going under, the Henryville simulates the commotion just by the way it sits.

Delta Wing Caddis (originated by Larry Solomon)

This fly was well known in the East even before the publication of *The Caddis and the Angler* by Larry Solomon and Eric Leiser. It was an important innovation in caddisfly patterns because it was the first pattern to intentionally mimic dead or exhausted adults in the surface film. By recognizing that not all caddisflies were high-bouncing fliers and that concentrations of flush-floating insects occurred, it opened up a new niche in adult imitations.

HOOK:	M-V 94840, sizes 14-20
BODY:	light-olive mink fur
WING:	two gray hen-hackle tips
HACKLE:	brown rooster hackle
	(colors can be altered to match any caddisfly adult)

Henryville Gary LaFontaine

Delta Wing Caddis Gary LaFontaine

The way the Delta Wing lies on the water, wings sprawled out at the sides, makes it a particularly effective fly during the mass returns of egg-laying females. Then, when many adults fail to fly away, it is deadly wherever the current gathers the drowned insects. Sometimes a very subtle twitch, just enough to make the wings fold momentarily against the body, helps draw attention to it.

Parkany Deer Hair Caddis (originated by Ken Parkany)

Ken Parkany and I have traded favorite or experimental patterns frequently, creating an East-West exchange of the latest ideas. He sent along a deer-hair imitation that quickly proved itself, not only in Montana but wherever it was used.

The Parkany Deer Hair Caddis is not just unique in appearance, it is one of the most durable, bouyant, and visible dry-flies available to imitate the adult caddisfly. Many patterns have these qualities and are praised as "rough-water" floaters, but they are unrealistically bulky in the intermediate sizes. The Parkany Deer Hair Caddis is not too bulky in these sizes. The body rides flush on the surface, but the wing, canted at a slightly higher angle than other caddisfly imitations, sticks up off the water.

HOOK:	Mustad 94843, 4XS (this type of hook has an extra-wide gap), sizes 8-16
BODY:	light-brown deer body hair (spun and clipped to shape)
WING:	mottled brown tips of deer body hair
HEAD:	deer body hair (the stubs of the wing hair are clipped flat on the top and the bottom and left flared out at the sides to act as outriggers)

This fly can be tied in any color combination. Rather than using it as an imitation of a specific caddisfly species, I use it generally on riffle sections of trout streams because it does not require a lot of fussing to keep floating. One day on the Madison River, Graham Marsh fished the Parkany Deer Hair Caddis and he caught and released over thirty trout without once changing or redressing the fly.

Spent Partridge Caddis (originated by Mike and Sheralee Lawson)

Mike and Sheralee Lawson tied this fly for a specific situation on the Henrys Fork: the selective feeding on small, spent caddisflies. They experimented with materials and tying techniques for a new fly, creating prototypes, and then Mike refined the ideas into a finished imitation by testing them on the river.

The usefulness of this pattern is not restricted to the Henrys Fork. It matches the silhouette and floating characteristics of many small caddisflies, and on slow-water rivers, where fussy trout often sip in spent females for hours, it is the consummate match for such activity.

HOOK:	Mustad 94840, sizes 16-22
BODY:	olive fur
WING:	mottled fibers of a partridge feather
HACKLE:	brown rooster fibers (palmered over the head; the hackle can be clipped flat on the top and the bottom)
HEAD:	peacock herl

Thompson Foam Caddis (originated by Ken Thompson)

Ken Thompson, a graduate student in aquatic entomology and a specialist on caddisflies, certainly has the background to appreciate the unique problems of this complex order. Many times entomologists are not anglers and have trouble translating their knowledge into solutions for anglers, but Ken was an accomplished fly fisherman and fly tier before he entered graduate school.

In initial form this fly was a terrestrial imitation, but then Ken discovered a new material, Ethafoam, and incorporated it into the pattern to transform the fly into a very effective adult-caddisfly imitation.

What does Ethafoam, a common packing material, add to a fly? It contains numerous air bubbles, and while these bubbles are not very reflective (because the

Parkany Deer-Hair Caddis (as shown from underneath)
Gary LaFontaine

Spent Partridge Caddis Gary LaFontaine

white foam surrounding them diffuses light rays) the foam is translucent enough so that when sliced thin it produces a look of soft illumination. When the material is used over the top of a fly, overlapping the sides of the body, this translucency along the edges recreates the effect of the wings of caddisfly adults.

HOOK:	Mustad 94840, sizes 14-28
BACK:	Ethafoam packing material (originally white, but made into any desirable color with a waterproof marker)
HALF WING:	mink hairs (tied in at the bend of the hook and extended off the rear)
BODY:	dubbed fur

In my tests this fly has been particularly effective when there have been large numbers of diving, egg-laying females under the surface. In these situations, when trout are snatching these returning, swimming adults in the film, the Thompson Foam Caddis represents the active insect arriving at the top.

Bucktail Caddis (originator unknown)

This large deer-hair dry fly is most popular in the Northwest, where it is often used to match the big autumn species of that area. Perhaps it has not become more widely known in the East because it is generally considered a rough-water type, better suited to the brawling western waters than the smaller eastern flows. But there are also big caddisflies in the East, fall emergers that are well matched by the Bucktail Caddis, and the pattern often works surprisingly well there on broken currents.

There are two color variations a fly fisherman should carry in the larger sizes, sizes 4, 6, and 8 especially, for both autumn fishing and midsummer night fishing no matter where he lives:

Thompson Foam Caddis Gary LaFontaine

Bucktail Caddis Gary LaFontaine

LIGHT BUCKTAIL CADDIS

HOOK: Mustad 7957-B
TAIL: light-tan elk hair
BODY: light-yellow fur (dubbed)
HACKLE: light-ginger rooster hackle (palmered over the whole body)
WING: light-tan elk hair (extending slightly past the bend of the hook)

DARK BUCKTAIL CADDIS

HOOK: Mustad 7957-B
TAIL: dark mottled deer hair
BODY: golden yellow fur (dubbed)
HACKLE: golden yellow rooster hackle (palmered over the whole body)
WING: dark mottled deer hair (extending slightly past the bend of the hook)

Kevin Toman markets an adaptation of the Bucktail Caddis. He ties flies so perfectly that they could never look bushy or sloppy. His patterns are very worthwhile when large imitations, sizes 6 through 12, are needed on smooth-flowing rivers in either the East or the West.

Kevin, a young Californian, is a highly acclaimed professional fly tier, supplying thousands of dozens of flies each year to discriminating commercial outlets such as the Henrys Fork Anglers and Kaufmann's Streamborn Flies. He is also a professional fly-fishing guide and an author, his first article appearing recently in *Fly Tyer* magazine.

ORANGE BUCKTAIL CADDIS
(color variation to match the Giant Orange Sedge [*Dicosmoecus*])

HOOK: Mustad 94840, sizes 6 and 8
BODY: bright-orange natural or synthetic fur (dubbed)
BODY
HACKLE: dark-ginger hackle (palmered over the whole body, tied in hackle-tip first)
WING: dark speckled natural deer hair (fine, long hairs, tied in neatly)
HEAD
HACKLE: dark-ginger hackle (not too bushy)
HEAD: brown fur

PEACOCK BUCKTAIL CADDIS

HOOK: Mustad 94840
BODY: peacock herl
BODY
HACKLE: brown hackle (palmered over the whole body; tied in hackle-tip first)
WING: light speckled deer hair (fine, long hairs tied in neatly)
HEAD: peacock herl

These recommendations give the angler a few more flies to carry (two more nymphs and six more dry flies) besides my patterns from Chapter 2, but the number

Peacock Bucktail Caddis Gary LaFontaine

still is not unreasonable. Every fly has right situations and wrong situations for it. It might be best to review briefly the specific moments for the patterns discussed in this chapter.

STRAWMAN NYMPH:	in the spring on streams in heavily wooded areas, when the water level rises and washes the stick larvae out of the bottom debris
BRASSIE:	when larvae with stone cases of yellow or metallic minerals are abundant and available
HENRYVILLE:	when female caddisflies that stay on the surface to lay their eggs, rather than dive underwater, are active
DELTA WING CADDIS:	near the end of or after heavy egg-laying activity, when dead or exhausted females are gathered into back eddies or dominant current lanes
PARKANY DEER HAIR CADDIS:	generally on the choppier, riffle sections of trout streams whenever sporadic caddisfly activity makes a downwing type a good searching fly
SPENT PARTRIDGE CADDIS:	on spring creeks and rivers, or on slow-water sections of freestone streams, when the females of any small species of caddisfly (sizes 16 through 28) are abundant and active
THOMPSON FOAM CADDIS:	when female caddisflies that lay their eggs underwater are active, swimming from and to the surface and creating a concentration in the meniscus
BUCKTAIL CADDIS:	during the summer at night or during the autumn in late afternoon or at dusk, when large caddisflies (sizes 4 through 8) are active

There are some notable absences in the selection. There are no patterns with upright wings. This type, generally recommended as an imitation of a fluttering caddisfly, is not very effective when trout are feeding selectively, even if the adults are fluttering. When the natural begins unfolding its wings it usually flies off very quickly and such a transitory moment is not worth imitating. The tent-wing fly is usually better because it imitates the insect at rest.

Another pattern type that is missing is the quill-wing adult imitation. Such flies, usually resembling the old Halford Caddis (originated by F. M. Halford) or the Kings River Caddis (originated by Buz Buszek), are effective; and, personally, I do carry them in my own fly selection, but they are very fragile. The wings tear apart so easily that each fly is only good for two or three trout at most. The quill-wing type can be considered optional on the list. For those who tie their own flies, or order them from a custom tier, here is the recipe for a good pattern:

TURKEY WING CADDIS (sent to me by Ron Zaworsky)
HOOK: Mustad 94840, sizes 14-18
BODY: brown fur
WING: section of turkey feather (cut to shape)
HACKLE: brown rooster

The Turkey Wing Caddis has been especially valuable as a match for species with mottled brown wings. On those occasions when trout have become super selective to the color of the wings, no other material has worked quite as well as turkey quill for precise imitation.

A final omission from the list is the Fluttering Caddis style of dry fly. This pattern, originated by Leonard Wright specifically for an active, twitching presentation, is a fine imitation also of the adult caddisfly. It requires a great deal of fussing, however, to keep it high and dry enough for fluttering on the surface.

Because the Fluttering Caddis demands so much attention it also must be an optional choice for the list; however, at least a few of these in an angler's carrying stock would not hurt. The original wing material, high-quality spade hackle fibers, is neither durable nor readily available. Mink-tail hair makes the fly more useful.

MINK-WING FLUTTERING CADDIS
HOOK: Mustad 94833, 3XF wire, sizes 10-18
BODY: fur (dubbed)
WING: mink-tail fibers
HACKLE: rooster fibers

Probably in total there are not as many patterns in this selection as the typical fly fisherman carries to match the various stages of the mayfly. And yet, throughout the season the contents of a well-stocked caddisfly box will handle more tough situations for the stream fisherman than a pattern assortment for any other insect.

Fishing the Larval Imitations

When I first began conducting caddisfly seminars I usually dealt with the larval stage of the insect fairly briefly: one, here are the flies, two, here is what they imitate, and three, go out and fish them like regular nymphs. One, two, three—after all, the fly fishermen attending these schools were not beginners and there was no apparent need for instruction in basic techniques.

During the on-stream sessions, however, even the very experienced anglers failed to take advantage of the incredible profusion of caddisfly larvae on the local rivers. Their efforts with the larval flies were hit-or-miss, without reason, because they not only did not grasp the importance of caddisfly larvae, they did not understand the basics of nymph fishing.

In later seminars the time spent teaching how to fish the larval imitations was increased to reflect the importance of this stage in the everyday diet of the trout. It seemed as if explaining the entomology and the flies was not enough, however; this part of the seminar eventually evolved into a very advanced nymph-fishing clinic.

1

The Dynamics of Nymph Fishing

How important are caddisfly larvae to the trout? Anyone preparing to nymph fish should probably understand two things: first, in many trout streams individual species of caddisflies can attain densities of 1,000 to 3,000 insects per square foot of bottom; and second, whenever trout see a continuous and large number of a particular nymph or larva they will tend to feed on that species to the exclusion of all others. Research by Neil Ringler at the State University of New York demonstrated how reluctant trout accustomed to feeding on one kind of forage are to change to something else. These fish, even when their regular food of mealworms was removed, refused to feed on unfamiliar prey at first. For brown trout it required 1,200 to 1,800 exposures to a new insect, in this instance crickets, over a four- to six-day period before they began to feed on them normally.

Now consider a hypothetical situation on a stream: a trout regularly forages in an area where it sees and successfully captures a particular type of caddisfly larva, the insect being a part of its feeding routine for days or even weeks; then an angler arrives on the scene with flies and tactics that cannot even remotely imitate the appearance or actions of that familiar prey.

What are the fisherman's chances? Oh, as soon as he exposes the fish to the unnatural fly 1,200 to 1,800 times over a four- to six-day period he will have virtually the same chance he would have had with a matching imitation in the first place.

It should be plain why the angler who understands underwater selectivity and can solve the problems posed by it has an advantage in fishing caddisfly imitations. Advanced nymph-fishing tactics capitalize on the selective situation rather than try to avoid it.

Selective feeding is simply a survival mechanism for fish. It is not the result of intelligence; just the opposite, it is due to a lack of reasoning ability, an instinct that has developed in trout out of biological pressures that have nothing to do with fly fishermen.

A trout feeds selectively because this is an efficient way to gather insects. In order to survive, the fish, possessing a very small energy reserve, has to gain more energy than it expends as it feeds. By holding in a single area of a stream and feeding in a set rhythm, selecting one type of food item and rejecting others, the trout accomplishes this economy of motion.

There is an equation that illustrates whether or not a concentration of a particular insect is important enough to trigger selective feeding:

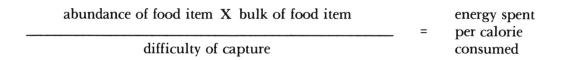

$$\frac{\text{abundance of food item} \ \mathbf{X} \ \text{bulk of food item}}{\text{difficulty of capture}} = \begin{array}{l}\text{energy spent} \\ \text{per calorie} \\ \text{consumed}\end{array}$$

As a trout feeds on a single type of insect it begins to key on a set or a sequence of visible characteristics, the recognizable features becoming the stimulae that trigger the feeding response. As long as the fish only responds each time to the recognizable stimulae, it does not waste energy by grabbing at pieces of stream debris. But because a trout lacks great intelligence it cannot pick and choose. It cannot reason, "Here comes a big stonefly. That'll make a nice change from the caddisflies I've been eating." It becomes locked into the visible characteristics of one type of insect and actually loses the ability to detect or respond to other kinds of prey.

The need for such a rigid feeding pattern, the instinct that keeps a fish from chasing all over a stream, is proportionate to the size of the trout, because the greater the size the more energy expended with the movement. The bigger trout therefore requires a heavier concentration of easily gathered prey before even shifting from a fish to an insect diet.

How strongly trout stick to a selective feeding pattern also depends on the velocity and clarity of the water. The clearer the water, the better the visibility for identification; the slower the water, the more deliberate the rise rhythm for better recognition.

Most fly fishermen know that when trout rise to take insects from the surface they often feed selectively, but these same fishermen, because they cannot see what happens underwater, fail to realize that trout foraging under the surface also feed selectively; to consistently catch them on a nymph the angler has to be able to answer four questions that solve the problems of selective feeding:

1. How are the trout feeding?
2. Where are the trout feeding?
3. What are the trout feeding on?
4. How can fly fishermen properly imitate the natural food?

With surface feeding, the first three questions—how, where, and what—can be answered by directly observing the activity. The fourth question is answered during moments of selectivity by matching the fly to the important visual characteristics of the natural insect. For the nymph fisherman these questions pose much greater problems. The answers, based on indirect observation at best, require a better knowledge of aquatic insects, a better understanding of trout feeding habits, and a better awareness of imitation.

How do trout feed on natural larvae and nymphs?

There are basically three ways trout feed on subsurface items in moving water. They grub insects from the bottom, pick insects from the drift, or pluck insects from the underside of the surface film. The dynamics of the feeding methods remain the same whether the main prey is mayflies, stoneflies, caddisflies, or midges. The mobility of the nymph or larva determines where it will be, but no matter what type it is, the flow characteristics of the water it is in determines the way a trout feeds.

Grubbing. Grubbing is either a vacuuming or a rooting action. The fish holds at a downward slant, snout pressed into the rocks or vegetation. During vacuuming a trout flares its gills, pulling in water and insects, and then squeezes out the water. During rooting it actually scrapes nymphs or larvae off the rocks or eats them along with bits of vegetation.

A grubbing trout pokes its nose among the rocks to root out insects.

As a trout grubs in the streambed, it is constantly twisting and turning to hold its position. The sunlight bouncing off its side sends off reflections that are visible to an observant fly fisherman. Tad Swanson

Either way its head is down in the still layer of water among the rocks and its tail is up in the faster water above, forcing it to constantly struggle to keep this position. The turning of the body causes flashes of gold or silver, reflections visible to the fisherman, that identify this form of feeding.

Some types of case-making caddisfly larvae are especially vulnerable to scraping and grubbing. Most immature insects remain under rocks or deep in crevices during the day, and thus are partially protected, but larvae such as the Grannom (*Brachycentrus*), with their four-sided cases, and the Little Tan Short-Horn Sedge (*Glossosoma*), with their turtle-shell cases, fasten themselves to the top of the rocks in riffles. There they can either be pulled off or knocked free by rumaging trout anytime.

Picking. The trout anatomy really is not ideal for grubbing; fish such as whitefish, suckers, and sculpins are much more adept at feeding nose down. Rather than forage in this manner, trout often stir up the bottom to loosen insects, and then swim quickly downstream and turn around to wait for the debris. This tactic allows them to feed with their tail down and head up.

Picking larvae or nymphs from the drift, those either carried naturally or stirred up by rooting, a trout holds comfortably in the quiet water and pokes its nose upward. It sidles back and forth in the current, performing gracefully as it intercepts passing fare.

This type of feeding often continues for hours when insects are drifting abundantly. Most of the trout's movement is from side to side, seldom upstream except to establish a new position. Sometimes, though, a fish hastily swims downstream to grab an item that it let pass, not the result of a sudden change in mind, as it seems, but because an insect slid into focus at the side.

One angling myth about caddisfly larvae is that only the free-living forms are available in the open currents. This is not true; many common trout-stream case-makers drift quite readily, case and all, and when they do they are worth imitating. At least two case-making genera, the Giant Orange Sedge (*Discosmoecus*) and the Little Tan Short-Horn Sedge (*Glossosoma*), regularly abandon their cases and drift completely helpless. Free-living larvae and net-making larvae, of course, are also available when they drift.

Plucking. An insect emergence strongly influences movement and foraging cycles of stream trout. During the late spring and early summer, when major hatches occur daily, fish begin feeding heavily a few hours before the hatch and continue gorging until the activity peters out. Afterward they settle to comfortable water to digest their meal.

Even during emergence the nymphs or the pupae of an insect often remain more important than the adults. With mayflies, a trout takes four nymphs for every adult. With caddisflies, few adults are actually ingested during a hatch. The reason for this difference is that mayflies ride the surface to dry their wings after discarding the nymphal shuck, but caddisflies keep their wings dry enough to pop from the underside of the meniscus right into the air.

When a trout actually feeds on the emergent stage, plucking an insect as it struggles to shed its skin, the way it works depends on the speed of the current at the surface. In slow-moving streams like spring creeks, a fish holds a few inches under the top and sips gently, but in faster water it rises all the way from the bottom. The method of the take is the same either way, but the tuck downward right after the capture controls the amount of bulge in the surface, the break more pronounced when a fish comes up from the bottom.

Caddisfly larvae do not emerge, of course; caddisfly pupae emerge. There is an intermediate stage of pupation in this order. Because they seldom leave the bottom areas of the stream, even when they are drifting, larvae do not cause this type of feeding.

A trout holds in the quiet water and pokes its nose upward to pick nymphs or larvae from the drift.

The fly fisherman has to be able to recognize all types of subsurface feeding to use larval imitations properly; the feeding motions may only be a clue that larval imitations and deep nymph tactics are not applicable.

Where do trout feed on larvae and nymphs?

This statement is repeated frequently: "Trout feed either at the top or the bottom of a river. The water in between is barren of both insects and fish." This has been written so many times, in one form or another, that it has become a cliche. Like many cliches, though, it is not only an oversimplification, it is wrong. There are not just two feeding levels in a trout stream.

Based on my scuba-diving experiences there are four separate feeding strata where insects become concentrated enough to trigger heavy trout activity. Each of these levels is a trap that holds the insect, at least momentarily, and allows a fish to key on the point of hesitation.

The surface tension of the water, the rubbery film called the meniscus, forms two of the feeding edges. The top of the film, the realm of the dry fly, supports insects, usually emergents breaking out of a shuck, by providing a tangible roof on the stream. The bottom of the meniscus is a barrier that insects must break through. Both of these edges form distinct points of hesitation.

Being able to recognize the difference between a true rise to an adult insect on top and a breaking roll to a pupa or nymph underneath is usually crucial. There is nothing more frustrating than fishing a dry fly among working trout only to have it be completely ignored; at the same time the proper floating pupa or nymph imitation would fool these fish.

The same, oddly, is not as rigidly true in the reverse situation. When trout are rising to take adult insects the proper dry fly is the best imitation, but a "damp" fly hanging in the film will still catch some fish. The reason for this is that enough of the naturals are temporarily in the transitional stage to cause a secondary layer of insects. There are not enough to cause selective feeding on them alone, but there are enough so that they are accepted as simply another form of the same food. (See the discussion of sequential selectivity in Chapter 6.)

There are two other important feeding levels in a stream, quite different from each other but both created by water flowing over a broken bottom. River currents are not uniform, of course, because of the friction of water against the solid bed. Even in a smooth, U-shaped sluice the currents are slower at the sides and the bottom, gradually becoming faster at the middle and reaching maximum velocity just under the top.

As water breaks over and around rocks, pushing out squiggling eddies, there is a quiet cushion left among the crevices and chinks of the bottom. This buffer space in the riffles serves as the primary production area in a trout stream, generating eighty percent of the insect life. It also provides the haven that allows a fish to hold and feed within a fast-water environment without exhausting itself.

This quiet water right at the bottom, harboring almost the entire insect community, is not the primary feeding zone for trout, though. It is an important level when trout grub, nose down, to vacuum or scrape insects from crevices, but grubbing is not an easy way for a fish to gather food. Every natural defense mechanism an insect possesses—protective coloration, inaccessibility, mobility—works to frustrate the feeding efforts of the trout.

The most important strata for insect concentration in a river is a level that can vary from a few inches to a few feet above the bottom. This zone is an interface, a joining of two currents of different force, that is formed when the unobstructed flow of the main stream meets the obstructed water of the bottom. When the eddies that swirl and break off the rocks hit the faster current above it, there is an intermediate buffer formed between them.

This interface captures insects that are involuntarily swept off the rocks. These insects, trapped in the current, are completely vulnerable, denied the chance to either hide or escape. The flow acts almost like a conveyor belt, carrying helpless prey to the fish.

This feeding level is the most important layer in the stream for nymph fishermen because of the amount of foraging time that trout spend there. Based on my underwater observations the feeding percentages for each of the four zones are roughly:

Surface (top of the film):	10 percent
Subsurface (bottom of the film):	10 percent
Drift level:	60 percent
Bottom:	15 percent
Stray feeding at nonconcentration levels:	5 percent

The statement, "Trout feed either at the top or bottom," by ignoring two layers in between, fails to explain seventy percent of trout activity. The fly fisherman, however, cannot afford to ignore these two crucial zones when trout are foraging on the concentrations of insects that gather in these areas.

Whenever there is a concentration heavy enough to trigger a spurt of selective feeding, there are two problems for the fly fisherman to solve, because not only do trout become selective to pattern with larvae or nymphs, but they also become selective to depth.

What are trout feeding on?

Sometimes, when trout are grabbing anything, this question only has to be answered generally because it is enough to know where the fish are working. At other times, when trout are singling out a prevalent insect, it has to be answered specifically because the feeding zone, the fly, and the action imparted to the fly are each important.

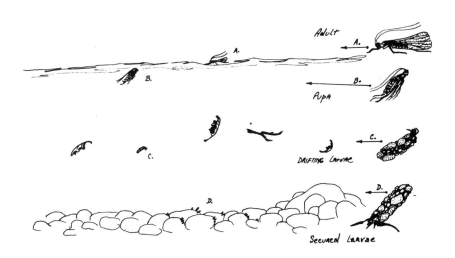

In a stream there are four main levels in which trout feed on caddisflies: (A) the top of the meniscus, where trout take floating adults; (B) the bottom of the meniscus, where trout grab struggling emergers; (C) the buffer zone, where trout pick up drifting pupae or larvae; and (D) the dead zone, where trout grub out crawling or clinging larvae.

The entomological knowledge that is most valuable to the fly fisherman, an understanding of the life cycles of the aquatic orders, pinpoints the times that insects are vulnerable to predation. These biological facts alone answer the how, where, what questions about trout activity.

Trout are opportunists, gorging themselves at moments of plenty until insects spill out their gullets. They prey on the easiest, most available concentrations of food, seeking the ideal situation: *the biggest insects in the largest quantity in the most vulnerable position.* And when this does happen, every large trout in the river works the concentration zones.

The periods that insects are most available in a stream vary according to season. In the spring the population reaches a peak, all the growth of various species during the previous winter attaining a preemergence bloom. During late spring and summer the daily hatches regulate the feeding of the fish, but they also deplete the bottom of mature nymphs and larvae. By the fall, after the last of the early hatches, only the few autumn emergers and those nymphs or larvae that have a two-year or a three-year life cycle remain to provide a sizable food source. The paucity of insect food late in the year forces trout to shift heavily to a minnow diet.

The relative abundance of insects at the various levels of the stream determines what fish are going to feed on. When there are neither drifting nor emerging forms available, a hungry trout scrounges on the bottom, but this grubbing is usually used more as a way of casual snacking than as a method of primary feeding. The phenomenon that supplies the principle opportunity for feeding on immature nymphs and larvae in a stream is free drift (divided into catastrophic and behavioral drift by entomologists).

When an insect loses its grip on the rocks or vegetation of the bottom it is swept into the buffer currents, temporarily lapsing into a state of shock. For a distance of fifteen feet or more, until it reaches a suitable patch of streambed again, it remains inert and helpless. Finally, if it has managed to escape the notice of a fish, it wiggles back to the safety of the bottom.

Catastrophic drift is caused literally by a catastrophe, one as major as a flood or as minor as a wading cow. It occurs when some influence disturbs the bottom and knocks insects into the current. This random drift induces trout to feed (a fact recognized by the fisherman's trick of kicking over rocks at the head of a pool and then fishing through it).

Behavioral drift, however, is neither a rare nor a random happening. During a twenty-four hour period approximately .003 percent of the total free-moving insect biomass of a freestone river gets plucked from the bottom and carried off downstream. The process, directly correlated to an overcrowding of the habitat, is a natural method of redistributing excess population as the age group of an insect species matures.

This drift also follows a predictable daily pattern. The amount of drifting that occurs depends on the amount of insect activity, and the amount of movement in turn depends on the amount of sunlight reaching the stream.

Aquatic insects regulate their feeding areas by the light. Many nymphs and larvae avoid it, a negatively phototropic reaction, and during the daytime they remain under stones or vegetation. At night they crawl around on top of bottom objects. A half-hour after dusk and a half-hour before dawn, when they come out in the evening or go back in the morning in hasty migration, these insects reach peak rates of behavioral drift.

*What are the trout feeding on? Often trout feed on the larvae of a common caddisfly genus such as the Little Plain Brown Sedge. (*Lepidostoma *case and larva shown at right.) Fish may take these insects by grubbing them from the bottom or by picking them from the drift.* Ken Thompson

The opposite is true of insects on a daytime cycle. Their rates of drift are higher during the day, the peaks controlled more by water temperature than by anything else. These larvae also tend to have minor increases in their drift rate at dawn and dusk.

The breakdown of which insects drift day or night is not simple, but here are possible generalizations:

nocturnal cycle:	mayfly nymphs, stonefly nymphs, free-living caddisfly larvae, some case-making caddisfly larvae
diurnal cycle (daytime):	some case-making caddisfly larvae
steady twenty-four-hour cycle:	midge larvae

For mature stonefly and mayfly nymphs, emergence has a major influence on this cycle. In the hours prior to hatching the nymphs become increasingly restless, drifting in considerable numbers regardless of the light intensity. This activity starts trout feeding well before the first adults reach the surface.

Although caddisfly larvae do not emerge, many of them become more active just before the pupation period. Some species migrate away from the larval habitat to more suitable areas before sealing off their cases. Both their general restlessness and movement result in higher rates of behavioral drift for the larvae.

How can fly fishermen properly imitate the natural food?

There are secrets to nymph fishing, secrets the angler needs to know before he can take full advantage of caddisfly populations. Every so often this is denied in an article or book titled, perhaps, *Nymph Fishing is Easy!* Such writings claim that the technique does not really require very much skill or knowledge. And in an obvious way these articles are correct because it is easy to catch an occasional fish on an artificial nymph.

Although it is easy to be a mediocre nymph fisherman, there is much more knowledge and skill needed to be a master. The secrets are the how, what, and where questions, information that is so much harder to get for nymphing than it is for dry-fly fishing, but the answers solve the problem of how to use a subsurface imitation properly.

The ability to understand what determines success or failure with a nymph, the use of knowledge rather than persistent flailing to catch trout, separates the master from the beginner. The deep understanding of the unseen stream and the unseen caddisfly larvae can make each drift of an imitation a planned attack instead of a guess.

2

Two Methods and a Magic Act

In the early 1900s the development of nymph fishing represented a departure from the older, wet-fly style of presentation—a method that mostly owed its credibility to the actions of emerging caddisfly pupae and egg-laying caddisfly adults. The greatest difference between the two methods was that the wet fly was fished actively and the nymph was fished passively. The fact that a dead-drifted nymph might be used to imitate caddisfly larvae was never considered; so unknowingly this new technique helped to separate caddisflies from the mainstream of fly-fishing theory.

George Edward Mackensie Skues explained nymph fishing in his first book, *Minor Tactics of the Chalk Stream* (1910), relating the method to the actions of insects on the chalksteams of England. His ideas were viewed as heresy, violating as they did an angling morality that restricted these Hampshire waters to dry-fly fishing, but it was a heresy that still followed the spirit, if not the letter, of that moral posture. Skues dictated that the nymph should only be cast upstream, and only to rising fish, the fly presented to a specific trout and the hook set following a visible take. This technique differed from dry-fly fishing only because the pattern drifted slightly below the surface film instead of on it. With these restrictions the nymph method was limited mainly to imitating emerging mayfly nymphs. Skues, in *Minor Tactics of the Chalk Stream*, never explored the possibility of imitating emerging caddisfly pupae with his dead-drift presentation, and, of course, since caddisfly larvae do not emerge and do not commonly drift in the surface film, his new method was not suitable for imitating them either.

Edward R. Hewitt corresponded with Skues. Later he visited the Hampshire region of England and accepted an invitation to fish with Skues on the Itchen. He observed tactics specifically suited to gentle waters, not the rougher streams of upstate New York. But this introduction nevertheless convinced him of the overall efficacy of the method.

He adapted his new technique to the unruly trout rivers of this country, but he significantly broadened the method, including downstream as well as upstream presentations. He also recommended fishing the nymph patterns blind, the angler covering the water rather than waiting for a bulging trout. This digression from the nymph fishing code of the English chalk streams was necessary because on freestone rivers a fly fisherman often did not see steadily working fish during the day.

These changes from the Skues method actually meant that Hewitt was mimicking a different nymphal activity with his dead-drift tactics. When he cast upstream and allowed the nymph to drift back toward him, the fly remaining in the water, instead of lifting and recasting as soon as it passed a specific, visible fish, he also provided time for it to sink to a deeper level. A nymph presented in this manner was simulating a natural insect caught in the current and drifting freely, not an emergent that had just swum to the surface. The Hewitt method was effectively taking advantage of the behavioral and catastrophic drifting of maturing nymph populations.

Hewitt surveyed the subsurface life of his water on the upper Neversink River, but his interest in entomology was never backed by formal study. He patterned imitations after his samples, creating both mayfly and stonefly nymphs. Oddly, although the river contained good populations of both case-making and free-living larvae, he did not try to imitate any immature caddisflies.

Later developments continued to link nymph fishing mainly with mayflies. Preston Jennings, in *A Book of Trout Flies* (1935), managed both to acknowledge and dismiss the importance of caddisfly larvae all in one sentence: "The Caddis worms, however, undoubtedly furnish a large proportion of the under-water food and for that reason are of more interest to the fish-culturist than the fly-fisher."

The first American book to describe caddisfly larvae systematically and to suggest a number of imitations (five patterns) was *Matching the Hatch* (1955) by Ernest Schwiebert. From 1955 until 1973, the publication date of Schwiebert's *Nymphs*, very little information was added to our knowledge of the larval stage. *Nymphs* included a fine chapter on the biology of the larvae, stressing the importance of free-living and net-making types. This book did not erase the lingering imbalance between mayfly nymphs and caddisfly larvae, but with its superb drawings it educated many anglers about the appearance of some of the larvae.

The Caddis and the Angler (1977) by Larry Solomon and Eric Leiser made the largest contribution to date to our knowledge of caddisfly larvae. It contained good biological sketches of each important family and a general review of effective tactics. In the Appendix it collected an impressive array of larval imitations from all regions of the country.

With this recent recognition, have caddisfly larvae become equal to mayfly nymphs in the minds of fly fishermen? Not anywhere near equal. This discrepancy could not be less justified, however, because when the populations are proportionate, trout feed more heavily on caddisfly larvae than they do on mayfly nymphs.

The way for American nymph fishermen to take advantage of the large caddisfly populations in their trout streams is to disregard the historical bias against caddisfly larvae. They are there; they are important—with an understanding of stream dynamics (see Part 1 of this chapter) and a selection of effective imitations, anglers only need two methods and a magic act to discover the potential of this form of nymph fishing.[2]

Two Methods . . .

In moving water trout generally feed on caddisfly larvae only two of the three subsurface ways: they grub them from the bottom or pick them from the current. Both of these feeding methods usually occur near the substrate, rather than at either of the two surface-feeding areas, but they are quite different. They are so different that a fly fisherman needs a method of presentation for each of them.

Two techniques are widely known and practiced. The first one, the Hewitt method, is probably more popular on eastern rivers; the second, the outrigger method, is definitely more popular on western waters. They are not interchangeable, however. Often one or the other is far more effective. The problem is knowing when to use which.

The Hewitt method (long-line method). Hewitt's articles and books on nymph fishing include instructions for actively manipulating imitations, but this method is limited here to the upstream presentation of the sunken fly. Particular actions separate this method from other dead-drift techniques—the distance of the cast, the quick mending of the line, the stripping in of slack—these are all delicate maneuvers that can mean the difference between minimal and great success. Here are the typical steps in this presentation:

Rigging up. The fly can be either weighted or unweighted. The leader should be between nine and twelve feet long, adhering to the sixty-twenty-twenty percent standard formula, with a tippet fine and soft enough for the fly to react naturally to the currents. The line for this technique can be either a floating double-taper or weight-forward, but some type of strike indicator on the end is helpful. The rod should be fairly long, eight feet at least, and have a medium action.

Casting. The cast is upstream or upstream and across, usually crossing as few bands of varying current speed as possible. With this method it is a great advantage to wade into the best position, placing the dominant current lane directly to the front. Ideally the fly, leader, and line all land on water moving at one speed, but if the current is at all broken by obstructions this is usually impossible.

The length of the cast varies, but between twenty-five and forty feet is a good distance. A typical mistake with the Hewitt method is casting too short a line, the fly hitting ten to twenty-five feet upstream from the angler. If the fly lands fifteen feet away and begins immediately coming back downstream with the current, it hardly has time to reach the prime depth. A longer cast allows the fly to sink, which might take up to four or five feet of the drift, and still lets it cover a decent length of bottom before the angler has to pick it up.

It is important to use a special type of cast when fishing a nymph with the Hewitt method. It is called a tuck cast because the angler overpowers the delivery and makes the fly kick back toward him, the leader tippet and nymph tucking underneath. This makes the fly hit the water closer to the caster than the line tip and gives it enough slack to sink. (This cast is described by Lefty Kreh in *Masters on the Nymph*, and it was developed by George Harvey and Joe Humphreys of Pennsylvania State University.)

Avoiding drag. The tuck cast momentarily delays drag, but as the fly sinks the floating line drifts downstream faster than it does, pulling slack out of the leader. The reason that fly and line do not travel at the same rate of speed is that they ride at

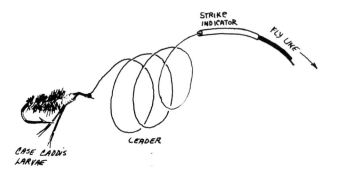

STRIKE INDICATOR

FLY LINE

LEADER

CASE CADDIS LARVAE

The setup for the Hewitt Method of presentation includes: (31) a weighted or unweighted larval imitation; (2) a 9-to-12 foot leader with a fine, supple tippet; (3) a strike indicator; and (4) a double-taper or weight-forward line.

By overpowering a cast, a nymph fisherman can make his fly tuck under.

different depths and water moves faster near the surface than it does near the bottom. As long as the fly is drifting deep it has to move slower than the line to move naturally.

To preserve the slack initially there when the line hits the water the fly fisherman mends, flipping extra line onto the bands of current. He begins mending immediately after the cast lands instead of waiting until drag actually starts pulling the fly out of position. If he mends correctly the fly never moves unnaturally in the water.

The more the cast is across stream rather than upstream the more mending is necessary. Often, these actions are quick and repetitive, with flicks of the rod tip counteracting the bellies formed in the line. It is an art almost forgotten—the inability to mend properly the reason that many fly fishermen fail to master the Hewitt method of nymph fishing.

Controlling line. The angler has to strip in line after casting upstream because it drifts back toward him. If he is right-handed he should keep constant control of the line with the index finger of his right hand, pulling in the excess with his left. He simply drops the slack at his feet or coils it in his hand after each strip.

It is absolutely necessary to gather in this extra line when using the Hewitt method, but it must be done carefully. Some fly fishermen have a great fear of slack on the water, probably because they worry about missing a strike, and yank every curl out of the line. Their overzealous tugs destroy the drift of the nymph because the strips lift the fly out of the feeding zone.

The rule for both mending and stripping line is that these actions should never be so vigorous that the floating line tip moves on the water. They have to be subtle, controlling drag and slack without negating the purpose of the cast.

There are numerous methods of dead-drift nymph fishing, but they all rely on the fact that trout tend to concentrate their feeding activity at specific depths, usually one of the three main subsurface levels. The effectiveness of any particular method depends on the fly reaching and staying in a zone—the zone it is designed to work at—for as long as possible. So it is necessary that the angler realize how fly depth is controlled with each technique.

The principle way it is controlled in the Hewitt method is simply by allowing time for the fly to sink; if the angler wants the fly to sink deeper he casts farther upstream of the target area. Proper presentation requires planning, demanding skill at reading water and judging current speeds. The fly has to enter the water far enough above the prime area to be near bottom by the time it reaches the spot.

The outrigger method (short-line method). This method has been publicized by

Chuck Fothergill through his articles in major magazines, in his chapter in *The Masters on the Nymph*, and in a letter outlining the history of the method, which appeared in *Challenge of the Trout*. Until recently the technique did not have a commonly accepted name, but in *The Masters on the Nymph* he wrote, " . . . angling professional Lefty Kreh mentioned that he was looking foward to coming to Colorado and joining me on the river to nymph-fish using the 'outrigger' technique. This description made me wish I'd coined the term."

"Outrigger" is very appropriate. The angler stands with a long rod, holding it out high in the air, and the leader hangs down into the water. The sight of a fly fisherman crouched in the middle of a trout stream this way is suggestive of an outrigger on a boat.

The technique is the antithesis of the Hewitt method—whereas the long-line method retains most of the fluid motions and delicate maneuvers of upstream dry-fly fishing, the outrigger method looks like a very clumsy way to fish. More than one fly-fishing friend has questioned the ethics of using this technique. One companion grumbled all day, maybe in part because it was the only method that was working, "That's nothing but glorified bait fishing."

Actions appear so unrefined with the outrigger method because instead of just a weighted fly, the angler must also cast a weighted leader, which means no pretty, tight loops, no false casts, no long-distance deliveries. All this method can do is catch fish. Here are the typical steps for making this presentation:

Rigging up. The fly should be weighted. The leader length can vary; twelve to eighteen feet is standard for the method, but the leader should be the knotted type rather than the knotless. The line should be a floating double-taper, one size heavier than recommended for the rod, with either a commercial or homemade strike indicator on the end. The rod can be slightly longer than the one suggested for the Hewitt method, but it should not be any longer than 9½ feet.

In addition to this basic outfit the fly fisherman needs either lead wire or lead strips. These pieces of lead are wrapped on the leader itself, the first piece eighteen inches above the fly, the second piece six inches above the first, and the third six inches above the second.

Casting. The lead weights spread along the leader make certain casting rules mandatory. The stroke has to be slower, with a pause to allow the backcast to straighten out completely. The loop of the unfolding line on the forward stroke (the space between the top and the bottom) has to be more open than normal to prevent tangling of the weights. Distance casting is impossible with this method.

Many times it is not necessary to cast at all. After the previous presentation is finished the fly fisherman can let the line go downstream until the fly and leader hang taut behind him in the current. Then he can lob the weights and line back upstream— gracelessly, perhaps, but effectively.

Although it is possible to fish straight upstream with the outrigger method, the angle of presentation is usually more across stream than upstream. The cast seldom needs to be more than thirty feet, including the length of the leader (twelve feet minimum) and the rod (nine feet normally). This leaves very little line actually on the water, and that is quickly lifted off.

Avoiding drag. One reason the outrigger method is so effective is that the set-up of weights on the leader works to eliminate drag. The strips of lead are heavier than the fly and sink faster. They bounce along in the slowest water, right at the bottom,

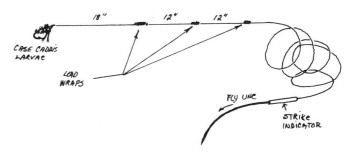

The setup for the Outrigger Method of presentation includes: (1) a weighted larval imitation; (2) a 12-to-18 foot knotted, compound leader; (3) lead weight spaced at intervals; (4) a strike indicator; and (5) a double-taper line.

and the fly follows them at the same speed.

The weights are so heavy that even a sloppy mend, one that tugs on the line tip, does not disturb the drift of the fly. Also, there is much less line lying on the surface to control; the quick mends to redistribute the line bellies are much easier to execute with this method than with the Hewitt method.

Controlling line. After the cast, as the fly drifts back downstream, the slack is controlled by stripping in line and raising the rod. With very short casts or lobs, ten to twenty-five feet up and across, slowly lifting the rod picks most of the slack off the water as it occurs. The cast is usually made off to the side of the angler rather than straight upstream, and by the time the fly drifts down to a position across from the angler only the leader is left in the current.

With his arm already extended above his head, it is nearly impossible to strike by moving the rod. Instead the angler has to use his left hand, the line-control hand for a right-handed caster, to set the hook. He does this by gripping the line just below his rod hand and pulling down quickly.

The most critical factor in the outrigger method is controlling the depth of presentation. This can be an intricate operation because the weights on the leader are not fixed amounts. There are no iron-clad prescriptions for how much to put on. Only experience can teach the angler how to judge the number of pieces he will need in a situation.

One lead wrap at each spot, eighteen inches, twenty-four inches, and thirty inches up a leader from the fly, is a good starting formula for a medium-speed riffle. To make the fly ride deeper or shallower means adding or subtracting some lead, but rather than removing or doubling one section entirely it is better to alter each one a little.

An expert working a stretch of pocket water is a skilled craftsman. He picks out a run and makes the first cast. If the fly does not drift at the right depth he pinches on or pinches off a piece of lead. On subsequent casts he keeps searching for the perfect amount of weight, trying to get the lead wraps "tapping" the rocks. Every time he moves to a new piece of water, even if it is only a few steps away, he usually has to adjust his weights all over again.

Achieving this "tapping" is the key to the outrigger method. If the weights are not knocking on the rock tops every few feet the fly is not at the right level. Then it usually fails to catch any trout at all because when the lead wraps are in the faster currents above the bottom the fly is being dragged unnaturally downstream.

Detecting a take when nymph fishing. It is not possible to teach someone how to detect a take through written descriptions; only hours of practice on the stream can bring the skills of observation and concentration that make a great nymph fisherman. It is possible, however, to discuss some of the subtle signs that indicate a trout has grabbed the fly.

Sometimes when a fish strikes it is not a gentle take. If a trout snatches the fly and moves with it, the signal to the fisherman is a quick jump of the line tip upsteam. Such strong strikes, however, are the exception because a trout usually accepts an artificial as it would a natural: confidently and unhurriedly.

There are two reasons that indications of a strike are generally more subdued with the outrigger method than with the Hewitt method. One, with the Hewitt method the cast is usually more upstream than across, so when the downstream progress of the fly is stopped the line tip is pulled abruptly back in the upstream direction, but with the outrigger method the cast is usually more across stream, so when the drift of the fly is stopped the line tip is pulled to the side, curling instead of jerking directly upstream. Two, with the Hewitt method there are no extra weights above the fly to interfere with the transmission of force from the fly to the line tip, but with the outrigger method the lead wrappings on the leader absorb some of the force from a strike because they are heavy and they must be moved before the power can continue to the line tip. With either method a "sixth sense," the ability to apparently know by intuition alone when to strike, is often necessary to consistently catch trout with a nymph.

Is it possible to teach a fly fisherman this sixth sense? It is easy to teach it on the stream. There is no mystery involved in the ability to detect a take even when there is no apparent indication. There is a tip off, but it just is not the usual vigorous pull on the line tip.

The first cast and drift a fly fisherman makes through a spot should be considered the "prototype" presentation. Then, on each subsequent cast and drift the line tip should react to the currents almost the same way it did the first time. It is important to imagine the path the line tip is supposed to follow—every little curl and every minor variation in speed—and if that projected movement fails to occur the fly fisherman should strike. The signal to set the hook is often not what the line tip does, but what it does not do.

Obviously, detecting and responding to such subtle indications demands a great amount of concentration. It means staring at the moving line tip and shutting out all the wonderful distractions of a trout stream. An expert nymph fisherman often enters a state of mind like a hypnotic trance.

I lead a gypsy life of fly-fishing, which gives me the chance to fish all over with many fine anglers, and I learned of these nymphing methods early. I practiced the Hewitt method with experts like Ken Parkany and Bill Crocker and the outrigger method with experts like Galen Wilkins and Wayne Huft. I saw these fly fishermen use their favorite methods effectively so many times that I never developed a strong preference for either technique. For a few years I went on using both, approaching a stream and deciding there on one or the other.

Occasional experiences with the two methods, however, began to indicate that they were not working equally well at all times. On some days, alternating them hourly produced strong performances for only one of the two; the other usually catching some fish but not nearly as many. Tests with two anglers, each using one of the techniques, also showed the momentary superiority of one of them. Each method apparently had an optimum period on the trout stream.

This last realization came at a time when I was studying the dynamics of stream currents—the main underwater experiment consisting of releasing white pellets at various levels and watching how the water carried them away. Once those little white balls revealed that there were two current zones near the bottom, instead of one, the link between dynamics and nymphing tactics became clear.

It seems as if both methods of presentation accomplish the same thing, both apparently putting the fly near the bottom, but they do not because they control depth of presentation differently. With the Hewitt method the sink rate depends on the weight of the fly. With the outrigger method the sink rate depends on the weight of the lead wrappings and the fly. As a result, each method actually holds the fly in different flow areas of the stream and at different levels of prey concentration. With the Hewitt method the front of the leader pulls the fly up; with the outrigger method the front of the leader pulls the fly down.

With the outrigger method the lead weights tap along the rocks in the dead cushion of water at the bottom. The fly may ride slightly higher, occasionally getting sucked into the buffer zone above the quiet area, but the downward pull of the leader brings it back. For most of the drift it stays deep, dropping momentarily into any pocket-size depression it happens to cross.

A fly acting like this works best when trout are holding and casually browsing in a riffle. It hits grubbing and rooting fish on the nose, slipping naturally into their downcast view. Even when fish are not actively foraging, an imitation presented this way offers such an easy meal it cannot be refused if it comes close enough (which is the reason for covering an area with painstaking thoroughness).

The Hewitt method presents a fly much differently. The weighted hook sinks toward the bottom and becomes momentarily trapped when it reaches the buffer zone. The swirling eddies of this interface carry the fly the same way it does a natural insect, but since the weighted imitation is heavier than an insect it tends to slip through to the dead zone below. When it does fall into the quiet water and slow down, however, the pull of the faster-moving leader from above picks it right back up. The fly rides most of the time in the buffer zone.

If the angler can spot trout and determine how they are feeding he will know which method to try. When they are grubbing on the bottom he should use the outrigger method, and when they are picking the drift he should use the Hewitt method. But if he cannot see the fish he will have to guess which method to try first—for this dilemma only the most general recommendations are possible. Usually trout pick insects from the drift early and late in the day, the change in light intensity causing night-active insects to drift more an hour after sunset and an hour before sunrise and causing day-active insects to drift more an hour before sunset and an hour

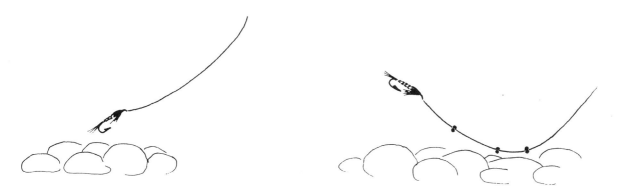

The result of nymph fishing with the Hewitt Method is shown in the left illustration. The right illustration shows the result of using the Outrigger Method.

after sunrise, so the Hewitt method will probably work best at these times. Usually trout grub on the bottom or browse casually more in the middle of the day when the sun is bright and no insects are moving, so the outrigger method will probably work best at such times. Still, an angler will often have to experiment to find out which method is best at a given moment.

There are other methods of dead-drift nymph fishing, of course, but these two take care of most situations for imitating caddisfly larvae in riffles. My work has been limited to understanding how these tactics present a fly, but any fly fisherman favoring a different nymphing technique is encouraged to study and experiment with it, determining which zone his method works best at so he can use it most intelligently.

. . . and a magic act. With a mastery of the two methods of deep nymph fishing, the Hewitt and the outrigger methods, the fly fisherman will have acquired the most important techniques for being an all-around angler. A deeply drifted nymph will be the best technique approximately twenty to twenty-five percent of the time, more than any other single type of presentation. It will give the angler the chance to catch fifty to sixty trout a day, because it is such a consistent way to fly-fish, not always producing trout quickly but virtually eliminating those dead stretches that even the best wet-fly (imparting motion to the fly) or dry-fly specialist encounters on a typical stream.

Can such an effective approach be improved upon? The research on the biology of caddisfly larvae uncovered a secret that makes the deeply presented imitation significantly more successful. In the right places on a trout stream it can turn a consistent method into a spectacular one. I called it a "Magic Act" because George Chouinard referred to it as such in a newspaper article. The technique, however, is the result of research.

My research began in Maine with a bit of historical detective work, and the investigation was not originally linked with caddisflies at all. It included interviews with many of the old-time wet-fly fishermen in that area. There was an old technique that fascinated me: their trick, used a lot in northern New England in the early part of this century, was to attach a piece of white sewing thread as a leader tippet. This single addition to their tackle often helped them produce the hundred-brook-trout-a-day catches of that era.

These old-time experts generally agreed on where the trick worked and when it worked, but none of them knew why it worked. The answer eventually had to come from the brooks and small rivers themselves. I fished, studied, and stuck my head in so many of them that the one thing they had in common finally became obvious.

These Maine waters all boasted heavy populations of black-fly larvae (Diptera). In the streams, clustered on rocks of the riffles, the larvae usually moved by alternating their grip from a posterior to an anterior sucker, but if they were swept away a white silk anchor line unfurled until the insect hung taut in the current. It then started to pull itself back upstream. The silk excretion, acting as a powerful triggering characteristic, explained the effectiveness of using a white sewing-thread tippet in these streams.

Caddisflies are also silk makers. The larvae can use silk for a variety of purposes—making the larval case, weaving a food-collecting net, or, like the black-fly larvae, spinning a safety line to protect themselves from dislodgment. Entomologists have noted this use of a safety line by three trout-stream genera of caddisflies, the

Green Sedge (*Rhyacophila*), Grannom (*Brachycentrus*), and Spotted Sedge (*Hydropsyche*). For two of these genera, the Grannom and Spotted Sedge, they have seen the lines not only used by the larvae to draw themselves back to the rock they were swept off of, but also for rappelling down to a new rock.

These observations make the white anchor line important as a triggering characteristic in a much greater variety of habitats than just those streams with an abundance of black-fly larvae. The three caddisfly genera known to use silk this way are among the most common in running waters, insuring that the tactic for imitating it is valuable almost everywhere.

In a riffle of a rich stream, where populations of Spotted Sedge or Grannom larvae might easily exceed 1,000 per square foot, a trout is surrounded by these food forms, but most of them are securely hidden in crevices. Everytime one of the larvae loses its grip and washes out of its safe hold, however, the trout sees the *anchor line and the larvae*. Since the anchor line is very distinctive, the trout many times notices it first, responding to this stimulus and swimming toward it even before recognizing the larva.

My initial attempts to use the larval imitations with the white sewing-thread tippet were disappointing. An eighteen-inch length of thread seemed to increase the effectiveness of the flies, but it also created problems. It was very difficult to tie thread to nylon monofilament; it is difficult to get materials with such varying stiffness securely together. Also, even after it was fastened, any advantage offered by the thread was lost because with its low breaking strength (approximtely one-pound-test) and lack of elasticity it could not absorb the shock of a hard strike. The trick of the white sewing thread, despite the fact that it added a powerful stimulus, was so much trouble it would never have been accepted by fly fishermen for general use.

Maybe it would have been excusable to abandon the idea of imitating the silk line, but every stomach sample loaded with the right type of caddisfly larvae was a reminder of how important it was to find a more practical answer—some method of quickly and easily adding white color to a leader tippet.

It was possible to dye tippets and get an acceptable shade of off-white, but this process was complicated and time consuming, and it also weakened the nylon material. What was needed was a marker of some sort, something to paint or coat a leader, a tube of something that the fly fisherman could keep in his vest and use to color his regular tippet whenever he fished the larval imitations. But apparently none of the marker companies was making white ones.

It was difficult to find a product not readily available on the mass market. The search was plodding work, thumbing through industrial catalogs, trying commercial supplies, questioning plumbing, building, and electrical contractors, and even

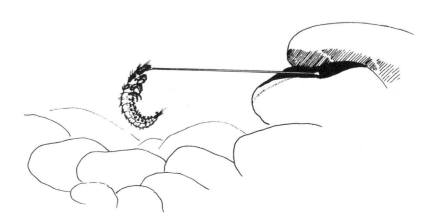

The silk anchor line and the larva are both distinctive characteristics of the insect as it dangles in the current.

hounding chemical manufacturers. Basically such a quest required faith that for some reason just about anything imaginable is made somewhere in the world.

It is: I found a marker named Mean Streak, distributed by the Sanford Corporation. Its original use is writing numbers on steel shipments at foundries, but it coats almost any material with a waxy, white substance that is thin, flexible, and impervious to water.

The Mean Streak marker is the basis of the magic act. There is no need for a fly fisherman to even change tippets, the white color easily wiped onto any monofilament surface. As long as he keeps a tube in his vest the fly fisherman is ready for situations where a white anchor line might be a significant factor.

When should a fly fisherman use the larval imitations? The how, where, and what questions about the basics of nymph fishing lead to this question about caddisfly larvae, and this is really the easiest question to answer. Just follow these basic rules.

One, sample the river bottom. See if caddisfly larvae are predominant in that part of the stream.

Two, if caddisfly larvae are predominant, and there is no evident hatch of aquatic insects or fall of terrestrial insects, match the most abundant species in the drift (see Insect Listing for breakdown of day- and night-drifting species).

Three, when and if a trout is caught, check the contents of his stomach to find out for certain what it has been eating.

The time to use a deeply presented nymph is when nothing is pulling the trout's attention off the bottom. A hatch—any significant hatch of caddisflies, mayflies, stoneflies, or midges—usually creates an abundance of easily secured prey, concentrated in specific areas, and decreases the importance of immature larvae or nymphs as food.

Periods when the water is blank, devoid of hatching insects, can be a significant part of the day on any stream. During these times trout may be quite willing to feed, and larval imitations bounced near the bottom are often the answer for consistent action.

A Mean Streak marker solves the problem of simulating the silk anchor line. Gary LaFontaine

Fishing the Pupal Imitations

Will the Real Caddisfly Pupa Please Stand Up?

My theories on how to imitate caddisfly pupae seem to run totally counter to anything else in angling literature. Once after a lecture at a fly-fishing club a member asked, "How can your opinions be so different from those of everyone else?"

I have wondered about that myself. Even my descriptions of how the natural looks and acts during its swim or crawl from the water differ completely from most popular accounts. The discrepancies are so great between mine and other fly-fishing versions that if the words "caddis pupa" were removed from them no one would guess that they were referring to the same insect. Fly fishermen, though, have to know how the natural insects act before they can mimic their movements with a fly.

A number of modern angling authors have been consistent in their descriptions of swimming pupae, portraying an insect that rises nonstop from the pupal case to the air like a missile. They have been explicit in these vivid accounts, creating a commonly believed scenario of emergence. It would have been easy to go along with this version, repeating it in my own writings, except for one fact: none of these descriptions was based on actual observation of the natural insect. Furthermore they were not really based on the few brief accounts in entomological papers.

The best method for observing caddisfly pupae in the natural environment was scuba diving. In my ten years of research on this insect and on new imitations and tactics, 211 hours were spent underwater. Of these, 54½ were spent primarily or secondarily studying the actual insect, determining the behavior of the free pupa after leaving the pupal case. Primary observation consisted of watching only the emerging insect; secondary observation consisted of watching the emerging insect and a related subject (for example, a feeding trout).

To see a small object clearly under the surface meant viewing it myopically, the distortion, even in clean or slow-running water, muting details from a distance, but these are the same restrictions placed on the trout. The first visual characteristics alerting an observer to a swimming pupa were the motion, and, in the instance of the swimming pupa, the brightness. Then the diver had to move to within inches for a closer look at the insect.

There was little doubt, even from the first dive, that what I was seeing in the swimming caddisfly pupa did not fit the common angling version. The insect neither looked nor acted like the popular "super caddis" that was supposed to pop straight out of the stream.

The emergence period could be divided into four segments:

One: after pulling free of the case the pupae drifted with the bottom currents. The duration and distance of this drift varied with the species, but on one occasion with the Spotted Sedge (*Hydropsyche* sp.) the pupae were carried nearly one hundred yards downstream before even beginning the ascent. If these pupae were struggling or swimming during this drift, the actions were so minor that they were unnoticeable.

Two: once an insect was ready to swim to the surface the actual ascent, the second phase, was usually fairly rapid, but the rate of the rise also varied from species to species. The larger species in general seemed to swim slower than the smaller ones.

Three: the third phase occurred just under the surface film, with the pupae hanging down and drifting. In no observed instances did an ascending pupa break through the meniscus and fly off as an adult without this period of hesitation. The time spent on the underside of the meniscus not only varied with species but also with the atmospheric conditions. On cold or wet days the drifting period was longer.

Four: after shedding the pupal skin and gaining the surface as an adult the observed caddisflies quickly flew off. This period was typically brief, consisting of a flutter or two.

This study certainly did not include all important trout-stream caddisflies, even with over fifty hours of observation, and exceptions are probable.

What do professional entomologists say about the action and appearance of an ascending pupa? There are excellent papers about the structure and functions of the pupa while it is still in the cocoon, but there are very few descriptions of what happens to it between leaving the anchored shelter and changing into an adult.

Why do some insect orders have a pupal stage and others do not? Pupation is an added step. The more advanced orders go through a complete life cycle: egg, larva, pupa, adult. The more primitive aquatic orders have only three stages: egg, nymph, adult. The advantages of pupation are that this intermediate step allows a greater

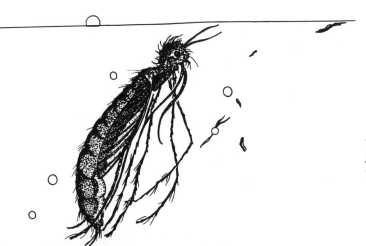

Caddisfly pupae sometimes drift for minutes, or even hours, just under the surface film.

physical divergence between the adult form and the larval form. A pupa occurs in the life cycle when the differences between larva and adult are so great that the muscle structure of the adult must be formed during a halfway stage.

A major benefit of pupation is that once freed from the requirement of having a body similar to that of the adult, the larvae of an order can evolve to survive in a wider variety of environments. This is one reason such orders as the caddisflies (Trichoptera) and the two-winged flies (Diptera) are more richly represented in the aquatic world than a primitive order such as the stoneflies (Plecoptera).[1]

Pupation is a period of metamorphosis for the insect. With caddisflies the process is similar to the change from caterpillar to moth in the closely related order Lepidoptera. The old larval case, or with free-living caddisfly larvae, a newly constructed case, is lined with a silk cocoon and sealed off with a mesh grating over the entrance. The transformation from larva to adult requires approximately two weeks for most species. The emerging caddisflies either swim or crawl to the surface.

Dr. Walter Balduf, in *The Bionomics of Entomophagous Insects* (1939), included a section on caddisflies. Although he did not carry out any original experiments, he researched both American and foreign literature thoroughly and included observations from scattered sources on emergence. He paraphrased C. E. Sleight: "The pupa of *Hydropsyche* is said *to crawl over the bottom for a short time upon leaving the case,* then shoots to the surface. As soon as they have reached the water surface, or after swimming about there for a while, the pupae of these families poke the dorsum of the thorax, and sometimes also the first abdominal notum, above the top of the water. *As soon as the exposed part is dry,* it bursts suddenly along a longitudinal median suture, and the adult issues promptly to the water surface and is able to run rapidly at once or even fly." (Italics mine.)

The two parts of C. E. Sleight's description that I italicized parallel pretty closely the two points of hesitation, phases one and three, in my observations. The discrepancy between his record of the *Hydropsyche* pupa crawling after leaving the case and mine of the pupa drifting could be due to a number of reasons, but it might simply be attributable to the fact that he transferred nearly mature pupae into an artificial stillwater environment for observation, whereas my observations were made in a natural running-water environment.

Dr. Balduf also translated the papers of the German entomologist G. Ulmer, "...[after] the pupa has left its case it seeks to reach the water surface by crawling or swimming. Sometimes, however, it may swim as long as several hours within the water."

This is a very fertile area for further investigation both for entomologists and fly fishermen because the way different caddisfly species emerge controls trout feeding. Fishery biologists especially have a need for such information to determine the part pupae play as a food source.

The insect that cuts free of the shelter and moves to the surface is actually a fully formed adult, but it is sheathed in the loose, transparent skin of the previous pupal stage. The only area in which this pupal skin is not flexible and filmy is along the back and head; this region is more calcified, or sclerotized. This is the section of the skin that splits when exposed to air.

One purpose of my underwater studies was to see not only how pupae acted but also how they looked. The physical appearance of pupae swimming to the surface was quite indistinct, really no more than a blob of silvery reflection with minor splotches of color, and no matter how close the other divers and I tried to view the naturals, it was impossible in even the calmest river to pick out many details. Every part of the swimming insect—head, wings, legs, body—was enclosed in that sheath, and minute air bubbles in between it and the insect produced the reflections that obscured most of these parts.

These observations were difficult for me to accept because of the total discrepancy between them and common angling lore. There was no way to reconcile what I had seen with the standard imitations available to fly fishermen. Where was the drab body or the opaque wingpads on the active natural that were a stock part of the pupa flies?

The dilemma was compounded, however, because there were many drawings and photographs showing caddisfly pupae with quite distinct features, and the pictures especially were strong evidence that this was how the natural looked. The photographs were not lying, but in this case they proved to be very deceptive because they were not of active, swimming pupae—they were of dead specimens. Maybe when viewing the natural in an aquarium or other artificial environment, or when using caddisfly pupae taken either prematurely from the cocoon or later from a trout's stomach for models, the drab body and opaque wingpads on standard imitations seemed plausible. Based on underwater observations, however, covering up the main identifying factor of the insect, the bright reflections of the air bubbles, did not make sense.

All of the scuba work left little doubt in my mind that fly fishing progress had slipped onto the wrong track with the caddisfly pupa, developing tactics based on a fanciful idea of how the natural emerged and creating flies based on inactive or dead models; and worse, it had prescribed an approach for fishing a caddisfly emergence that most fly fishermen knew from frustrating experiences did not work very well.

Where did fly fishing theory fail? Many older styles of flies could possibly pass as rough imitations of emerging caddisflies, especially the sparse, soft-hackled patterns of early fly-fishing history. For the most part, however, this important stage of the insect was either ignored or overlooked. It was not until the late 1930s that a group of New York anglers began to recognize the caddisfly pupa as a specific problem.

This coterie of fly fishermen and fly tiers, centered loosely around the famous Angler's Roost shop in New York City, was interested in all aspects of the sport, but they were especially involved with the aquatic life that seemed to control the trout. They experimented with and brought out many new imitations during their creative association, exchanging ideas freely while working at the fly-tying benches at the Roost. They developed patterns not only for such well-known trout foods as the mayfly, but also for many of the lesser insect forms. Many of these flies were later included by Jim Deren in a popular paperback book, the *Noll Guide to Trout Flies*.

Jim, owner of the Angler's Roost, devised one of the first imitations of a pupa, the Devastator, using a popular material of the time, floss, for the body. In a note to me he commented, "I didn't put the name on that Caddis Pupa in the 1930s. I forgot who did, but I think it was old Ed Hewitt."

Ed Sens, a fly tier at the Roost, created one of the best known of these early pupa imitations. He used naturals taken from pupal cocoons and from trout stomachs as models, tying imitations with wool bodies and small, duck-quill wing slats. As a serious student of entomology he was well aware of the loose pupal cuticle and the air bubbles of the natural insect, but he also knew that he could not imitate the brightness of the pupa with the fly-tying materials of his era.

Ray Ovington, in his book *How to Take Trout on Wet Flies and Nymphs* (1953), featured Ed Sens and his pupa imitation, listing specific color recipes for two eastern species *Psilotreta frontalis* (Dark Blue Sedge) and *Rhyacophila lobifera* (Green Sedge). Ernest Schwiebert, with a review of many important caddisfly genera in *Matching the Hatch* (1955), and Charles Wetzel, with the first mention of the genus *Hydropsyche* (Spotted Sedge) in his book, *Practical Fly Fishing* (1943), continued expanding the knowledge of caddisfly entomology.

At this point, fly-fishing was at a threshhold, ready to recognize and seriously consider this stage of the caddisfly. Unfortunately the sport slipped into a virtual Dark Ages in the post World War II years, a time when spin-fishing swept the country and fly-fishing wallowed in confusion over undecipherable line weights and rod balances. It seemed also as if the positive aspects of caddisfly theory were lost to the fly-fishing public during these times.

The revival of fly-fishing in the late 1960s and early 1970s failed to inspire new research and experimentation with the caddisfly pupa. Sadly, even though there was no new knowledge on the subject, this did not stop angling writers from blithely discoursing on the how, where, when, and what of a caddisfly emergence. Misconceptions about caddisflies were spread during these years, mainly in books that talked mostly of other aquatic insects but offhandedly threw a few pages to caddisflies.

Edward Sens had said it when he indicated that we had gone as far as we could go with what we knew and what we had. And the writings in the early years of the current revival of fly-fishing did not have the cogent reasoning that pointed the way to future progress.

Advanced Tactics for Imitating the Emerging Pupa

The first discoveries and theories resulting from my research in caddisflies began coming out of Montana early in 1973, most of the information going directly back to members of my home fishing club, the Connecticut Fly Fishermen's Association, through my writings in their newsletter. The new pupal imitations and the accompanying tactics were introduced there because this group contained so many fine and knowledgeable fly fishermen that they were the perfect audience. Their responses would tell a lot about the acceptability of such radical ideas.

This initial exposure of my theories on emerging caddisflies was only a beginning. The ideas later reached much larger audiences in articles and books, national awareness really starting with the publication in 1976 of my book, *Challenge of the Trout*. The mention there of Antron and Creslan yarns for simulating the air bubbles carried by the emerging insect began to guide pupal theory out of the dead end it had reached in the area of imitations.[2]

Learning to Recognize a Caddisfly Hatch

Aren't effective flies and realistic techniques all that fly fishermen need to meet the challenge of a caddisfly hatch? There is one more important thing. Before they can fish an emergence of caddisflies, they have to know it is happening.

As my pupal imitations and tactics became better know it became obvious from the questions that were being asked that many people, including some very skilled anglers, did not know when to use them. These fly fishermen were generally split into two groups—those who could not recognize an emergence; and those who could not recognize an emergence but thought they could. There are three signs that indicate when a caddisfly hatch is happening:

One, a trout occasionally leaps into the air. When a trout jumps it is not playing, it is feeding. The jump happens during a caddisfly hatch when a trout follows a pupa from the bottom and the trout's momentum carries it into the air.

Two, most of the feeding trout are bulging or splashing. Usually trout grab pupae from the underside of the surface film and turn downward, this porpoising roll causing a bulge or, after vigorous pursuit, a splash. Bulges, splashes, or occasional jumps can happen when trout are feeding on other types of insects, but when they occur together it is a good indication that they are concentrating on caddisfly pupae.

Eric Taverner, in *Trout Fishing from All Angles*, includes a good description of this splashy riseform and associates it with emerging caddisflies: "The pyramid rise-form is the projection of a column of water upwards and at an angle with the surface of the water. The tiny column is considerably broader at the base and ends in a kind of brush; it is more often seen in the dusk and at night than at any other time and shows up very white against a dark background, just when the light is too poor for accurate observation.

The jumping and rolling movements of trout signal a caddisfly emergence.

A fast-charging trout breaks the surface as it pursues a caddisfly pupa. Tad Swanson

The pyramid-rise form is a splash of spray into the air.

"At one time I thought pale watery duns were the flies responsible for this rise-form and one evening when these duns were coming down and the rise-form was in full swing, I tied on a fly with a pale blue hackle and a hare's poll body. It was entirely successful, but to my surprise the stomach-contents of the trout I caught consisted almost exclusively of a green-bodied sedge in the act of hatching; and to many individuals the pupal shuck was still adhering."

How many times do fly fishermen see mayflies on the water and falsely attribute caddisfly activity to their presence? This mistake happens all the time. It is another reason anglers believe that mayflies are more important to them than caddisflies.

Three. There are no insects on the water. The absence of visible insects, along with the feeding activity of the trout, is a strong clue. Even during the heaviest part of a caddisfly hatch there are usually very few adults resting on the water; the emergents fly off quickly because they do not have to dry their wings as mayflies do. If the hatch is happening alone, without a simultaneous mating flight of other caddisflies, there will not be many adults in the air either because they do not dally long over the water.

It is because of the lack of surface insects that many fly fishermen fail to recognize a hatch. Even when all three signs are present it is not guaranteed that fish are feeding on swimming pupae, but at those times it is usually smart to try pupal imitations on faith, testing various colors and sizes if a natural insect cannot be captured for a model.

Some fly fishermen, once they have learned a little about caddisflies and have started looking for them, use the pupal imitations when they see adults in the air. The flying hordes, beating upriver, do not mean that the pupae are emerging. They do not even mean that adult females are about to lay their eggs. These adult flights are composed mostly of males, so while they may coincide with ovipositing activity they are not necessarily an indication of it.

One way for a fly fisherman to recognize egg-laying activity is by observing the water, if necessary putting his head down next to it so he can see along the surface. He watches for females that either dap like a bouncing Ping-Pong ball or dive straight into the stream. He also has to be able to recognize those species that lay their eggs by crawling under the surface rather than diving through it, but he can easily spot an important species of this type because the females swarm over any object protruding from the stream.

With experience a fly fisherman should usually be able to tell the difference between the egg-laying period and the emergence period, both of which excite trout, but he might also encounter situations where the pupae and adults are active at the same time. When trout are very selective, each fish choosing only one form of the insect, the unfortunate fly caster often cannot tell which stage a fish is concentrating on.

Larry Solomon and Eric Leiser reported on this phenomenon in *The Caddis and the Angler.* They discovered an article by entomologist Philip Corbet; just as importantly they realized the significance of Corbet's findings, which were that the emergence and egg laying may coincide. They wrote, " . . . upon inspection and dissection of captured insects [taken from an emergence trap], it was noted that many of the insects captured were adult females that had just returned from ovipositing. As mentioned earlier, the females of the species in group A pass through the surface to lay their eggs on the bottom, returning to land after their task has been completed.

"An even more interesting fact was that the schedule of the returning ovipositing species was quite consistent with the period of emergence of the same species; that is, the ovipositing females returned during a hatch of pupae. Now this was news!"[3]

What can a fly fisherman do when this happens? It can be a very challenging situation. Since the riseforms of feeding trout to either swimming pupae or swimming adults will be virtually identical, the only thing an angler can do is experiment when he suspects such dual activity, if necessary changing imitations for each fish.

TACTICS

The way to fish any imitation intelligently is to copy the movement of the natural insect in or on the water. The swimming emergers are usually the most important to fly fishermen, but not all pupae swim to the surface and fly off. There are even variations on the general swimming behavior—with some species the pupae reach the top, but instead of emerging from the water they swim just under the surface to a protruding object and climb out; with others the pupae emerge from the water and shed the pupal skin, but instead of flying off the adults run across the surface.

The other major way pupae emerge is by migrating to the shore and crawling out. During the slow trip into the bank, as the insects clamber over the rocks, they are completely vulnerable to any waiting fish. Even after reaching land the crawlers require more time than the swimmers to escape the pupal skin, taking ten seconds or more to emerge and two minutes to fly.

All these different forms of emergence mean that the fly fisherman needs a variety of tactics, not just one or two standby methods. No other stage in the life cycle of caddisflies presents more complexities—but no other presents as many opportunities either.

Tactics for swimmers

My patterns and tactics for matching swimming pupae are based on my own observations, and as a result of that research the recommendations differ markedly from most methods prescribed in angling literature. My techniques are based on the different phases of the emergence of the natural pupa.

There are two points of hesitation in the ascent of the natural—the dead drift near the bottom and the struggle under the surface film—and trout key on these levels. To properly simulate these moments of hesitation and to effectively fish a caddisfly hatch, the angler needs tactics that will keep the fly in these prime zones for as long as possible.

Fishing the entire hatch first requires flies that are physically able to stay either at the bottom or near the surface; this demands two patterns to match a caddisfly pupa: a weighted version and a semidry version. Each of these flies is fished during a different stage of the hatch, the deep version working best at the beginning of the emergence and the surface version becoming more effective later on. My imitations, the Deep

Sparkle Pupa and the Emergent Sparkle Pupa, are designed to accommodate this split situation.

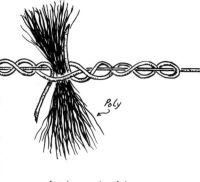

There are two major types of presentation, one passive and one active, that work these flies efficiently in the prime spots. The older approach is the upstream, dead-drift presentation—basically nymph fishing with the Deep Pupa and semidry fishing with the Emergent Pupa. The slack line presentation of a weighted pupa imitation keeps the fly floundering near the bottom for as long as possible, where trout pick up the freshly emerged pupae. The surface, no-drag presentation with a buoyant pupa imitation keeps the fly awash in the meniscus, where trout porpoise and intercept the escaping pupae. The dead-drift tactic is effective with either type of pupal imitation, especially when the insects are riding inert with the current for long distances.

There is a little trick that is especially useful for the Emergent patterns. These flies sit low in the water and, in smaller sizes, they can be difficult to see. In these situations a tuft of white or orange polypropolene, greased with floatant and tied in at the first blood knot of the leader, serves as a very visible strike indicator.

A piece of white or orange polypropylene may be tied in at the first blood knot of the leader to serve as a strike indicator.

The stutter-and-drift method (active presentation). Many types of caddisfly pupae do not ride quietly with the current even during the periods of hesitation. They bend and flex, beating their legs ineffectively. Such struggles produce minor movement, and this movement alerts trout to the insects.

A similar movement of the fly, a slight but noticeable progress *against and across the current,* is often critical in imitating such pupae. It must be a delicate motion rather than a wild jog across the stream, and it must be followed by further drift. Done properly, such action advertises the fly as suitable prey.

My method used to initiate this subtle motion with the Deep or Emergent Pupa patterns is called the stutter-and-drift. It differs from other forms of active presentation because the fly moves not only upstream (a twitch presentation) but across stream. It is designed solely for the purpose of initiating a sideways "struggle" because this motion, even more than the upstream motion, is very deadly with the submerged or partially submerged fly. The method is predicated on the observation of natural pupae, which showed that the feeble actions of the underwater insect usually only helped it slip across minor bands of current rather than against the full force of it. There are three skills required for the stutter-and-drift:

Casting. The angler has to be able to cast a slack line with a curve. The presentation is made slightly up and across, the fly landing downstream of the leader and line and drifting dead for the first few moments. The line lies loosely on or in the water until the current drag begins taking the slack out.

Mending. One key to the method is what is usually considered bad mending. With a "good" mend the fly does not move, but with a "bad" one it hops up and across the currents. Bad mending is much easier than good mending; the angler simply makes an upstream arc with the rod tip, taking slack line already on the water to throw the line in an upstream belly. An important feature of the stutter-and-drift, however, is to make this bad mend prematurely, before the fly actually starts dragging, so that only a small bit of power reaches the fly.

Stutter drifting. The bad mend transmits a slight tug to the fly, pulling it in a tantalizing, sidling movement. There is now not enough slack left on the water, however, to allow further dead drift, so follow-up drift is extended with the quick release of more line.

The angler insures the stutter, the pause of the fly between the mending

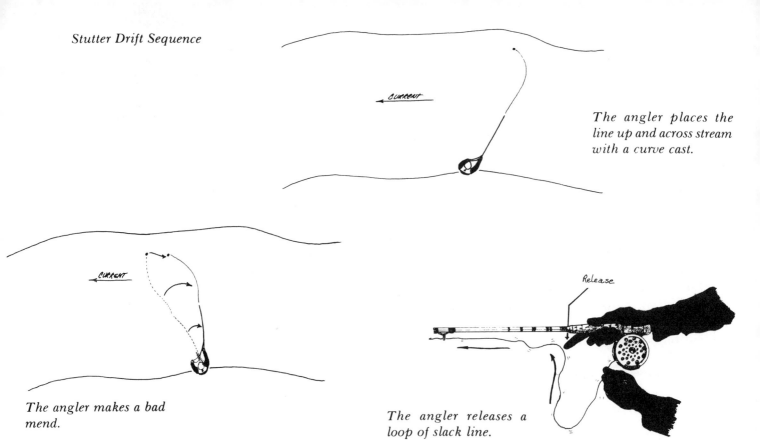

The angler places the line up and across stream with a curve cast.

The angler makes a bad mend.

The angler releases a loop of slack line.

movements, by first holding the line under the index finger of his rod hand. With his other hand he strips a foot or so of slack from the reel, and after fully completing the mend he lifts his index finger on the rod hand and slides the excess slack onto the water, allowing the fly to drop farther downstream.

The bad mend-and-slack release sequence is repeated until the fly passes the angler and swings completely downstream. It is a highly effective method of teasing trout into taking when they are keying on the struggling motion of caddisfly pupae, the strike usually coming as the imitation resumes its dead drift. The hit is generally hard and there is no problem detecting it.

The Emergent Pupa pattern, riding the surface, is fished with a floating line. The Deep Pupa pattern, settling near the bottom before the manipulation begins, is fished with a regular sinking tip line with a ten-foot sinking section or a high-density sinking-tip line, also with a ten-foot sinking section. The method of presentation is virtually the same with either fly.

Older methods for active presentation. Two of the classic methods have always been effective during emergences of swimmers. These older techniques were inventions of necessity, both tributes to the ingenuity of fly fishermen, partially solving the problem of how to catch selective trout without effective pupal imitations. They accomplished this by minimizing the importance of the fly.

Fly fishermen found out that the older patterns, either the Sens Pupa or the soft-hackled style, could not be fished too slowly. With methods such as the dead drift or the stutter drift, where trout would have a chance to examine an imitation, these flies often proved inadequate. The repeated failures of these artificials when fished slowly probably contributed to the myth of the "super caddis," that myth explaining why a slow-moving fly would not work.

One way to overcome a poor imitation was to present it so close to the fish that he never had the chance to see it. Another way was to show it so quickly that the fish never had the chance to see it well. This was how these methods fooled fussy trout in spite of the fly.

In my talks with many older fly fishermen, including Charles Haspel (80 years old) and Merle Jones (88 years old), the technique they prescribed for "those jumping trout" is the hit-them-on-the-head method. It is actually an ancient wet-fly trick for catching rising fish, a method used to circumvent the need for a surface imitation before dry flies became widely popular. (This technique was later adapted for dry-fly use by George LaBranche in *The Dry Fly and Fast Water*.)

With this method an angler, surrounded by feeding trout, false casts until one of them rises within range. Then, as quickly as possible, he slaps the fly right on top of the riseform, hoping that that fish will snatch at another tidbit.

If the fly lands quickly enough and close enough the fish often reacts out of reflex. It does not matter what the fly looks like because the fish is reacting to the commotion of its landing; the fish never has a chance to look at it. The tactic works especially well when fish are feeding in a frenzied manner, as they often do on swimming emergers, because then they respond immediately.

The major benefit of this method is that the visible characteristics of the fly are unimportant, at least for the split second after it lands. A pattern should hit with a soft plop rather than with a splash, however, so a small, light fly such as an Emergent Pupa is an immediate advantage. Also, if the fly is not snatched instantly, a good imitation provides a better chance for a delayed take.

James Leisenring, through his writings, strongly influenced both my fishing tactics and my fly-tying. One reason I never seriously considered putting wingpads on my own Deep Pupa imitations was his unequivocal statement in *The Art of Tying the Wet Fly* (1941); "I could always, and still can, catch more fish on a wingless imitation."

The ideal qualities he touted for a subsurface fly—sparseness and translucency— would have been frustrated by stiff, thick, and opaque materials. His patterns had to match his method of fishing; both were parts of a delicate and precise system for fooling trout by simulating the motion of an emerging insect.

Motion is an important factor in imitation because anything that moves against or across the current, as long as it does not take off with unusual alacrity, announces itself as alive and available. The movement attracts the attention of the trout, becoming a triggering characteristic, and by doing so lessens the impact of other visual characteristics of a fly.

The Leisenring lift method of nymph fishing is not a scattergun method for covering water, but a way to tease fish into striking. It saves the attractiveness of motion for a specific moment in the presentation. The fly does not even begin swimming until it reaches the spot where the trout is most likely to feed.

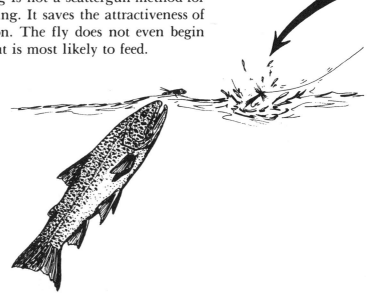

Wet-fly specialists used the "Hit-them-on-the-head" method to catch jumping trout.

The angler stalks fairly close to his target, usually a visible fish but sometimes just a nice-looking pocket, and casts fifteen to twenty feet above it. He lets the fly sink and drift downstream on a slack line, all the time pointing at the fly with the rod tip. When the sunken fly approaches the target, he simply stops following it with the rod, allowing drag to take over and lift the fly up in front of the fish.

This method works best in the slower waters of a trout stream. In pools, flats, and soft riffles the drag puts subtle tension on the fly rather than pulling it uncontrollably, the illusion of life vibrating through the hackles as the imitation rises and swims. If it begins at the right moment, such movement can persuade a fish that an easy victim is escaping.

A drawback with both of these methods is that neither of them covers the feeding zones efficiently. The hit-them-on-the-head method is effective the moment after it hits, and if the fish has left or is not receptive the entire presentation is a loss. The Leisenring lift method is effective only if the fly kicks to life at a precise spot, teasing a specific fish, and if that fish ignores the opportunity the entire drift-and-rise sequence is a loss. Both have to work to individual trout rather than to areas of insect concentration.

They are still valuable tactics. Whenever it is possible to observe and approach actively feeding fish, especially if some of them are large, these methods provide the chance for one-on-one confrontation, angler versus trout. If a fly fisherman is patient and does not mind doing more searching than fishing, these methods are two of the best ways to hunt trophy trout.

Tactics for crawlers

Maybe the crawlers are not as important overall as the swimmers, trout feeding on them a smaller part of the time simply because a smaller number of caddisflies emerge in this manner. But when an abundant species does begin hatching and migrating to shore it becomes the attraction of the moment. The pupae can pull fish into the shallows to intercept easily captured prey.

It is not always possible to predict such migrations, but the fly fisherman usually has no trouble recognizing one when he stumbles onto it. The telltale signals are the trout stacked in the shallows, nosing the gravel in completely exposed areas even during the day. They spook easily at these times, and the first indication of such feeding activity may be flushed fish rushing back to deeper water. The main obstacle for a fly fisherman is believing that these fish are there to feed.

I have botched such opportunities many times, showing a lack of observation,

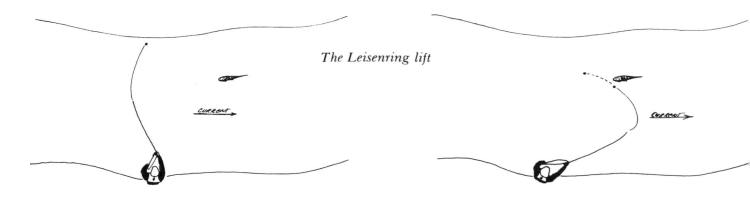

The Leisenring lift

*The angler points his rod tip at the fly and follows it until it reaches the trout's position.
Then he stops following, letting the drag tease the imitation into life.*

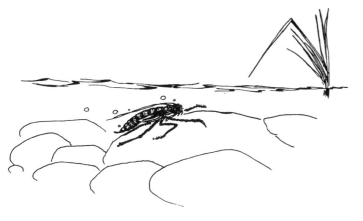

Many types of caddisfly pupae will crawl into the shallows and onto·exposed rocks to emerge.

inquisitiveness, and creativity. I would scare out trout from under my feet, vaguely note the incident, promise to move a bit more stealthily, and then start fishing the "good-looking"water as if nothing had happened. What I should have done was find another shallow gravel area crammed with trout, but these blunders usually occurred in the fall when I was hunting spawning brown trout, so I would go back to casting my 3/0 streamers.

This shallow-water feeding has not been noted very often and has never been linked with migrating caddisflies, but it is not uncommon. Especially in the fall, when many of the big case makers (family Limnephilidae) start crawling into the banks, trout jam up over gravel bars in inches of water to wait for the pupae.

One particular place trout congregate is at the inside bend of a curve in the stream. The biggest fish usually hang at the break between the deep and shallow water, lesser fish arranged by size in toward the bank, but there can be exceptions to this hierarchy because any depression or pocket in the gravel might shelter a large fish.

Sometimes a dead-drift presentation picks up a few fish in these situations, but usually the fish prefer an imitation that is creeping toward shore, crossing their noses just like the natural. While it might not be possible to make a fly scrape the bottom like a crawler, there is an effective technique that can slow it down enough to imitate the activity.

I call it the limbo method; this name describes the main principle as well as anything. The goal is to get all parts of the terminal tackle—the fly, leader, line, and rod tip—suspended underneath the faster current of the surface. If any section stays on top a downstream belly of drag can ruin the presentation.

Tackle includes a weighted Deep Sparkle Pupa in appropriate size and color; a short leader, four to five feet, the entire length treated with a sinking agent; an assortment of sinking lines; and an eight- to nine-foot rod, preferably not bamboo (it is going to be slightly abused).

The method requires a bit of stealth, the angler creeping out into the water and kneeling or crouching just upstream from the fish. Since the trout are peering intently at the bottom, rather than at the surface and into the air, slow movements even fifteen or twenty feet in front of them usually do not frighten them, but they are very sensitive to the vibrations of heavy steps or the waves of a splashy approach.

From this position the line is cast across and slightly upstream but no more than twenty-five feet, including the leader; just enough for the fly to hit three feet beyond the break between shallow and deep water. In very large rivers, where the shallow shelf might extend out more than twenty-five feet, it is better to wade out closer to the break than to make a longer cast.

As soon as the weighted fly lands and begins to sink, the fly fisherman thrusts the rod tip underwater against the gravel. He lets fly, leader, and line drift downstream until they are below him and next to the feeding fish. Then he begins retrieving with a hand-twist motion (also known as a figure-eight retrieve) and continues until the fly has swung completely into the shallows.

Here is what happens underwater during this procedure: thrusting the rod underwater allows the entire connection, from the fly to the spot where the line enters the rod tip, to get near the bottom. When the fly first hits it is beyond the break between shallow and deep water. Since the water farther away from the bank is

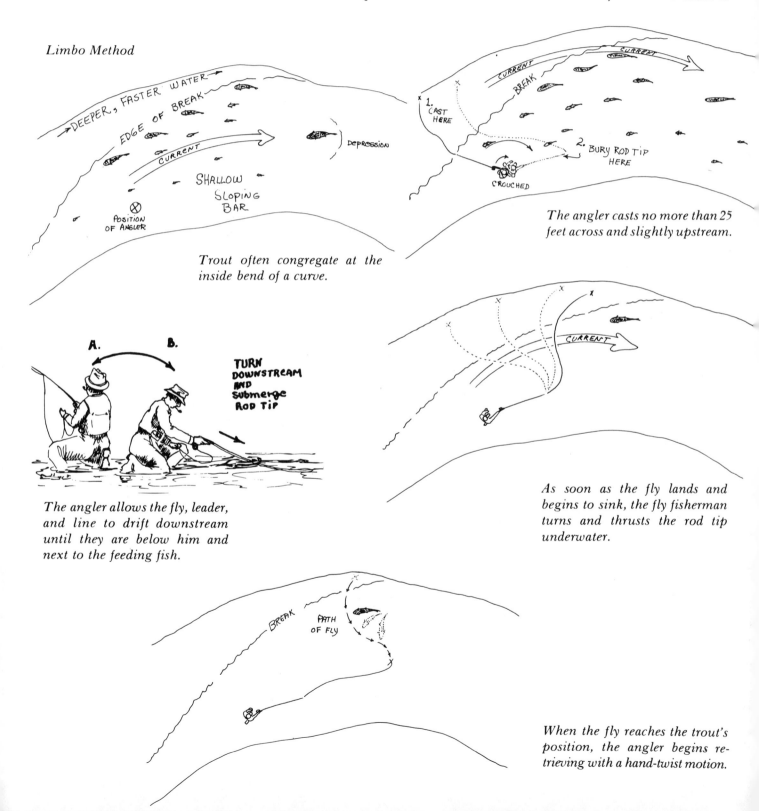

Limbo Method

Trout often congregate at the inside bend of a curve.

The angler casts no more than 25 feet across and slightly upstream.

The angler allows the fly, leader, and line to drift downstream until they are below him and next to the feeding fish.

As soon as the fly lands and begins to sink, the fly fisherman turns and thrusts the rod tip underwater.

When the fly reaches the trout's position, the angler begins retrieving with a hand-twist motion.

usually moving faster than the water closer in, even as the fly sinks it gets pushed slightly farther downstream than the leader and line. As the fly drifts past his position the fly fisherman begins the hand-twist motion. With the rod tip pointed downstream this retrieve brings the fly around and into the shallows at a crawl in front of the trout.

The fisherman carries an assortment of sinking lines for the limbo method because the depth and current velocity at the break can vary from stream to stream. Usually it does not vary so much from spot to spot on the same stream that he has to change lines everytime he moves to another gravel slope. A sinking line makes it possible to work the fly at a crawl because it gets under the surface currents. The sink rate of the line has to be matched to the conditions at the break so it can sink to the bottom between the spot where the fly hits and the spot where the retrieve begins. Because the current at a curve in a stream is partially controlled by centrifugal force, the inside areas usually are not extremely fast, but on larger rivers the break can be deeper than four feet. In these spots commercial lead-core lines are valuable.

Execution of the limbo method is fairly easy. The main element of success is making the crossing crawl begin just as the fly reaches the break, the area where the biggest fish usually wait for the migrating pupae.

Tactics for the oddball emergers

A number of caddisfly species deviate from the usual patterns of emergence. They rise to the surface like most swimming pupae, but instead of flying off they behave differently. They can be divided into two types: runners and paddlers.

The runners shed the pupal skin once they reach the surface and then, as freshly emerged adults, sprint across the top with amazing agility, the tension of the meniscus supporting them quite well. They keep their wings folded while moving, the back edges sliding on the water like skate blades.

A quick clue that trout are feeding on these running adults is an absolutely explosive rise; not the clean jump of a fish taking an emerger and continuing into the air, but the churning and splashing of a fish engulfing both the insect and a portion of the surface. Adults on the water, highly visible as they scramble about, help verify what is happening, especially if a trout obliges by grabbing one that is being observed.

This type of feeding activity actually requires a dry fly that imitates an adult rather than a pupa pattern. A fly creating the correct impression on the surface film, such as the Dancing Caddis, skittered on top with a fast retrieve, usually draws the same kind of violent strike as the natural.

The paddlers do not shed their pupal skin as do the runners after reaching the surface. They swim with a vigorous breaststroke to the bank or to a protruding object and climb out of the water. They emerge there as adults, as do the crawlers. When they are swimming near the surface like this the insects are not readily visible to an observer, and therefore offer no clue to the aberrant activity, but the feeding manner of the trout is often very distinctive. The fish identify the emergence method for the angler, leaving long wakes as they chase the pupae, the trout looking like miniature

After shedding the pupal sheath, the emergers of some caddisflies run across the surface instead of flying off.

Some emerging caddisflies move toward the shore by swimming just under the surface of the water.

marauding sharks. The fish speed up as they come up behind the insect, or a matching fly, and push up an even higher ridge of water. When it is the fly that these fish are closing in on this surge often causes an angler to strike too soon.

A fly tied in the style of the Deep Pupa, but without the lead weight on the shank, can be used to imitate these paddling pupae. Greased with floatant to keep it near the surface and retrieved with long pulls to make it swim across stream, a fly can be cast to intercept the path of visible, cruising trout.

Possibly the advantage gained by emerging either of these two ways, instead of flying off, is that the insects are momentarily safe from birds. The extra time spent in or on the water, however, gives fish more opportunity to feed on them. These moments of availability during a hatch help make the oddball emergers important. They encourage especially frenzied feeding by trout, attracting a greater percentage of the fish to the surface because of the increased amount of insect activity there.

How often should a fly fisherman be using pupal methods? On many trout streams this is the way to fish as much as fifty percent of the time. The caddisfly pupa is the insect to imitate, in manner and appearance, not only during a hatch, but whenever a familiar form is needed to tempt trout, because caddisflies are so prevalent that the cumulative effect of the pupae of numerous species continually hatching ingrains the general characteristics into the mind of the fish.

Fishing the Adult Imitations

The Dry Fly Takes Its Place

The dry fly reigns supreme in the hearts of American fly fishermen. It is the easiest way to catch trout; it is the most exciting way to catch trout; and at the proper moment it can be the most effective way to catch trout.

The "glue" of this love affair between the dry fly and the angler, however, has usually been the mayfly. Since the Nineteenth Century pronouncements of Frederick Halford, who tried to restrict dry-fly presentation to the upstream dead-drift on the chalkstreams of England, the methods themselves have been suitable more for imitating the gentle ride of the mayfly dun than the more boisterous behavior of caddisflies.

The opinion of most fly fishermen is that mayflies are taken as surface food more often than caddisflies, meaning, naturally, that mayflies are more important than caddisflies as dry flies. Maybe these two ideas should be examined separately, however.

Is it a fair assessment to say that mayflies are more available on the surface than caddisflies? The supposed predominance of mayflies as forage is not true under the surface, where caddisfly larvae and pupae are so important, but it probably is true on top of the water. The reason mayflies are taken more there is that during their adult stage they have two extra periods of availability. First, when they emerge as duns they generally ride serenely with the current while their wings dry, the distance they travel depending on weather conditions and water type. Second, when the females of most species lay eggs as spinners they flop and die on the water, washing away with the surface drift.

Caddisflies are usually not so available on the surface. During emergence the

period of hesitation is underneath the meniscus, not completely on top of it, and this slight difference is critical. It generally makes the dry fly a poor choice when caddisflies are hatching. The main exception to this is when the adults of some species run across the water, but even then the proper presentation is not the typical dead-drift method. During egg-laying the females of some species do fall to the surface, providing excellent dry-fly fishing, but even for this second period of availability most species dive or crawl underwater.

So caddisflies are on the surface much less than mayflies during both emergence and egg-laying. The only time that they are there when mayflies are not is when the adults return to the stream to drink water. This can be significant because caddisflies may live up to three months after emerging and they need liquids a number of times each day. Mayflies die within a few days after emerging and cannot take in water or nourishment because the mouth parts atrophy in adults. This added exposure of caddisflies on the surface, however, does not compensate fully for the extra moments of mayfly availability.

If mayflies are taken from the surface more than caddisflies, isn't it also true that mayflies are more useful as dry fly models than caddisflies? It certainly seems as if there should be a great disparity in relative importance, but fortunately for dry-fly anglers the trout are not so predictably logical.

In recent angling literature there has been a lot of conjecture about the place of caddisfly-adult imitations. No one can ever doubt that these flies are important, their consistent effectiveness providing solid empirical evidence of their value on all types of trout streams, but some thoughtful anglers seem almost apologetic about recommending the adults as dry fly models because they do not understand why or when fish should be interested in a food item they see so seldom on the surface.

A close look at the activities of caddisfly adults is necessary to explain when they are and are not readily available to trout:

Even in the bright light midday, the shaded wat of the Wise River in Mo tana is a good place to try caddisfly imitation becau fish are accustomed to t flitting and bouncing the adult caddisfly. Ga LaFontaine

One, when swimming pupae emerge and shed their pupal skins, the adults sometimes flutter once or twice on the surface before flying off. These preliminary hops are usually brief, affording trout very little chance to take the insect. The dry fly is not important here, except with those species that run rather than fly to reach shore.

Two, during a hatch there are natural cripples that cannot fly away. After drowning, these adults drift with the currents, eventually gathering in areas where foam and debris pile up. The dry fly is important here, especially after a heavy, concentrated hatch.

Three, after emerging and escaping to the safety of the streamside vegetation, the adults can live for weeks, or even months, but they need liquid to prevent dehydration. Sometimes they drink nectar from flowers or trapped water from boles of trees, but usually they return briefly to the stream.

This type of activity is continuous near dark, sheltered areas because the adults of many species congregate in these spots during the day. Wherever low-hanging limbs, undercut banks, or cliff ledges extend over the water, the trout become accustomed to seeing and feeding on caddisflies.

The dry fly is important here, especially as a midday searching fly in the damp and dark areas.

Four, different species of caddisflies lay their eggs in different ways. The females of some types paste their egg masses on rocks or vegetation next to or over the water, not in it, and let the rain wash the eggs into the stream. These females are not available to the fish at all during egg laying, but few important trout-stream species belong to this group.

The females of some common species carry their eggs in a ball at the end of the abdomen. They dap or collapse on the surface, releasing the packet to sink to the bottom. The time they spend on the water can vary with the species, but the females of some sprawl out and drift unstruggling with the current, spent from the rigors of egg-laying.

In the most common manner of egg-laying, the females dive or crawl under the surface. They crawl around on the bottom until they find a suitable place, and there they lay a string of eggs. These adult females often survive their submersion, swimming back to the surface and flying off, possibly repeating the process a number of times.

The dry fly is not important for the first type of egg-laying female, but very important for the second. It is the third type, the divers, that provide the surprise.

Some female caddisflies carry a ball of eggs at the tip of the abdomen.

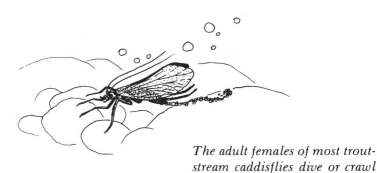

The adult females of most trout-stream caddisflies dive or crawl to the bottom and lay a string of eggs on a solid object.

*The diving females
hit the surface hard.*

If trout only took dry caddisfly imitations when caddisfly adults were on the surface, then caddisflies would be much less important than mayflies as dry-flies.

During my own fishing, however, it seemed as if downwing dry flies were doing much better than they should in at least two situations: as imitations when diving adults were abundant and as general all-around patterns even during the middle of the day on open water. If there was some reason for adult caddisfly patterns to work at these times, their value relative to mayfly patterns could not be judged by comparing the number of *naturals* taken from the surface.

It turned out that the two mysterious periods of effectiveness were related. The subsequent investigation into odd preferences by trout for surface imitations, even when the predominant available food was not on the surface, forced me to rethink my general ideas and add two wrinkles to the theory of selective feeding—sequential selectivity and carry-over selectivity—to explain these phenomena.

It was clear that the diving females spent most of the time during egg laying under the water rather than on it. Their longest period on the surface was when they tried to dive through the rubbery meniscus, flying as high as twenty feet up and hurtling down to hit with a fearful impact. They often failed to break the surface tension at all, but even when they did they would lie half in and half out of the film, momentarily stunned.

If observations had shown that the trout, for some reason, were concentrating their feeding efforts on the disoriented adults at the surface, that might have quickly explained the effectiveness of dry flies, but they did not show this at all. The fish were taking the insects in a pattern: first, they picked up drowned or struggling females drifting near the bottom; second, they rose for females swimming toward the surface; and third, they searched the surface for any freshly fallen females.

They were feeding at three levels—the buffer zone, the underside of the meniscus, and the topside of the meniscus—in a regular sequence. The feeding on struggling females near the bottom seemed to last until a swimmer caught the eye of a fish, triggering a rise, and then after capturing this insect on the underside of the meniscus the fish would stay there and wait for one to fall on the topside. If the current at the surface was not too swift, the trout often lingered there to take a number of crashing females.

It is important to emphasize that the fish work one level at a time. There is no hopscotching around; a fish usually does not grab an insect at one level, rush to another, and then return to the first. It is generally a very patterned feeding action progressing from bottom to top and then back, the fish spending a certain amount of time at each level.

The fish are actually responding to a sequence of different visual stimulae when they feed like this even though they are taking the same insect all the time, because the insect looks different at each level. The motion of the insect, the angle the fish views it from, and the background the fish sees it against all change. This is why, possibly, the mind of the fish may be telling it that it is taking a series of different insects, but as long as there is a steady sequence it can continue to feed selectively.

Trout exhibit the same sequential selectivity with some other insects. They feed on emerging mayflies this way, taking nymphs drifting, nymphs emerging, and duns floating in a regular order. But here there is an important difference between mayflies and caddisflies: mayfly duns spend much more time on the surface than diving caddisfly females. So there must be a special reason why caddisfly adults still trigger a strong feeding response.

But consider another question now: do trout feed sequentially on emerging caddisfly pupae? Generally not. The fish stay at one level of insect concentration even if there are occasional adults on the surface after emergence. There is an answer to this question and it explains why the dry fly works during caddisfly egg-laying but not during caddisfly emergence or why it works at all.

It does not matter how much time diving adults spend on the surface. They might not be staying there any longer than the emergers, but the emergers are going and the divers are coming. Once an emerger reaches the surface it is on the verge of escaping, whereas when a diver splashes down it is remaining in the water. This is the difference.

It is the splash-down itself that makes the adult caddisfly important on the surface. When the insect hits the meniscus an explosion of light radiates from the bottom of this rubbery mirror. This simulus is so powerful that it breaks the fish from one stage of selective feeding, the capture of swimmers on the underside of the meniscus, and kicks it into another.

The initial splash alerts the trout to the fact that an insect has arrived. It is a signal that brings the fish charging, but by the time a fish reaches the spot the female caddisfly may be breaking through the surface film or actually swimming downward. Most of diving egg layers, even here, are probably not taken on the true surface, but just under it; nevertheless, it makes little difference in the effectiveness of the dry fly. When the fish rushes over to investigate, it is hunting an adult caddisfly and will take it or an imitation wherever it finds one.

The fact that fish are actively searching, instead of passively waiting for the current to bring the natural item, lessens the importance of concentration level in their feeding. So no matter what percentage of naturals fish take from the surface during egg laying, the dry fly remains a very effective imitation.

The attention of the trout might be on the surface a good part of the time during egg laying, but the fish is usually not looking for a typically presented dry fly. A delicate drop and a dead-drift float fail to recreate the fuss an adult caddisfly makes on the water; nothing diminishes the effectiveness of an imitation more than a standard dry-fly technique. At times a delicate drag-free float is useful with caddisfly patterns, but not when the divers are crashing.

This is the situation in which to use an active, twitch presentation. The fly should slap down fairly hard, spreading the same shower of light streaks as the insect. If it lands down and across stream from the casting position, that first splash of light can be reproduced by moving it with periodic upstream twitches.

Other methods of fly-fishing also work when caddisflies are laying eggs. Various wet and semidry techniques, described in the next section on tactics, can be as effective as the active dry-fly presentation, but usually they are not more effective. The powerful attraction of something live moving on the meniscus, an action that can be duplicated with a surface imitation, pulls trout from such a wide area that it makes up for any lack of insects on the water.

My fishing experiences indicted a second situation where dry flies were working inordinately well. At times, in the middle of the day, when there were no insects at all on the surface, the trout were demonstrating a strong preference for caddisfly patterns. They were being selective even when there was nothing to be selective to. This was happening on certain rivers during certain months.

On streams that have heavy populations of caddisflies there is a one- or two-month period each summer when the combined egg laying of various species can overwhelm any other activity. Every evening the clouds of females come down, bouncing, skittering, and crashing on the water. If this happens for enough days consecutively—if no sudden change in weather conditions interrupts the egg-laying pattern—the trout become used to taking active insects near the surface.

Fish can become conditioned to the splash and fuss of egg-laying caddisflies and lose their ability to recognize other insects as surface food. They often ignore imitations or naturals unless there is movement. The trout may also refuse these items when they are fluttering, turning away at the last moment, if the downwing silhouette is missing.

This selectivity can carry over once it becomes part of the trout's routine. Even when the surface currents of a stream are barren the fish may be unable to respond to any insect except a caddisfly. In these situations any pattern that fails to at least vaguely mimic a caddisfly is going to perform poorly when compared to a proper caddisfly-imitation.

An angler switching from a wet fly to a dry fly, or vice versa, can become momentarily confused. Different optical laws and different forms of selectivity control the way fish react at each level. The fly fisherman actually has to shift his mental perspective if he wants to be completely successful with either type of fly; changing methods without changing perspectives just as quickly can hurt performance so much that it becomes obvious why some anglers prefer to always fish a dry fly or always fish a sunken fly. Purism, in this sense, becomes more a case of practicality than snobbery.

The dry fly has a definite place in caddisfly tactics. Methods might range from a delicate upstream presentation when trout are sipping drowned stragglers to a vigorous stripping action when they are chasing running adults. Probably the most useful technique for imitating caddisflies, however, is the twitch-and-drift sequence, the fly moved in a short upstream skip and then allowed to float down to a fish that has been notified of its presence.

What is the value of adult caddisflies as dry flies? How they actually rank in importance depends on the stream, but they are probably not quite as valuable as mayflies when their populations are equal. There is no type of trout habitat, however, where they can be ignored completely as dry-flies. The failure to use tactics and patterns that can successfully cope with adult situations costs an angler exciting dry-fly fishing over the length of a season.

Wet and Dry Tactics for Imitating Adult Caddisflies

A virtue of fly-fishing entomologies is that they cannot discuss tactics without giving a rationale for using them. The biological information on the insects provides basic clues on where and how the fly should be presented and links methods with the rhythms of the stream. This is a much more useful approach than the practice of randomly listing techniques.

Fly-fishing entomologies have another obligation: tactics cannot be separated from the way trout perceive the natural insect. Entomologies must explain how the sensory faculties of the fish, especially the senses of sight and feel, control feeding, because flies and tactics have to change everytime the manner of recognizing food changes. Trout recognize surface food one way and subsurface food another; they recognize drifting food one way and struggling food another.

The insects affect the way trout see them by where they are and what they do. Where they are can be described by the main categories of dry and wet; what they do can be described by the main categories of passive or active. At any given moment an insect can be dry and passive, dry and active, wet and passive, or wet and active (four possibilities in all).

The fly fisherman, matching a particular insect, must choose the tactic that fits the actions of that insect. If he picks the wrong one, the fly, no matter how much it may resemble an insect in brightness, size, color, or shape, can look wrong. The trout may not recognize the fly because it will be perceiving the naturals under a different set of optical laws.

In the area of tactics adult caddisflies create some fascinating challenges because they can be dry or wet and passive or active. A particular species might fit any one of the four possible combinations of these categories.

A fly fisherman cannot decide how to fish as soon as he spots an adult caddisfly. How much simpler it is, for example, with mayfly spinners; they can be matched with an upstream dead-drift presentation almost all the time. But when egg-laying caddisflies arrive at the stream the fly fisherman has to spend time observing both fish and insects before he can proceed.

Dry-fly tactics (passive presentation)

The recent emphasis on active presentations has raised what used to be a minor approach to a major one. This readjustment has been beneficial both because twitching and skating methods mimic the way many caddisflies act during egg laying. But maybe this crusade has been a little too successful; many fly fishermen now believe that caddisfly-adult imitations should be fished actively all the time, and this is not true.

There are important trout-stream caddisflies that float along very quietly. Some adult egg layers, especially the type that expel their eggs on the surface instead of swimming underwater, need to rest before flying away. Even the swimming females, after pasting their eggs and returning to the surface, sometimes sprawl exhausted and drift long distances.

Trout adjust their feeding rhythm accordingly when the adults stop fluttering and skipping in typical caddisfly fashion. Instead of rising with a splash every time, they slow down to more methodical selection. They no longer rush toward the commotion on the meniscus like they do with active females. They stay in their holding lie and let the current bring insects to them.

Trout either hold near the bottom and rise or hang just under the surface and sip when they feed on these passive adults. There are many factors that determine which way they work, but two of the most important ones are the number of insects on the water and the speed of the current at the surface.

There usually has to be a lot of insects available before fish can sip efficiently. Holding near the surface, even in the slower areas of a stream, requires a large expenditure of energy, but if there are enough insects passing overhead a trout can take them with a very quick rhythm, tipping slightly every few moments and opening its mouth. As surface currents become increasingly faster there have to be more, or

John Randolph captured a caddisfly "blizzard" in this photograph taken on the Matapedia River in Canada. "Billions of flies were backlit by the sun, producing the snowstorm effect in the picture," he wrote. "Twenty miles of river were snowed in by the caddisflies. The quaking aspen along the banks were abuzz with the myriad tiny bodies and fluttering wings. The whole river seemed to hum with the soft whir of wings."

Behavior during egg laying varies between the different types of caddisflies. Here is a "rogue's gallery" of important caddisflies and their egg-laying habits.

*Little Black Sedge (*Chimarra aterrima*) Category: Dry and passive. The females ride the surface quite serenely after egglaying. They are often the cause for sipping rises.* Ken Thompson

*Scaly-Wing Sedge (*Ceraclea resurgens*) Category: Dry and active. The females lay their eggs on the surface, and usually flop and flutter while doing so.* Ken Thompson

*Spotted Sedge (*Hydropsyche bronta*) Category: Wet and passive. The females lay their eggs underwater. When they are finished, they release their hold and drift with the current.* Ken Thompson

*Rush Sedge (*Phryganea sayi*) Category: Wet and active. The females choose slow-water areas for egg-laying sites. However, they almost seem to recognize their vulnerability in these quiet habitats as they swim strongly and quickly to-and-from underwater cover.* Ken Thompson

larger, insects available to make this feeding style feasible. No matter how much food is on the surface, sipping becomes impractical when current speed is more than .50 to .75 feet per second, which is still fairly slow-moving water.

When the water is fast or the insects are sparse it is easier for a trout to wait near the bottom. It can rest there in the dead currents, often behind an obstruction that breaks the force, and swim up when it sees the insect approaching. The fish takes it with a head-and-tail rise and returns quickly to the holding position.

Fly fisherman have to be able to cope with both sipping and rising activities. The same general upstream approach does not work equally well for both of them.

When fish are rising all the way from the bottom the standard dry-fly method works fine. The main problem is to mark the general vicinity of the holding spot and cast far enough above it so that the fly drifts naturally over the fish. If an angler sticks to the center portions or deeper areas of a stream, where the surface currents normally flow faster, it might be possible for him to use this one method all the time.

But on the silky flow of spring creeks, or even on the quieter flats and edges of freestone streams, trout hold and sip inert drifters for hours, leaving small rings on the surface. They take the quiet egg layers in a preoccupied manner that makes a general technique like the standard dry-fly method ineffective.

There are two things that make sipping unique as feeding behavior—and also make the standard approach a poor way to take these fish. First, there are usually an incredible number of insects present—millions floating over the head of the fish. Second, the fish have a very tiny field of vision, demanding very precise placement of the fly.

The upstream-and-across approach does not work well because it requires a long cast (which is difficult to put exactly on a lane of drift) and a long float by the fly (which is time consuming). As a result it is inefficient, failing to cover fish accurately or frequently enough to raise the odds in an angler's favor.

The fly fisherman needs special tactics to take sippers consistently. If he understands the optical laws that govern the way a fish sees, and uses them to his advantage—sometimes the same laws that make this situation so tough—he can overcome the problems of abundant naturals and a narrow feeding lane. Here are three methods for overcoming these problems.

Stalker's method. Why won't sipping trout move far to take either a fly or a natural? Because if an object is floating a bit off to either side a fish does not see it. A sipping trout, holding just under the surface, has a smaller window (the area of the meniscus it can see through) than a fish that is deeper. By the same rules, a trout near the surface cannot see much of the outside world (for example, an approaching fisherman).

The optical laws of light entering the water were first discussed by Alfred Ronalds in *A Fly-Fisher's Entomology* (1836), but he only pointed out how this affected the way the trout might view the angler. Dr. Francis Ward, in both *The Marvels of Fish Life* (1911) and *Animal Life under Water* (1921), approached the problem from the perspective of the trout capturing food and included an elaborate illustration showing the "cone of vision," explaining how this inverted cone narrows or widens as a fish rises or sinks (see accompanying illustration).

The stalker's method makes use of this information. It requires much patience and stealth, but it is worth the effort. The fisherman starts his approach from directly in back of the trout and wades slowly toward it, careful not to push a bow of water

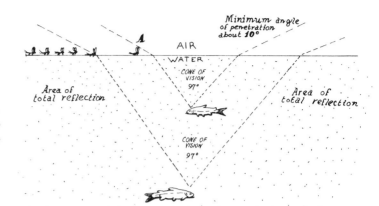

In The Marvels of Fish Life, Dr. Francis Ward was the first to explain how trout perceive objects floating on the surface.

With the Stalker's Method the angler approaches very close to the sipping trout.

upstream ahead of him. By approaching from the rear he is taking advantage of the blind spot the fish has directly behind it. The fisherman is able to move to within ten feet—so close that he can almost touch a rising trout with his rod tip as it feeds.

In the casting technique, the rod is kept in a perfectly straight, up-and-down plane during the casting motion because any sidearm action would let the fish see the waving stick. Also, the angler stops casting if the fish turns sideways—for example, when it drops back with an insect. The casts are short and quick, the fly landing a few inches upstream of the sipping trout each time.

Being this close to the fish provides three advantages to the angler. First, the nearness gives the caster the chance to present his fly many more times than he could if he were farther away. Second, being this close means that it is easier for him to be accurate. And third, he is so close that he can watch every move of the fish and cast so that his fly lands just as the sipper is tilting upward to take an insect. With quick, accurate, well-timed casts the angler can put his fly over the fish with such great efficiency that an imitation has a chance among the millions of naturals.

When the water behind a sipping fish is too deep to wade, the angler has to stalk his target from the side. By crouching as low as possible and changing to a sidearm cast he keeps his profile under the line of the trout's vision, and if he can get close enough to the fish he gains the same advantages as with the rear approach.

The stalker's method is popular with those Henrys Fork fishermen who seek the bank sippers, big rainbows that gather in pods of three or more over the shallow shelves near the shoreline. The approach itself is exciting because it puts the caster so near to twenty- to twenty-five-inch trout, and if these incredibly selective fish refuse imitations it is nice for the angler to know that he can lean over and whack the offender (although we never do).

I learned this method on the Henrys Fork from Fred Arbona, who guides on the river, during a mixed autumn hatch of *Baetis* and *Pseudocloeon* mayflies, but since that initial experience I have also used it all over the country for caddisfly situations. I have needed it so many times—for example, with the famous Little Black Sedge (*Chimarra*) egg-laying fall on the Au Sable in Michigan or with the Little Red Twilight Sedge (*Neureclipsis*) egg-laying fall on Big Flat Brook in New Jersey—that I consider it an essential dry-fly technique.

Downstream-release method. One benefit of my work as a guide is that the days are a learning experience for me. The people who come to fish in Montana do not leave their favorite methods at home. It does not matter where they are from, either; with the growing sophistication of fly-fishing, tactics are being developed or refined everywhere to cope with tough situations. These new approaches are usually applicable on waters outside of their original areas.

The downstream-release method is practiced quite effectively in California on the weedy and slow-moving sections of the Fall River. The anglers there, fishing from boats, needed a practical way to place the fly on a precise lane of drift because the sippers would not move out of their narrow feeding slots. If a dry fly did not pass right over the nose of one of these trout it was ignored.

The angler begins the downstream-release method by picking out a rising fish and wading, walking, or rowing to get above it. He does not cast directly to the trout, but to a spot slightly long and off to one side of it. Then he slowly draws back and lifts his rod, pulling the line upstream, and positions the fly on the exact lane two or three feet above the sipper. When he drops the rod tip he produces enough slack for the fly to drift downstream over the fish. If it is refused the first time he draws it off to one side and retrieves.

This is such a simple method for catching tough sippers that it gives even beginners at spring-creek fishing a chance for some success. There are still skills required, mainly stealth and patience, but it eliminates the need for perfect casting accuracy. It can be used for any fish if the angler can get into suitable position upstream from it. The wading or bank-walking fisherman might find only a few of these perfect approach areas during a day, but it is a good technique to remember for those situations.

Reaction method. The two previous techniques, the stalker method and the downstream-release method, can solve the problems of abundant naturals and narrow feeding lanes, but sipping activity nearly always creates another problem, extreme selectivity, and they do not minimize it. This might seem to be a problem for fly-tying, and usually it is, but there is also a technique that can serve well at such moments.

This method, developed long ago by professional fly fishermen on the spring-fed rivers of France, deals with the problem of selectivity by avoiding it. Instead of putting

*The angler casts beyond
and to the side of the fish.*

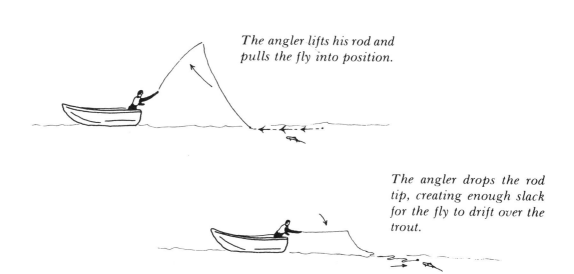

*The angler lifts his rod and
pulls the fly into position.*

*The angler drops the rod
tip, creating enough slack
for the fly to drift over the
trout.*

the fly where it must appeal to the sense of sight, it puts it where it will appeal to the sense of hearing.

Fly pattern does not matter much with the reaction method, as long as it is small enough to hit with a gentle splat. It can be either a wet or a dry fly, since it never has a chance to sink, but if it is a dry fly it should not have hackles that will make it float down too softly. A size 16 Parkany Deer Hair Caddis has all the necessary qualities for creating a nice plopping noise.

The fisherman creeps as close as possible to a trout, from either behind or the side, and casts with a curve cast. He drops his fly about three inches from the fish, off to one side and just behind its eye, hopefully at the rear edge of its sight. At the sound of something hitting, the fish spins around and snatches the hook without ever seeing it clearly.

This is what happens when it works. In my experience the times it failed and spooked fish could often be attributed to obvious mistakes—the fly landing too close or too hard, for example—but many times when the drop seemed perfect it still failed. The frustration of not knowing why it failed or succeeded almost led to my abandonment of the tactic.

I used to save this method as a desperation measure. Its success rate was twenty percent, which might not seem too poor considering that this rate was for each cast, but unfortunately one cast was all a fisherman would get. I would either trick the fish into reacting blindly and taking the fly, or else I would scare it badly.

Rich Colo, an optometrist and a fly fisherman, and I sat and talked until 3 A.M. one morning after a Connecticut Fly Fishermen's Association meeting—or actually, Rich talked and I listened because he had a fascinating theory on how fish react to visual objects and it bore directly on the reaction method.

His idea, from his observations, was that when fish feed on surface items they make the initial recognition with one eye (monocular vision), not both, and that even a regular dry-fly presentation should be placed either slightly to the left or the right of a trout's holding position. He speculated on possible reasons for this phenomenon: One, fish might have a dominant eye, and be left-eyed or right-eyed just as humans are left-handed or right-handed, and prefer to take things off that side; or two, fish might take a food item that is on the side away from the sun, rather than look into the brightness.

After our talk I started looking for this eye preference and noted it a number of times. I even observed fish that were feeding in the shade choosing food from one side or the other, and I often saw fish swim to the side of an approaching item to view it. All of these incidents were random, not systematic, so they were not proof, but they showed that Rich's ideas were worthy of being tested.

The most immediate benefit for me was with the reaction method. Simply by observing which side a trout was feeding on I could double my success rate. I was no longer automatically dropping the fly to the right side of the fish simply because I was a right-handed caster. Instead I was putting it where it was most likely to draw a response, off the dominant eye.

The feeding on passive caddisflies is characterized by the riseform. The head-and-tail rise means that the fish is coming all the way up from the bottom; the dimple rise means it is sipping. Either of these two actions are distinguishable from the feeding on active caddisflies, which is characterized by splashier activity and the pyramid riseform.

These sippers pose the ultimate challenge for fly fishermen. Usually it is the smaller caddisflies, requiring size 18 to 28 flies, that create these situations. On the slick waters where these insects become important the fly fisherman must be versatile; he has to use all three methods, choosing the best one for each situation.

Dry-Fly Tactics (Active Presentation)

It is sometimes said that the dry fly actively fished is somehow less skillful or less delicate than the dead-drift presentation. The negative connotations of the word "drag" are sometimes applied to this type of fishing; but is the fly really dragging?

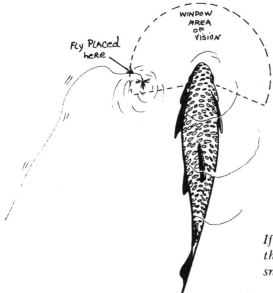

If the fly hits at the right place, the trout whirls around and snatches it.

By strict definition it is not, because the angler does not let the fly move out of control, so call it induced motion instead. Drag happens when a belly is pulled into the line, which tugs the fly downstream faster than the currents. Induced motion happens when the fly is pulled upstream against the current at the proper moment. The difference is primarily a matter of direction.

In most instances induced motion has to be delicate. It looks right to the fish only if the fly simulates the movement of an insect, and it takes a lot of skill to make a fly reproduce the dashes of light made on the meniscus by a living insect. The fly must dance, skid, twitch, or streak on the surface to imitate an insect bouncing, sliding, fluttering, or running.

Considering the development of dry-fly fishing, and the precedent of wet-fly tactics, the downstream active dry fly probably predated the upsteam dead-drift dry fly, but this transitory step was never hailed as a separate method. It was fishing the upstream dry-fly that became the "heresy"—and needed explaining.

The active dry-fly method was well known at the turn of the century in England, but it was always relegated to a minor position. George Skues, in *Minor Tactics of the Chalk Stream* (1910), recommended active presentation as one of the "minor tactics" on the spring creeks of that country. Eric Taverner, in *Trout Fishing from all Angles* (1919), wrote, "If a dry sedge is dropped gently on quiet water and after floating there a moment is given a twitch, so that it moves in a jerk an inch or two along the surface, it is imitating very closely the movement of the natural insect."

Many American writers—including G. LaBranche, E. Hewitt, S. Gordon, C. Wetzel, E. Schwiebert, C. Fox, V. Marinaro, and A. J. McClane—have also explored ways of recreating movement. They again relegated it to a much subservient role, but by explaining many innovative methods they broadened the applications. Of these writers the two who expounded most on it were E. R. Hewitt and A. J. McClane. Edward Hewitt explored active presentations of two types; subtle twitching movements for regular dry flies and Bi-visibles and steady retrieves for his Skating Spiders. A. J. McClane, in *The Practical Fly Fisherman* (1953), devoted a full chapter to describing times and places where the twitch presentation was both effective and practical.

Richard Alden Knight began the task of boosting this approach to a proper perspective with his book, *Successful Trout Fishing* (1968). He made a commitment to the active downstream dry fly as a method of imitation, rather than as just a random technique, and emphasized wider correlations with the behavior of naturals for this type of presentation.

Leonard Wright, Jr., in *Fishing the Dry Fly as a Living Insect* (1972), forwarded views on the active approach in a provocative manner and instructed a new generation of fly fishermen in the techniques. He concentrated on both the twitch presentation and caddisflies, devising special flies (the Fluttering Caddis series) for the active imitation of this insect order.[1]

The modern acceptance of the moving dry fly is recognition that for many insects, and especially adult caddisflies, the action of the imitation becomes just as important as its appearance. By creating the streaks of light on the surface, a fly reproduces the initial triggering characteristic (and for fast-charging fish the only necessary characteristic) of the insect.

It is possible to divide the known techniques for active presentation into three categories: methods in which the fly is manipulated as it dances at the end of a taut

The Dancing Caddis is the ideal imitation for active presentations because it floats completely above the surface of the water.
Gary LaFontaine

line, but is not cast—bushing and dapping; methods in which the cast itself initiates a flash of light—skip cast and tick cast; and methods in which the fly is manipulated after it is on the water—twitch method and rapid-retrieve method.

Bushing and dapping. These two methods are among the oldest fly-fishing strategies. The simplest tackle—a long willowy rod, a heavy line, and a short leader—similar in function to the reeless set-up recommended by Dame Juliana Berners in the *Treatise of Fishing with an Angle*, can be used to catch trout in this manner.

The principles are the same with both methods. The line and leader hang down from the tip of the rod and the fly is touched lightly and repeatedly on the water. Dapping is done from the bank, the angler kneeling or lying on the grass and poking the rod over the water to work the fly. Bushing, so quaintly named by the English, is done from an overhanging tree, the angler climbing up a likely tree and manipulating the fly from his high perch. These methods mimic the bouncing activity of adult caddisflies perfectly.

An explanation of bushing sometimes prompts the question: Who in the hell is going to climb a tree to catch a fish? Almost no one. This explains the effectiveness of the approach.

This method, like so many of my favorite tactics, is geared to the demands of eastern trout fishing. No matter how many experiences I might have now on rivers in the West or in the South, my early lessons on Connecticut streams have ingrained a certain philosophy that affects the way I look at any fly-fishing situation. Fly-fishing in the East can require radical methods because a stretch of popular stream is often hit by fifty or more anglers during a day. Each of them will fish every obvious or productive-looking spot, but odds of catching a trout out of such a place decrease with each fisherman.

The secret is to look for the spots that are too tough for everyone else to fish. This is where the best trout in the stream lurk, unmolested by the passing horde. With a little extra effort, and maybe an unorthodox approach, these fish suddenly become chumps.

Bushing works best where the trees are clumped together next to the water. Climbing into one, even to the height of a few feet, gives a fisherman access between the branches. He can dap a fly in places near the bank where no cast can ever reach. He may see a fish come out and hold under the dancing fly, ready to pounce on it as soon as it drops, and in these situations the angler can tease a trout to complete distraction.

Fly fishermen everywhere, when first approaching a stream, should search for the prime dapping and bushing places. Overlooking the simple ways to mimic the

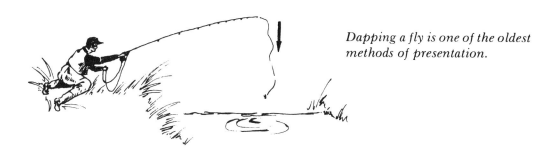

Dapping a fly is one of the oldest methods of presentation.

motion of caddisflies is usually a mistake. These can be the best methods for reaching the deep and dark recesses where caddisflies flit around all day.

Tick cast[2] and skip cast. The premise of all active presentations is that they call attention to a fly before the fish even sees it. Certain casting tricks make this bid for attention by forcing the fly to hit the water in such a way that it creates an explosion of light on the meniscus.

The fly slapping on the water reproduces the fuss of a landing or bouncing insect. The difference between success or failure with these techniques is making the fly hit close to the fish, or at least close to a good holding spot, so that the commotion is seen right away by a trout. When done properly, either of these casts can trick a fish into moving toward the point of impact.

The tick cast solves the problem of how to make a realistic dash of light when the angler is casting upstream. In this situation it is necessary to have the fly, at least for the initial moment, skip away from the caster so that the dash can streak upstream and look similar to the movement of an insect. This is possible with the tick cast because the fly does not land; it only touches the surface for an instant.

The angler false casts and aims down toward the water. On each false cast he makes the fly barely flick the surface just above a rising fish or a piece of prime water. He never lets it stay there, not even for a moment, repeating this ticking four to ten times, or for as long as he has the skill and patience.

The fish see this series of light flashes and are drawn long distances to the spot. Often more than one swims over to investigate. Sometimes a fish swirls or jumps at the tantalizing fly, occasionally catching it, but even a missed strike increases the frenzy. When the fly finally drops on the water, it is taken savagely by the first trout to reach it.

An angler uses the same principle for the skip cast as a boy uses for skipping rocks. He casts sidearm, making the unfolding line on the forward stroke move almost parallel to the surface. The cast is driven hard, with a tight loop and even a line haul if necessary, so that the fly hits the water hard. Because of the angle of impact it caroms off the water and skitters six inches to eighteen inches farther.

With modern equipment it is an easy cast to execute. More responsive and quicker rods make it simple to throw a tighter, faster loop of line. Finer and more flexible leaders help the fly kick around faster. A good average for a good caster with proper tackle is three successful casts out of four attempts, or even four out of five.

There are two benefits from this cast. The flash of light caused by the fly skipping over the surface is the major plus. The second advantage is where it goes. It is an invaluable method for fishing any stream that has undercut banks or overhanging bushes. The skip cast hits at the edge of these hazards and slides the fly right underneath them. It puts the fly where the fish hide, and provides that warning flash in addition. For midday use, when big trout have left the open water, this is a cast to attempt on almost every presentation.

Rapid-retrieve method and twitch method. With all that has been written

The skip cast makes the fly carom off the surface of the stream. The impact produces a shower of light sparks below the meniscus.

SKIP

recently about active dry-fly presentations, anglers have gotten the idea that all there is involved in fooling trout is making the fly move upstream. But this general method is not a panacea for all active caddisfly sitations.

There is an aspect of manipulation that should be understood by anyone hoping to master active tactics: *the amount of movement imparted to the fly must vary to match the actions of the insect.*

A fly fisherman can no more step into a stream and start blithely casting when active caddisflies are about than he can when any other type of insect is on the water. He has to use the same saving attribute—his powers of observation—that should always precede his first cast.

The movement of an adult on the surface can vary from a feeble struggle to a frantic sprint. The manipulative tactics, the rapid-retrieve method and the twitch method, are versatile enough to match all degrees of motion once an insect is on the surface. The casting tricks, the tick cast and the skip cast, are still needed to match the initial splash of the falling adult.

The rapid-retrieve method was popularized by Edward Hewitt for fishing his Skating Spiders. He wrote about the development of the high-riding Spider in a 1935 issue of *Spur Magazine,* suggesting it as an imitation of a butterfly. The fly and the method subsequently proved effective both on the glides of freestone streams and the flats of spring creeks whenever there were bouncing or running insects around.

This method is good for imitating those adult caddisflies that run across the surface, but it works better with a Dancing Caddis dry fly than with a Skating Spider because the former better reproduces the distinctive twin streaks made by the wing edges of the insect. A fast, steady retrieve makes the fly slide across the flats or hop from wavelet to wavelet on broken water.

The reason for keeping a fly moving steadily rather than erratically is that the body of a trout is not built for maneuverability. A stop-and-go or side-to-side motion draws strikes, but too often the fish misses the imitation completely. The best retrieve, accomplished with either a fast handstripping of the line or a rapid cranking of the reel, moves the fly up and across stream evenly. The rod is held straight up so that the tip can absorb a hard strike.

The twitch method can be used to match every insect action short of the frantic run. As the name indicates, it is a stop-and-go sequence rather than a retrieve. The fly twitches upstream and then falls back with the current in dead drift. Any strikes usually occur when the fly is floating quietly. This method may never be as popular as the upstream dead-drift presentation. This is not because it is less effective, but because many fishermen cannot learn to do it properly. They fail because the downstream casting is too difficult for them. There are prerequisites with this method, and approximately sixty percent of the fly fishermen cannot use the twitch method with full effectiveness because they either do not understand or do not know how to execute the proper downstream cast.

The direction of the cast can vary from across stream to almost straight downstream, but it is important that there is slack in the line and leader and that there is a curve near the end of the line. The curve, either left or right, hooks the fly around so that it lies straight downstream from the line tip. The slack allows the fly to drift dead until the angler is ready to move it.

Accuracy and control are critical because for best results the fly has to move just before it enters the trout's window. If the fly does not land on a lane of current that can carry it to the trout, or if there is not enough slack for the fly to drift down to the fish, the presentation usually fails. The twitch is an attention-getting device, and it has to be performed in the right place at the right time to look realistic.

A common mistake beginners make with the twitch method is putting too much twitch and not enough drift in the presentation. This overemphasis on movement stems partly from the misconception that this technique involves nothing more than dragging the fly. Most of the time the method is much more effective if movement is used only to advertise the fly, the dashes of light on the meniscus acting as the initial visual characteristic instead of the only one. The purpose is to alert the trout so that it is keyed in on the approaching fly.

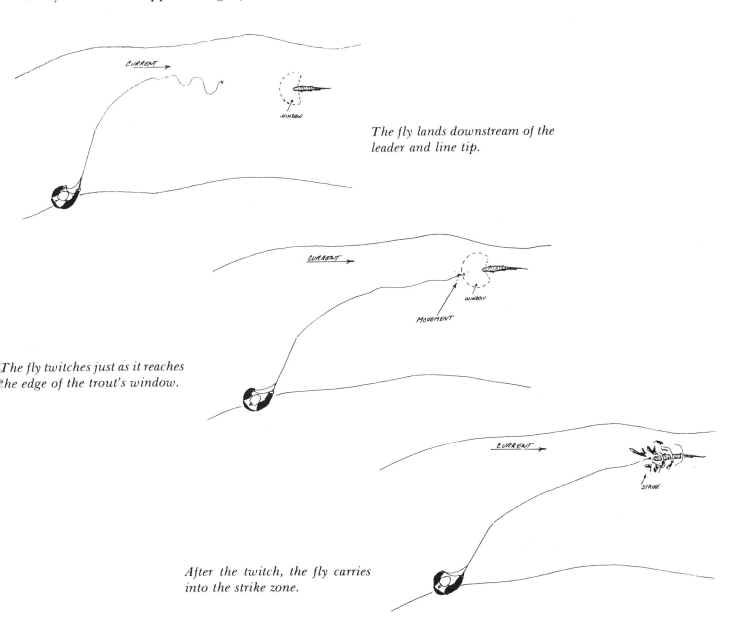

The fly lands downstream of the leader and line tip.

The fly twitches just as it reaches the edge of the trout's window.

After the twitch, the fly carries into the strike zone.

It is a familiar sight to see a fly fisherman changing flies, trying one pattern after another. At the same time he never thinks to change his tactics. His faith that a different size, color, or silhouette of dry fly alone can make trout begin striking is incredible. It is usually wiser to try a technique—something that can show the fly in a different way or different place—than to continue in such an unthinking rut.

There is a major rule for dry-fly fishing: if passive presentations are not working, do not just change flies, change to an active method (and vice versa).

WET—FLY TACTICS

The wet fly can be used throughout the entire egg-laying period, but many fly fishermen prefer to fish a dry fly if it is effective—and during heavy activity it will be. The wet fly usually works better at the beginning of egg laying because a trout's first awareness of the diving females happens at the bottom when the bright insects start passing its nose and because enough insects have not arrived to create a concentration at the surface.

Trout see a fly differently as soon as it breaks through the meniscus. There is no more window, and likewise there are not more light dots to betray movement. The fly is not always seen from underneath so it has to have a correct three-dimensional form. The way the materials respond to the actions of the water suddenly becomes important.

The angler must take all of these factors into consideration before making a choice about flies and tactics because trout are also viewing the natural insect differently. Some very basic characteristics become either more or less critical. Coloration probably has to be matched more exactly while size probably does not have to be matched as precisely. Any list of triggering characteristics for an insect has to be rearranged when changing from a wet to a dry fly, even though both are imitating the same insect.

These are the differences between dry and wet with any insect. With adult caddisflies there is a much greater transformation because they bring a glittering collection of air bubbles underwater. The proper imitation must have the same bright overcoat covering the wings, but one that still allows color to show through.

The Diving Caddis wet fly is an effective imitation because it both looks and acts like the natural. It can be fished deep, where the trout begin feeding, and later it can be fished higher in the current. It is versatile enough so that with the right technique it can simulate egg layers anywhere underwater—and versatility is the major reason for using a wet fly at all.

Before he begins considering techniques, however, the angler has to decide whether to use a single fly or a dropper rig with two or three flies. Each set-up works best with certain methods, each offering advantages in many instances not available with a dry fly.

Dropper-rig presentations. The first thing Galen Wilkins and I would do when we were instructing a group of anglers in what we called "total fly-fishing" was give a quick demonstration of the major approaches—dry fly, nymph, streamer, and wet fly. We would take turns fishing the Big Hole River; he would catch a trout with a dry fly, I would catch one with a streamer, he would catch one with a nymph, and finally I would catch one with a wet fly on a dropper rig. It usually took us no more than twenty minutes to show the students the effectiveness of all four types of fly.

These fishermen were always surprised that the dropper rig could catch any fish at all, which is ironic because if it had been necessary for us to choose one of the four methods as a "guaranteed' approach, this would have been the one. The dropper rig, with its ability to imitate an insect when it is active or passive and dry or wet, gave us a better chance because of its unique versatility.

What ever happened to the dropper rig, or "team of flies," to make it such a forgotten technique? Less than a hundred years ago it was the most popular method of fly-fishing in America, but then came the dry fly, the nymph, and the streamer. In many instances these pattern types definitely were better than any wet fly for imitating natural items, so a reappraisal of the dropper rig was justified, but instead of reappraisal the technique was relegated to complete oblivion. When the imitative philosophy became the prime direction of fly-fishing, it left the wet fly and the dropper rig behind.

With the recent emphasis on caddisflies in American fly-fishing, the dropper rig is overdue for a revival. Both the fly type and the method have a right to be considered in an imitative context because they are invaluable for matching the appearance and actions of adult caddisflies. Somehow the great bulk of fly fishermen who now dismiss the dropper rig as a quaint trick must be made to realize that it has a place in modern tactics.

There is one thing a dropper rig can do that no other method (with the possible exception of techniques such as dapping and bushing, which have limitations because no casting is involved) can do: it can make a fly rise and fall, touching the water just like an egg-laying caddisfly. It can do it because the fly at the end, called the tail or the stretcher, acts as an anchor. When the angler pulls the rod up, the line and leader come momentarily taut and the dangling dropper flies jump up and down as the tension is decreased or increased. The flies can be made to twitch, skip, or bounce completely off the water (see accompanying sequence of illustrations).

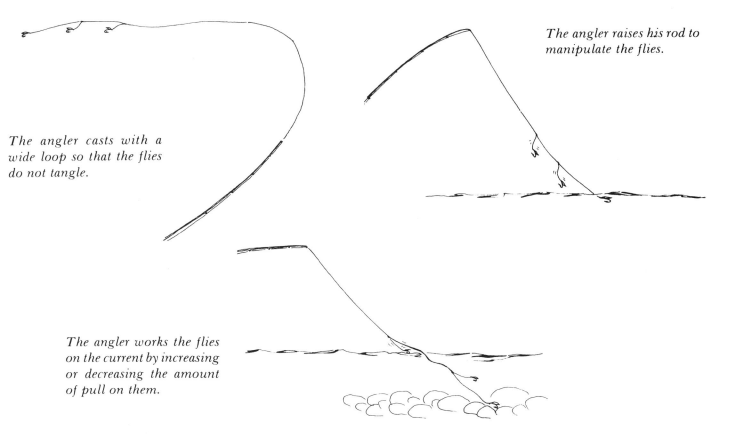

The angler casts with a wide loop so that the flies do not tangle.

The angler raises his rod to manipulate the flies.

The angler works the flies on the current by increasing or decreasing the amount of pull on them.

It is also possible to use the dropper method with a Diving Caddis wet fly on the stretcher and one or two dry flies on the dropper lines. Then when tension is released and the droppers fall, they float instead of sink. Active manipulation can be interspersed with periods of dead drift. The dry flies not only draw strikes during these times, but they also act as an indicator if the sunken wet fly is taken. Patterns such as the Thompson Foam Caddis, the Parkany Deer Hair Caddis, or even the Emergent Sparkle Pupa (which works as an adult imitation) are good. The Dancing Caddis is not suitable for dropper duty because the upright hook snags too easily on the leader.

The bouncing and hopping technique is not the only way to use a dropper rig. The sunken flies can be fished completely dead drift, with either an upstream or downstream presentation, or they can be cast across stream and fished with a pulsing retrieve. During a single presentation they can be worked in any combination of these techniques.

There are basic reasons for using any fly-fishing method. Among the most important are that it is effective, exciting, and challenging. The dropper rig, one of the most fascinating, works on all three counts. When it is used with proper patterns during caddisfly egg-laying activity there is also a rational imitative purpose.

Single-fly presentations. The dropper rig is such a favorite tactic of mine that I seldom use a single wet fly, but there are special circumstances where one fly is more practical than two or three. Two reasons for not using the single-fly presentation are that it limits the action that can be created on the water and it limits the number of different patterns that can be shown to the fish. On the plus side, however, the single fly can be presented with more delicacy and precision than a dropper rig, which makes it more useful when using a dead-drift approach or using a very small fly.

Some egg-laying caddisflies create a situation where the single fly is a definite advantage. The females of certain species, instead of diving into the water, crawl down a rock or other obstruction. They enter the water on the downstream face of the object, avoiding the force of the current, and paste their eggs on the bottom. Usually these crawlers cannot or do not climb back up the way they climbed down. They release their hold and drift away with the currents.

The trout quickly gather behind obstructions to feed on these drifting adults, focusing their attention on the currents that pass to each side of the object. During heavy egg-laying activity, when the rocks and logs in the middle of the river attract so many fish that it can be futile to cast anywhere else, a smart fisherman skips the intervening water and moves upstream from obstruction to obstruction. These selective situations occur commonly in a stream with good populations of caddisflies.

The single fly is more effective than the dropper rig at these times because the upstream cast and dead-drift technique (the Hewitt method), often with imitations as small as sizes 18 and 20, require a delicate presentation. The fly is delivered upstream with a tuck cast and allowed to sink and drift, first at one current wing and then the other. With each subsequent set of casts the presentation is made a little farther upstream, until the entire area behind the object is covered. The main purpose of such slow, patient fishing is to catch and gently scare off the smaller trout feeding at the rear so that the largest fish, in the best foraging zone close to the obstruction, can be taken afterward.

The single fly can also be used with a wide range of general techniques elsewhere in the stream when scattered egg laying is underway. Many of the same methods recommended for the active pupa, such as the Leisenring lift and the stutter drift, are effective with the Diving Caddis wet fly. The same types of motion that help a fly act like a swimming pupa also help the proper imitation mimic the swimming adult.

In the final analysis the theories of imitation and presentation come together very nicely. Step one is a point for presentation: observe the trout and pick a tactic that covers their feeding area. Step two is a point for imitation: study one of the individual insects and pick a fly that matches the important characteristics. Step three, a rational streamside approach, joins the two: pick the imitation and the presentation that work together to make the fly look and act like the insect in the trout's feeding zone.

The effort a fly fisherman puts into understanding caddisfly adults brings great rewards. His knowledge gives him the chance to catch trout even when everyone else is frustrated by selective feeding. The flogger with his one-fly and one-technique approach usually fails to fool as many fish as the angling entomologist simply because there are so many possibilities with the adults. At these moments it is not only the relative importance of caddisflies that makes them worth studying, it is also their complexity (the very reason most often given for not studying them).

The fly fisherman must use his entomological knowledge to choose effective tactics and patterns. Here is a summary of approaches to fishing caddisfly-adult patterns:

One, trout that sip or rise to passive adults require flush-floating dry flies— Thompson Foam Caddis, Parkany Deeer Hair Caddis, Solomon Delta Wing Caddis, or Lawson Spent Caddis—and a dead-drift presentation. Sipping trout often demand special techniques such as the downstream-release method or the stalker's method.

Two, trout that slash at active adults require high-riding imitations— Henryville, Bucktail Caddis, or, especially when adults are intermittently active and passive, the Dancing Caddis—and active presentations. The manipulations of the fly have to match the actions of the adult. The main techniques once the fly is on the water, are the rapid-retrieve method and the twitch method.

Three, trout that feed underwater require a sunken fly, the Diving Caddis, and active methods if the adults are swimming or passive methods if they are drifting with the currents. Either a dropper-rig with two or three flies, or a single-fly presentation can be used.

Heresies for the Practical Caster

There are fly fisherman who will be able to go out and effectively use the flies and tactics that have been described in this book; others, however, will be unable to make the ideas work on the trout stream even if they have fully accepted them. Usually the people who will have trouble are the experienced fishermen. It is their experience, mainly with upstream dry-fly methods, that makes the adjustments difficult.

If every presentation were straight upstream, the line falling on a single lane of unvarying current, fly-casting would be fairly simple. Only rarely, however, does an angler encounter such basic situations. Usually, even with a general upstream presentation, the cast is also angled across stream, the line landing on currents of different speed. When this happens there has to be slack in the line and leader to delay drag.

Does the fly fisherman have to cast differently when he uses caddisfly imitations? Many of the recommended techniques, especially for pupal and adult situations, require across-stream or downstream presentations. As the angler rotates, casting more and more at a downstream angle, there has to be an increasing amount of slack line on the water to achieve the same distance of drag-free drift.

Fly fishermen should be ready to present a fly in any direction, but many cannot break the upstream habit. They can neither produce nor handle slack line. They are intimidated by it. This hurts their angling performance anytime they must cope with drag, but it virtually makes across-stream or downstream, dead-drift presentations impossible.

It is almost a major heresy to suggest that anglers cast so that the fly is presented efficiently. There is a cult in fly-fishing that makes fly-casting something separate from catching fish. Fly-casting itself has gathered a full set of rigid taboos and rules. The formula for a correct cast has developed into the tyranny of the tight-loop, high-speed delivery of line. Actually, this "correct" delivery does not help the angler catch trout on a stream; it usually hinders that effort by eliminating slack.

Every cast on a moving stream has to be unique. The presentation should be suited exactly to a specific lane of drift rather than to random coverage, with drops and mends working to counter the negative effects of any current between the target and the caster. This is the reason why the taboos of the high-speed, tight-loop formula, a wide loop and slow speed, are what should be achieved rather than avoided for many downstream techniques. These factors might be bad for distance casting, but they are good for dropping a sloppy mess on the currents.

The term slack-line casting means putting out extra line, enough curls and loops should be drifting with the current to horrify any fly fisherman who likes his line to look neat. The skill that separates slack-line casting from just plain bad casting, however, is the ability to drop that slack on particularly troublesome water and still place the fly with pinpoint accuracy.

How does a fly fisherman practice this style of casting? Unlike distance casting, which is best done on a dock or a lawn, the only place to learn slack-line presentation is on the stream itself. It is necessary to practice devising different patterns of slack to counteract the action of moving water. It is an exercise in problem solving: the problem is drag, how to use it and how to avoid it.

The mechanics of casting cannot be stressed so much that the purpose of casting is forgotten. Students should start on or quickly move to a river where the reasons for casting are made apparent by the problems of catching trout. Spending more than a few hours casting on a lawn or a pond at the beginning can actually be detrimental to future progress.

Even fundamentalists, who drill their students for days before letting them put on a fly, admit that this is true—they know that they are teaching fly-casting, not fly-fishing. The advantages of on-stream practice are undeniable. As one instructor conceded, "You can teach casting that way if all your're interested in is catching fish."

Controlling slack

Can fishing downstream be that different from fishing upstream? Consider just one basic habit of upsteam presentations. When the fly lands it immediately begins coming back toward the angler, so he pulls in line to keep control. Turn that angler downstream, however, so that the fly begins going away from him, and then he must

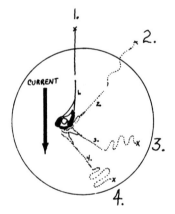

As the angler rotates, casting more and more at a downstream angle, there has to be an increasing amount of slack line on the water to achieve the same distance of drag-free drift.

stop pulling in line; and as a matter of fact, he should take extra line off the reel and feed it through the rod guides. The habit of pulling in line, either with short strips or a continuous hand-twist retrieve, is so ingrained in many fly fishermen that they cannot stop doing it. They can never effectively use a drag-free downstream presentation because they unconsciously destroy the slack they need for drifting the fly.

The spaghetti leader. The standard leader formula (butt: sixty percent; taper: twenty percent; tippet: twenty percent) is designed for proper turnover, not for handling the drag problems that ordinarily occur with downstream presentations. It is adequate for upstream or taut-line tactics, but it is too stiff to produce much slack.

Twenty to thirty inches of one of the softer leader materials (Nylorfi, for example), added on as an extended tippet, changes a typical leader into a "spaghetti leader." This long piece of flexible nylon creates a buffer of slack between the line and fly; and what is the use of slack in the line if any minor split in the currents can exert drag on the first ten inches of the tippet?

Mending line. The purpose of mending line is to extend a float, but when the fly is pulled out of its path of drift and skittered sideways across currents during mending, it defeats the purpose.

A bad mend happens when the fisherman, gathering in line to roll forward, simply lifts the rod and pulls in line already on the water. This "bad mending" maneuver is an integral part of at least one method, the stutter drift, but even with this method the mend is followed by the release of more slack. The stutter drift is such an odd way of imparting a drift and twitch sequence of motion to a fly that it can take advantage of what would otherwise be a mistake.

To get a longer drift without moving the fly during a downstream presentation it is necessary to put more line out, not take it away. The slack that is already on the water has to be left there because there is no way to gather it without disturbing the free ride of the fly. Extra slack is pulled from the reel and rolled out onto the water.

During an upstream presentation, slack is formed as the fly drifts back toward the fisherman, so no additional line is needed from the reel. The mend simply puts the original supply of line back out, a rolling loop pushing it upstream or across stream.

The correct mending motion begins with the rod lowered to the water. After slack is stripped from the reel and shaken out through the guides (for a downstream presentation), or gathered as the fly drifts back (for an upstream presentation), the angler rolls this excess line forward with a thrusting, half-circle motion of the rod.

A master of the mend technique varies the momentum of the rolling loop of line so that it collapses wherever needed on the current. The curls of line already on the water from the regular slack cast act as a cushion ahead of the rolling mend and prevent the fly from being jerked away from its drift.

Dick Fryhover was the man who put all the elements of slack-line casting together for me, as much by what he did as by what he said. Whenever we fished together he caught incredible numbers of trout, often punctuating his success with streamside lectures. "Get the fly on the water and keep it there. You can't catch fish waving it back and forth in the air."

Teachers of varying opinions have influenced my casting methods, but it has always been the advocates of the slack-line presentation who were most convincing because they could prove the effectiveness of their methods by catching trout.

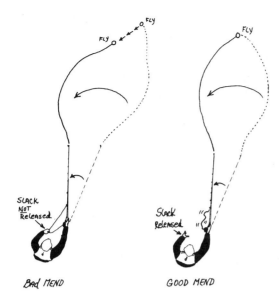

A bad mend (left) *makes the fly move in or on the water. The proper mending motion* (right) *rolls a compensating loop of line into the current without disturbing the fly.*

Why bother delaying uncontrolled drag? Why are ten short drifts worse than one long one? Sometimes the quick, short drifts are almost as good as an extended one, but they can never be quite equal to it because of the time the fly spends in the air. Short drifts, however, may work almost as well when trout are rising quickly.

But there are times, because of the distance insects drift, when trout choose or refuse in a deliberate manner. They come leisurely towards either the natural or the imitation, falling back with it before taking it. There are other times when trout recognize and select a food item many feet upstream of their actual holding position, keying on an item only if they spot it coming toward them from a distance.

Under these circumstances the added effectiveness of the extended drift may be minor (ten percent more effective when trout are rising quickly), or intermediate (thirty percent to fifty percent more effective when trout are feeding deliberately). But there are other times when the length of free drift is almost the total reason for success or failure.

There are moments when the slack-line fanatic, finagling drifts of ten feet or longer, consistently catches fish because he can delay uncontrolled drag. At the same time and place, the straight line, "pop-pop" caster catches nothing because trout are taking a fly only after it has floated ten feet, and he is unable to get a drift of even five feet.

The extended drift can also be an advantage when trout are shy and spooky. On smooth water, where the plop of even the most delicate fly and tippet creates a shock area around itself, the fish may flush wildly or just ignore any item that lands too close. The slack line presentation solves the problem because it lets the fly drop outside the caution zone and drift into the area of receptiveness.

Caddisfly tactics can never be completely separated from general fly-fishing theory, but there is more emphasis on downstream methods with this insect order. Slack-line casting would add to the effectiveness of a fly fisherman even if he never tried to match a hatch or egg-laying fall of caddisflies, but for any angler seriously trying to meet the challenge of this insect the practical heresies of slack-line presentation can be considered necessary adjustments.

(For instruction on the different slack-line casts recommended here, see *Fly Casting with Lefty Kreh* (1974) by Lefty Kreh.)

Stillwater
Caddisflies

The Northwest is justifiably famous for its trout rivers, but the lakes of this region are quickly gaining a notoriety of their own. The dedicated anglers who specialize in these stillwater habitats are developing a strong new tradition, a spirit of innovation and ingenuity dominating this type of fly-fishing. A healthy exchange of ideas between local groups in the Northwest is not only homogenizing tactics and patterns, it is accelerating the overall progress.

It is still possible to find an occasional fisherman using flies and methods that reflect older, outside influences: the dropper rig of Irish loch fishing, the streamer tactics of Maine pond fishing, or even the gawdy spoon-wing wet flies or popping bugs of eastern brook-trout and smallmouth-bass fishing. But it is amazing how quickly these methods, which dominated western lake fishing as recently as fifteen years ago, are disappearing. The dropper rigs and streamer flies at least may undergo a modest revival, but only because they have a place in the new system. The attractor flies are probably gone permanently on the tougher lakes.

The new wave sweeping stillwater fishing is based on the entomlogy of these habitats. It has taken over even more completely on lakes than similar entomological philosophies have on streams because the need is more critical. While it might be possible for someone adamantly opposed to the entomological approach to fly-fishing to ignore insects on the freestone streams, because there always seems to be at least a few fast-water fish willing to take anything, it is frequently impossible to do the same on lakes. The tough, continuous problems of stillwater selectivity are making the conversion to entomological principles complete.

Entomology is also indispensible in lake fishing because just finding trout can be very difficult. Ninety percent of the bottom area is generally devoid of fish at any given time, and in the ten percent holding fish, only ten percent of that area might be holding most of those. Such concentrations of trout make random prospecting, no matter what the tactics or flies, very unproductive. What fly fishermen need is a system for finding fish.

Understanding the insect fauna of a lake can help with all the problems of stillwater fly-fishing. This knowledge can reveal how and where concentrations of available insects occur, and finding their food is one way to locate trout. It can reveal what the insects are doing and what they look like, and knowing how the natural moves and appears in the water makes it easier to select the right fly. This information, providing a short cut for catching trout, is the reason for studying all the important food sources in a lake.

There are three main ways of finding trout in lakes: the wind-drift method, the surface-search method, and the bottom-association method. Each of these is part of an overall plan for locating the concentrations of insects that fish feed on. The system works for most insects in lakes.

How important are caddisflies in stillwater habitats? In the cold-water lakes of the Northwest they are second only to two-winged flies (Diptera) as a year-round food source. During the months of heavy emergence activity, May and June, they are the most important food item. The larvae are available to fish foraging on the bottom all the time. When the pupae and adult are abundant they cause such rigid selectivity that fly fishermen cannot realistically ignore them.

The system works so well with caddisflies that it would be silly not to use these insects. They are so valuable as a food source that finding concentrations of them by one of the three methods nearly guarantees finding some trout, also.

Wind-drift method

Insects in lakes can be divided roughly into two forms: those that are in control of their movements and those that are at the mercy of the currents. The second group is the basis for the wind-drift theory. These inactive insects are helpless. They drift with the top few inches of lake surface, a layer that moves wherever the wind pushes it, and if there is even a moderate breeze in one direction they soon get stacked up against the windward shore. They become concentrated in a splash zone, a band of flotsam that forms a few inches off the bank, in incredible numbers.[1]

This is one of those ideas that came as an instant revelation, rather than after a long process of experimentation and testing. It has proven so valuable since a particular day on a high-country lake, experiences that I wrote about in my "Primer of Entomology" series in *Fly Fisherman* magazine (see the February/March, 1973 issue) and in *Challenge of the Trout*, that I have no doubt that it is the most important segment of the overall system.

This is the main method, the one that fly fishermen should try first when approaching a new lake, but it does not involve caddisflies as much as it does other insects. The most important inactive forms are *Chironomid* midge pupae, the primary trout food in high-country lakes, and drowned terrestrials. These provide the bulk of wind-drift fare.

Nevertheless, there are at least three times in their life cycle when caddisflies can become an integral element of this lake drift. It can happen when a heavy emergence produces a percentage of cripples that never get off the water. These dead or dying insects get piled against the windward shore, collecting in the foam line, and become important after the main hatch is over. An Emergent Pupa pattern in matching size and color or a flush-floating dry fly, such as a Thompson Foam Caddis or a Solomon Delta Wing Caddis, fished with the gentlest of twitches, works well in these situations.

The egg-laying activity of species that have a high mortality rate can also create concentrations. Three genera—the Somber Microcaddis (*Ochrotrichia*), Vari-Colored Microcaddis (*Hydroptila*), and Salt and Pepper Microcaddis (*Agraylea*)—of the small caddisflies (Hydroptilidae), a family well represented in the lake fauna, are normally dependable sources of drift fare. The Salt and Pepper Microcaddis (*Agraylea*) particularly can occur in large numbers in weedy, northern lakes, and in midsummer, when they oviposit at night, they are typically the main insect in the foam early the next morning. Any such build-up of spent females encourages very selective feeding by sipping trout, and only flush-floating imitations perfectly matched to the size of the naturals work effectively at these moments.

One very odd phenomenon happens every spring and contributes enough food to the drift to spur trout into a mad feeding binge. When the ice goes out on the northwestern lakes, the larvae of the Great Late-Summer Sedge (*Onocosmoecus*) migrate toward shore to recolonize the shallow margins. Apparently air bubbles get trapped inside their cases, because the larvae float to the surface.

Michael Winterbourn, in his paper "The life histories and trophic relationships of the Trichoptera of Marion Lake, British Columbia," studied the feeding habits of rainbow trout. He noted, "The May stomach samples were dominated by *Onocosmoecus* sp., which in May 1969 was the most abundant and widely distributed species present in the final instar. Throughout the month large numbers of larvae were found floating, often in clumps of more than 100 individuals, on the surface of the water."

I have seen this mass drift of larvae in many British Columbia lakes during fishing trips for Kamloops rainbows, but it is not limited to that area. I have also found it to be a common occurrence in Montana and Idaho lakes, although generally in early June rather than in May, and since *Onocosmoecus* is widespread throughout the Northwest I would be surprised if it is not important elsewhere in the region. These floating larvae need a special, bouyant imitation:

FLOATING CASED LARVA

HOOK:	Mustad 94840, size 2-6 (bent to shape)
CASE:	brown speckled deer hair (spun on and clipped to shape)
INSECT BODY:	cream cotton chenille (one wrap just above deer hair)
HACKLE:	speckled grouse fibers (tied down and back)
HEAD:	light-brown marabou fibers or fur

The cased larvae, lying in or just under the meniscus, can be very difficult to see. Unless the angler strains the foam areas with a net or seine, he may overlook them. A quick check, however, against the windward shore should reveal for sure if this amazing surface drift is underway.

The feeding on these wind-drift items is often very subtle. The fish learn that there is no rush to grab these helpless insects, so they generally take them with gentle sips. For bigger forms, such as the floating larvae, they might roll, causing a bulge on the surface, but for the smaller caddisfly pupae and adults that end up in the drift, the trout hold under the foam line and feed quietly. It is necessary to consider even the

The Floating Cased Larva matches the drifting Onocosmoecus *larva.*

most minor of disturbances as a sign of a big fish.

Certain places along the windward shore are better for fishing than others because of their physical structure. A point or a bend, jutting out into the lake, is not a particularly good area because the incoming insects get pushed around it. The indentations, however, ranging from small cuts to large coves, are very good because they act as traps and collect the drifting items. The ideal place is at the back of a bay with a funnel configuration (a wide mouth and a narrow end).

The best way to cover the narrow band of foam is by casting parallel to the shore. The angler drops the fly on the outside edge of the drift line. He lets it rest motionless for a few moments in case any fish is attracted by its fall, and then he begins working it with feeble twitches. If the spot is good or if the trout are visibly feeding, he should retrieve the fly no more than a foot in ten minutes. This patient approach is usually much more enticing in these areas than a faster technique.

Surface-search method

A fisherman uses this method to spot any signs of surface activity, but it involves more than the cursory glance many anglers give the water before starting to fish. Instead of arriving and looking for random rises, a lake fisherman should take ten or fifteen minutes to pinpoint both major concentrations of feeding fish and the positions of the biggest fish.

A pair of binoculars is necessary for searching the water. From a high vantage point—a hill, a cliff, or even a tree if it is the only such point available—it is possible to do more than just see rises; it is possible to plot any pattern of movement by a school of surface-feeding trout. And with binoculars it is possible to study the riseforms so closely that a good observer can tell what type of activity—active or passive, dry or wet—the trout are concentrating on even before he gets near them.

Caddisflies can prompt good open-water surface feeding either as adults or as pupae, but the rises to each are usually distinctive. Trout feed on adults with the simple head-and-tail rise if the insects are sitting still and with an erupting swirl or jump rise if the insects are running. They take the swimming pupae anywhere from the bottom to the top in stillwater, but it is the rolling break of the fish capturing naturals just under the meniscus that signals what is happening.

Pupae. The visible feeding on pupae normally indicates only a small percentage of the activity taking place, most of it occurring underwater, so during an emergence a sinking pupa imitation ought to work better than the buoyant Emergent Pupa. The Emergent pattern, however, fished with or without movement, exhibits the same, strange power over trout in lakes as it does in streams.

Robert Ince of England wrote to tell me about some experiences he has had with the Emergent on the reservoir fisheries in his country (where stillwater fly-fishing has been developed to a high art): "We have always found that the sign of a *really* effective stillwater surface pattern is when trout will take it static as well as when moved. Many times last summer I just cast out the fly and left it, only to see a good brown (especially browns) or rainbow take it as if it was the last meal it was going to get—quite incredible! It is a most excellent general sedge pattern as well as a specific pattern.

"It is ideal, we have found, for multiple hatch situations. Last July I was fishing a reservoir with my brother during a very heavy sedge hatch. They were in our hair, sunglasses, everywhere. Well, it was a multiple hatch of Longhorns, Grousewing, and the Great Red, our biggest sedge [anterior wing length up to twenty-eight millimeters]. We had the time of our lives; they wanted that emergent like there was no tomorrow."

It is during an emergence that many abundant lake species, such as the Black Dancer (*Mystacides alafimbriata*), the Brown Checkered Summer Sedge (*Polycentropus cinereus*), and the Long-Horn Sedge (*Oecetis inconspicua*), become important for the first time in their life cycle to fish. These insects are relatively secure from trout as larvae, but when the pupae begin swimming to the surface they are completely exposed. In May and June these caddisflies provoke intense rises for a short time, usually two hours or less, every day they emerge.

Adults. The adults can be found on the surface in large numbers either after emerging or during egg laying. In some species they sit on the water quietly before flying off. They might occasionally stretch their wings, but generally they remain inactive until ready to leave the water. Unlike drowned forms they are not mired in the surface film. They ride high and dry.

No matter how serenely the adults are resting on the water, the best form of presentation is the twitch. Some kind of slight movement is needed to attract attention. Especially when trout cruise, their typical way of feeding on scattered insects, an ocasional hop of the fly produces the light streaks that help them locate it.

Adults of other species, many of which never have any intention of flying, start running toward the nearest dry object immediately. They cause more sporadic feeding than either emerging pupae or stationary adults, but when the fish are watching for these naturals, any practical imitation, such as the Dancing Caddis, pulled rapidly across the surface is very effective. A dropper rig, with dangling flies that can tap dance on the surface, is also a deadly method in these situations.

The large adults in the family Phryganeidae all seem to share this running habit. Their activity triggers the most explosive of riseforms, trout bursting into the air in wild jumps. The end result of such an uncontrolled attack, a thumping splash, is quite different from the rolling motion made by trout taking emerging pupae or the head-and-tail rise made by trout taking inactive adults.

From early summer to early fall this type of feeding happens when the adult of such Phryganeidae genera as the Giant Rusty Sedge (*Ptilostomis*), Great Dive-Bomber Sedge (*Agrypnia*), Traveller Sedge (*Banksiola*),[2] and Rush Sedge (*Phryganea*),

The predaceous larvae of Agrypnia *are an important part of the still-water insect community. The insect specimen shown is 27mm long.* Ken Thompson

common insects in western lakes, are completing emergence or egg laying. Instead of flying away they sprint quite rapidly across the water in a sinuous path, but they are not fast enough to escape a determined trout. Often an entire section of a lake, usually over a weed bed, is pocked with periodic eruptions at dusk or at dawn.

The surface-search method is usually the second technique to use for locating trout. Even if the angler notices rising fish, he should carefully check the wind-drift areas of the lake first, because unless there is a great amount of food spread on the surface the larger trout may still be in one of those collection areas secretly sipping in drowned naturals.

Bottom-association method

When nothing else is happening it is time for fly fishermen to begin searching. If the fish are not concentrating on drifting or active insects, they are probably scrounging larvae and scuds near the bottom. But any lake has a lot of bottom area and when the surface is blank, locating feeding spots can be difficult. Without some way to use the feeding habits of the trout to eliminate most of the lake, the deep-dredging method of fly-fishing necessary to cover these places can quickly turn into a grueling exercise in futility.

One of the best approaches for distinguishing between productive and unproductive areas is the bottom-association method. The angler uses a two-step plan: first, he figures out which caddisfly species trout are feeding on; and second, he fishes the bottom type where the larvae of that species are prevalent. As long as he can associate trout with particular bottom features—such as weeds, mud or leaf accumulation—it is possible for him to look into the water, if it is not too deep or too cloudy, or drag anchor across the bottom and identify the areas where trout are most likely to be.

How does an angler know which caddisfly larvae the trout are feeding on? They consistently prey on the largest available larval form present in any number. In a lake, with different species maturing at different times, the largest larva is usually a major species in families such as Phryganeidae and Limnephilidae in the last developmental instar. Just before pupation these larvae can be from twenty to forty millimeters long.

In Marion Lake (British Columbia), for example, species become the dominant prey in a predictable sequence. In early spring, just after the ice disappears, the most important larvae are the fully developed Giant Rusty Sedge (*Ptilostomis ocellifera*),

Bottom-association method: certain types of lake bottoms are more productive at specific times of the year. In northwestern lakes, trout work weed beds heavily during late spring and early summer since the caddisfly larvae that inhabit these areas reach their maximum size at this time.

Dark Brown Still-Water Sedge (*Lenarchus vastus*), and Early Summer Lake Sedge (*Clistoronia magnifica*), which overwinter in the fifth instar (the last stage of larval development). By April, when the submergent plants begin to appear in the lake, the largest and most available prey are the larvae of the Early Summer Lake Sedge (*Clistoronia magnifica*), Traveller Sedge (*Banksiola crotchi*), and Great Late-Summer Sedge (*Onocosmoecus* sp.). In May, as the Great Late-Summer Sedge (*Onocosmoecus*) larvae grow to full size, this genera becomes the main caddisfly in the trout's diet. After the Great Late-Summer Sedge (*Onocosmoecus*) and Early Summer Lake Sedge (*Clistoronia*) pupate and emerge, the largest larvae available through the early weeks of June are Traveller Sedge (*Banksiola crotchi*). By the end of June the only sizable available larvae left in the main lake are those of the Long-Horn Sedge (*Oecetis inconspicua*). In late summer and early fall, after the major species have emerged, caddisfly larvae are no longer an important item for trout.

This sequence makes the bottom-association method very easy for fly fishermen; all they have to do is fish the areas that dominant larval types inhabit. Anglers can break a lake down into the most productive types of bottoms—weed beds, open flats, inlets, and outlets—and concentrate on the one that supports the main prey of the trout (see Marion Lake chart).

Outlets. At the natural outlet of a lake, net-spinning larvae of the family Hydropsychidae are generally very abundant. This area, where the gathering current runs over a sloping gravel bar, forms the ideal environment for filter feeders that can trap drifting algae.

During June and July important species of Spotted Sedge (*Hydropsyche*) and Little Sister Sedge (*Cheumatopsyche*) mature, and fish from both the lake and the stream migrate to the gravel bench of the outflow. They feed on emergents and egg layers when they are active and grub among the rocks for the larvae during the midday lull.

Inlets. The mouth of an inlet stream is a dumping ground. As the currents from the stream spread out into a lake, the drifting leaves and sticks drop and accumulate in the bay. The area, littered with this decaying material, becomes populated with the types of larvae that feed on these nutrients. An inlet is a good place to check anytime, even when the resident insects are not abundant or available, because the current also carries drifting or hatching stream forms into the lake.

Often the inlet harbors caddisfly species found nowhere else in the lake. Running-water larvae that have drifted downstream live restricted existences along the edge of the incoming current, unable to migrate upstream and unable to disperse. Genera such as the Giant Cream Pattern-Wing Sedge (*Hydatophylax*), Giant Orange Sedge (*Dicosmoecus*), Pale Western Stream Sedge (*Chyranda*), Little Plain Brown Sedge (*Lepidostoma*), and Snow Sedge (*Psychoglypha*), trapped in this thin zone sometimes become important enough to attract bottom-foraging trout.

Open flats. The areas of the open sediment in a lake support good populations of such species as the Brown Checkered Summer Sedge (*Polycentropus cinereus*), the Long-Horn Sedge (*Oecetis inconspicua*), and the Black Dancer (*Mystacides alafimbriata*), the total numbers of larvae comparable to densities on other bottom types, but during most of their development these insects live in the sediment rather than on it. In its final larval instar the Long-Horn Sedge (*Oecetis inconspicua*) becomes more available, coming out to roam on top of the bottom during June, but otherwise, unless one of the abundant species is emerging, the open flats are not an especially good area.

Weed beds. The major species of the weed beds, the large Phryganeidae and Limnephilidae insects, are the most important larval prey in the lake. The fish cruise over the vegetation, picking off or rooting out the cased insects. Throughout the early-summer months the weed beds remain a primary foraging area.

These big larvae are not always slow-moving crawlers. The primitive case makers of the family Phryganeidae readily abandon their leaf houses if disturbed and scuttle away rapidly. Whenever genera such as the Traveller Sedge (*Banksiola*) or the Giant Rusty Sedge (*Ptilostomis*) are the predominant caddisfly, an energetic retrieve and an imitation of the pale yellow uncased larvae can be appropriate.

Trout feed on many types of bottom organisms, but only damselfly nymphs and *Gammarus* scuds compare with caddisfly larvae as a food resource from this area. Neither of these invertebrates is as richly represented in as wide a variety of stillwater environments as caddisflies. As a daily tool for locating trout with the bottom-association method, caddisflies are the most valuable element of the lake fauna.

A fly fisherman can cover bottom areas with a count-down retrieve. He casts and lets his fly and line sink while he counts: one thousand and one, one thousand and two, and so on. He increases his count by one number after each cast, letting the fly sink deeper and deeper every time before beginning the retrieve. When the fly starts ticking the bottom or snagging the weeds, he backs up one number so that on subsequent retrieves the fly barely skims over these hazards.

This methodical technique is not my favorite way to catch trout. The slow hand-twist retrieve, the repetitious casting, and the blind striking all detract from the enjoyment. Often in lakes there is no choice, however, because when there are no emerging pupae or egg-laying adults for the trout they quickly concentrate on those patches of bottom that hold insects. At these times other methods are useless.

Fly fishermen in this country have paid much less attention to trout in lakes and ponds than they have to those in streams. Many still believe that lakes are better fished with spinning or bait-casting methods, but this attitude is changing as people discover the advantages of the fly rod. No other method can better imitate what trout eat.

MARION LAKE, B.C.
(data from M. J. Winterbourn study)

MONTH	PREDOMINANT CADDISFLY LARVAE	HABITAT
late March/early April	*Ptilostomis ocellifera* *Lenarchus vastus* *Clistoronia magnifica*	all three species: before submergent vegetation appears these larvae are spread out in the deeper areas.
mid-April/early May	*Banksiola crotchi* *Clistoronia magnifica* *Onocosmoecus sp.*	all three species: submerged and marginal vegetation

May	*Onocosmoecus sp.*	submerged and marginal vegetation; at mouths of inlet streams
early June	*Banksiola crotchi*	submerged and marginal vegetation
late June/early July	*Oecetis inconspicua*	open sediments

The scientific approach to lakes is just beginning. It is much too early in the study of these fisheries to propose a comprehensive plan for attacking them. The basic research, both by anglers and biologists, still has to be done; not only for a wide range of insects but also for animals such a leeches, baitfish, scuds, and crayfish, all prey for trout, before fly fishermen can undertand the interplay of the food chain.

Much of the recent scientific interest by fly fishermen has centered on lakes in the Northwest, but there are also fine lake and pond fisheries elsewhere that should be investigated by modern angling entomologists: the historic brook-trout and landlocked-salmon lakes of Maine, the source of inspiration for innovative streamer and bucktail imitations of smelt; the Great Lakes, reborn as trout and salmon fisheries; the ponds and seepage holes of the Upper Peninsula of Michigan, waters so lovingly eulogized by Robert Traver; and the new cold-water impoundments of the mid-South.

Just listing these fisheries raises so many questions. There are plenty of unsolved puzzles, even with caddisflies, about the trout food in these lakes for fly fishermen to work on. What are the major species? What is their sequence of importance? What are their emergence and egg-laying habits?

Let me make a prediction: the next great wave of interest in stillwater fly-fishing is going to be in two-tier trout lakes. Lakes that stratify in summer and winter are called two-tier fisheries because they support populations of warm-water fish—bass, bluegills, bullheads—in the upper temperature layer, and cold-water fish—trout and salmon—in the lower one. The trout stay in deep water during the summer, but in the spring and fall, when the layers mix, or "turn over," these fish cruise the shallow margins of the lake. At no other time of the year is there such a fabulous opportunity for fly fishermen to catch large trout in heavily populated states. The task now is to discover a predictable pattern of movement and feeding for these fish.

Advances in the art of lake fishing are possible whenever there is a study done such as the one on Marion Lake. The information on food preferences of trout and distribution of insects can be put together in the three-part system—wind-drift, surface-search, and bottom-association—to locate feeding fish. It is not hard for anglers to do the same type of survey by collecting the insects from their local lakes.

Recent books have been using the entomological approach for solving the problems of lakes. They should be on the reading list of any angler who is serious about stillwater fly-fishing: *The Art and Science of Lake Fishing with a Fly* by Randall Kaufmann and Ron Cordes, *Fly Fishing Still Waters* by Don Roberts, *Stillwater Trout* edited by John Merwin, and *Kamloops* by Steve Raymond.

Why should fly fishermen bother with lakes at all if there are so many problems? It is important to focus attention on stillwater fisheries. In our ever more crowded world of fly-fishing these habitats are a great resource. Rich lakes and ponds can grow so many trout so fast, the phenomenal growth rate producing fish with tiny heads and thick bodies, that they can provide challenging, quality experiences even in areas where angling pressure is great. Maybe because of our wealth of trout rivers lakes have not been fully appreciated yet, but for fly fishermen willing to work at understanding them, they are there waiting.

Part Two

The Biology
of Caddisflies

The Biology
of Caddisflies[1]

The origin of the name caddis, or caddice, is a mystery, its roots lying in the common tongue of Britain rather than in the more easily traceable Latin. But considering the reputation of these insects as an angling enigma, this seems almost fair.

In a deft bit of linguistic detective work, the British entomologist N. E. Hickin traced the word as far back as Shakespeare's *The Winter's Tale* (1611), the term "cadysses" referring to itinerant vendors. These men stuck patches of cloth to their clothing, acting as walking billboards for their wares, and were also called "cadice men" in the early Seventeenth Century, possibly as a parallel with case-making caddisfly larvae.

Izaak Walton, in *The Compleat Angler* (1653), referred to the insect by the name caddis, but he also called it a "cod-worm." This term and the common modern names, rock worm, stick worm, stone creeper, periwinkle, and, for the free-living *Rhyacophila* larva, green worm, all are derived from the immature aquatic form of the insect.

The adult stage also inspires nicknames, including sedge, shad fly, grannom, miller, and dancer. The scientific name of the order, Trichoptera, describes the mature insect, derived from the Greek *trichos* (hair) and *pteron* (wing), referring to the dense mat of microscopic hairs covering the wings of the adult.

The study of caddisflies is the graduate school of an angler's education. They are usually not the first insects that a fly fisherman tries to understand. As a matter of fact, there are many angling experts on trout-stream mayflies that cannot even recognize the connection between larvae, pupae, and adults of caddisflies. Some honestly declare that they would just as soon never find fish feeding on them.

One reason for the seeming reluctance to learn about these insects is that a halfhearted approach to this important group is usually not enough. Broad descriptions, lumping all species together, tell the fisherman very little. Such general pap cannot begin to make order out of the diverse types that inhabit trout waters. The only way to put caddisflies into a workable framework is to understand their basic biology completely. This eliminates much of the confusion that surrounds them, providing the angler with rational explanations for much of their behavior. With the proper information as a foundation they become much less a mystery.

Caddisflies are a complex order, with many species in all types of water, but the number of individuals important to fly fishermen are not an impossible number. The identification of the commonly recognized trout-stream species is already well underway, and many caddisflies are becoming familiar to the layman.

The Trichoptera are one of the largest groups of aquatic insects. There are more than 1,200 species in 142 genera and 18 families now known in North America; there are more than 7,000 known species in the world. This abundance is basically due to a broad diversity within the order, an incredible variety of forms and habit, with species specialized to exploit most aquatic environments.

Present evidence suggests that approximately 200 million years ago caddisflies shared a terrestrial ancestor, a flying insect with net-veined wings, with both the order Megaloptera (alderflies and dobsonflies) and the order Lepidoptera (moths and butterflies). The evolving caddisfly larvae lost their spiracles for air breathing and became fully aquatic. The early ones were probably hunters, slender and mobile, prowling under the stream rocks much like their ancient cousin, the *Corydalis* hellgrammite, the larval form of the dobsonfly.

The dawn of the modern caddisfly, recorded in fossil specimens, began in the mid-Jurassic Age, 150 million years ago. The insect was an inhabitant of cool-running streams initially. The early species, with primitive respiratory systems, were limited to this environment by their dependence on highly oxygenated water.

A study of the morphology and body structure of modern species reflects this restricted origin. The genera that retain the most ancestral characteristics are still found in running-water, or lotic, environments. Those that possess derived characteristics—evolutionary adaptations—are able to cope with warm and still water, or lentic, environments.

The temperature line between cool-water and warm-water groups is naturally an arbitrary figure, but the caddisfly fauna changes significantly when the maximum

There are more than 1200 species of caddisflies in North America. Each species represents a distinct population whose males and females are capable of breeding only with mates of the same species. An adult of Frenesia missa, *the Dot-Wing Winter Sedge, is shown above.* Ken Thompson

water temperature extends beyond the sixty-five- to sixty-eight-degree Fahrenheit range. Primitive genera are restricted to streams where the temperature does not exceed sixty-eight degrees. Advanced genera are able to inhabit warm-water streams, cool-water lakes and ponds, warm-water lakes and ponds, and even temporary bodies of water.

Caddisflies, with all the changes from that early terrestrial ancestor, basically owe their diversification in the aquatic world to the ability to make silk. This is the evolutionary tactic, a wonderfully functional tool, that has been used in so many ways to solve problems of dislodgment, food gathering, respiration, and protection.

Looking strictly at the larvae first, the wholly aquatic stage, it is possible to see how movement into various habitats has been aided by the "silk economy." An understanding of the evolutionary trends in silk usage by the larvae provides a biological map of their distribution in various water types. For the angler such a study removes much of the complexity of the order. It divides caddisflies into major groups, each suited to life in specific types of water, and it highlights the species that are most important to the fly fisherman.

The Net Makers (superfamily Hydropsychoidea)
families Philopotamidae, Psychomyiidae, Polycentropodidae, Hydropsychidae

The earliest splits from the ancestral Trichopteron followed two evolutionary lines: a sedentary strategy, where larvae built a fixed retreat and/or a net; and a mobile strategy, where larvae built a portable case. The adaptations of caddisflies are a record of net making and case making.

The net makers use silk as a food-gathering and a shelter-providing tool. The larvae live in the crevices between and under rocks, the interstitial habitat of the streambed, most weaving intricate nets that collect drifting fare from the current. They build permanent shelters of silk, stones, and plant debris, or, in one genus, a silk-lined burrow in the sediment, coming out only to repair and clean the nets. Food normally consists of algae and fine organic particles, but some species prey on smaller insects.

The general net designs include elongated tubes, trumpetlike bags, and mesh fences. These silk structures depend on flowing water, and most just collapse into shapeless masses if removed from the stream. The specific nature of these nets restricts each species to a certain environment; each net possesses a mesh diameter geared to trapping a certain amount and size of drift particles and a structural design suited to withstanding a particular velocity of current.

The use of silk in this way generally restricts the evolutionary push of this group to moving-water habitat—streams, either cool or warm, and wave-washed lake edges. In running-water environments, however, net makers are often the dominant caddisfly because the type is so well adapted to that biological niche, and there are species that reach great abundance in suitable habitats.

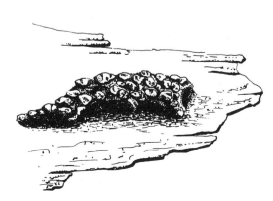

The larvae of the genus Lype *do not build cases; they build tunnel-like retreats instead.*

Some genera of the net-making family Polycentropodidae have specialized enough to cope with stillwater environments. In the amazing genus *Polycentropus* (Brown Checkered Summer Sedge) the net may be used as a filtering device if current is available to convey the food, or as a trap that functions like a spider web if current is not available. When prey is detected by the vibrations on the outer strands, the highly predaceous larva comes out to attack the victim.

The Free-Living Forms (superfamily Rhyacophiloidea)
family Rhyacophilidae

The free-living Rhyacophilidae are the most primitive representatives of the order. The members of this family, although the larvae are not case makers, are the forerunners of that very diverse group. The subsequent adaptations of case making are portable, rather than fixed as is the retreat of net spinners, following the free-moving lifestyle of the Rhyacophilidae larvae.

The larvae are restricted to running-water environments, lack of prominent gill development in most species making them dependent on cool, oxygenated currents. Most of the family are predaceous, but a few are herbivorous, the insects roaming the streambed in search of food. Everywhere they move the larvae leave a silken line draped over the rocks as protection against dislodgment, a safety thread that helps them withstand the current.

Although little changed from the earliest caddisflies, the Rhyacophilidae are among the most successful larval forms. The genus *Rhyacophila* (Green Sedge) is the largest in the order with more than a hundred North American species. In cool, headwater trout streams these bright green larvae are the major free-moving predators.

The Saddle-Case Makers (superfamily Rhyacophiloidea)
family Glossosomatidae

This group is so closely related to the free-living Rhyacophilidae that until recently taxonomists included it in that family. The Glossosomatidae larvae construct a loose-fitting dome that resembles a turtle shell. The rigid case has a broad strap dividing the front and rear openings on the bottom. The evolution of case making is thought to have begun in this family with the precocious formation of the pupal shelter of the Rhyacophilidae.

There are many differences between the primitive saddle cases of this group and the specialized tube cases of the more highly evolved larvae. The Glossosomatidae cases are simply an aggregation of rocks, gaps in the covering allowing circulation of a current over the larva. The cases of advanced forms, often called true case makers, are built around a matrix of spun silk and have a rear opening for water circulation.

The saddle case is a specialization that allows the larva to exploit a very particular area, the current-swept surfaces of rocks, in the stream environment. The shelter first of all provides a roof with a low flow resistance, the insect being able to feed entirely underneath the case, swapping ends at will between the two openings. It also affords protection against predaceous insects.

*The larvae of the Green Sedge (*Rhyacophila*) do not build cases or retreats before pupation.*

Like other primitive families the Glossosomatidae mainly inhabit cool, rapidly running water. Marginal numbers sometime exist along lake edges and in cool springs, but the high population densities mostly occur in the riffles of streams with highly oxygenated flows.

The Purse-Case Makers (superfamily Rhyacophiloidea)
family Hydroptilidae

Along with Rhyacophilidae and Glossosomatidae, this family is part of the super group Rhyacophililoidea. These microcaddis are not on the direct line between the free-living larvae and the tube-case makers, however, but represent a situation of parallel evolution. The development of this family includes specialized adaptations that aid survival in warm and stillwater environments.

The life cycle of these insects is unique among caddisflies because the larvae do not build cases for part of the aquatic period. The early forms are small, inconspicuous crawlers, growth apparently stunted until the final larval stage. Then the insect builds its case and increases quickly in size, gaining the bulk of its energy reserve just prior to pupation.

The cases of the hydroptilid caddisflies are an evolutionary advancement over the rough turtle-shell form of Glossosomatidae. The larvae primarily use silk, a spun matrix, as the base for construction. Also, these insects, unlike the Glossosomatidae, are able to expand their cases to accommodate growth.

The distribution of this family shows the biological push to fill warm-water niches. In tropical regions they are widespread, often the dominant type in the caddisfly fauna. They are also, however, well represented throughout the northern tier of the continent, some genera common to abundant in cold-water streams and lakes.

The Tube-Case Makers (superfamily Limnephiloidea)
families Phryganeidae, Brachycentridae, Limnephilidae, Lepidostomatidae, Beraeidae, Sericostomatidae, Odontoceridae, Molannidae, Helicopsychidae, Calamoceridae, Leptoceridae

This diverse group carries case making to its highest development. In both running-water and stillwater environments the silk-making potential solves problems, engineering of cases providing " . . . streamlining, ballast, buoyancy, structural rigidity, camouflage, internal water circulation, external water resistance, protection from predators that would swallow the case and from those that would intrude, and so on."[2]

One of the larval body characteristics that maps the evolution of case making is the anal claw. In the free-living forms it is long and flexible, suited to grasping

The saddle-case makers (genus Glossosoma, above) can forage on the current-swept surfaces of rocks.

surfaces. It begins to shrink in the saddle-case makers, becoming less of a hook. In the tube-case makers it is no longer functional as an external gripping tool, up-and-down movement being lost, but it is perfectly adapted for securing the body to the silk matrix of a tight-fitting case.

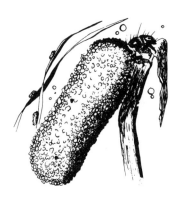

The larvae of the Hydroptilidae family build cases that look like miniature purses (genus Hydroptila, above).

The evolution of case making is the story of growing dependence on the case. The saddle-case makers survive very well if removed from their shells, at least during the short period it requires for them to construct a new one. Even the larvae of a primitive tube-case making family, the Phryganeidae, may abandon their cases when disturbed, but the larvae of the more advanced families are helpless, many of them unable to build a new shelter or to live independently if separated from their tubes.

A major biological advantage of the tube case, preparing the larva for life in water that has lower concentrations of dissolved oxygen than a cold, rushing stream, is its function in respiration. It acts as a ventilation chamber, the undulations of the larva creating a flow from front to rear—this self-generated supply of fresh water passes continuously over the gills and replaces stream current as a source of oxygen renewal.

The production of silk in the form of a case, providing the remarkable increase in respirational efficiency, permits exploitation of food items unrelated to current. The tube-case makers take advantage of this flexibility by feeding on a wide variety of items. They shred dead wood and leaf material, scrape algae and fine organic particles, prey on other aquatic insects, and search sand and silt deposits.

Caddisflies, mainly in the development of tube-case makers, rank second only to Dipteran forms as successful members in the insect fauna of stillwater environments. In trout streams there are abundant larval populations of many genera also, not only of the average-size (six- to fifteen-millimeter) species, but of the giants of the stream communities, species of thirty to thirty-five millimeters (the equivalent of a size 2 or 4 hook).

Life Cycle of the Caddisfly

Larva

The larvae of the genus Goera (family Limnephilidae) build a true tube-case. The large stones on the sides of their cases serve as ballast.

The typical North American caddisfly, with the complete egg-larva-pupa-adult cycle, lives one year and passes through five instars as an aquatic larva. At the end of the larval stage the insect seals the case or retreat and undergoes a change, this period generally lasting two to three weeks. The pupa swims or crawls to the surface to emerge. Adults usually mate two or three days after emergence. The female dives or crawls into the water, or less frequently daps the surface, to lay the eggs. Some females even oviposit above the water.

The typical caddisfly, of course, is a myth; variations from the general are more the rule than the exception. The life cycle is modified in species to suit the demands of particular habitats, both aquatic and terrestrial, their survival depending on such specializations.

In advanced families, the tubecase of the larvae acts as a ventilation chamber (patterned after the A. Odum illustration in Dr. Wiggins' Larvae of the North American Caddisfly Genera).

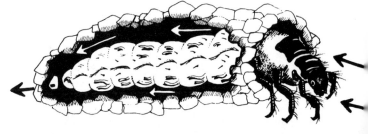

Although a one-year cycle is the normal requirement, the length of the larval stage does vary considerably. Some species follow a bivoltine schedule, producing two separate broods a year. Others, mainly in the tube-case makers, remain in the aquatic environment longer than a year. A few species stagger groups, overlapping generations emerging throughout the year.

Feeding habits

The specific distribution of species in streams and lakes often depends on methods of feeding. Just as the evolutionary adaptations provide a key to the macrohabitat, the broad restrictions enforced by environment, the feeding mechanisms provide a key to microhabitat, specific areas within an environment.[3]

The major caddisflies fall into broad groups: shredders, collectors, scrapers, and predators. The larvae are part of the aquatic food chain, transferring plant and animal material to a higher trophic level, and in turn becoming prey to larger insects, crustaceans, or vertebrates.

Shredders. The shredders feed on leaves and woody materials that fall or wash into the water. These larvae utilize this food form not so much for the energy in the woody materials, which is not easily digestible, but for the energy they derive from the associated micro-organisms, the fungi and bacteria, consumed in the process. The dead organic matter along with the associated micro-organisms are collectively

5mm

A typical caddisfly larva passes through five instars, or stages of development, before pupation. The five larval instars and the pupa of an important lake species, Clistoronia magnifica, *are shown above.* Jon Spier

Shredder larvae produce the lacework design seen on decaying leaves in a stream. Jon Spier

5mm

referred to as detritus. Shredders do not directly release nutrients, but in the act of shredding they increase the surface area of detritus, which in turn allows for more micro-organism colonization and therefore more "food."

In both streams and lakes the greatest populations of shredders occur where detrital debris is deposited by flow or wave action. Such a restricted diet usually results in concentrations of the larvae in prime areas, this abundance attracting gamefish to such places during vulnerable periods in the insect's life cycle.

Notice, for example, how narrowly a biological description of a dominant Eastern genus, *Pycnopsyche* (Great Brown Autumn Sedge), a tube-case maker in the family Limnephilidae, places the insect for an angler. This information, gleaned from scientific papers, provides a map of local distribution: "This genus inhabits running-water environments, but typically only the upland streams and small rivers of hardwood forests. The autumn leaves collecting in these waters provide a food source for the new brood, larvae living for one year and pupating in September or October. These shredders work actively all winter in the eddies and pools of streams, areas where the leaves accumulate, processing the detrital material, but the dangerous time for the larvae is the spring when the intermittent spurts of stronger current flush these slack backwaters."[4]

Most of the shredders live in headwater streams or lake margins, where quantities of leaves fall and sink intact. Farther down the river, where trees no longer form a canopy over the water and the grinding action of the current and earlier shredder processing has broken any leaves drifting from upstream into particles too small for these insects to feed on, the shredders peter out and give way to other types of caddisflies.

Predators. Many caddisfly larvae ingest some form of animal material in the course of indiscriminate browsing or collecting, but few types are strictly carnivorous. This is a biological niche that is often better filled by other insect orders. There are only a few hunting specialists among caddisfly genera.

In fast-water habitats the family Rhyacophilidae virtually dominates this feeding role for free-moving larvae. These crawlers are basically restricted to riffle areas, but they are well adapted for prowling the crevices among the stones. Often closely related species are biologically separated in a stream environment by preference for a specific type of prey.

In the family Phryganeidae, primitive tube-case makers restricted to stillwaters or slow-moving waters, nine of the ten North American genera are partially or wholly predaceous as larvae. The large crawlers, well camouflaged in stick or leaf cases, inhabit areas of organic trash accumulation or standing weed beds at stream or lake margins, hunting the smaller insects that live there.

Species of the genus *Oecetis* (Long-Horn Sedge), family Leptoceridae, are the other specialized hunters of still or slow-current areas. The larvae have long, single-blade mandibles for attacking prey organisms. They are often abundant in lakes and gentle streams.

Usually predators are free moving, either the free-living or tube-case forms, but some net makers also subsist on animal fare. These include fast-water types, such as the genus *Arctopsyche* (Great Gray Spotted Sedge) of the family Hydropsychidae, that snare insects drifting in the current, and slow-water forms, such as the genus *Polycentropus* (Brown Checkered Summer Sedge) of the family Polycentropodidae, that trap insects moving over the bottom.

Caddisflies are often specialized in the way they obtain food, but they are also typically eclectic in the forms of food they can assimilate. The exceptions to this generality are often found in the predator species, many of these larvae dependent on a particular type or size of victim. Such species naturally congregate wherever the desired prey organism is abundant.

Scrapers. The scrapers, mainly case makers, graze the rocks. In most genera the teeth on the mandible are fused together into a continuous edge, an adaptation for this feeding process. The larvae scrape the mandibles over the stones, peeling away the diatoms and algae that coat the surfaces.

The major habitat is running water, where the periphytic scum forms over the bottom. This food base is seasonal, increasing in summer, and the emergence and egg-laying of most genera occur from late spring through midsummer, rather than in the fall as is the situation with many of the shredders. This cycle provides the newly hatched eggs with a burgeoning food supply.

One of the exceptions to summer egg laying is the western genus *Dicosmoecus* (Giant Orange Sedge), an autumnal emerger and egg layer in the family Limnephilidae, but these huge orange caddisflies are not typical scrapers. In the early larval instars they build cases of plant material, suggesting possibly a slow-water microhabitat and a detritivorous diet for the young stages. Only during the final instar do the larvae build the stone cases that allow them to hold in faster currents. Such a change in what they eat and where they live partially explains the survival tactic of a fall beginning.

The scrapers include some of the most important species found in trout streams. In waters where the boulders are greasy with algae, indicating an ideal environment, populations often reach high densities. The larvae cling to the rock surfaces in fast currents, the cases of species that frequent the uppermost edges flattened or rounded to offer less resistance to the water. They stay on top of the boulders during the day and retire to the undersides of the stones at night.

Collectors. The feeding mechanism of collector larvae is linked to the amount of organic material suspended in the current. These insects depend on the flow to work as a conveyor, washing food into their capture area. Different species, however, are suited to different levels of stream enrichment; so as a watershed progresses toward the ocean and increases in size, picking up nutrients, the predominant species of collectors also change.

Net makers are not the only caddisfly larvae that feed this way. The family Brachycentridae has groups that fasten their cases to tops of stones and hold their middle and hind legs out to the sides, the hairs filtering drift items from the current. These larvae are not strictly collectors because they also function as scrapers. They exploit the environment with both methods.

Many situations other than the natural build-up of productivity create an enriched habitat in running water. Spring streams or spring rivers, fed through a carbonate aquifer, are particularly fertile. Rivers below either man-made or natural lakes receive the microflora funneling from these stillwater basins. Many watersheds become mildly enriched by the nitrogen and phosphate wastes of civilization. Such trout-stream environments containing sufficient current velocity and riffle habitat may support high populations of collector feeders.

The study of the larval stage is valuable for all anglers fishing caddisfly imitations, even for dry-fly purists who may never use subsurface flies, because of its control over subsequent life stages. The pupa usually emerges in the vicinity of the larval habitat. The adult female usually stays close to the general site, and in many families it also lays its eggs in types of water specifically suited to survival of the species.

At the completion of the larval existence the cycle normally progresses steadily through the pupation, emergence, and egg-laying activities, establishing the next generation in the stream or lake, but in some species there is a delay so that the beginning of the young larval instars coincides with more favorable aquatic conditions.

There are three ways delays can occur in the cycle. In some species the microscopic larva remains in the gelatinous matrix of the egg for as long as eight to nine months, leaving the temporary environment to build a case only when a change in the external habitat signals better conditions. In other species there is a gap between the spring emergence and autumn egg laying, the onset of sexual maturity in the adult delayed through summer until the shorter days, and photoperiods, of fall. In other species, and possibly for all autumn caddisflies with a one-year cycle, the larva reaches full growth in early summer, but then it seals the case, its development suspended, and pupal metamorphosis does not occur until fall.

The first two of these tactics are often adaptations for inhabiting temporary pools and streams, the delay allowing the insect to survive the dry period, but the prepupal delay, or diapause, is utilized by some important trout-stream caddisflies. It not only times the cycle for fall egg laying, but it also synchronizes the emergence of a species in a coordinated blitz.

Such a blitz is a survival mechanism for some aquatic insects. Instead of emerging sporadically, the entire adult population of the species erupts, a percentage of the group living to mate and reproduce because this glut satiates or overwhelms both fish and birds.

Major hatches of caddisflies include autumn genera, such as *Dicosmoecus* (Giant Orange Sedge) and *Neophylax* (Autumn Mottled Sedge), both members of the Limnephilidae family, that emerge and lay eggs during the daylight hours. In these instances the delay serves as a crucial regulator of the life-cycle and creates an important opportunity for both trout and fly fishermen, and therefore, it is necessary for anglers to know which species go through it.

Pupa

At the end of the larval stage most caddisflies attach their cases, or with the non-casemakers, especially constructed shelters, to solid objects on the bottom, but a few burrow into sand or organic muck. Some species migrate to specific areas to pupate, but most simply remain in the larval habitat.

Using the word "pupa" to describe the entire period between the larva and adult is actually inaccurate. The metamorphosis of the insect, lasting two to three weeks, consists of three stages: prepupa, pupa, and pharate adult. The prepupal existence begins with the closure of the case and the cessation of normal larval activity, the insect in a resting state for four to six days.

The insect is called a pupa only during its metamorphosis. The developing

The pupal enclosure of a Rhyacophila *(Green Sedge) caddisfly is shown cut open on one side to reveal the developed insect inside.* Ken Thompson

structure pulls away from the larval skin, or cuticle, until the underlying parts no longer correspond to the previous features. The insect at this stage assumes the typical pupal shape.

The alterations continue, however, with the insect again developing a new body structure and separating from the pupal cuticle. It is then no longer a pupa in strict entomological terminology, but a pharate adult. The mature insect inside the skin controls all functions, its muscles moving the overlying parts such as the mandibles and swimming legs of the pupal cuticle.

The term "pharate" comes from the Greek word *pharos*, meaning garment, and it is important for the fly tier or fly fisherman to realize that the thin and flexible sheath is like a loose garment. The insect that cuts its way out of the cocoon and swims or crawls to the surface is not a pupa but an adult in a transparent pupal covering.

The pupal cuticle, once the emergent insect bites through the silk grate blocking the case opening, still serves two purposes: it keeps the adult dry and it acts as an inflatable bag. Until the insect escapes completely from the cocoon it cannot generate air bubbles, since they would anchor it in the shelter, but after pulling free of the silk matrix it begins to fill the cuticle with gases.

In running water the emergent rides with the current for some distance before beginning the ascent. The length of this drift varies with the genera; some, such as *Rhyacophila* (Green Sedge), starting the rise after a few feet, and some, such as *Hydropsyche* (Spotted Sedge), remaining near the bottom for longer distances.

The rate of ascent through running water also varies considerably. The air bubbles in the pupal sheath add buoyancy, but even then the insect does not generally shoot up through the currents. The gas and the oar-shaped legs propel the emergent to the surface, its progress marked by the rhythmic stop-and-go beat of the swimming stroke.

The insect hesitates for a period when it reaches the surface, the adult struggling to escape the pupal shuck. It pushes through the meniscus and then uses the surface tension to wriggle free of the cuticle. During this effort, half in and half out of the water, the emergent drifts downstream with the flow.

Studies were conducted with a Green Sedge species, *Rhyacophila bifila*, the fastest emerger in my tests, in a crude but effective homemade fluvarium to determine the distance the insect was carried by the current. The velocity of the water was very slow, approximately one-half inch per second at the surface. The depth of the water was two feet. A number of observations produced an average escape pattern:

1. Distance of bottom drift after escape from the case: 4½ feet
2. Distance of downstream drift while swimming through water column: 1¼ feet
3. Distance of surface drift (time struggling free of pupal cuticle): 9 feet
4. Distance of surface drift (free adult resting on surface; including preliminary hops): 2 feet

The baffling part of the experiments was a wide daily divergence in the distance of surface drift from the average figure. The emerging insect's struggle to shed the cuticle sometimes lasted from a minimum of 5½ feet to a maximum of sixteen feet. On individual days the drift usually ran either consistently longer or shorter.

Dick Calvin, a hydrologist commenting on the experiments, suggested a possible cause for these great variations. He wrote, "Atmospheric conditions, changing from day to day, affect the thickness and elasticity of the meniscus. The barometric pressure, for example, affects the degree of molecular crowding at the water and air interface."

Since the surface film serves as not only the barrier the insect must break through, but also the sheet it must grasp to free itself from the pupal cuticle, a relationship between the distance of drift and the changeable meniscus seems very plausible. And a difference in the time the insect spends trapped in the water, of course, alters the way trout feed on a particular day.

During an emergence there is a naturally occurring percentage of cripples, deformed insects that never escape. After leaving the case they either fail to rise, drifting near the bottom, or, after reaching the surface, fail to extract themselves from the cuticle. The percentage of cripples is generally low, but during a heavy hatch enough of them get concentrated at the two levels to provide a significant food source.

There are other ways caddisflies emerge besides swimming up and flying off. Some species, instead of emerging after rising, swim just under the surfce and climb out on the shore or on an upright object. Many of the big tube-case makers, generally stillwater or slow-water types, crawl over the bottom and climb out, shedding the pupal cuticle on partially exposed rocks, logs, or plants.

Adult

Larry Solomon and Eric Leiser wrote in *The Caddis and the Angler*, "Newly emerged adults quickly fly to land, where they rest and dry their wings."

Steve Raymond, reviewing the book for *Flyfisher* magazine, disagreed with that statement. Raymond wrote, "Even a casual observer during a caddis hatch will note that an emerging caddis spreads and dries its wings before it flies."

Any fly fisherman reading these statements might think that there should be a simple answer as to who is correct. But there is not. Larry Solomon and Eric Leiser were correct if they meant "dry" with reference to the internal structure of the insect. Dr. Glenn Wiggins noted on my original draft of this chapter, "Drying in this context involves not external wetting but the physiological need for expanding wing tissue to become sufficiently firm to support flight; [for caddisflies] wings remain physiologically soft (or wet) for some time even after capable of sustaining flight."

It is doubtful if the adult needs to dry the outside of its wings at all. There are at least two things that keep them from getting wet externally: the pupal cuticle, enclosing the insect until the last moment, keeps water off during the ascent, and the wings themselves, with the dense mat of hairs, resist wetting.

The stretch, flutter, and hop of the adult before leaving the surface probably helps it to unlimber the muscles. In streams and rivers the open-water emergers hesitate momentarily on the surface, but they seldom ride long distances on the currents as do mayfly duns. Once out of the pupal cuticle most caddisfly species fly off relatively quickly.

There are exceptions to the flying habit even among the swimming emergers. Many large adults run across the water instead of taking off. For such lumbering slow fliers, birds in the air evidently pose a greater threat to survival than fish in the water.

Most caddisflies of average size are strong fliers, however, darting from the surface to nearby bushes or trees after emerging. The adults live days to months, drinking water or plant nectar to prevent dehydration, and generally remain near the larval habitat.

Probably the greatest complaint against caddisflies as far as the fly fisherman is concerned is that they are mostly nocturnal. Such a generalization, however, suffers from many inaccuracies. Many major groups avoid bright sunlight, and thus are called negatively phototrophic, but most are not actually nocturnal. The greatest activity, for both emerging and egg laying, occurs during subdued light, not dark, and triggers major dawn and dusk feeding periods by fish.

Graham Marsh kept very detailed and very illuminating notes during 1975, a year in which he spent 140 days on a tail-water stretch of the Missouri River. He recorded the hours of heavy daylight feeding, up to a half-hour past sunset, on both caddisflies and mayflies. Between May 20 and October 28 he verfied with stomach samples 448 hours of caddisfly emergence or egg laying, a 3.2 hours per day average, and 392 hours of mayfly emergence or egg laying, a 2.8 hours per day average. When both insects were available, the rainbow trout and the brown trout showed a feeding preference for caddisflies. Whitefish, on the other hand, showed a feeding preference for mayflies.

The area he sampled, below Holter Dam, is an incredible insect factory. It has important populations of Hydropsychidae and Hydroptilidae caddisflies, but it also has major mayfly populations, especially in the Baetidae and Tricorythidae groups. This river fairly represents a tail-water environment.

Adult caddisflies prevent dehydration by drinking water or plant nectar.

Adult caddisflies huddle in dark and moist hiding places until ready to mate. The large swarms form near the water, usually in the cool hours of evening, and beat upriver five to fifteen feet above the surface. During these flights the insects stay in the air, seldom hitting the water even by accident, and they are not available to the fish.

These vast flights have contributed to the poor reputation of caddisflies. Angling writers have continually disparaged such a seemingly unproductive abundance; Preston Jennings, in *A Book of Trout Flies*, wrote, " . . . [I] cannot recall ever seeing a trout definitely rising for the winged fly."

One of the most important stages for fly fishermen, however, is the egg laying, or ovipositing, that follows the swarming activity. Although the females usually return to the water sporadically, rather than en masse, the commotion they create can tempt fish to the surface.

The eggs are deposited in one of four ways: below, on, near, or above the water. Some species paste the egg masses under branches or bridges, the hatching larvae dropping to the water. Others lay them on objects near the stream. Neither of these actions exposes the females to fish predation.

Many species develop a ball of eggs, the mass protruding from the abdomen, and they must touch the water to release this packet. These females either dip down to lightly skim the surface or actually flop momentarily onto it. They are vulnerable while releasing the eggs, or, in instances where an exhausted female collapses, until finally escaping to the air.

The most common means of egg laying in trout streams occurs below the water, the female diving or crawling to the bottom. The insect, carrying bubbles of air under and around its tightly folded wings, drags its abdomen over rocks and leaves a sticky string of eggs. Then she attempts to return to the surface.

Dr. Donald Denning once timed the underwater period for a microcaddis, *Agraylea multipunctata* (Salt and Pepper Microcaddis), as one hour and eight minutes. Its successful return to the surface attests to the water-repellent nature of the hairy wings and to the swimming ability of the adult.

On the Missouri River in the fall the diving activities of various microcaddis takes place every day, often steadily for eight or nine hours. So many of the females collect on the flats while trying to either get under or get off the water that the water looks as if it has been sprinkled with pepper.

Some females survive the ordeal, actually laying eggs two or three times before dying, but the mortality rate is high. Many of them are swept away and drowned;

This greatly-magnified egg mass from a female of the Limnephilidae family is the type deposited near, rather than in or on, the water.
Jon Spier

many are captured by fish. Some never break through the meniscus, washing flush in the film. The dead and the dying become concentrated during this type of egg laying, making this final stage an important food source for trout.

Entomology is confusing only if it consists of a lot of unrelated scientific names. An understanding of basic distribution patterns, macrohabitat restricted by evolutionary adaptations and microhabitat restricted by food resources, provides the framework that simplifies study for the layman.

The Latin names are arranged in a hierarchical system. The listing for a common Grannom species, for example, would be as follows:

Kingdom: Animalia (contains all animals)
Phylum: Arthropoda (contains all animals with exoskeletons and jointed appendages)
Class: Insecta (contains all arthropods with three pairs of legs and compound eyes)
Order: Trichoptera (contains all caddisflies)
Superfamily: Limnephiloidea (contains caddisflies that build a tube case as larvae)
Family: Brachycentridae (contains tube-case makers whose larvae lack spacing humps)
Genus: *Brachycentrus* (Brachycentridae that are morphologically similar)
Species: *americanus* (only one form fits into this group; final determination usually based on structural differences in genitalia of adult males)

The system of scientific nomenclature may be likened to a tree, with each branch containing fewer individuals. It continues to the final designation of species, which contains one type of individual capable of reproducing only with members of that group.

The best way for fly fishermen to assimilate caddisfly facts is to first gain an overall view of the order, a mastery of the generalities, and then begin to progressively narrow their attention. Each step down the classification system will eliminate possibilities of form and habit.

9

Caddisfly Habitat

Every trout stream is a complex ecosystem where many different factors, interrelated like a giant web, work together to influence the structure of its insect community. By creating an overall habitat that is either favorable or unfavorable for some larvae, these environmental features allow certain caddisfly species to dominate the fauna.

An undertanding of how such factors affect distribution (water temperature, bottom structure, current speed, and alkalinity among others) makes it possible to play a simple guessing game: if a person is given a set of major facts about a stream, he can, without even seeing it, provide a rough profile of the insect community; likewise, if he is given a list of the insects present, he can provide a rough description of the stream.

Once he knows that *Glossosoma* (Little Tan Short-Horn Sedge) is a major genera in a stream he can assume that the stream has gravel-bottomed riffles because this is a necessary feature for this insect; he can also assume that warm water, consistently above seventy degrees Fahrenheit, is not a problem because this would be a limiting factor. Or, to play the game the opposite way, once he knows that this stream possesses the proper physical features, and that it has a suitable water-temperature range, he can guess that *Glossosoma* is an important component of the insect community.

What determines how abundant a species is in the stream? When there are no negative features in an environment to limit distribution, the availability of food and space control population densities. The fact that each stream type provides certain kinds of food and habitat makes the predictions possible.

The Distribution of Common Caddisfly Genera
of North American Trout Streams

The symbol _____ designates environments where a particular genus might be found. / The symbol ********** designates where the genus would probably be most abundant. / The complete graphic for a genus might look like the following **********.

The mark ← means that the genus is also well represented in headwater streams (not shown on the chart). / The mark → means that the genus is also well represented in warm water rivers (not shown on the chart).

The terms Large Stream, Small River, and Large River correlate to the very general classification system set up for fly fishermen in Chapter 9, *Caddisfly Habitat.*

SCIENTIFIC NAME/ COMMON NAME (NUMBER OF KNOWN NORTH AMERICAN SPECIES IN PARENTHESES)	MAIN FEEDING METHODS	MAIN DIETARY ITEMS	PRIMARY COLD AND COOL WATER HABITAT		
			LARGE STREAM	SMALL RIVER	LARGE RIVER
Superfamily Hydropsychoidea					
Family Philopotamidae					
genus *Chimarra* (17) (Little Black Sedge)	collector	leaf particles, algae, animal matter		******************************* → (abundant in some spring fed and some tailwater rivers)	
genus Dolophilodes (8) (Medium Evening Sedge)	collector	leaf particles, algae, animal matter	***************** (the larvae inhabit riffles with rubble-size gravel)		
genus *Wormaldia* (13) (Little Autumn Stream Sedge)	collector	leaf particles, algae, animal matter	← ************ (common in riffle areas of large streams)		
Family Psychomyiidae					
genus *Lype* (1) (Dark Eastern Woodland Sedge)	collector	leaf particles, algae, animal matter	************ (found only in the East and North Central regions, where it can be especially abundant in woodland streams)		
genus *Psychomyia* (3) (Dinky Purple-Breasted Sedge)	collector	leaf particles, algae, animal matter		********************************** → (abundant in a wide range of running water habitats, from woodland streams to large, warm rivers)	
Family Polycentropodidae					
genus *Neureclipsis* (5) (Little Red Twilight Sedge)	collector/ predator	smaller animals	***************** (found in areas of slower flow)		
genus *Nyctiophylax* (8) (Dinky Light Summer Sedge)	collector/ predator	smaller animals		***************** (found in areas of slower flow)	
genus *Polycentropus* (40) (Brown Checkered Summer Sedge)	collector/ predator	smaller animals		** (can be common in slack current areas in almost any size stream, but this genus is generally more common in cool, clear lakes)	

SCIENTIFIC NAME/ COMMON NAME (NUMBER OF KNOWN NORTH AMERICAN SPECIES IN PARENTHESES)	MAIN FEEDING METHODS	MAIN DIETARY ITEMS	PRIMARY COLD AND COOL WATER HABITAT		
			LARGE STREAM	SMALL RIVER	LARGE RIVER
Family Hydropsychidae					
genus *Cheumatopsyche* (40) (Little Sister Sedge)	collector	algae, leaf particles, animal matter	•••••••••••••••••••••••••••••→ (abundance depends on amount of algae produced in the stream or river)		
genus *Hydropsyche* (70) (Spotted Sedge)	collector	algae, leaf particles, animal matter	•••••••••••••••••••••••••••••→ (the genus as a whole prospers in a wide variety of streams and rivers, but the individual species usually have more restricted habitat needs)		
genus *Arctopsyche* (4) (Great Grey Spotted Sedge)	collector/ predator	smaller animals	←•••••••••••••••• (can be common in even larger rivers if the water is cold and swift)		
genus *Macronema* (3) (Glossy Wing Sedge)	collector	algae, bacteria			••••••••••→ (most abundant in larger and generally warmer rivers)
Superfamily Rhyacophiloidea					
Family Rhyacophilidae					
genus *Rhyacophila* (100+) (Green Sedge)	predator (primarily)	smaller animals	←••••••••••••••••••••••• (can be common over a wide range; amount of dissolved oxygen and current turbulence are usually controlling factors)		
Family Glossosomatidae					
genus *Glossosoma* (25) (Little Tan Short Horn Sedge)	scraper	algae, leaf particles	←•••••••••••••••••••••• (this genus is very sensitive to siltation; it is generally abundant in fast, cold, and clear running water)		
Family Hydroptilidae					
genus *Agraylea* (3) (Salt and Pepper Microcaddis)	piercer	algae			•••••••→ (frequently common in slower moving areas of large rivers; can be very abundant in spring creeks)
genus *Hydroptila* (60) (Vari-Colored Microcaddis)	piercer/ scraper	algae	••••••••••••••••••••••••••••••••••••→ (this is a very diverse genus; different species are adapted to almost any type of freshwater habit)		
genus *Leucotrichia* (3) (Ring Horn Microcaddis)	scraper	algae		••••••••••	(the larvae inhabit very strong currents)
genus *Oxyethira* (30) (Cream and Brown Microcaddis)	piercer	algae			•••••••••• (common in slow-moving areas of large rivers; more abundant east of the Mississippi River)
Superfamily Limnephiloidea					
Family Phryganeidae					
genus *Phryganea* (2) (Rush Sedge)	predator	smaller animals		••••••••••••••••••••••→ (frequently common in slow-moving areas of large rivers)	

SCIENTIFIC NAME/ COMMON NAME (NUMBER OF KNOWN NORTH AMERICAN SPECIES IN PARENTHESES)	MAIN FEEDING METHODS	MAIN DIETARY ITEMS	PRIMARY COLD AND COOL WATER HABITAT		
			LARGE STREAM	SMALL RIVER	LARGE RIVER
genus *Ptilostomis* (4) (Giant Rusty Sedge)	predator	smaller animals		*****************	
			(frequently common in weedy, large rivers)		
Family Brachycentridae					
genus *Amiocentrus* (1) (Little Western Weedy Water Sedge)	shredder	leaf particles	**************		
			(found only in the West; the larvae are usually associated with moss and rooted aquatic plants)		
genus *Brachycentrus* (9) (American Grannom)	collector/ scraper	algae, leaf particles, smaller animals		******************	
			(most abundant in streams and rivers with good algae production)		
Family Lepidostomatidae					
genus *Lepidostoma* (65) (Little Plain Brown Sedge)	shredder	leaf particles	**********************		
			(found in slow areas of cool streams and rivers, usually in association with leaf accumulation; some species are also locally common in backwaters of large rivers)		
Family Limnephilidae					
genus *Dicosmoecus* (5) (Giant Orange Sedge)	scraper	algae, animal matter, leaf particles	*****************		
			(found only in the West; abundant in fast riffles of rich rivers)		
genus *Onocosmoecus* (7) (Great Late Summer Sedge)	shredder	leaf particles	*****************		
			(this genus inhabits roughly the same range of running water environments as the closely related genus, *Dicosmoecus*, but it is usually found in slower currents)		
genus *Ecclisomyia* (3) (Early Western Mottled Sedge)	shredder	leaf particles, algae, animal matter	*************		
			(found only in the West, where it inhabits the riffles of small streams and rivers)		
genus *Neophylax* (15) (Autumn Mottled Sedge)	scraper	algae, leaf particles	*************************		
			(the heavy stone cases of the larvae help them exploit the fast currents of streams and rivers)		
genus *Oligophlebodes* (7) (Little Western Dark Sedge)	scraper	algae, plant fragments	←**********		
			(the larvae inhabit the rapid sections of mountain streams in the West)		
genus *Frenesia* (2) (Dot Wing Winter Sedge)	shredder	leaf particles, woody materials	***************		
			(found only in the eastern half of the continent; prime habitats are cold, woodland streams and rivers)		
genus *Hesperophylax* (6) (Silver Stripe Sedge)	shredder/ scraper	algae, plant fragments	*************************************		
			(the single eastern species, *H. designatus*, is found mainly in streams, but some of the western species are abundant in rich rivers)		
genus *Limnephilus* (95+) (Summer Flyer Sedge)	shredder	leaf particles		*************************→	
			(this genus is mainly adapted for stillwater environmants, but some species are found in running waters. These species can sometimes be important in slow stream and spring creek habitats)		

SCIENTIFIC NAME/ COMMON NAME (NUMBER OF KNOWN NORTH AMERICAN SPECIES IN PARENTHESES)	MAIN FEEDING METHODS	MAIN DIETARY ITEMS	PRIMARY COLD AND COOL WATER HABITAT		
			LARGE STREAM	SMALL RIVER	LARGE RIVER
genus *Platycentropus* (3) (Chocolate and Cream Sedge)	shredder	leaf particles	**************************	************	
			(this eastern genus inhabits quiet areas of streams and rivers; the larvae are very tolerant of warm temperatures)		
genus *Psychoglypha* (15) (Snow Sedge)	shredder	leaf particles, animal fragments		*******************	
			(found in a large range of running water habitats, but cool water is a requirement for the larvae)		
genus *Pycnopsyche* (16) (Great Brown Autumn Sedge)	shredder	leaf particles	←************************		
			(most prevalent in cool streams and rivers of woodland areas in the East and Midwest)		
genus *Goera* (6) (Little Grey Sedge)	scraper	algae, fine leaf particles	←***********		
			(the larvae inhabit riffle sections of streams)		
genus *Chyranda* (1) (Pale Western Stream Sedge)	shredder	leaf particles, moss fragments	←******		
			(can be very common in small spring brooks and mountain streams in the West)		
genus *Hydatophylax* (4) (Giant Cream Pattern-Wing Sedge)	shredder	woody materials	←*********		
			(*Hydatophylax* is an important processor of decaying sticks and bark in small streams)		
genus *Apatania* (15) (Early Smoky Wing Sedge)	scraper	algae	******************		
			(can be abundant in riffles of streams and small rivers)		
genus *Ironoquia* (4) (Eastern Box Wing Sedge)	shredder	algae, leaf particles	←***********		
			(found only in the eastern half of the continent; can be locally common in stream areas where leaf materials accumulate)		
Family Odontoceridae					
genus *Psilotreta* (7) (Dark Blue Sedge)	scraper	leaf particles, algae		****************	
			(the larvae burrow into the gravel of the riffles; this genus is represented only in the eastern half of the continent)		
Family Molannidae					
genus *Molanna* (6) (Grey Checkered Sedge)	scraper/ predator	algae, leaf particles, algae, smaller animals		********************	
			(especially important in the sandy-bottomed, spring fed rivers of the upper Midwest)		

SCIENTIFIC NAME/ COMMON NAME (NUMBER OF KNOWN NORTH AMERICAN SPECIES IN PARENTHESES)	MAIN FEEDING METHODS	MAIN DIETARY ITEMS	PRIMARY COLD AND COOL WATER HABITAT		
			LARGE STREAM	SMALL RIVER	LARGE RIVER
Family Helicopsychidae					
genus *Helicopsyche* (4) (Speckled Peter)	scraper	algae, leaf particles, animal matter	●●● (often common wherever incoming springs influence streams and rivers; the larvae can survive in very warm temperatures)		
Family Leptoceridae					
genus *Ceraclea* (34) (Scaly Wing Sedge)	collector shredder/ predator	leaf particles, fresh water sponges	(especially abundant in the tailwater river of the Midsouth; some species feed on freshwater sponges)	●●●●●●●●●●●●●●●●●●●●	
genus *Mystacides* (3) (Black Dancer)	collector/ shredder/ predator	leaf particles, smaller animals	(mainly found in ponds and lakes, but can be abundant in slow rivers; the larvae require a cool-water environment)	●●●●●●●●●●●●●●●●●●●●	
genus *Nectopsyche* (12) (White Miller)	collector/ shredder/ predator	leaf particles, smaller animals	(usually found in areas with slow currents; can be especially abundant in streams and rivers with rooted aquatic plants)	●●●●●●●●●●●●●●●●●	→
genus *Oecetis* (20) (Long Horn Sedge)	predator	smaller animals	(a widespread genus; often abundant in rivers with slow currents)	●●●●●●●●●●●●●●●●●●●●●●●●●	

Professional entomologists can do this guesswork quite easily, often supplying amazingly detailed analyses of a biotype or an insect community. They consider the environmental features and use their knowledge to judge how each one benefits or harms particular types of larvae.

Even such amateur naturalists as fly fishermen can quickly learn to group certain insects and stream environments together by applying some basic principles. They only need to know generally why different kinds of insects live in different kinds of trout streams and how the fauna changes as habitat changes in the water's downward course to the ocean.

The purpose here is to discuss the caddisflies that live in a basic array of trout streams. For each major classification—large stream, small river, large river, limestone spring creek, and tail-water river—there is a "prototype." All five of the typical waters included here are very good trout fisheries in their own right, but they have been chosen because they also illustrate caddisfly distribution in many similar waters.

For polluted streams and rivers no example is provided. Instead there is a general discussion of how various pollutants affect an insect community. For headwater streams, no example is given either, but a general discussion of typical insect fauna is provided. For the five "prototypes" the following waters were chosen:

Large stream: Woods Creek (Wisconsin)
Small river: Mt. Hope River (Connecticut)
Large river: Yellowstone River (Montana)
Limestone spring creek: Henrys Fork of the Snake (Idaho)
Tail-water river: White River (Arkansas)

Polluted Streams and Rivers

There is a statement that has appeared in one form or another so often in angling literature that it is widely believed by fly fishermen: *caddisflies are becoming increasingly important because growing pollution and wider use of pesticides are taking a higher toll of the relatively fragile mayflies while sparing the more rugged caddisflies.*

Doesn't it sound a bit absurd for insects, in this instance caddisflies, that evolved over millions of years in natural habitats to suddenly start prospering in environments degraded by industrial poison? It should.

This concept of caddisfly invulnerability seemed so unlikely to me that I began searching scientific papers, looking for information in industrial and agricultural reports, that might either confirm or deny the "ruggedness" of caddisflies. None of the papers confirmed it; just the opposite, many of them cast doubts that this insect order possessed any particular immunity to poisonous pollutants. They stressed that trout streams degraded by nonorganic sources of pollution usually suffered a drop in overall productivity, the populations of all major aquatic insect orders declining as conditions worsened.

In one well-documented case a spray plane accidently wiped out the entire insect population on four miles of the Miramichi (New Brunswick, Canada) by dumping the pesticide DDT on the river. The first insects to return to the blighted stretch were *Chironomid* midges (one year later), the second were mayflies (two years later), the third were stoneflies (3½ years later), and the last were caddisflies (four years later).

In another stream, Silver Bow Creek, source of the Clark Fork River, Montana, extensive reclamation of waste water by the Anaconda Company greatly reduced mining pollution. Biological surveys demonstrated that prior to 1950, when the watershed was still being used to transport effluents, there were no algae or aquatic insects present in the stream. In 1973, representatives of aquatic beetles, midge larvae, and mayflies were found below the town of Gregson. By 1975, blue-green algae, yellow-green algae, and diatoms were found throughout the entire length of Silver Bow Creek below Butte, and stonefly nymphs, caddisfly larvae, and crane fly larvae, as well as the previously mentioned insects, were collected near Gregson. Recovery progressed slowly for all aquatic orders because of residual pollutants, but none of the insects prospered from the copper, zinc, and iron precipitates.[1]

When I began studying caddisflies I wanted a simple yes or no answer to the question, "Is it true that caddisflies can withstand more pollution than mayflies?" I kept asking entomologists about this. And I kept getting perplexed looks and hesitant responses; it was as if they were having trouble understanding this angling question at all. In my naivete I failed to see why these experts could not give a simple, concrete answer to what seemed like a simple question. As I learned more about caddisflies I began to realize why the experts were having trouble comprehending it; to them, with their knowledge of this order, the statement was so oversimplified that it did not make sense.

There is no way it can be answered with a yes or no. There are three words in it that make a response impossible: caddisflies, mayflies, and pollution. Each one of these terms is too general. What type of caddisfly or mayfly or pollution is the statement talking about? It is going to make a big difference.

Consider the example of a contaminant much milder than chemicals. Siltation, a physical waste resulting from erosion, even in small amounts quickly decreases the population of *Glossosoma* larvae (a type of caddisfly) in an area. It does not affect *Baetis* nymphs (a type of mayfly) very much.[2]

For chemical agents there could be thousands of combinations—a mayfly species hardier or a caddisfly species hardier, depending on the pollutants. Maybe if more were known about how different toxins affect different larvae and nymphs there could be a comprehensive chart of the possibilities, but as recently as 1979, in their article "Ecological Diversity in Trichoptera," R. J. Mackay and G. B. Wiggins stated, "Relatively little is known about the effects of chemical factors [on caddisfly larvae]."[3]

One group of effluents has to be considered separately from chemicals and pesticides. They are still pollutants, but in controlled amounts they are not toxic. These substances—the organic wastes of municipal sewage and the nitrogen and phosphorous compounds of agriculture—can fertilize a stream, increasing algae and weed growth, the same way they fertilize a garden.

Eric Leiser, in *The Caddis and the Angler*, commented on one of my letters to him, "In the first chapter of this volume comment was made concerning the hardiness of caddis as opposed to the mayfly. Gary LaFontaine in his *The Challenge of the Trout*, disagrees. He claims that both are equally hardy, and the reason for the increase or seeming preponderance of caddis flies in our streams is due to the increase of organic leachings of civilization, giving many filter-feeding Trichoptera species, the netmakers, a competitive advantage over mayflies. Many netmaking caddis, such as *Hydropsyche*, are more abundant because nutrient-laden currents now deliver greater quantities of drift food into their feeding nets. This is an interesting observation and I for one am glad to hear that our tampering with nature has had at least some benefits for aquatic insects and trout."[4]

A little bit of such enrichment can be good; a lot of it can be bad. How much of it is helpful depends on the original condition of the stream. The main hazard of fertilizing an ecosystem is that the action of bacteria on the nutrients can use up so much of the dissolved oxygen that fish and insects suffocate. A cold, tumbling river, low in primary productivity, can efficiently oxidize more effluents than one that is warm, slow-moving, or already enriched. A sterile stream can benefit from the added nutrients that might degrade an already fertile one.

The Bow River, a Canadian trout stream that is one of the finest dry-fly fisheries in North America, owes its great productivity to man-made fertilization. Above Calgary, this Alberta river is cold and pure, but it is not a very good trout stream. Starting in the city itself, near the outflow of the sewage plant, the river becomes a giant insect factory. It produces spectacular hatches, enough insects emerging every day of the summer to make even four- to seven-pound trout feed on the surface.

How do these nutrients raise productivity? The initial benefactors of these wastes are single-cell organisms, bacteria and algae. They are at the base of the food chain; many insects consume these organisms and in turn are consumed by other animals (including fish). An increase in algae and bacteria can, in a suitable stream, result in more insects and, consequently, in more trout.

Certain insects species increase dramatically when a watershed is beneficially fertilized with organic wastes. These types, naturally abundant in rich trout streams anyway, are mainly the collectors and scrapers that feed on algae. This includes many species of caddisflies, especially in common genera such as *Hydropsyche* (Spotted Sedge), *Cheumatopsyche* (Little Sister Sedge) and *Brachycentrus* (Grannom); in general, the aquatic order benefiting most from trout stream enrichment might be caddisflies. Other orders also have species that may benefit, however, such as true-fly species in the genus *Simulium* (black fly) and mayfly species in the genus *Isonychia* (Mahogany Dun).

Many trout streams in America have become organically richer over the last thirty years because of farming and housing development in their watersheds. Definitely, some major species of caddisflies have increased in abundance—not because of any resistance to toxic substances, but because of the additional productivity of these waters. The importance of these caddisflies in the fly-fishing scenario has also increased.

Headwater Streams

One way to categorize running water and the changes that occur when it moves toward the sea is with an age scale. The trickle in the mountains, fed by melting snows, is young; as it runs downhill it grows older. The young stream is a different environment than the old river, and each has its own insect fauna.

In the youngest type of mountain habitat, the runoff rivulets, the water is sterile, lacking both mineral and organic nutrients because it is basically the same as its main components—rain and snow. The miniature stream bounces and gurgles down the steep slope of the mountain, turning into a little torrent during the spring thaw and shrinking to a pitiful ribbon during the summer. At this point the environment is so inhospitable that it does not support very many insects.

Physical changes happen gradually as the trickle drops in elevation. It grows as other trickles and underground seepages feed into it until it can be properly called a stream. As it increases in size it becomes able to support a resident population of trout. The gradient of a stream, if looked at in overall profile from its origin to its end, decreases throughout its course, the current becoming slower as the slope lessens. The temperature of the water steadily increases. As a direct result of decreasing gradient and increasing temperature, the amount of dissolved oxygen in the water begins to decrease. In its course, as it changes from a mountain trickle to a headwater stream to a large stream to a small river and finally to a large river, it may cease to be a cold-water trout fishery and become a warm-water bass river.

The aging of a stream from mountain to sea is characterized, in a most general fashion, by the following physical changes: one, increasing size; two, decreasing gradient; three, increasing water temperature; and four, decreasing dissolved oxygen.

The food base, the organic matter that insects eat, also changes as a stream ages. In its original state, rainwater has a slightly acidic pH of approximately 6, and is too pure to encourage much plant growth. Even as it rushes downhill or seeps through sand and gravel it cannot, if the rock is of volcanic origin, pick up many nutrients; thus, even after growing into a small headwater trout stream, it does not contain enough dissolved solids to promote a luxuriant aquatic garden of algae and rooted plants. The amount of inorganic nutrients in suspension increases slowly as the stream erodes stone and soil during its downhill trip, this enrichment process proceeding much faster if it hits calcium-rich sedimentary rocks such as limestone. It is possible to plot another gradual change during the progression from youthful to aged habitats, a fifth physical change: increasing dissolved solids.

Headwater streams can be absolutely delightful fisheries. The quarry, generally wild brook or cutthroat trout, may measure no more than six to nine inches, but they battle with a frantic ferocity. The thrills they provide serve as a bonus to the charm of these small-stream environments.

Do trout in headwater streams feed selectively? Not usually, and this lack of discrimination on their part removes the main reason for studying the insect fauna in these waters. The trout snatch any bit of food, or any vaguely credible fly, passing by their nose—so a fly fisherman has no need to imitate caddisflies here except in the most general fashion.

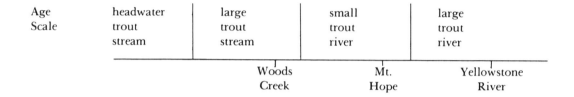

Age Scale	headwater trout stream	large trout stream	small trout river	large trout river
		Woods Creek	Mt. Hope	Yellowstone River

Large Streams

If the production of algae is limited in headwater streams, and even to a certain extent in large streams, what is the primary food source for insects? As much as ninety-nine percent of the energy input in these environments can come from the leaves and sticks that fall from trees. Aquatic insects process this basic energy by eating the decaying materials, releasing the nutrients locked up in them.[5]

The type of food available in a stream greatly influences the composition of its insect community. When the major food resource is decaying leaves, then most of the insects in that environment are going to be the kind that eat leaves. In woodland brooks, shadowed by a canopy of trees, shredder and collector species, not only among caddisflies but also among other aquatic insect orders, that feed on large pieces of plant material dominate the fauna.

As the stream grows larger the amount of dissolved solids, and subsequently the production of algae, increases and the insect fauna changes. This shift continues throughout the course of our hypothetical trout stream; insects that feed primarily on decaying leaves are the most important vegetarians in the sterile headwaters and insects that feed primarily on algae are the most important vegetarians in rich rivers.

The larvae of most caddisfly species feed on a broad selection of food types, eating whatever is available, but they usually gather food in a specific manner; they are shredders, scrapers, collectors, or predators. The way the larvae of a caddisfly species feed often makes them very dependent—if not totally so—on a particular food

In a tree-lined stream leaf-shredding larvae, such as the Pycnopsyche *larvae shown in the drawing, are usually very abundant.*

resource; hence, shredders may eat anything from algae to dead fish, but they cannot become abundant unless there is a supply of decaying leaves.

In a large stream the vegetarian insects are still generally dependent on leaf fall, but there is enough algae production, especially in midsummer, to support species that feed on this resource. The food supply is fairly diverse, and the list of species from such an environment is fairly large—in Woods Creek, the example for this type of environment, there are seventy-eight species. But the important vegetarian species (marked with stars on the accompanying list) feed mostly on dead leaves.

The environments that are being used to illustrate the progression from stream to river have been chosen because they demonstrate the shift from leaf-eating to algae-eating insects. The large stream, Woods Creek, supports in good numbers species that depend on leaves; the small river, the Mount Hope, supports some species that depend on leaves and some that depend on algae in good numbers; the large river, the Yellowstone, supports species that depend on algae in great numbers.

Woods Creek — Wisconsin (Florence County)

There really is no "typical" stream or river; they are all unique—and Woods Creek is certainly so. For one thing, the gradient and the current speed of Woods Creek is not as great as in a Rocky Mountain or even an Appalachian trout stream of similar size. Upper midwestern waters often originate in relatively low-elevation swamps and marshes and do not tumble down mountain sides. Still, in Woods Creek the gradient averages fourteen feet per mile, and while not a torrent, this rates as a steady flow.

The Wisconsin Department of Natural Resources, in their publication *Wisconsin Trout Streams*, lists Woods Creek as a top-rated, Class I trout water. It is eighteen miles long, with a combination of pools and riffles. Hardwood trees line both banks and in many places nearly touch overhead. This fine little stream supports a good population of wild brook trout.

My basic species list for Woods Creek comes from a study, *Aquatic Insects of the Pine-Popple River, Wisconsin*, conducted by the department of natural resources. Jerry L. Longridge and William L. Hilsenhoff did the work on caddisflies for this bulletin. Three of my fly-fishing friends—Tom Poole, Tory Stosich, and Vern McArthur—did a great job collecting caddisflies from Woods Creek so that I could make a determination on the importance of various species.

In Woods Creek the leaf-feeding larvae are especially conspicious in the spring before they become inactive (diapause) or begin pupating. Trout prey heavily on them at this time, stomach samplings usually recovering the leftover debris of the cases as well as insect parts. This probably explains why a large Dark-Cased Caddisfly pattern works well in slower areas of the stream early in the season.

SPECIES LIST FOR WOODS CREEK

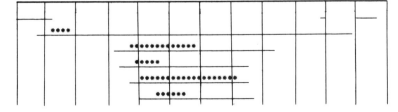

	JAN.	FEB.	MAR.	APR.	MAY	JUNE	JULY	AUG.	SEPT.	OCT.	NOV.	DEC.
Frenesia missa												
* *Dolophilodes distinctus*		****										
** *Glossosoma nigrior*					******************							
** *Limnephilus submonilifer*					*****							
* *Cheumatopsyche pettiti*					*********************							
* *Brachycentrus americanus*					******							

SPECIES LIST FOR WOODS CREEK

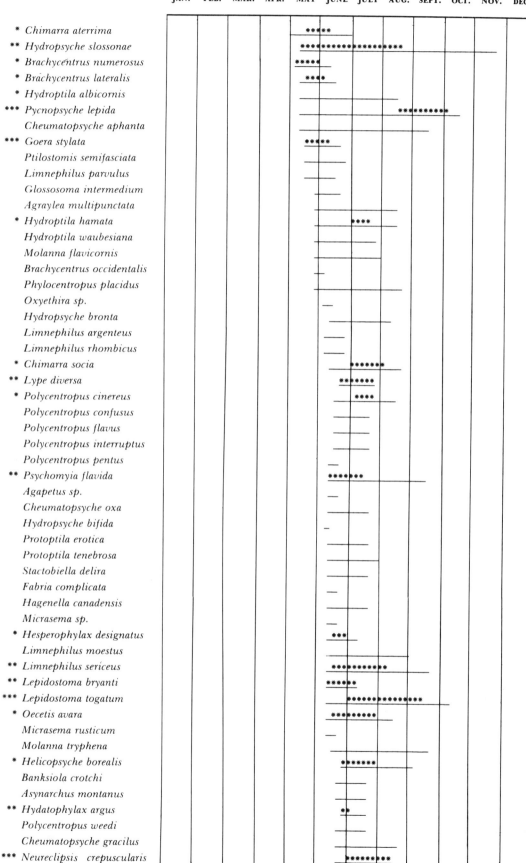

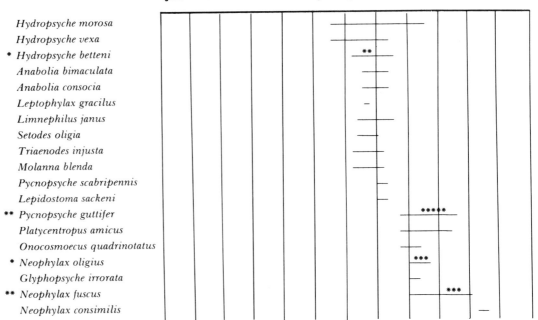

SPECIES LIST FOR WOODS CREEK

	JAN.	FEB.	MAR.	APR.	MAY	JUNE	JULY	AUG.	SEPT.	OCT.	NOV.	DEC.
Hydropsyche morosa												
Hydropsyche vexa												
* *Hydropsyche betteni*							**					
Anabolia bimaculata												
Anabolia consocia												
Leptophylax gracilus												
Limnephilus janus												
Setodes oligia												
Triaenodes injusta												
Molanna blenda												
Pycnopsyche scabripennis												
Lepidostoma sackeni												
** *Pycnopsyche guttifer*									*****			
Platycentropus amicus												
Onocosmoecus quadrinotatus												
* *Neophylax oligius*									***			
Glyphopsyche irrorata												
** *Neophylax fuscus*										***		
Neophylax consimilis												

The major shredders, the genera in order of descending importance to the angler are: *Lepidostoma* (Little Plain Brown Sedge; two common species, both with peak emergence in late June and early July), *Pycnopsyche* (Great Brown Autumn Sedge; peak emergence in September), *Hydatophylax* (Giant Cream Pattern-Wing Sedge), *Platycentropus* (Chocolate and Cream Sedge), and *Limnephilus* (Summer Flyer Sedge). The number of *Limnephilus* species collected from Woods Creek might be deceptively high because there are marshes near the stream, and adults could have flown in from these adjacent areas, but at least two species, *L. sericeus* and *L. submonilifer*, are common in the main stream and often present in fish stomach samples during July.

Some of the net-spinning larvae also depend on detritus as a food source. The most common species of *Hydropsyche* (Spotted Sedge) in Woods Creek, *H. betteni* and *H. slossonae*, are both indigenous to streams and small rivers rather than to large rivers, and feed to a certain degree on leaf particles they filter from the drift. *Chimarra* (Little Black Sedge) larvae, which build their nets under rocks, are not discriminate feeders, eating detritus, algae, or insects, but in woodland streams, where leaves are the main source of food, they depend on leaf particles almost exclusively. *Psychomyia* (Dinky Purple-Breasted Sedge) and *Lype* (Dark Eastern Woodland Sedge), the latter always associated with areas of heavy tree growth, also feed on decaying leaves and woody materials.

Three scraper-feeding genera, *Goera* (Little Gray Sedge), *Glossosoma* (Little Tan Short-Horn Sedge), and *Neophylax* (Autumn Mottled Sedge), are common in riffle sections of Woods Creek. They crawl over the rocks, peeling the film of organic matter, including small fragments of detritus, off the surface of the rocks. The species *Goera stylata*, emerging in late May and June, is especially abundant in this stream.

There are also important predators in Woods Creek and while they do not consume plant material they do depend on it to sustain their prey. These hunters are usually the third step in the food pyramid.

Since there is a certain amount of waste and loss of energy in each step up the

Woods Creek, a fine Wisconsin stream, is populated with wild brook trout. Gary LaFontaine

The giant caddisfly, Hydatophylax argus *(Giant Cream Pattern-Wing Sedge) has a distinctive pattern of colors on its wings. It is an easily recognizable part of the late-summer caddisfly community on Woods Creek.* Ken Thompson

pyramid, and since not all vegetarian insects are going to be eaten, there have to be a greater number of prey animals, or potential victims, than there are predators to form a food pyramid.

The most common carnivore, and the only one with more than a one-star rating, is *Neureclipsis crepuscularis* (Little Red Twilight Sedge). This species also consumes some algae, so it is not completely dependent on animal food. The larvae build trumpet-shaped nets on branches or plants standing upright in slow currents, the gentle character of Woods Creek providing many suitable sites for these caddisflies.

What is missing in Woods Creek? The fauna is typical of woodland streams throughout the East and Midwest. In similar waters the same genera of caddisflies are going to predominate in Minnesota, Pennsylvania, or New Jersey. In Western states the caddisfly community might consist of some different genera, leaf shredders such as *Chyranda* (Pale Western Stream Sedge) and collectors such as *Arctopsyche* (Great Gray Spotted Sedge), but they fill the same roles as their Eastern counterparts. (The reader can find out which western caddisflies are important in streams of this size by checking the Distribution Charts.)

The fast-water predator, *Rhyacophila* (Green Sedge), is not common in Woods Creek; according to Dr. William Hilsenhoff it is not common at all in Wisconsin. The scarcity of this genus is possibly due to the lack of brawling, turbulent waters in the state. The absence or rarity of some other caddisflies in Woods Creek might also be attributable to the low altitude or unspectacular gradient of the stream.

Many of the physical factors that make streams a good environment for some caddisflies can slightly limit other types. The steady flow, the cool temperature, and the oxygen saturation of the water might not suit certain genera, but these really are not very much of a deterrent to most caddisflies. As a result, large streams, with the pools supplying slow-current areas and riffles supplying fast-current areas, provide the right biological conditions for many different species. It is only later in the downstream progression of the watershed, when higher temperatures, slower currents, and less dissolved oxyten act as real limiting factors, that the number of species and the diversity of the insect community begin to decline.

In most streams the large number of species often means that caddisflies must be considered collectively as well as individually. When the trout see many insects of roughly similar silhouette and size all doing just about the same things, minor differences in characteristics become secondary to the overall picture that defines caddisfly—and thus food—to the fish. As long as there are not two or three distinctive species on the water in large numbers, the finer points of selectivity never become ingrained in the mind of the trout.

The wisdom of matching the general appearance of caddisflies, especially during their pupal stage, is one of the important lessons in Ernest Schwiebert's *Nymphs.* "Several species are often present together," Schwiebert notes, "and in spite of each emerging in relatively small numbers, their aggregate populations are large enough to trigger a rise of fish."

Often the key to catching trout on large streams is collecting all the active caddisflies and matching the size and color best represented in the hodgepodge of species. The angler can then present his general imitation to working fish, either ignoring or specifically targeting those strays that demonstrate a greater degree of fussiness.

Small Rivers

Size is not the only difference between a large stream and a small river. Streams are usually not as slippery as rivers—the slick boulders that make wading so treacherous in larger waters are covered with a slimy coating of algae. Certain rivers gain a reputation: there is a little man, a mythical caretaker, who goes out every night and greases the rocks.

The increased production of algae in rivers means that there is a fundamental change in the food base; this in turn means that there are changes in the caddisfly fauna. Most small rivers are still heavily influenced by the input of leaves and still have impressive numbers of shredders, but algae-feeding collectors and scrapers also become common. These larvae dominate the riffles of rich, cold-water habitats.

The collectors serve as especially fine indicators of the changing conditions. Two genera, *Hydropsyche* (Spotted Sedge) and *Cheumatopsyche* (Little Sister Sedge), show up with more species—and the species represented become more important. These genera both belong to the family Hydropsychidae and this family can be considered in its entirety. The number of individual larvae rise as a watershed becomes richer and produces more algae. Density figures for the larvae of all genera in this family increases steadily: headwater streams: 100 per square foot in prime habitat; large streams: 200 per square foot in prime habitat; small rivers: 400 per square foot in prime habitat; large rivers: 1,000 per square foot in prime habitat; spring creeks and tail-water rivers: 2,000 or more per square foot in prime habitat.

The prime habitat for these net makers in a stream is a riffle. The larvae need current to convey their food, but most of them also need the cobblestone bottom that this current creates when it blows out debris from between the rocks. These spaces, known as interstitial habitat, are where the larvae build their nets and retreats.

Mount Hope River — Connecticut

The Mount Hope River, the example for this type of habitat, experiences some enrichment from both its source (the outflow of Morey's Pond) and the organic input of suburbs and towns along its route. These outside influences probably nudge it a little farther up the age scale than it would be naturally, but in this respect the watershed is not much different from most small freestone trout rivers in southern New England and New York. The stream is classified AA, the highest water-quality rating, by Connecticut's Department of Environmental Protection, indicating that the minor additions of organic pollutants pose no threat to the trout fishery. Another sign that nutrients have not caused any stress in the stream is the great diversity of the caddisfly fauna (at least ninety-three species).

The Mount Hope is bordered by hardwood trees—white ash, maple, oak, alder, sumac, and black cherry—but it is wide enough so that the branches cannot form a canopy and shut out the sun. Enough light penetrates the clear water and reaches the bottom to stimulate the growth of algae, creating an important secondary food resource for insects during the summer.

The river bounces through pools, riffles, and runs, offering many different current speeds for insects. It remains cool and saturated with dissolved oxygen all summer. There are no drastic limiting factors in this type of stream and, as in such habitats as Woods Creek, the variety of biological niches provides space and food for

There are quiet, tree-shaded flats on the Mt. Hope. Ken Thompson

shredders, scrapers, collectors, and predators. There are important species from all four groups.

There is an excellent professional paper on the river, *Energy Budget for the Late Winter Aquatic Insect Community from the Mount Hope River* by Peter J. Dodds and Kenneth W. Thompson. It describes the physical characteristics and food resources of this ecosystem. It also summarizes the general insect fauna, listing all the aquatic orders in the river, most to genus level.

Ken Thompson, in one of the many tasks he did for this book, collected the caddisflies on the Mount Hope. He used a light trap and a sweep net to capture specimens, taking samples virtually every day of 1979, and compiled a list of ninety-three species (including many first-time records for Connecticut).[6]

SPECIES LIST FOR THE MT. HOPE RIVER

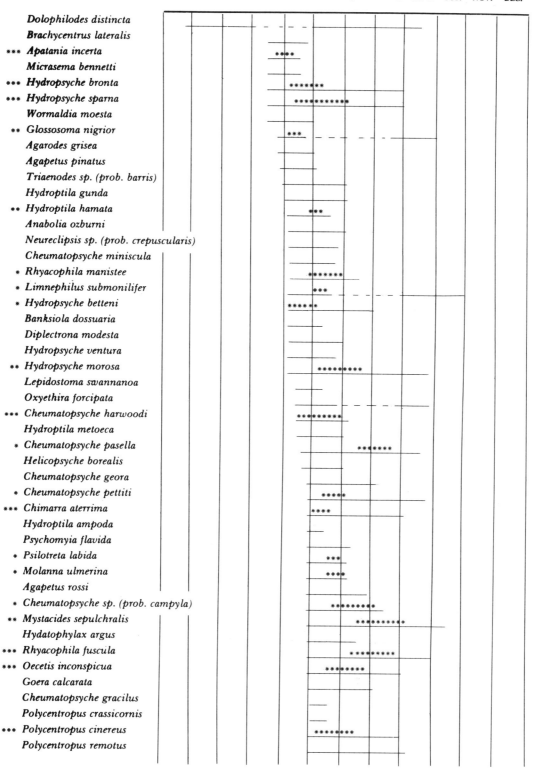

| | JAN. | FEB. | MAR. | APR. | MAY | JUNE | JULY | AUG. | SEPT. | OCT. | NOV. | DEC. |

Dolophilodes distincta
Brachycentrus lateralis
*** *Apatania incerta*
Micrasema bennetti
*** *Hydropsyche bronta*
*** *Hydropsyche sparna*
Wormaldia moesta
** *Glossosoma nigrior*
Agarodes grisea
Agapetus pinatus
Triaenodes sp. (prob. barris)
Hydroptila gunda
** *Hydroptila hamata*
Anabolia ozburni
Neureclipsis sp. (prob. crepuscularis)
Cheumatopsyche miniscula
* *Rhyacophila manistee*
* *Limnephilus submonilifer*
* *Hydropsyche betteni*
Banksiola dossuaria
Diplectrona modesta
Hydropsyche ventura
** *Hydropsyche morosa*
Lepidostoma swannanoa
Oxyethira forcipata
*** *Cheumatopsyche harwoodi*
Hydroptila metoeca
* *Cheumatopsyche pasella*
Helicopsyche borealis
Cheumatopsyche geora
* *Cheumatopsyche pettiti*
*** *Chimarra aterrima*
Hydroptila ampoda
Psychomyia flavida
* *Psilotreta labida*
* *Molanna ulmerina*
Agapetus rossi
* *Cheumatopsyche sp. (prob. campyla)*
** *Mystacides sepulchralis*
Hydatophylax argus
*** *Rhyacophila fuscula*
*** *Oecetis inconspicua*
Goera calcarata
Cheumatopsyche gracilus
Polycentropus crassicornis
*** *Polycentropus cinereus*
Polycentropus remotus

SPECIES LIST FOR THE MT. HOPE RIVER

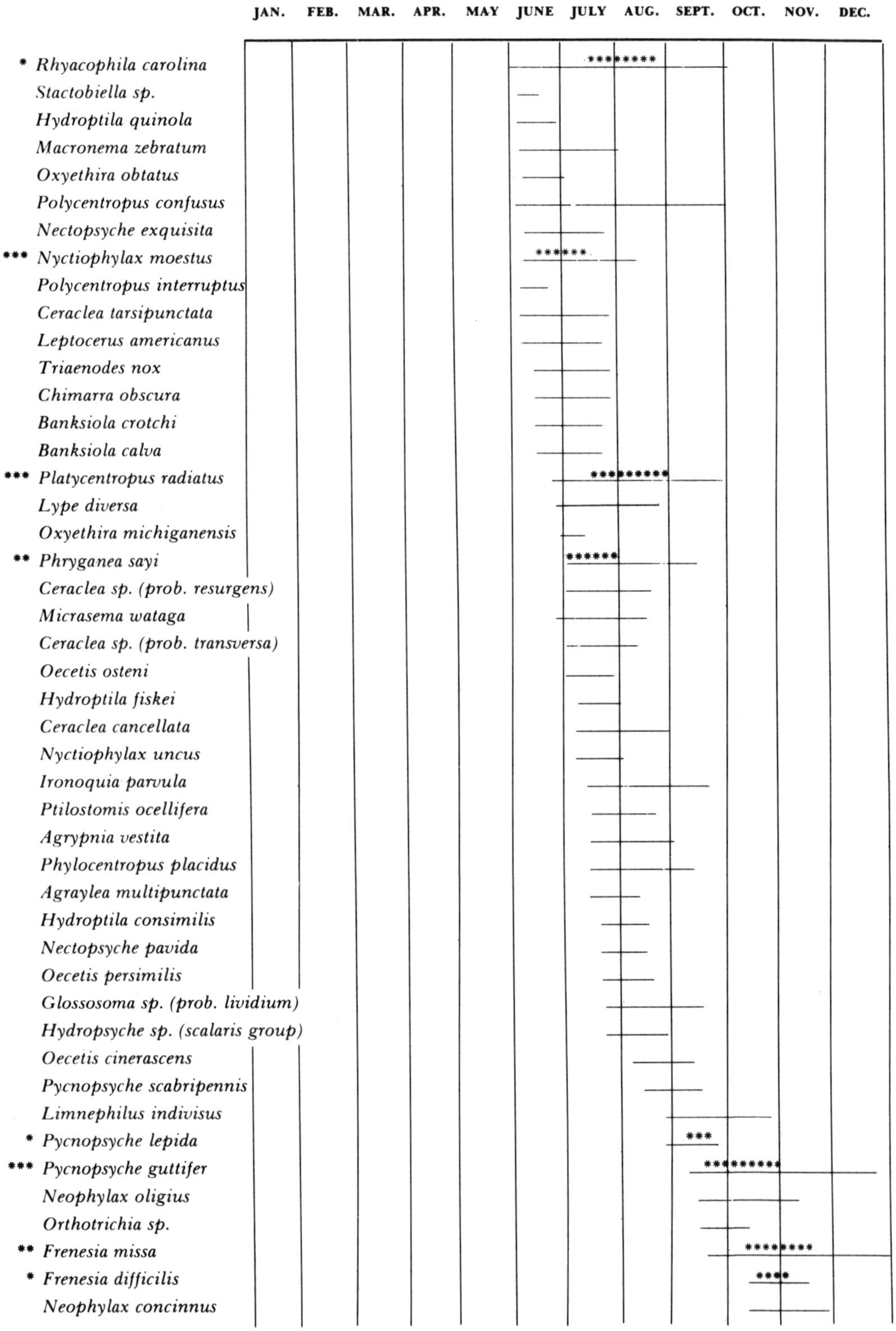

| | JAN. | FEB. | MAR. | APR. | MAY | JUNE | JULY | AUG. | SEPT. | OCT. | NOV. | DEC. |

* *Rhyacophila carolina*
Stactobiella sp.
Hydroptila quinola
Macronema zebratum
Oxyethira obtatus
Polycentropus confusus
Nectopsyche exquisita
*** *Nyctiophylax moestus*
Polycentropus interruptus
Ceraclea tarsipunctata
Leptocerus americanus
Triaenodes nox
Chimarra obscura
Banksiola crotchi
Banksiola calva
*** *Platycentropus radiatus*
Lype diversa
Oxyethira michiganensis
** *Phryganea sayi*
Ceraclea sp. (prob. resurgens)
Micrasema wataga
Ceraclea sp. (prob. transversa)
Oecetis osteni
Hydroptila fiskei
Ceraclea cancellata
Nyctiophylax uncus
Ironoquia parvula
Ptilostomis ocellifera
Agrypnia vestita
Phylocentropus placidus
Agraylea multipunctata
Hydroptila consimilis
Nectopsyche pavida
Oecetis persimilis
Glossosoma sp. (prob. lividium)
Hydropsyche sp. (scalaris group)
Oecetis cinerascens
Pycnopsyche scabripennis
Limnephilus indivisus
* *Pycnopsyche lepida*
*** *Pycnopsyche guttifer*
Neophylax oligius
Orthotrichia sp.
** *Frenesia missa*
* *Frenesia difficilis*
Neophylax concinnus

Three genera of caddisflies—*Rhyacophila*, *Oecetis*, and *Phryganea*—fill the role of free-roaming predators in the Mount Hope. Current speed determines where each one is important. *Rhyacophila* (Green Sedge) thrives in the faster, highly oxygenated flows; *Oecetis* (Long-Horn Sedge) and *Phryganea* (Rush Sedge), lacking adaptations to prevent dislodgment, prefer the quieter areas. In a river with a varied, pool-and-riffle mixture of water, such as the Mount Hope, species of all three genera can be common to abundant.

Two genera of net-making predators are also very important in this river. *Nyctiophylax* (Dinky Light Summer Sedge), which spins a silk roof over a depression in a log or stone, and *Polycentropus* (Brown Checkered Summer Sedge), which spins either a tube or a bag retreat, both inhabit the pools and gentle flats of the Mount Hope. *N. moestus* and *P. cinereus*, one species in each genus, rate three stars because of their high value to anglers.

The leaf shredders include caddisflies such as *Pycnopsyche* (Great Brown Autumn Sedge) and *Platycentropus* (Chocolate and Cream Sedge), which are both important items in the trout diet early and late in the fishing season. In the spring the huge larval forms of these insects are often washed into the drift by rising water, and imitations of these cased caddisflies are deadly tools in the right places. In the late summer and fall, when these giants emerge, they are preyed on heavily by trout. Overall the ratings for these shredders might be only one or two stars, but at specific times their value is much higher.

In the Mount Hope the genus *Hydropsyche* (Spotted Sedge) probably predominates over the genus *Cheumatopsyche* (Little Sister Sedge), with three major species, *H. bronta*, *H. morosa*, and *H. sparna*, in the former and only two, *C. harwoodi* and *C. pettiti*, in the latter, but both of these Hydropsychidae collectors are so numerous that fish can become selective to the general characteristics of either genus. Whichever one is on the water at the moment usually controls the feeding actvity of the trout.

Neither *Psilotreta* (Dark Blue Sedge) nor *Brachycentrus* (Grannom), two major spring caddisflies, rates three stars in the Mount Hope. Basically both of these genera are more abundant in larger trout rivers, such waters as the Beaverkill and the Esopus in New York typifying ideal habitat for them. Smaller freestone rivers generally are not quite rich enough to produce the profuse hatches that are so famous on other eastern rivers. In the Mount Hope the most important spring-time genus is *Apatania* (Early Smoky Wing Sedge), which rates a solid three stars for this stream.

Caddisflies are a valuable food item for trout throughout the season in small rivers. The larvae are in constant supply, emergence dates staggered enough so that as soon as one major species has hatched out another is reaching maturity. The emergents and egg layers are plentiful all season also, mostly in the afternoon during spring and fall and in the morning or evening during the summer (and of course in the dark hours during hot weather).

The selectivity of feeding trout is generally greater in rivers than it is in smaller waters, mainly for three reasons: first, in richer habitats the important insect species are present in greater abundance and an emergence creates heavier concentrations; second, the reduced gradient of larger rivers results in more pools and flats, where fish can better inspect drifting objects; and third, the species of trout found in larger

A small river with both fast and slow currents can support a variety of predators. Oecetis larvae (Long Horn Sedge) prowl the pools and flats of such waters.

waters, rainbows and browns, are more likely to be selective than the brooks and cutthroats of streams. On small rivers it becomes important for fly fishermen to know their caddisflies to species levels because situations arise where the finer points of matching the hatch can mean the difference between success and failure.

This need to cater to the whims of trout is a trend that continues as the river system grows in size. Because of the increasing fussiness of the fish a very large trout river can be tough to master, a few major species dominating the caddisfly fauna and producing incredibly heavy hatches. When trout do rise they quickly become attuned to the actions, size, shape, and color of the insect.

Large Rivers

There are normally a large number of caddisfly species in unpolluted streams and small rivers; for example, there are seventy-eight in Woods Creek and ninety-three in the Mount Hope. In many large rivers, however, a complete species list may consist of only thirty to forty different caddisflies. Even in the healthiest watersheds environmental factors often make downstream sections unsuitable for many species.

The natural changes that occur as a river travels toward the ocean—decreasing dissolved oxygen, increasing water temperature, decreasing gradient, decreasing current speed, and increasing enrichment—eventually become drastic enough to limit the diversity of the entire caddisfly fauna. The species that do remain are usually the ones that have adapted to the special rigors of life in such an environment.

No longer does the water tumble from pool to pool, splashing into the air and rushing over the rocks. In many large rivers it flows in a smooth sheet or a broad riffle, generally slower and deeper than in smaller streams. Rapids occur when the great volume of water is pinched into a steep canyon, but overall the amount of fast-current area is low in proportion to the amount of slow-current area.

The larvae of various caddisfly species disappear with the downstream progress of a trout river. The water temperature may rise too high for cold-water forms, the current speed may become too slow for fast-water forms, or the amount of dissolved oxygen may decrease too much for saturated-water forms. These changes, sometimes associated with the lower portion of a trout river, are negative factors for many of the more primitive caddisfly species.

There are also a limited number of caddisfly species in a large trout river when there is a lack of physical diversity in the environment. If it does not break into the bouncing pool-and-riffle sequence, instead flowing deep and uniform or shallow and slow, the river does not provide a variety of bottom types—microhabitats—for different forms of aquatic insects.

Yellowstone River—Montana

By the time it leaves Yellowstone Park at Gardiner the Yellowstone River is already a large river. It rumbles through Yankee Jim Canyon, producing a minor set of white-water rapids, and then transforms into a deep powerful river, looking like anything but trout habitat. Althought it is greatly enriched and quite broad at this point, the temperature of the water remains cool. It supports good populations of both cutthroat trout and brown trout, as well as large numbers of whitefish.

The area for the insect study begins at Corwin Springs. The trout fauna changes with the downstream passage, rainbows starting to replace the cutthroats below the town of Emigrant. Past Greycliff the river enters a transition zone between a cold-

The Yellowstone River is large, even in its upper stretches. Mike Seymour

water and a warm-water fishery, rough fish such as carp sharing the habitat with trout. The lower limit of good trout fishing, and the end point for the study area, is at the town of Laurel.

The basic species list and most of my information on the composition of the caddisfly fauna comes from the *Yellowstone River Study* by Robert L. Newell. This excellent report contains data on all the aquatic insects, not just caddisflies, from twenty sampling stations between Corwin Springs and the North Dakota border (although the species list used here only includes the collections from 1 through 8, 8 being Laurel, the end of the decent trout fishing).

I did the supplementary collecting on the Yellowstone River, a simple task for me since I regularly guided on the Corwin Springs to Emigrant portion. I used my larval and adult samples to determine the importance to fly fishermen of each caddisfly species and in some instances to make judgments on distributions and flight periods, but I did not add any species to the list in the *Yellowstone River Study* .

In spite of the cool temperatures in the upper reaches of the study area there are apparently still factors detrimental to the more primitive, cold-water caddisflies—a point emphasized by the relative scarcity in my collections of genera such as *Arctopsyche* (Great Gray Spotted Sedge), *Glossosoma* (Little Tan Short-Horn Sedge), and *Rhyacophila* (Green Sedge). The only sections of the river where these caddisflies are common are in the rapids of Yankee Jim Canyon and in scattered patches of fast water in other areas. Current speed, as well as temperature, probably affects their distribution in this instance.

SPECIES LIST FOR YELLOWSTONE RIVER
—May through October

	JAN.	FEB.	MAR.	APR.	MAY	JUNE	JULY	AUG.	SEPT.	OCT.	NOV.	DEC.
* *Brachycentrus occidentalis*					***	peak of abundance mainly in late April						
*** *Hydropsyche cockerelli*								*****************				
*** *Hydropsyche occidentalis*					*******							
Agraylea multipunctata												
Glossosoma velona												
Polycentropus cinereus												
* *Oecetis avara*						******						
** *Lepidostoma pluviale*						****						
Arctopsyche grandis												
Helicopsyche borealis												
*** *Cheumatopsyche campyla*						********						
* *Hydropsyche oslari*						***						
Amiocentrus aspilus												
*** *Brachycentrus americanus*							*******					
Ceraclea⁷ sp.												
** *Psychomyia flavida*							****					
Rhyacophila bifila												
* *Cheumatopsyche pettiti*							**					
Glossosoma traviatum												
Oecetis disjuncta												
Cheumatopsyche enonis												
Hydroptila waubesiana												
Lepidostoma veleda												
Nectopsyche⁷ sp.												
Hesperophylax incisus												

Another possible negative influence for these insects might be the turbidity of the river and the resulting siltation. Periodic landslides in the Lamar River, a major tributary, can muddy the Yellowstone badly anytime of the year. The river also tends to carry a lot of silt as late as August when there is high runoff, which often diminishes the importance of caddisflies that emerge in June and early July.

Two species of caddisflies, *Amiocentrus aspilus* (Little Western Weedy-Water Sedge) and *Helicopsyche borealis* (Speckled Peter), can be locally abundant. They are both found around the mouths of spring-creek tributaries, especially below the streams entering the Yellowstone near Livingston. When these species emerge or lay eggs many trout move up from the river to feed on them.

Of the ten species that are widespread and important throughout the river, eight of them are collectors. There is one leaf shredder, *Lepidostoma pluviale* (Little Plain Brown Sedge), but it is restricted mainly to the coves and backwaters, areas where faster currents deposit detrital materials. The major predator among caddisflies is *Oecetis avara* (Long-Horn Sedge), but it also inhabits the quieter areas of the river. The collectors include the Grannoms, *Brachycentrus americanus* and *Brachycentrus occidentalis*, which also feed by scraping algae off the rocks. The remaining six species, all net-spinning collectors, attain varying degrees of abudance: *Hydropsyche occidentalis*, *Hydropsyche cockerelli*, *Psychomyia flavida*, and *Cheumatopsyche campyla*, the most important caddisflies, produce as a group great, overlapping fly-fishing opportunities from the end of high water through to the fall.

The transition zone, defined here as between Greycliff and Laurel, has many interesting slow-water insects. The net makers, especially *Cheumatopsyche campyla* (Little Sister Sedge), dominate the caddisfly fauna almost completely in this brown-water stretch, and along with major mayflies, such as *Traverella albertana*, produce the main hatches. At times insects are so available and abundant on this big flat water that the carp join some very large trout in the surface feeding.

It is easy for fly fishermen to master the sequence of hatches on the very large trout rivers in their area because there are usually a limited number of species. It is also critical that they do so; the great profusion of these hatches means that trout quickly become attuned to the insect. The need for exact imitation frequently becomes critical.

Some of these rivers are so powerful and so deep that when there is no hatch trout are often not susceptible to the surface fly. The fish hold near the bottom then, and weighted streamers and fast-sinking lines are the only way to reach them. In these fisheries the ability to anticipate the appearance of major insects is especially valuable for anyone who wants to cast for rising fish.

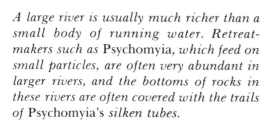

A large river is usually much richer than a small body of running water. Retreat-makers such as Psychomyia, *which feed on small particles, are often very abundant in larger rivers, and the bottoms of rocks in these rivers are often covered with the trails of* Psychomyia's *silken tubes.*

Such rivers might not fit the idyllic image of fly-fishing for trout. On very big western waters, and even on some eastern ones, wading is not always pracitical. Anglers use a boat to get to places where they can wade, or else they fish from the boat. The tactics are different on these rivers, but the rewards can be spectacular.

Limestone Spring Creeks

Within a twenty-five-mile radius of my home in Deer Lodge, Montana, there are many spring creeks. Such streams in this area include a cold-water flow, fifty degrees at its warmest, smothered in beds of watercress; a mysterious stream that disappears into the floor of the valley and pops out again full size a couple of miles farther on; and a river, augmented by bubbling sulphur pots, with a pH between 8.3 and 9.5.

My studies and collections on just the streams in this one valley, all with the same external influences of climate and altitude, point out something about spring creeks: the name is not very descriptive. By itself it does not tell enough about a habitat.

R. A. Muttkowski, writing about springs, explains why spring creeks might even begin with different characteristics, "One could employ a dozen different criteria for their classification and still not exhaust them. One could classify them according to size and temperature; as for the latter, the springs range from icy chillness to boiling point. One might arrange them according to color, which not only differs among different springs, but often in the same spring at different times. Again, one could classify them according to substances in solution, such as carbonates, arsenates, chlorides, silicates, sulphides, etc., or according to substances in suspension, such as sulfur, mud, sand, silt, etc."[8]

What about limestone spring creeks? Would there be similarities among them if the definition was restricted to the fly-fishing image of such habitat (an image probably patterned after Pennsylvania's Letort)? The concept would become a bit more manageable. There would still be differences; for example, those three streams near Deer Lodge are all limestone waters, but each supports slightly different insect communities and each holds different kinds of trout. By understanding the affect that their similarities have on the biological makeup, however, it becomes possible to explain the general structure of these environments.

The nature of spring creeks and their similarities result from two main characteristics: high alkalinity and consistent flow. The almost unbelievable productivity of these streams is due to the alkalinity, or "hardness" of the spring water, an attribute that makes soap suds curdle rather than lather. The pH of a good limestone trout stream is more than 7.75.

The subterranean water becomes alkaline as it percolates through the pourous limestone rock. It collects carbon dioxide from underground, the soil being richly supplied with this gas, and the combination of water with carbon dioxide forms carbonic acid. The acid works on the carbonates in the limestone, making them go into solution.

The addition of these calcium nutrients to the water raises the productivity of the stream by stimulating the growth of algae and, if pockets of silt and quiet areas are available so they can root, aquatic plants. The food base in limestone streams is highly favorable to the herbivorous insects, both scrapers and filter feeders, that utilize these materials.

The constant rate of flow in spring creeks also contributes to their high productivity. The water bubbling out of the ground is the overflow of a vast underground aquifer. The volume of the flow may rise or fall a little, but most springs that form trout streams parcel out their water steadily throughout the year. These creeks do not turn into roaring floods with the runoff of melting snow and they do not shrink to midsummer trickles. The constant water levels allow insect populations to utilize all suitable areas between the banks.

Generally a limestone spring seeps out near the base of the foothills, spilling onto a valley floor or a plateau rather than out onto the steep slopes of the mountains. In these flatter areas the stream meanders gently. The slower-moving currents are suitable for some insect species that cannot live in fast freestone streams, and they often support abundant populations of lake species not ordinarily found in trout rivers.

A species list from a slow-moving spring creek, however, is usually fairly small. There are only a few major species because the number of biological niches in these environments is limited. There are not a lot of different current speeds or bottom types for insects to choose from.

A stream with high overall productivity and a restricted number of species results in incredibly heavy hatches of the major insects. The dominant caddisflies, mayflies, and two-winged flies in these habitats are available in unbelievable numbers. These insects help foster the mystique of spring-creek fly-fishing by concentrating enough vulnerable food during emergence and egg laying to make even large trout rise freely.

Sometimes a spring creek flows off a flat bench of land and down a steep slope. Although the water might still have most of the characteristics that it had in the slow-moving stream—stable temperature, high alkalinity, constant flow—it becomes a different habitat. Many of the fast-water insect species that could not live in the typically gentle spring flow because of their need for such physical factors as heavy current, oxygen saturation, or boulder bottom, survive quite well in these rapid streams. The caddisfly fauna is much more diverse.

The Henrys Fork of the Snake River — Idaho (Fremont County)

At first glance the Henrys Fork might not seem like a good example of this type of stream. It is not only big, more of a spring river than a spring creek, but it also passes through Island Park Reservoir. There are, however, influences that make it more typical of a spring-water than a tail-water fishery, even below the dam. The river originates from springs above the lake, rather than from runoff, and below the lake more springs and a major tributary, the Buffalo River, add their water. In the famous Railroad Ranch area the insect community is very similar to the insect communities of many smaller spring creeks in Montana and Idaho.

The Henrys Fork makes an especially good study area because there are fast-water and slow-water sections with very different caddisfly populations. As soon as the river comes out of Island Park Reservoir it enters the Box Canyon, a five-mile piece of fast, rough water. As it approaches the small town of Last Chance it slows down and enters the weedy, meandering Railroad stretch. The level fluctuates some in both sections because of the dam, but there is a base flow from tributaries and springs even when the upstream water is shut off completely.

The Railroad Ranch section of the Henrys Fork is a slow, weedy spring creek. Dave
Engerbretson/Joe Dvorak

I collected adult caddisflies every three days from July 1 to October 1 at three sites
along the river: in the Box Canyon, just above the Railroad Ranch, and in the
Railroad Ranch, and in the Railroad Ranch near Osborne Bridge. I gathered
specimens mainly by netting, but I also used a formalin/oil trap very successfully on
two occasions. (see Chapter 12, Collecting and Identifying Caddisflies).

Bill Blackburn often accompanied me on trips to the river and captured many of
the adults. Fred Arbona, Mike Lawson, and Kevin Toman made supplementary
collections for this study. Fred Arbona also graciously supplied a comprehensive set
of June specimens from his own Henrys Fork series.

The one-, two-, and three-star ratings, indicating the abundance and availability
of a species, only apply to the Railroad Ranch area. Some of the fast-water caddisflies
that are uncommon in the Ranch are very important in the Box Canyon. Heavy
emergence and egg-laying activity of such species as *Rhyacophila bifila* (Green
Sedge), *Glossosoma velona* (Little Tan Short-Horn Sedge), and *Neophylax rickeri*
(Autumn Mottled Sedge), as well as those species of the Hydropsychidae and

SPECIES LIST FOR THE HENRYS FORK

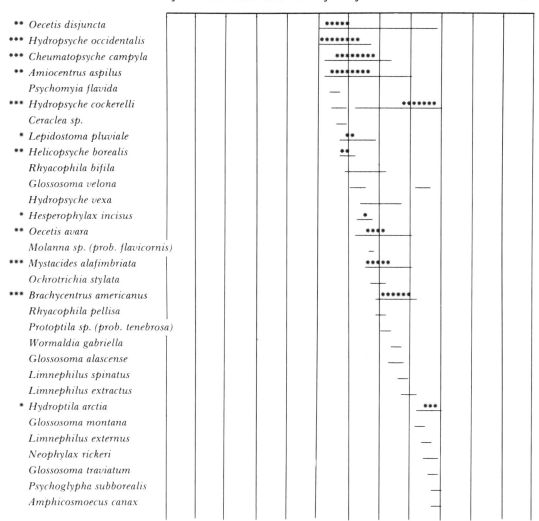

	JAN.	FEB.	MAR.	APR.	MAY	JUNE	JULY	AUG.	SEPT.	OCT.	NOV.	DEC.
** *Oecetis disjuncta*						*****						
*** *Hydropsyche occidentalis*						********						
*** *Cheumatopsyche campyla*						********						
** *Amiocentrus aspilus*						********						
Psychomyia flavida						—						
*** *Hydropsyche cockerelli*						—		********				
Ceraclea sp.						—						
* *Lepidostoma pluviale*						**						
** *Helicopsyche borealis*						**						
Rhyacophila bifila						—						
Glossosoma velona						—		—				
Hydropsyche vexa							—					
* *Hesperophylax incisus*						*						
** *Oecetis avara*						****						
Molanna sp. (prob. flavicornis)						—						
*** *Mystacides alafimbriata*						*****						
Ochrotrichia stylata							—					
*** *Brachycentrus americanus*							*******					
Rhyacophila pellisa							—					
Protoptila sp. (prob. tenebrosa)							—					
Wormaldia gabriella								—				
Glossosoma alascense								—				
Limnephilus spinatus								—				
Limnephilus extractus									—			
* *Hydroptila arctia*									***			
Glossosoma montana									—			
Limnephilus externus									—			
Neophylax rickeri									—			
Glossosoma traviatum									—			
Psychoglypha subborealis									—			
Amphicosmoecus canax									—			

Brachycentridae families that are widely distributed in both sections, create great fly-fishing opportunities in the upper water.

There were no surprises in the collection. The types of caddisflies that should have been abudant in a western spring creek were abundant.[9] Wherever there was enough current to clean off the gravel there were tremendous larval populations of net-making caddisflies, *Hydropsyche* (Spotted Sedge) and *Cheumatopsyche* (Little Sister Sedge), and scraping caddisflies, *Brachycentrus* (Grannom). In gentler areas there were large larval populations of stillwater and slow-water forms, *Mystacides* (Black Dancer), *Oecetis* (Long-Horn Sedge), and *Amiocentrus* (Little Western Weedy-Water Sedge).

The larvae of the genus *Lepidostoma* (Little Plain Brown Sedge), which feed mainly on dead leaf material, were distributed somewhat oddly. They were concentrated above the Railroad Ranch, but they were still in the slow-moving meadow stretch of the Henrys Fork. There were no trees to drop leaves or pine needles into the river in that immediate area. Possibly the source of their food was the fast water coming out of the tree-lined canyon, the detrital material settling and accumulating as the current slowed down at the head of the flats.[10]

Microcaddis, represented in the species list only by *Hydroptila arctia* and *Ochrotrichia stylata*, were probably not accurately accounted for in the collections. Many times they may have been overlooked simply because of their small size. Some species may have also been active before or after the collection period.

The Henrys Fork is a great caddisfly stream. This is ironic because it is well known mainly for its mayfly hatches, many visiting fly fishermen ignoring caddisflies even when the trout are feeding exclusively on them. During the early season, from June 15 to July 15, the hatching and egg-laying of seven major caddisfly species overlap into a continuous blizzard of insects and make themselves collectively the dominant food item for the fish.

Mike Lawson, the resident expert on this spring river, has stated, "Even considering mayfly hatches like the green drake (*E. grandis*) and brown drake (*E. simulans*), caddisflies are the more important insect for fly fishermen until about mid-July."

Where do spring creeks fit into the age profile? They can gush into life as fully developed trout streams from a single source. Often they flow only a short distance before dumping into a larger river. In their brief existence many spring creeks never have a chance to change. They are blessed with an ageless maturity.

Most spring creeks support substantial populations of caddisflies. The species, and even the genera, might be different in eastern and midwestern waters than they are in the Henrys Fork, but the factors determining distribution remain the same.

For some reason caddisflies have never been strongly linked with spring creeks. In all the books and articles extolling the special kind of fly-fishing experiences provided by these streams there is very little about the magnificent caddisfly hatches. There can no longer be any excuse for ignoring the fine fly-fishing available at these times.

Vincent Marinaro, in *A Modern Dry Fly Code*, briefly mentioned the heavy mating flights of caddisflies on the Yellow Breeches, in Pennsylvania but he never identified the species. He wrote, "On the Yellow Breeches Creek, before the first Hendrickson is seen the caddis flies have already put in their appearance. The variety and number of caddis at this time of year is astounding. Light-colored ones and dark ones, small and large, they fill the air above the water in countless hordes, dipping, fluttering, and flying aimlessly as caddisflies will. They are often so thick that the form of an angler a hundred feet away is reduced to an indistinct blur. It is not unusual for an angler to leave the stream after a day's fishing at this time and discover that his waders, from top to toe, are covered with a solid mass of green egg sacs, acquired from the deposit of the industrious caddis. The memory of such an experience is indelibly inscribed on the mind of the unlucky angler when he discovers the tenacious character of these egg sacs in his futile attempt to remove them."

Rex Wheeler, a Pennsylvania friend, made some collections for me on the Yellow Breeches on April 15 this past season. The specimens he sent were identified as *Cheumatopsyche campyla* (Little Sister Sedge), the most prevalent species, *Brachycentrus numerosus* (Grannom), *Hydropsyche slossonae* (Spotted Sedge), *Chimarra aterrima* (Little Black Sedge), *Helicopsyche borealis* (Speckled Peter), and *Goera sp.* (Little Gray Sedge); plus there was a smattering of other, less common species in the sampling. What a wealth of caddisflies!

In such habitats as spring creeks fish feed ultra-selectively. The need for both exact imitation and proper presentation is critical in these places because general patterns and tactics fail so completely. This is why it is important to know and understand the caddisflies that are a major element in spring creeks.

Tail-Water Rivers

Let me admit to a bit of hypocrisy: whenever a dam is proposed I try through individual effort and membership in conservation organizations, to stop its construction; but if I had to make a list of my favorite trout fisheries it would include many tail-water rivers—some of them resulting from the very dams I worked hard to prevent.

A dam can completely change the character of a river. There might be little or no trout fishing at all before it is built either because the water is too warm or too muddy, but the dam forms a lake that can eliminate both of these problems. The lake acts as a settling basin and removes the silt. It also stratifies the water, creating a cold layer at the bottom. Below the dam the river rushes out clear and cool.

These lakes destroy resources that are just as valuable as a new trout fishery, wiping out long stretches of free-flowing river and drowning acres of fertile flood plain. The loss to man and wildlife often cannot be justified for these projects on either economic or moral grounds.

This sad fact, however, does not stop me from fishing, studying, or appreciating these unique rivers. Once the damage is done by a dam there is no reason to ignore the compensating features. In truth the tail-water rivers provide such incredible fly-fishing for anyone who makes the effort to understand them that it is sometimes easy to overlook the tragic aspects.

A lake, besides clearing silt and creating a cold-water layer, also enriches the river. The wide expanse of stillwater produces a steady supply of phytoplankton and funnels this primary food through the outlet. Even when there is only a small dam and a small lake, the enrichment changes the stream into the equivalent of a big river system in terms of food base.[11]

Small-particle collectors generally flourish in tail-water environments. The species may vary from region to region, but genera such as *Psychomyia* (Dinky Purple-Breasted Sedge), *Cheumatopsyche* (Little Sister Sedge), and *Hydropsyche* (Spotted Sedge), all net spinners, abound in trout rivers of this type nearly everywhere. Two other net spinners, *Chimarra* (Little Black Sedge) and *Macronema* (Glossy Wing Sedge), are restricted more to the Midwest and the East, but they are usually abundant in the rivers of these regions. *Brachycentrus* (Grannom), which uses the hairs of the legs as filtering devices, is particularly profuse in more northerly rivers.

The large, beautiful caddisfly *Macronema zebratum* (Glossy Wing Sedge) is found in the larger rivers of the East and Midwest but generally in waters that, being naturally warmer in these climates, support smallmouth bass rather than trout. In tail-water rivers, however, the larvae cluster on small and medium-size rocks in the riffles, their nets (with the finest mesh of any hydropsychid) efficiently straining plankton from the drift. When the pupae emerge, generally in May or June, such an abundant supply of big, slow insects prompts spectacular evening rises on these trout streams.

Directly below a dam the collector-feeding larvae from all genera frequently attain densities of 5,000 or more per square foot. These populations decrease as the river flows away from the lake, the fauna that is almost monotypically collectors at the spill basin of the dam becoming more diverse downstream, although filter-feeding caddisflies remain important as long as the river provides the proper water temperature and bottom structure.

Species of another caddisfly genus, *Ceraclea* (Scaly Wing Sedge), can also be abundant in tail-water rivers, but not for the same reason as the collectors. The larvae of some *Ceraclea* species burrow into and feed on colonies of freshwater sponges; these curious animals in turn thrive in many tail-water situations, especially in the mid-South. The large population of certain *Ceraclea* species can be directly attributable to an abundance of the prey animals.

The diversity of the caddisfly fauna in tail-water rivers, just as in spring creeks, can be limited, but it does not have to be. If the gradient at the dam is very steep with the river churning into white water, fast-current species survive quite nicely. If there is a large input of another food source, such as leaf fall from tree-lined banks, other types of feeders prosper in the river.

From the results of my insect collecting it seems that very cold water discharges from a dam, consistently running below fifty degrees, limit the abundance of caddisflies. In these tail-water rivers, two-winged flies, mainly Chironomidae midges, dominate the fauna—possibly because they are the only insects that can complete their life cycle quickly enough under the cold-water conditions that slow down life-cycle processes.

White River (below Bull Shoals Dam) — Arkansas

There was barely time to mourn the loss of one of the great smallmouth-bass rivers in the country before it blossomed as a cold-water fishery. Planted rainbows and browns grew at phenomenal rates in the White River, this and other tail-water streams in the region suddenly turning the mid-South into a trout mecca.

The White River is now producing world-record fish. Fly fishermen matching the insect hatches cannot realistically hope to catch thirty-pound monsters, these trout gorging on the rich supply of crayfish and minnows, but there are plenty of free-rising fish up to four or five pounds that feed heavily during the early-morning and evening activity.

Starting at the end of March and continuing through April and May, caddisflies appear in successive waves. Eight important species, each appearing in incredible numbers, overlap in May. Some of these caddisflies have very long emergence and flight periods, spread out over months, and remain important throughout the summer. In the fall the numbers of caddisflies begin to decline. Midges gradually become the primary insect to imitate late in the winter, and fly-fishing continues to be an effective method.

The White River is one of the places that I consider a "home stream" because I fish it so often. I stay on it for at least two weeks every year, and I usually manage to stop and try it a few additional times each season during my cross-country trips. I collect insects there regularly.

My sporadic records were augmented by Joe and Cindy Mackicich. They visited the river an average of once a week from March to October in 1979, gathering thousands of specimens. Bob Anderson helped Joe and Cindy, and also collected by himself on three occasions.

The fabulous White River below Bull Shoals Dam is one of the finest trout fisheries in the country. George Purvis (courtesy of the Arkansas Fish and Game Commission)

These samples were used to single out important species and define flight periods. They were not used to compile a species list; that information came from collection records in a professional paper, "A preliminary list of the Arkansas Trichoptera," by J. D. Unzicker, L. Aggies, and L. O. Warren.[12]

The main surprise in our collections was the complete absence of any caddisflies in the family Brachycentridae. Why weren't they there? Or were they there and just missed in the samplings? In other tail-water rivers in other sections of the country certain species, especially in the genus *Brachycentrus*, are well represented; for example, in Montana rivers such as the Ruby and the Beaverhead there are great populations of two western Grannom species, *B. occidentalis* and *B. americanus*. Is this absence of *Brachycentrus* a regional phenomenon or is it just a fact in this particular river? It is a mystery.

The flight periods of four species of *Ceraclea* (Scaly Wing Sedge) overlapped in June, often making it difficult to determine the abundance or value of any single one

SPECIES LIST FOR THE WHITE RIVER

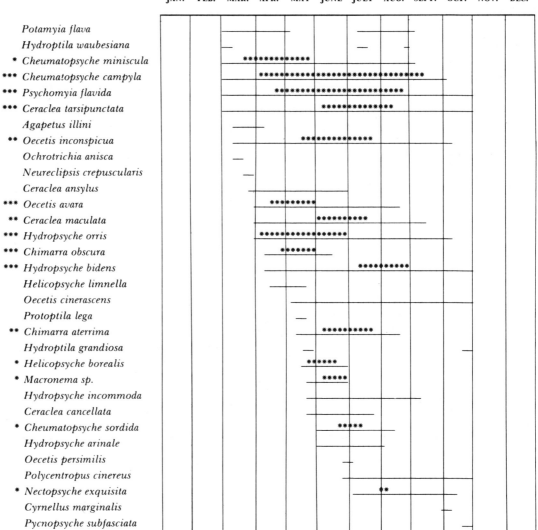

	JAN.	FEB.	MAR.	APR.	MAY	JUNE	JULY	AUG.	SEPT.	OCT.	NOV.	DEC.
Potamyia flava												
Hydroptila waubesiana												
* *Cheumatopsyche miniscula*												
*** *Cheumatopsyche campyla*												
*** *Psychomyia flavida*												
*** *Ceraclea tarsipunctata*												
Agapetus illini												
** *Oecetis inconspicua*												
Ochrotrichia anisca												
Neureclipsis crepuscularis												
Ceraclea ansylus												
*** *Oecetis avara*												
** *Ceraclea maculata*												
*** *Hydropsyche orris*												
*** *Chimarra obscura*												
*** *Hydropsyche bidens*												
Helicopsyche limnella												
Oecetis cinerascens												
Protoptila lega												
** *Chimarra aterrima*												
Hydroptila grandiosa												
* *Helicopsyche borealis*												
* *Macronema sp.*												
Hydropsyche incommoda												
Ceraclea cancellata												
* *Cheumatopsyche sordida*												
Hydropsyche arinale												
Oecetis persimilis												
Polycentropus cinereus												
* *Nectopsyche exquisita*												
Cyrnellus marginalis												
Pycnopsyche subfasciata												

in a particular situation. The star ratings had to be very speculative for these species, but there was no doubt about the overall importance of the genus. They occurred in such numbers that they were considered a nuisance by people living along the river. Much of the activity for this genus, including emergence and egg laying, took place during daylight hours even under the brightest conditions, often causing tremendous late-morning or early-evening feeding sprees by the trout.

In general the flight periods of caddisflies in this river are very extended. Most of the major species are around as adults for at least four months. This could be attributable to the mild climate of the mid-South, which may allow longer survival of the adults, or to the constant temperature of the water released from the dam, which may spread out the emergence dates of the pupae in the first place. The result is a wide selection of caddisflies for trout to choose from. This is no problem when the trout are feeding on them in a fair, democratic manner—come one, come all—but let these fish become selective, each one restricting itself to one species of caddisfly, and the situation gets very sticky. The poor fly fisherman has to change flies to match the particular preference of almost every trout.

The best time to hit the caddisfly hatches on the White River is in April and May. More of the activity then occurs during the day instead of early in the morning or late in the evening as it does later in the summer. If the weather is overcast, or even drizzly, the insects emerge and lay eggs all day and the trout rise steadily, except during the release of great amounts of water from the dam.

One aspect of tail-water fishing that anglers have to adapt to in some rivers is the daily flush of high water. The level of the stream rises so suddenly that fishermen often have to scramble for the bank, but as long as they are not totally oblivious to what is happening around them they usually have enough of a warning.

The sudden rise of water happens during early afternoon below electricity producing dams. The extra water is released at that time to generate a surge of power for the peak period of daily energy consumption. The river remains swollen for two or three hours and then subsides in time for the evening hatch. The short period of high water each day is small inconvenience for the fishing below these dams.

There are now great trout rivers in states that have never had any substantial trout fisheries, Oklahoma and Texas just two examples. Fly-fishing is becoming a big sport in many areas of the South because of these tail-water rivers. Even in regions that already have great trout fishing, these waters are producing more, and often better, angling opportunities.

Caddisfly Habitat—final comments. Even in its most general form the guesswork game of matching caddisflies to habitats, or vice versa, can be very helpful to fly fishermen. With it they can quickly figure out which genera are going to be important in the waters they fish. This is the first step in anticipating major hatches.

The *Distribution Chart* preceding this chapter is a reference tool for the guesswork game. The *Insect Listing*, Chapter 13, should also be considered a reference section. Probably all of Part II should be used like an encyclopedia—when a fly fisherman discovers an important caddisfly species in his stream he can look it up, collate the information, and apply it to the angling situation.

10

Caddisflies as a Food Resource for Trout

Why all the fuss about caddisflies? Why, after all these years, are books and articles suddenly appearing about this insect order? The answer is simple: written accounts about caddisflies are increasing because there is a growing interest in them on the part of fly fishermen.

The dramatic surge of interest in caddisflies by anglers can be partly attributed to a basic piece of equipment known as the stomach pump. This device, consisting of a plastic tube with a rubber bulb at one end, uses suction to recover some of the contents from the stomach of a trout. It provides fly fishermen with an easy way to check what fish have been feeding on, and it allows this without requiring that fish be killed and gutted.

Imagine the chagrin of fly fishermen when they began analyzing what the trout in their local streams were eating. The revelations they were being made privy to nearly everytime they used a stomach pump spurred the grassroots interest in caddisflies. So much tangible proof of the value of these insects made anglers wonder about the prevailing attitudes, and inevitably made them ask which was really more important—mayflies or caddisflies?

Scientific studies cannot settle the argument about which aquatic insect is the most important. Entomologists and biologists have been analyzing the contents of fish stomachs for many years, but for anglers the problem with professional studies is that the data in them does not provide an answer for all trout streams. Usually a scientific paper deals with the feeding habits of trout in one stream—and that is all the

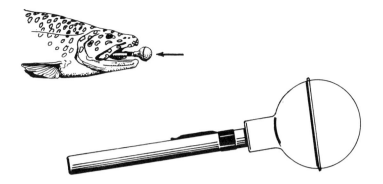

A stomach pump provides reve-
lations everytime the angler
samples a trout.

researcher expects it to cover; fly fishermen, however, often look at the same study and disregard its limitations, wrongly interpolating all kinds of far-reaching conclusions.

No study has been quoted more often by fly fishermen than the one by Dr. Paul Needham in *Trout Streams*, and as a result no study has created more misconceptions. The fallacies are not in the research, but in the use of the data by anglers as a general answer about caddisfly importance.

Dr. Needham never claimed that his study was any more than a limited sampling based on stomach analyses of 377 trout from small streams in upstate New York. Fly fishermen were the ones who took the information out of context and used it to make statements about the comparative importance of the aquatic insects in all streams.

What did this study really prove? It was conducted on brooks with neutral or slightly acid pH and low to moderate productivity. It included only 377 stomach samples total, the collections spread over twelve months. It did not distinguish between wild trout and stocked trout, which would have had greatly different feeding preferences. The trout in the study were mostly between three inches and nine inches. (When was the last time you stalked the mighty three-inch trout?)

The figures on caddisflies as a forage item were impressive enough, ranking them as the most important aquatic insect overall in the streams surveyed. But if anything, the Needham study was slanted *against* caddisflies. It showed that they made up 21.3 percent of the population and constituted 44.7 percent of the aquatic foods taken by trout, but these findings came from a type of habitat where caddisflies were not the dominant order. If the study had included a wider range of trout-stream habitats, or even larger rivers in New York, caddisflies would probably have been more significant.

Other professional papers also have to be considered for what they are: research on specific habitats, often with many unknown or uncharted variables. As long as these limitations are taken into account, there is nothing wrong with utilizing the information in them. Some of the well-known studies contain very interesting observations on the feeding habits of trout.

Here are brief synopses of two American papers:

1. "Bottom fauna and temperature conditions in relation to trout management in St. Mary's River, Augusta County, Virginia." Eugene Surber. July 1951. *The Virginia Journal of Science.*

The St. Mary's River, a tributary of the South River, is a mountain stream. The quantity of potential fish-food organisms is average for freestone streams in the area. There is no breakdown of the percentages of each aquatic order in the St. Mary's, but both caddisflies and mayflies are well represented, the study noting that these insects play an important part in the ecology of all of the mountain streams in Virginia.

Dr. Surber examined the stomach contents of thirty-seven brook trout and fourteen rainbow trout during the open angling season, which was from May 15 to

June 15, in 1936. Overall, terrestrial insects were more important than aquatic forms during the study month. For the brook trout, forty-one percent contained caddisflies (all stages), thirty-eight percent contained stoneflies (all stages), and twenty-two percent contained mayflies (all stages). When all the aquatic insects in the stomachs were considered by number, the caddisflies were most numerous. For the rainbow trout, which did more bottom grubbing than brook trout, seventy-nine percent contained stoneflies, fifty-seven percent contained caddisflies, fifty percent contained two-winged flies. In spite of their importance in the fauna, mayflies were not found in enough rainbow-trout stomachs to be listed.

2. "A preliminary survey of the food of Oregon trout." R. E. Dimick and D. C. Mote. 1934. *Bull. Oregon Agric. Expt. Sta.*, 323: 1-23.

This was a very broad survey, the trout samples coming from a variety of water types in Oregon. There were not enough specimens for a valid breakdown of the information, and even the conclusions in the paper were very general: "Caddisflies are important organisms in the diet of cutthroat, rainbow, and eastern brook trout in Oregon streams and lakes throughout all seasons of the year, particularly in the larger trout. When the pupae leave their cases and swim to the surface of the water to emerge as adults, they fall prey in large numbers to the feeding trout. Then again, as the females are depositing eggs on the water, they are often fed upon by the fish."

"Larger trout" in this study meant fish more than eleven inches long. This study concurred with other general surveys on the gradual shift in diet from midges for very small fish (one to five inches) to mayflies for mid-sized fish (five to ten inches) to caddisflies and stoneflies for large fish (over eleven inches) in running-water habitats.

One of the most comprehensive investigations on the feeding habits of trout was not done in America; the study was conducted on the River Don in Scotland by R. M. Neill. The method of research was so complete that it became the model for future food-preference analyses. The bottom fauna for the area was compared with the organisms recovered from the stomachs of fish feeding in the same area over the same period of time. The ecology of the River Don was charted so carefully that it was possible to describe not just the percentage of each food type eaten, but also the predatory relationship between the brown trout and its environment.

Caddisflies were not a very significant order in the River Don, comprising only about five percent of the total bottom foods. Two-winged flies, mainly black flies (*Simulium*), were the most abundant organism in bottom samples and also the predominant aquatic insect in the stomach samples. Mayflies were second in both abundance and importance. But the surprising fact revealed by this survey was that during the month of July, pupal and adult caddisflies constituted almost thirty percent of the food items eaten. Nothing could better illustrate than this study how the availability and vulnerability of caddisflies increase their desirability to trout out of proportion to their numbers.[1]

Citing studies that show how important caddisflies can be in particular situations is not meant to diminish the role of any other food organism. A check of all feeding surveys points out that on different types of trout water the most important dietary item can be caddisflies, two-winged flies, mayflies, stoneflies, or terrestrial insects. But they also demonstrate that, overall, caddisflies do not deserve a secondary place in the hearts of fly fishermen.

The point that becomes obvious after reviewing a number of studies is that the results are more meaningful when there is a comparison between the percentage of foods available and the percentage of foods taken in a trout stream. This relationship between population and predation can be expressed by a formula that determines a forage ratio.[2]

R. L. Usinger, in *Aquatic Insects of California*, explained how the forage ratio reflects feeding preferences, "A forage ratio of 1 indicates than an organism is being taken at random according to its relative abundance in the environment; a forage ratio of more than 1 indicates that an organism is either being selected in preference to other organisms, or that it is more available than others; and a forage ratio of less than 1 indicates that an organism is either less preferable or less available."

In most studies the forage ratio follows a general pattern; caddisflies are taken more than their percentage in the fauna, two-winged flies are taken slightly more than their percentage in the fauna, mayflies are taken slightly less than their percentage in the fauna, and stoneflies are taken significantly less than their percentage in the fauna. This means that in most stream environments caddisflies, considering all stages of the life cycle, are going to be so available and so preferable that their importance cannot be judged by their numbers alone.

The forage formula also suggests a system for comparing the relative importance of caddisflies and mayflies. By understanding in which environments each order is the dominant form, it is possible to make rough estimates of their value to trout. Caddisflies are going to be important almost everywhere because of their great diversity, but surveys of habitat types reveal where they are normally going to dominate the insect community. Wherever the two orders are equally well represented in the fauna, caddisflies can be rated higher overall than mayflies as a food resource because of their higher forage ratio.

Caddisflies are almost always extremely abundant in tail-water rivers, especially the family Hydropsychidae, and two-winged flies such as midges, not mayflies, are second in total number. Below some dams caddisfly larvae make up to sixty percent of the insect count. The only environmental factors that seem to decrease caddisfly numbers, and in proportion raise the value of two-winged flies in these rivers, are constant cold temperatures and/or wide fluctuations of the outflow water. In tail-water streams, caddisflies are generally the most valuable forage organism.

In any watershed, as the stream gathers tributaries and grows in volume, usually with a corresponding increase in algal drift, caddisflies become more abundant than mayflies in the fauna. In large trout rivers, or even in smaller ones that are mildly enriched from organic pollution, the food-collector species of caddisfly larvae enjoy a competitive advantage, and this is a biological niche well filled by many caddisfly species. In these habitats caddisflies are again the most utilized forage organism.

Where are mayflies the dominant order? In headwater streams they make up a greater percentage of available insects than caddisflies; in those small streams surveyed by Paul Needham the population percentages were 36.9 percent mayflies compared to 21.3 percent caddisflies. This numerical advantage for mayflies continues at least until the stream increases in size to a small freestone river. As long as they are at least ten percent more abundant than caddisflies, mayflies remain more or just as important as a food resource.

Mayflies are also abundant in spring creeks. How they compare to caddisflies in number depends on many other physical factors of the environment—dissolved oxygen, water temperature, current velocity—but generally burrowing and swimming mayfly species thrive in these waters. As forage they are usually not as important to trout as noninsect organisms such as scuds and sow bugs even when they are the dominant insect, but they rate favorably against caddisflies. This probably does not hold true in very alkaline spring creeks, such as the Firehole or the upper Clark Fork, where caddisflies become the dominant order.

These judgments on comparative value are made without any breakdown of the general data. There are many ways to divide the information into categories: percentages the trout eat of each stage in the life cycle, differences in the feeding habits of trout of various size, shifting patterns of predation during different months or even during different times of the day, food preferences of each species of trout.

Any detailed analysis might point out instances where mayflies or caddisflies were particularly important. If the information on feeding was divided into surface and subsurface activity, caddisflies would rate higher as subsurface fare, which includes the predation on larvae, but not as high as mayflies as surface fare. Mayflies are taken more often from off the top of the surface film because of the suicidal drift of the dun, and it is this characteristic that assures the mayfly's position as the darling of the fly-fishing world.

There are many comparisons that would make studies on feeding especially valuable to fly fishermen, but when there are only a few hundred trout in the entire sampling this degree of refinement becomes impossible. It requires thousands of stomach samples, not hundreds, before there are enough fish to split into categories and still guarantee validity.

Would it be possible for fly fishermen, using nothing more sophisticated than stomach pumps, to do their own study? In many ways it is easier for fishermen to gather data in a consistent and comprehensive manner on the feeding habits of trout than it is for professional researchers. In most scientific studies the stomach samples are taken from fish caught by hook and line, not by electroshock equipment. The biologists usually approach anglers along a given stretch of stream and ask if they can gut their dead fish, or else they gather trout by fishing themselves. A large enough group of fly fishermen, working together to sample a particular river or stream, can escape the limitations on time and money that prevent a biologist from fishing, or even collecting stomachs, hundreds of days in a season. Then, with the help of professional entomologists, they can analyze their findings.[3]

The Missouri River Study

Graham Marsh became interested in caddisflies through the same process of discovery that had hooked many other fly fishermen. When he moved to Deer Lodge, Montana, he began using a stomach pump on the brown trout he caught from the upper Clark Fork and found that as much as sixty percent of their diet consisted of caddisfly larvae, pupae, and adults. Since he was not catching as many fish as he thought he should be catching, he started looking at his imitations, the usual array of mayfly and stonefly dry-fly and nymph patterns, as a possible reason for his failures. He suddenly wanted to know a lot more about caddisflies—why, where, when, and how trout feed on them.

Graham took over part of the planning and work for me on a study designed to answer some of these questions. He directed the efforts of eighty-six fly fishermen who come each year from out of state to fish the Missouri River, an informal group of our friends known as the Missouri River Boys. He wrote letters and made telephone calls all winter, finding out when each man or woman would be fishing the river. When they arrived he coordinated their fishing hours and areas like a dictator, leaving nothing to random.

None of the group minded the directions. They were the most important part of the study, out there with stomach pumps and glass vials. They took their work very seriously, even if one of them occasionally moaned a little when he found out he had the dawn shift. "I haven't been out at dawn," John McGrotha said once during the study, "since I gave up stump-knocking for bass."

They started out with a set goal: to sample 2,000 trout between May 1 and October 31. They exceeded that number, catching 2,341 trout (1,879 rainbows and 462 browns). Every vial the group brought in, each containing food organisms from one trout, was marked with the date and hour the fish was caught and the length and species of the fish.

All of the fish were taken with flies, except for seventeen trout that our group gutted for lure and bait fishermen. The majority of the fish collected ranged in size from twelve to twenty inches, but there were trout up to twenty-eight inches (9½ pounds) in length in the sampling. Trout less than twelve inches long were not sampled and not included in the catch total because of the possibility of injury to small fish with the stomach pump.

Description of study area

By the time the Missouri River reaches Holter Lake it has already passed through three dams, Toston, Canyon Ferry, and Hauser. Each of these, and finally Holter Dam itself, acts as a settling basin and removes silt from the river. When it flows out of Holter the water is clear no matter what the month, but it is also greatly enriched by the algal production of the lake. The pH of this section varies from 8.1 to 9.0.

The gradient of the river in this area is gentle. The currents are steady, flowing at approximately 20 to 40 centimeters per second in midriver. For such a large river, more than a hundred yards across in places, it is not very deep on the average, but there are some large fifteen-foot-deep holes. Much of the bottom is gravel, interspersed with beds of rooted vegetation.

With its unbroken surface and weedy channels, the Missouri River is a giant stretch of what fly fishermen call dry-fly water. There is no doubting its productivity as a trout stream. There are a lot of fish and there are big fish; the Montana fish-and-game biologists estimate that in some sections there is a twenty-inch or larger trout for every four square feet of bottom area. Because of the rich insect life and placid character of the water, even these large trout feed on emerging caddisflies, mayflies, and two-winged flies.

Russ Pillen, an aquatic biologist, surveyed the insect fauna in early May just before the beginning of the big summer hatches. He sampled all the bottom types (gravel runs, silt pockets, and weed beds) and combined the numbers into a rough profile of the insect community—mayflies: 36.2 percent, caddisflies: 33.6 percent, two-winged flies: 18.3 percent, miscellaneous: 11.9 percent. The minor insect orders of this river, placed in the miscellaneous category, included beetles (Coleoptera), true bugs (Hemiptera), damselflies and dragonflies (Odonata), stoneflies (Plecoptera), and aquatic moths (Lepidoptera). Other food organisms such as snails, crayfish, leeches, scuds, and slow-swimming fishes were also captured in the sampling, and throughout the season they were a significant part of the trout diet, but no estimates were made of their populations.

The insect samplings showed that caddisflies dominated the fauna immediately below the dam, but that downstream, after the input of numerous large springs and a small tributary, Little Prickly Pear Creek, the populations of mayflies and caddisflies were more balanced. To prevent any distortion of the feeding survey the upper waters, near Holter Dam, were not included in the ten-mile collection area.

Feeding survey

The insects recovered from the stomachs were tabulated numerically, each specimen no matter how small or large counting as one. They were divided into orders, and whenever possible identified to the family or generic level. The insects were also divided into where they were probably taken by the fish: surface or subsurface. The information on food preferences was only broken down into months, but when the data showed more specific feeding patterns the trends were noted in the written record. No totals were made for the year since the entire sampling period only covered six months.

May—
Almost all the surface feeding during May (thirty-four percent of the stomach contents) was on Chironomidae midge pupae and adults. The fish would start rising in the afternoon and continue until just before dark. Nothing else was really available in any numbers for the trout until the last week of May, when a few stray caddisflies began emerging.

The bottom feeding was not focused on any single bottom organism, but the bulge in the "others" category could be attributed to the water boatmen (Hemiptera) in the stomachs during the first week of May. Among caddisflies, the larvae of *Hydropsyche* (Spotted Sedge) were most abundant in the samplings, but this might have been due to their general predominance in the bottom fauna and not to any selectivity on the part of the trout.

Which are more important here: mayflies or caddisflies? There is a cycle on Rocky Mountain rivers—it is the same on the Missouri as it is on the Henrys Fork, North Platte, or Madison (to name a few). June and July are the months when caddisflies are overwhelmingly important, such major genera as *Hydropsyche*, *Brachycentrus*, *Amiocentrus*, *Helicopsyche*, *Lepidostoma*, and *Cheumatopsyche* contributing to the blitz. Right after the Giant Stonefly (*Pteronarcys californica*) finishes its emergence and egg-laying spree on the rivers, at least on the ones that have good populations of the species, caddisflies take over.

MAY	JUNE
caddisflies: 27.1%	caddisflies: 51.2%
mayflies: 17.3%	mayflies: 22.3%
two-winged flies: 36.0%	two-winged flies: 17.6%
other aquatic insects: 19.6%:	other aquatic insects: 8.9%
subsurface: 66%	subsurface: 52%
surface: 34%[4]	surface: 48%

June—
On the Missouri, which lacks the *Pteronarcys* hatch, the caddisfly activity began building up in the second week of June and replaced the Chironomidae midges as the main surface target. By June 15 the heavy flights, especially of *Hydropsyche*

occidentalis (Spotted Sedge), started in early afternoon and lasted until nightfall. The stomach analyses from rising fish indicated heavy feeding on the pupae and adults of the species that were on the water at the moment.

During June the larger *Hydropsyche* larvae also became more significant in the subsurface feeding. Possibly this indicated greater restlessness, and therefore greater drifting, by those larvae that were about to begin pupation. In the stomachs of trout caught in certain gravel runs the *Hydropsyche* larvae were the only organisms present, demonstrating a high degree of selectivity in the feeding.

July—

In the first two weeks of July the caddisfly activity continued unabated, but as the month grew warmer their emergence and egg laying started a little later each day. There was a long period of sunny weather, not unusual for this time of year in Montana, and by the end of July caddisfly activity was happening in the evenings. The mayfly hatches did not start getting heavy until the last two weeks of the month, but with their afternoon emergence period they began dominating the midday surface feeding.

The percentage of feeding on subsurface insects began going down, possibly reflecting the steady depletion of the insect community by the successive hatches. Mayfly nymphs became a more important item in underwater feeding as their activity increased with their approaching emergence dates.

August—

During the month our fishermen killed a few trout in order to check the volume of food in whole stomachs. The purpose was to compare the total weight of all organisms in the stomachs with the weight of all organisms in whole stomachs taken from fish in late June. The volume of food, and almost certainly the numbers of organisms, was about forty percent less than in previous months.

JULY
caddisflies: 50.8%
mayflies: 36.1%
two-winged flies: 7.0%
other aquatic insects: 6.1%
subsurface: 39%
surface: 61%

AUGUST
caddisflies: 36.3%
mayflies: 45.3%
two-winged flies: 8.2%
other aquatic insects: 10.2%
subsurface: 30%
surface 70%

Is there any doubt why trout are harder to catch in August? Even if there are as many fish in the stream as there were in the spring and early summer, the chances of finding them in a feeding mood decrease by forty percent.

The mayfly hatches were steady during the first week of August, but they decreased in intensity after midmonth. Much of the surface feeding in the last two weeks, a hot spell, began at dawn and stopped after only an hour or two. Crane-fly adults, while never abundant, were particularly active and noticeable in these early hours, and they showed up frequently in the samplings.

September—

Beginning early in September there were insects emerging or laying eggs all day long. The activity began at dawn, with the emergence of three Limnephilidae and a Hydropsychidae species. Between eight and nine o'clock in the morning the *Tricorythodes* mayfly spinner fall started, an unbelievable profusion of these small mayflies dying on the water. *Baetis* mayflies hatched in the afternoon. In the evening, starting at six o'clock, clouds of two or three caddisfly species appeared over the river.

It was possible for a fly fisherman to cast to rising trout for fourteen hours a day. The members of the group collecting stomach contents were surprised that subsurface food made up even thirty-six percent of the diet. They expected the percentage of surface food to be even higher than it had been in August, but apparently the increased feeding activity in September also meant more bottom scrounging by the trout. The caddisfly larvae in the samplings included the smallest of the order, three-to five-millimeter *Hydroptila* microcaddis, and the largest of the order, thirty-millimeter *Hesperophylax* limnephilids.

Were there any differences in the feeding preferences of brown trout and rainbow trout? In both July and September, when there was surface food available from morning until dark, there were very noticeable differences. The rainbow trout rose all day, no matter how bright the sun; unless it was cloudy the brown trout rose mainly in the evening when the light was fading. The feeding periods of the brown trout coincided perfectly with the emergence and egg-laying of the caddisflies during these months. Not surprisingly, a greater percentage of their food was caddisfly pupae and adults.

SEPTEMBER
caddisflies: 36.8%
mayflies: 41.7%
two-winged flies:15.5%
other aquatic insects: 6.0%
subsurface: 36%
surface: 64%

OCTOBER
caddisflies: 34.3%
mayflies: 31.5%
two-winged flies:23.5%
other aquatic insects: 10.7%
subsurface: 33%
surface: 67%

October—

The morning emergence and evening egg laying of the predominant *Hydropsyche* species (probably *H. cockerelli*) triggered most of the early and late surface activity. As October progressed the pupae began emerging a little later each day until by the end of the second week, when the hatch petered out, they were coming off the water at noon.

Mayflies, represented by *Baetis* and *Pseudocloeon*, were the main midday insects early in the month. In the third week a concentrated emergence of a multi-brooded caddisfly, *Glossosoma velona* (Little Tan Short-Horn Sedge), made its last appearance, showing up in both pupal and adult stages in the stomach samples. Near the end of October very small insects, the only surface fare available, in the form of microcaddis (family Hydroptilidae) and midges, became important dietary items.

Maybe the late-season feeding on tiny, three- to five-millimeter insects can be partly attributed to the slow-moving nature of the river, which allows fish to feed efficiently even on these small organisms, but it also seems as if the trout keep rising out of habit. They are apparently addicted to feeding on the surface, because even fifteen-inch to twenty-inch trout sip in midges for hours when there are no larger insects on the water. The free-rising tendencies of the fish might be due to conditioning or to a genetic mechanism bred into these wild trout over generations.

General observations on the Missouri River study

The study raised as many questions as it answered. It did not end the argument about which one, caddisflies or mayflies, was a more important food resource for trout, but for this one river it did identify specific moments when one or the other was the dominant aquatic insect.

There may have been a built-in bias in the study against fish that fed near the bottom. Most of the anglers gathering samples preferred to use dry flies, or at least patterns that could be fished in, on, or very near the surface film. Also, on the Missouri River there were weeks in midsummer when, because of drifting weeds, it was impossible to use anything but a dry fly. Many times a trout grubbing deep might not be caught or sampled. Maybe with a different method of procuring specimens the percentages on subsurface feeding would have been higher, but to counteract the preponderance of dry-fly specialists, the nymph, streamer, and wet-fly fishermen in the group worked especially hard.

There were other food items in the stomach samplings besides aquatic insects. Fish and crustaceans made up eighteen percent of the total number of organisms. In early May, sucker fry were an especially important food resource, sixty-four percent of the browns and rainbows sampled containing one or more of them. With the size of the trout in the study (from twelve-inches up), probably the only reason large food items were not utilized even more was because of the great insect populations in the river.

Terrestrial insects constituted seventeen percent of the food items in the stomach samples. In studies on other rivers terrestrials have been as much as sixty percent of the total diet, but that was on smaller streams where the nearby land area had a greater impact. On the Missouri River, with its expanse of water, the insects falling from the banks were distributed over a larger area and among more fish.

The percentages of all food organisms for the six months of the study were, aquatic insects: sixty-two percent; fish and crustaceans: eighteen percent; terrestrial insects: seventeen percent; miscellaneous: three percent.

A number of whitefish (*Prosopium williamsoni*) were also caught and sampled during the study. These fish, often considered a nuisance by anglers seeking trout, were also heavily dependent on surface food, but the stomach checks showed that they seldom fed on caddisfly pupae or adults. Even during a big emergence or egg-laying fall, whitefish ignored caddisflies almost completely. They fed on the drowned cripples collected in the backwaters after the activity, but unless the caddisfly species happened to be one that drifted motionless on the surface they did not feed during the main flush of it.

Maybe the struggling movements of healthy pupae and adults made it difficult for the whitefish to capture them with their tiny mouths. When mayflies were available the whitefish worked steadily, so much so that sometimes it was difficult to find trout during a hatch. One of the secrets for avoiding whitefish and catching trout, when both mayflies and caddisflies were on the water, was to imitate the latter.

Maybe the whole question of relative importance has to be broken down into a region-by-region accounting. Are caddisflies more important than mayflies in the East? Are caddisflies more important than mayflies in the West? Water is water no matter where it is; and streams with the same characteristics and food base are going to support roughly the same types and densities of caddisflies regardless of location. Nevertheless, the answers might be different.

One common angling belief about caddisflies is that they are generally nocturnal. For any fly fisherman who dislikes night fishing this is enough to discredit them. There can be little doubt that if it were true, this would greatly diminish the value of caddisflies to the average fisherman. But it is only part true, and it is even less true in some regions of the country than in others.

There are many species of caddisflies that are active only during full daylight, retiring to hiding places as soon as it becomes dark. Most of the others are not strictly nocturnal, their greatest activity occurring during the reduced light of dusk and dawn. Records of flight periods reveal peaks at sunset and sunrise, the peak at sunset the greater of the two, and show that full darkness actually inhibits flight activity.[5]

Air temperature and humidity probably have as much control over the movements of caddisflies as light intensity. Many species that have emergence and flight periods extending over months bear this out; the adults are active during the day in spring, at dusk in early summer, and at night in midsummer. They emerge and lay eggs when the atmospheric conditions are suitable. When the temperature is so cold that it would freeze them or so hot that it would dehydrate them, they do not fly.

The time of emergence and egg laying for a species can vary not only with the season, but also with the latitude and altitude of the stream. A species that flies actively only during the night in an equatorial climate is often active during the day in a cooler northern region. Maybe it is fortunate for fly fishermen that there are not many trout streams at the equator.[6]

There is a reason that caddisflies might be even more important to fly fishermen in a Rocky Mountain state than they are in an eastern one. During the summer in Montana the daytime temperature can be warm, but as soon as the sun sets it plummets. There are not many nights when caddisflies can move without risk of freezing. There is an apt bumper sticker for the state: "There are only two seasons in Montana; winter and four weeks of bad skiing."

My own observations on the Clark Fork River also showed a definite relationship between air temperature and flight periods. During summer the adults usually became active when the temperature either rose or dropped to sixty-five degrees Fahrenheit. They almost always stopped flying, no matter what the level of light intensity, when it fell to between forty-five and forty degrees.

Similar observations on emergence periods did not reveal such a direct link with air temperature alone. The data seemed to suggest that emergence was controlled, at least in part, by a balance between water temperature and air temperature. The activity ceased entirely when the air temperature was lower than the water temperature, even when the air temperature seemed to be in the ideal range.

Even in the East the early-season species are daytime fliers. As late as June and July the bulk of the activity still occurs in the evening or morning. By the hot spells of August, maybe caddisflies are nocturnal, but anyone familiar with eastern trout streams knows that in the middle of a scorching summer day there are very few aquatic insects flitting about. Mayflies and stoneflies, as well as caddisflies, have important species that emerge and lay eggs during the night in August.

It is not surprising that the various studies on the food preferences of trout do not end up with exactly the same conclusions. They are conducted on different waters, each a unique environment that controls not only which insects are available but also how trout can feed on them. The trout are going to capture insects differently in a fast, broken-water stream than in a slow, smooth one, and differently in a deep, steep-sided stream than in a shallow, spread-out one. There are many types of trout habitat.

Fly fishermen can apply the findings of these studies to their own fishing, but why should they stop with general information? Using a simple stomach pump, one person, or even better a small group, can discover the food preferences of the trout in their own favorite stream. They can outline blocks of time, days or weeks, when the fish selectively concentrate on one kind of insect.

Stomach sampling is a natural extension of angling entomology. Anyone interested in the insects of trout streams can use his knowledge better because the stomach contents reveal what is available and what is vulnerable. In the process, the fly fisherman might also find out why there has been so much fuss about caddisflies lately.

Emergence and Egg-laying Charts

The Emergence and Egg-laying Charts cover the top twenty-five species in each of five regions—East, Midsouth, Midwest, Rocky Mountain, and Pacific Coast. Each species list includes the most important caddisflies from a wide variety of water types, from large streams to major rivers, in a particular region and designates the main emergence periods and the egg-laying periods for these species.

The exact dates of emergence will vary with altitude and latitude (see Chart A). They will even vary from season to season because of the effect of weather conditions on emergence. The sequence in which the species emerge, however, will remain the same from year to year.

the symbol _____ indicates the general period when adults can be present in significant numbers

the symbol ********** indicates the prime periods of emergence and egg-laying

When will a particular species emerge within a region? Emergence charts from a number of different streams seem to show the following pattern for latitude if all other factors are roughly equal—a spring species appears earlier in the southern section of a region than it does in the northern section; a midsummer species appears at approximately the same time in either the southern or northern sections; a fall species appears later in the southern section of a region than it does in the northern section.

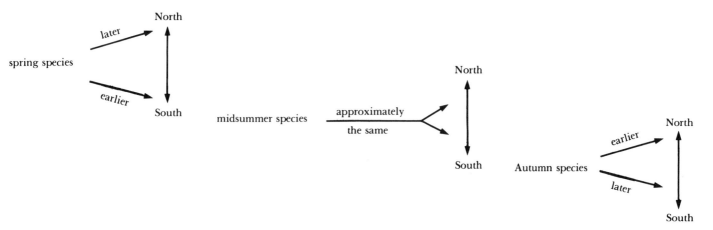

There is a "focus area" given for each region. These focus areas are roughly in the center of their regions; for example, in the East the focus area is northern Pennsylvania. The hatches to the north or south of the focus areas are usually on a slightly different timetable; a fly fisherman can adjust the schedule to fit his home waters.

EAST
(these emergence and egg-laying dates apply specifically to northern Pennsylvania)

| | JAN. | FEB. | MAR. | APR. | MAY | JUNE | JULY | AUG. | SEPT. | OCT. | NOV. | DEC. |

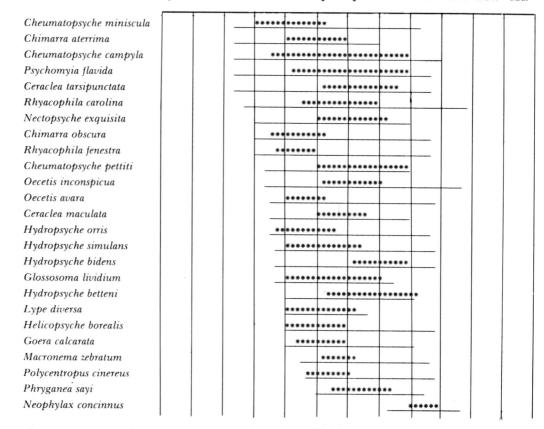

Apatania incerta
Limnephilus submonilifer
Cheumatopsyche pettiti
Brachycentrus numerosus
Lepidostoma vernalis
Chimarra aterrima
Glossosoma nigrior
Hydropsyche bronta
Hydropsyche sparna
Cheumatopsyche harwoodi
Helicopsyche borealis
Hydroptila hamata
Platycentropus radiatus
Hydropsyche morosa
Psilotreta labida
Rhyacophila fuscula
Oecetis inconspicua
Mystacides sepulchralis
Hydatophylax argus
Psychomyia flavida
Polycentropus cinereus
Nyctiophylax moestus
Ceraclea transversa
Pycnopsyche guttifer
Frenesia missa

MIDSOUTH
(these emergence and egg-laying dates apply specifically to eastern Tennessee)

| | JAN. | FEB. | MAR. | APR. | MAY | JUNE | JULY | AUG. | SEPT. | OCT. | NOV. | DEC. |

Cheumatopsyche miniscula
Chimarra aterrima
Cheumatopsyche campyla
Psychomyia flavida
Ceraclea tarsipunctata
Rhyacophila carolina
Nectopsyche exquisita
Chimarra obscura
Rhyacophila fenestra
Cheumatopsyche pettiti
Oecetis inconspicua
Oecetis avara
Ceraclea maculata
Hydropsyche orris
Hydropsyche simulans
Hydropsyche bidens
Glossosoma lividium
Hydropsyche betteni
Lype diversa
Helicopsyche borealis
Goera calcarata
Macronema zebratum
Polycentropus cinereus
Phryganea sayi
Neophylax concinnus

MIDWEST
(these emergence and egg-laying dates apply specifically to the lower peninsula of Michigan)

	JAN.	FEB.	MAR.	APR.	MAY	JUNE	JULY	AUG.	SEPT.	OCT.	NOV.	DEC.
Limnephilus submonilifer				*******								
Cheumatopsyche pettiti				************								
Brachycentrus numerosus				****								
Chimarra aterrima				************								
Glossosoma nigrior					*********							
Brachycentrus lateralis				******								
Hydropsyche sparna					*********							
Rhyacophila manistee					*****							
Goera stylata					*****							
Platycentropus radiatus					******************							
Helicopsyche borealis					************							
Hydropsyche slossonae					***************							
Neureclipsis crepuscularis					*******							
Molanna uniophila					**************							
Ptilostomis ocellifera						*****************						
Lype diversa						*************						
Nectopsyche albida						*******************						
Limnephilus sericeus						******************						
Lepidostoma togatum						*************						
Oecetis inconspicua						***************						
Hydatophylax argus						******						
Hydropsyche recurvata							******					
Pycnopsyche lepida							*****************					
Pycnopsyche guttifer								*************				
Neophylax fuscus									******			

ROCKY MOUNTAIN
(these emergence and egg-laying dates apply specifically to Wyoming)

	JAN.	FEB.	MAR.	APR.	MAY	JUNE	JULY	AUG.	SEPT.	OCT.	NOV.	DEC.
Psychoglypha subborealis										*****************		
Brachycentrus occidentalis					*******							
Dolophilodes aequalis						******						
Oecetis disjuncta						*****						
Glossosoma traviatum						******						
Hydropsyche occidentalis						**********						
Arctopsyche grandis						*******						
Cheumatopsyche campyla						****************						
Amiocentrus aspilus						*******						
Limnephilus spinatus						*********						
Hydropsyche cockerelli								**********************				
Cheumatopsyche pettiti						******************						
Glossosoma alascense						********						
Lepidostoma pluviale						****************						
Helicopsyche borealis						***********						
Rhyacophila bifila						***************						
Hesperophylax incisus						****************						
Oecetis avara						************						
Leucotrichia pictipes						****						
Hydropsyche oslari							*******					
Psychomia flavida						********						
Mystacides alafimbriata							*******					
Brachycentrus americanus							**********					
Rhyacophila coloradensis							***********					
Dicosmoecus jucundus								*******				

PACIFIC COAST

(these emergence and egg-laying dates apply specifically to Oregon)

	JAN.	FEB.	MAR.	APR.	MAY	JUNE	JULY	AUG.	SEPT.	OCT.	NOV.	DEC.
Brachycentrus occidentalis				**********	*****							
Glossosoma traviatum					**********							
Hydropsyche occidentalis					**********							
Cheumatopsyche campyla					*****	**************	*****					
Amiocentrus aspilus					**********							
Hydropsyche cockerelli								*****	**************	*****		
Hydropsyche californica						************						
Cheumatopsyche pettiti						************						
Rhyacophila grandis						******						
Helicopsyche borealis					*************							
Lepidostoma rayneri						******						
Glossosoma califica						**********						
Rhyacophila bifila						**********						
Oligophlebodes sierra						*********						
Hesperophylax incisus						************						
Oecetis avara					**************							
Lepidostoma unicolor							**************					
Mystacides alafimbriata					************							
Chyranda centralis						************						
Brachycentrus americanus						************						
Rhyacophila vaccua							************					
Dicosmoecus atripes									*******			
Dicosmoecus gilvipes									*******			
Neophylax splendens										*****		
Neophylax rickeri										*****		

Insect Listing

A fly fisherman is not interested in all caddisflies. He is concerned with the ones that are important to his success. When he is out on his favorite water he is looking for those species that are abundant enough and vulnerable enough to control the way fish feed.

In this section the list is further restricted to caddisflies that are important in trout streams. The decision on which families, genera, and species to include is based on the thousands of collections done for this book all over this country and Canada. Even so there are undoubtedly some important species that have been overlooked during the search.

All the caddisflies listed here can be dominant enough to force trout into a pattern of selective feeding in one or more types of trout streams. Some genera are more widespread and overwhelming than others; for example, the genus *Hydropsyche* (Spotted Sedge) is not only the most important trout-stream caddisfly but also, as a group with so many common species, overall the most important trout stream insect of any type in North America. All the genera that have been included, however, can be critically involved in fly-fishing success at some time and place. The comments on the individual species use the terms—in order of ascending rank—common, abundant, and very abundant to define their importance.

Common names

Many fly fishermen prefer to use common names rather than scientific ones. A few caddisflies are already well known to the angling public. The terms Grannom (*Brachycentrus*), White Miller (*Nectopsyche*), and Dark Blue Sedge (*Psilotreta*) all refer to specific genera. But caddisflies have never been comprehensively covered in angling books and articles beyond the family level. Many important genera that need common names have never had one. A rough system of nomenclature has been used here to name the adults of these genera. It follows a few simple rules to make the descriptive terms more explanatory.

Size. Any reference to the size of an adult insect is correlated to both a hook number and length:

DESCRIPTIVE TERM	MATCHING HOOK SIZE	LENGTH OF INSECT
dinky	18, 20, and smaller	3mm to 6mm
little	14, 16	8mm to 10mm
medium	10, 12	11mm to 13mm
great	4, 6, 8	14mm to 19mm
giant	2 and larger	20mm and larger

The family Hydroptilidae is not included in this sizing scale. All of the genera in this particular family are referred to by the term microcaddis, a name used by professional entomologists.

Wing characteristics. These insects can often be very easy to identify to family or generic level just by their external appearance. The wings of some caddisflies have a very distinctive shape or structure, and for these there is a description of the feature; for example, the Eastern Box Wing Sedge (*Ironoquia*).

The color in a name usually refers to the top wing of the adult. The word can either mean a pattern of colors, for example, spotted or speckled, or the actual color itself, for example, brown or black. The only irregular terminology found here is the word "blue," an ancient fly-fishing substitute for dark gray; for example, the name Dark Blue Sedge for the genus *Psilotreta*. The terms "light" or "dark" before a color describe the shade of that particular color.

Body color. Adult insects are referred to by the color of their body in only three instances, and with each caddisfly it is because the body color is so distinctive: Green Sedge (*Rhyacophila*), Giant Orange Sedge (*Dicosmoecus*), and Dinky Purple Breasted Sedge (*Psychomyia*).

Physical traits. For some genera a very distinctive physical feature suggests a descriptive name. For example, Long Horn Sedge refers to the exceptionally long antennae of the genus *Oecetis* (and can actually refer to all the family Leptoceridae).

Geographic distribution. In genera where all species are restricted to a single part of the continent the terms "eastern" or "western" are sometimes used. "Eastern" includes the provinces and states from the Atlantic Coast west to approximately Minnesota, and "western" includes the provinces and states from the Rocky Mountain region west to the Pacific Coast. This split is a recognition of the fact that the Great Plains, referred to by early settlers as the American Desert, forms a geologic barrier that in the past and currently prevents some caddisflies from spreading across the continent. An example of this nomenclature is the Little Western Dark Sedge (*Oligophlebodes*).

Seasonal designation. When all the species in a genus emerge in one season the terms "spring," "summer," "autumn," and "winter" are sometimes used to designate the times they are important to anglers—for example, the Dot Wing Winter Sedge (*Frenesia*).

Time-of-day designation. When the activity periods for both emergence and egg laying for all species in a genus occurs mainly at one time of the day there is a qualifying term such as "morning" or "twilight;" for example, the Little Red Twilight Sedge (*Neureclipsis*).

Environmental preference. The type of stream or terrestrial habitat a genus is found in is designated when all species are restricted to a particular environment; for example, the Dark Eastern Woodland Sedge (*Lype*).

Habit. Some caddisflies have peculiar habits that help fly fishermen recognize them. The lake genus, *Banksiola*, is commonly known as the Traveller Sedge in the Northwest because the adults run across the surface.

Synonomy

Sometimes the scientific name of an insect changes and this causes all kinds of problems for fly fishermen. For one thing it means that an angler reading an older fly-fishing book cannot check the information in it about a species such as *Stenophylax scabripennis* in any modern angling book because they will probably list it only under a new genus, *Pycnopsyche*. Names change because the study of insects is still a young and growing science. Professionals are constantly learning new facts and, as they do, they revise and refine the system of scientific nomenclature.

What can modern angling writers do to help their readers? In their books they can use the same system of nomenclature that is used in the most modern text on the subject. Then they can identify their source material so that future readers can trace the names. Also, they can list the widely used previous names of a particular species.

Reference to scientific keys

Professional entomologists use scientific keys to identify specimens to species level. More fly fishermen all the time are learning how to do the same thing. For the convenience of anyone who wants to identify his own specimens the entomological books and papers with the best keys for the male adults of each genus are listed after the section on it (for more information on using scientific keys see Chapter 12, Collecting and Identifying Caddisflies).

The foresight method of using this book

Fly fishermen should ask themselves two questions before a fishing trip:

One, what type of stream will I be fishing? Answer the question and check both Chapter 9, Caddisfly Habitat, and the Distribution Charts, to find out which caddisflies are going to be in that kind of trout water.

Two, what time of year will I be fishing? Answer the question and check the Emergence Charts for the correct section of the country to find out which of the caddisflies found in that stream will be active then.

The answers to these two questions can tell fly fishermen which flies to use and how to use them. Anglers can look up those caddisflies that will be present and active in the Insect Listing that follows, finding out there which patterns and tactics are recommended. If they feel it is necessary they can also review Part One, the discussions on tactics, before the trip.

Family Brachycentridae (tube-case maker)
(represented by 6 genera in North America)

Shelter type: larvae build a case of plant material or pebbles; for some genera the case is rectangular and for others it is round.

Typical feeding habits of the larvae: larvae filter particles from the drift by holding up their legs or scrape organic matter from rock surfaces.

Typical method of emergence: pupae swim to the surface and emerge in open water.

Typical egg-laying habits: females either swim underwater or flop on the surface and release a ball of eggs.

This is the only family among the North American tube-case makers whose larvae lack a prominent hump either on the top or the sides of the first abdominal segment. Without this spacing hump the larvae cannot efficiently create a self-sustained flow of water through the case, a renewable source of dissolved oxygen, and in part because of this they cannot survive in stillwater habitats. They are restricted to moving-water environments, either streams or the wave-washed shores of lakes.[1]

The two major trout-stream genera are *Brachycentrus* (Grannom) and *Amiocentrus* (Little Western Weedy-Water Sedge). *Brachycentrus* can inhabit swifter currents than *Amiocentrus*, the larvae of some species fastening their cases on the exposed surfaces of rocks in flows of 100 centimeters per second or more. *Amiocentrus* attaches its case to moss or rooted vegetation in quieter areas, these larvae reaching their greatest abundance in spring creeks and weedy rivers of the Northwest. Both genera are very dependent on algae, mainly the hard-shelled diatoms, as a food source, but plant particles and animal matter are also in their diet.

genus *Amiocentrus* (Little Western Weedy-Water Sedge)
(1 known species in the genus)

Generalized description of the adult:
adult length up to 7.5mm
WING: dark brown
BODY: greenish brown
LEGS: brown

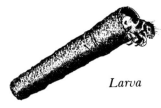

Larva

Amiocentrus

Adult

The single species in this genus, *A. aspilus*, has a wide range throughout the West. It is especially abundant in spring creeks and spring rivers, the larvae found on rooted weeds and in bottom mosses. The larvae, pupae, and adults are all worth imitating—there are incidents in my angling notes of trout feeding fussily on them from the Fall River in California to the Beaverhead River in Montana (and, of course, see the Henrys Fork species list).

Aquatic biologist Rich Hafele commented on the distribution of *A. aspilus* in Oregon for me, "The Metolius in central Oregon, the Deschutes in the eastern part of the state, and the McKenzie in the western part are examples of the weedy types of habitat that have populations of this species. The emerging pupae get some lovely fish feeding just under the film during the evening hatches in these rivers.

In a study by Dr. N. H. Anderson on the Metolius River the larvae of *A. aspilus* were found in densities of up to 700 per square foot in beds of *Ranunculus* weeds. They drifted at very high rates, case and all, during spring and early summer.[2]

Important species
(The only species, *A. aspilus*, used to be included in older taxonomies in the genus *Micrasema*.)

A. aspilus W
(= *Micrasema aspilus*)
The emergence and egg-laying periods are spread out from March to October. My series of collections from Montana and Idaho streams show a main peak in late June and a smaller one in early September.

General imitations for *Amiocentrus*:

LARVA:	Dark Cased-Caddis Nymph (sizes 12, 14, 16)
PUPA:	Brown and Bright Green Deep Sparkle Pupa; Brown and Bright Green Emergent Sparkle Pupa (sizes 16, 18, 20)
ADULT DRY:	Lawson Spent Partridge Caddis; Henryville (sizes 16, 18, 20)
ADULT WET:	Brown and Green Diving Caddis (sizes 16, 18, 20)

ADULT KEYS:

Denning, D. G. 1956. "Trichoptera." Pages 237-270, in *Aquatic Insects of California*, R. L. Usinger, ed. Univ. of California Press, Berkeley. This book has good illustrations of the identifying characteristics for *A. aspilus* (under the old generic name *Micrasema*).

genus *Brachycentrus* (American Grannom)
(9 known species in the genus)

Generalized description of the adult:
adult length up to 13mm

WING:	varies from almost white to tan to greenish brown
BODY:	varies from bright green to greenish brown
LEGS:	vary from brown to almost black

Larva

Brachycentrus

Adult

Brachycentrus *larva rapelling*

The famous Grannom wet fly, an imitation of a British species of this genus, was originated by Charles Bowlker and included in *The Art of Angling* (1780). With its dubbed body of rough fur and scraggly wing, it accounted for many trout on the chalkstreams before wet flies were banned from these waters.

The current minirevival of downwing wet flies in this country is due to the continued effectiveness of such flies. They remain a good imitation of drowned adult egg layers, insects that lack the silvery coat of air bubbles possessed by living underwater swimmers. With *Brachycentrus* the mortality of females seems to be high, the adults sprawling helplessly in or just under the surface film. Specific Grannom imitations are effective when fished dead drift in the same area.

It is no fluke that this was one of the first caddisflies to become commonly known to American fly fishermen. It is a showboat insect, popping out in midafternoon in full glory on some of the most famous Eastern rivers—angling shrines such as the Beaverkill and Esopus. Who could miss the vast flights or the resulting gluttony of the trout? (Not such angling entomologists as Louis Rhead or Preston Jennings, who, although they lamented their inability to catch the actively feeding fish, recognized the importance of the Grannom.)

The abundance of this genus has long been a mixed blessing for eastern fly fishermen. It was evident from both stomach samplings and direct observations that all stages—larva, pupa, and adult—were part of the trout's diet, but for years the standard flies produced the same poor or mediocre results. Only the old style wet patterns consistently caught fish when the adults were so evident on the water. Many anglers refused to use these flies because they considered them anachronistic attractors. Such misconceptions came from a failure to understand the egg-laying habits of caddisflies.

The first effective dry fly for matching the spent females was Larry Solomon's Delta-Wing Caddis, this pattern achieving much of its initial word-of-mouth reputation because of its deadliness during the Grannom flights on the Beaverkill. It worked when higher-floating downwing styles did not, mimicking the collapsed position of the natural by the way it sprawled flush in the film.

My own Sparkle Pupa series, especially the Emergent, gained much of its early popularity in the East because it solved the enigma of the pupal stage on the renowned rivers. Everytime someone used a matching pupal fly and caught fish during the emergence period, there were enough other anglers around asking questions to quickly spread the news about these imitations.

The Dark Cased-Caddis Nymph, clipped into a four-sided shape, and the trick of mimicking the white anchor line were a deadly combination on eastern rivers last year. When the season opened in April, this fly and a white leader, fished deep with either added lead wraps or a sinking line, worked extremely well on the big Beaverkill below Roscoe.

The larva builds the rectangular, chimney-shaped case so familiar to anyone who has picked up rocks from the stream bottom. Most of the time the insect keeps its case attached to the rocks, fastening the front lip down with silk in a ten-to twenty-minute procedure. During the day it feeds by scraping algae off the bottom, but at night it holds up its second and third pairs of legs and filters drifting particles from the current.

G. W. Gallepp, in his 1974 paper "Diel periodicity in the behaviour of the caddisfly, *Brachycentrus americanus* (Banks)," noted how the larvae use an anchor line "After fastening the beginning of a silk-like line to the substrate, they released the substrate, holding only the line. By lengthening the line, larvae moved downstream until they encountered a suitable substrate and again began crawling." The fine observations in this paper are my source on the activities of the larvae.

Gary Borger, in *Nymphing* (1979), was the first angling author to report this rapelling activity for *Brachycentrus* larvae. In this book he used his training as a biologist to make many other good observations on the appearance and behavior of various aquatic insects.

The pupae emerge in the surface film, apparently drifting for fair distances before they can fly away. In my general fly-fishing experiences all important species have had this prolonged period of hesitation, but this conclusion is based on the methodical way trout feed on them rather than on actual observations of pupae themselves.

I have only watched one specimen emerge, a pupa of *B. americanus*[3] that I scooped up during an August hatch on the Yellowstone River. I timed the escape process and made notes: "The insect lay in a puddle in my palm. It quickly pulled one wing free, but it rolled over on its side as it struggled to loosen the other. Once both wings were out of the sheath it began wriggling convulsively, the shudders beginning at the thorax and working back down the abdomen. Between periods of pulling the insect remained still, apparently in a state of exhaustion. While it was working it slowly slipped forward and up out of the pupal skin. After an elapsed time of thirty-seven minutes it extricated itself completely and began spreading its wings."

The adult females become very important during egg laying. They carry a ball of eggs at the tip of the abdomen. They either land on the surface and drop this egg mass or they swim underwater and deposit it. They drift for a long time, often dying in such great numbers that the water is littered with the spent bodies.

The egg laying of *Brachycentrus* can create a problem when other caddisflies are doing the same thing. The females of this genus might ride the surface serenely, but those of most others do not—they dive, swim, and kick about vigorously. When *Brachycentrus* egg layers and those of another major genus are on the water in roughly equal abundance, they present a choice to feeding trout. Frequently the result with dual, or even multiple, egg-laying flights is that one fish will be selectively taking one caddisfly while his neighbor is selectively taking another.

During a conversation we had at a Theodore Gordon Flyfishers luncheon, Larry Solomon proposed the best theory I have heard yet to explain why the trout do not all feed on the same insect: "The fish will stay with the one he sees the most of at first, and depending on his position in relation to the currents that might be either active or inactive egg layers."

What a fly fisherman must do in these situations is either pick out one trout and work on him, changing flies if necessary to match its performance, or else he can make a presentation to many rising fish and just skip the ones that refuse his particular imitation.

The American Grannom rates second only to *Hydropsyche* (Spotted Sedge) as an important caddisfly for trout-stream fly fishermen. It is distributed from coast to coast, with major species in the East, Midwest, and West. Its habits as a pupa and adult are tailored to the needs of both trout and angler: it appears in heavy concentrations, it is active during daylight hours, and it is very vulnerable to predation. It deserves its fame.

Important species

B. americanus E, M, W
(= *B. similis*)
This species is richly represented in medium and large trout rivers throughout the West and Midwest, and to a lesser degree in the northern regions of the East. It emerges early in the morning during July and August (creating such great fly-fishing that it is almost a joy getting up before dawn).

Almost any major trout river in the West could serve as an example of prime habitat, from the Klamath in California or the Cowichan in Vancouver to the upper Pecos in New Mexico or the Black in Arizona. In the Midwest it is not only abundant in big rivers but also in smaller ones; for example, a survey by Wisconsin biologists reveals good populations of *B. americanus* in rich watersheds such as the Plover, Deerskin, and East Branch of the Eau Claire.

B. fuliginosus E, M
This species has been written about more than any other in the genus by angling authors, but its fame might be overrated. For example, Larry Solomon has informed me that *B. fuliginosus* was relatively rare in the eastern specimens he sent to Dr. Oliver Flint for identification. In my own samplings and in entomological records it has not been a very common species.

B. lateralis E, M
B. lateralis and *B. numerosus* are closely associated in eastern and midwestern rivers, with the former inhabitating deeper and faster sections. Both species have very concentrated emergence periods, appearing in successive waves. *B. lateralis* usually follows its sister species by one to two weeks.

B. numerosus E, M
Which species produces the famous May hatches on the Beaverkill, the Esopus, the West Branch of the Ausable—or on most other eastern trout rivers? It is *B. numerosus*. Emergence begins in the afternoon and egg laying starts in the early evening. These activities happen each year with a wonderful predictability on waters from Quebec to North Carolina.

B. occidentalis W (also found in the Midwest, but not as commonly)
Every spring, fly-fishing friends around the West have reported great hatches of a dark, brown-and-green species. The activity was described as so heavy and so widespread that, if all accounts were about the same insect, it had to be a very common caddisfly in the Rocky Mountains. But which one was it?

The fine fly-fishing caused by this mysterious caddisfly occurs in late April or early May, a special time in the West—the rivers are clear because the runoff has not begun yet and there are no crowds, even on the most popular streams, because the tourist season has not begun yet. Most of the rivers are open year-round for fishing.

I received the same reports about abundant insects and feeding trout on the following streams from the following anglers: Ruby River (Montana), Nevin Stephenson and Dick Williams; North Fork of the Platte (Wyoming), Barry Hawkins; South Fork of the Platte (Colorado), Lew Tarrows; Henrys Fork of the Snake (Idaho, near St. Anthony), Mike Lawson; and the McKensie River (Oregon), Dick Pine.

Such a wide geographical distribution indicated that this caddisfly was probably important in most of the large, cool trout streams of the West, from Canada south to Utah, sharing this type of habitat with *B. americanus*.

Last spring I traveled and collected samples, confirming that it was indeed the same species in all regions, *B. occidentalis*. On many of the streams I also had the chance to fish, finding superb action with both Emergent Pupa and Dancing Caddis imitations.

General imitations for *Brachycentrus*:

LARVA: Dark Cased-Caddis Nymph (sizes 10, 12, 14)

PUPA: Brown and Bright Green Deep Sparkle Pupa; Brown and Bright Green Emergent Sparkle Pupa (size 10, 12, 14, 16)

ADULT: Brown and Green Dancing Caddis, Solomon's Delta Wing Caddis in appropriate colors (size 10, 12, 14, 16)

ADULT WET: Brown and Green Diving Caddis (size 10, 12, 14, 16) (For lighter-colored species the ginger series of pupal and adult imitations can be substituted.)

ADULT KEYS:

The information for identifying the species of this genus is not available in any single paper or book, but the angler can find keys for the important trout stream species in the following books:

Ross, H. H. 1944. "The caddis flies, or Trichoptera, of Illinois." *Bull. Illinois Nat. Hist. Surv. No. 23.*

Denning, D. G. 1965. "Trichoptera," in *Aquatic Insects of California*, ed. by R. L. Usinger, pp. 237-270. Berkeley and Los Angeles: University of California Press.

Family Glossosomatidae (saddle-case maker)
(represented by 6 genera in North America)

(in older entomologies this group was often included in the closely related family, Rhyacophilidae)

Shelter type: larvae build a portable, turtle-shell-like case. This is a simple case of small stones, lacking the inner matrix of spun silk found in the cases of the more advanced families.

Typical feeding habits of the larvae: the larvae are scrapers, grazing on tops of rocks in riffles.

Typical method of emergence: the pupae swim to the surface.

Typical egg-laying habits: the females dive under the surface and paste their eggs to the rocks.

The six genera of this family can be roughly separated by water-temperature and oxygen requirements, progressing from colder to warmer in the following order: *Anagapetus, Glossosoma, Matrioptila, Agapetus, Protoptila,* and *Culoptila.*

The debut from relative obscurity for this group did not occur until a 1972 article in my column, "Primer of Stream Entomology," in *Fly Fisherman* magazine. That piece featured the dominant trout-stream genus, *Glossosoma*, outlining the general biology and emergence habits of western species.

This family is the most primitive of the case makers, but like some other primitive groups it thrives in environments that it is ideally adapted to exploit. All the genera show up in trout-stream samplings, although only two, *Glossosoma* and *Protoptila*, become generally abundant. *Protoptila* is found mainly in the warmer rivers of the central basin, important in the riffle areas of some smallmouth-bass waters and marginal trout streams. *Glossosoma* is the major representative in trout waters.

Protoptila is not listed under the generic sections, mainly because its warmer water habitat and very small size (hook size 26, 28) diminish its importance to the trout fisherman, but future researchers might find situations where even the tiny imitations of the larvae, pupae, or adults could be needed. H. H. Ross, in *Evolution and Classification of the Mountain Caddisflies*, provides the clues to where midwestern angling entomologists should look, "They frequent a definitely warmer type of stream and often abound in some of the cool, large rivers. Apparently clear water during most of the year is a prerequisite for their existence, as is also a fairly rapid flow."

Dr. George Roemhild of Montana State University has also found that *Protoptila tenebrosa* is common in some of the thermal trout streams of his area, waters such as the Madison River and Firehole River, but that even in these steams the genus is overshadowed by more abundant caddisflies. An equally small but much more numerous microcaddis, *Leucotrichia pictipes* (Ring Horn Microcaddis), emerges and lays eggs at the same time as *P. tenebrosa*.

genus *Glossosoma* (Little Tan Short-Horn Sedge)
(25 known species in North America; all but 3 in the mountain West)

Generalized description of the adult:
adult length up to 10mm
WING: varies from a very pale tan to a medium brown
BODY: greenish brown
LEGS: varying shades of brown

Larva

Glossosoma

Adult

Surely, in this age of imitation, every important trout food has been at least identified and copied with some sort of pattern. In the course of all the recent research on nymphs and larvae it could not have been possible, for example, to completely overlook a predominant insect in the trout diet. Or could it? Surprisingly, a caddisfly larva that is extremely abundant, vulnerable, and available has never even been mentioned as worth imitating; and yet this insect often forces trout into selective subsurface feeding during the summer and fall.

The inconspicuous species of *Glossosoma* have never been highly rated even among caddisflies, possibly because they are case makers as larvae and sporadic emergers as pupae. They are not particularly prominant as adults either. They are easy to dismiss overall as only a secondary food source for trout, one of little consequence to the fly fisherman.

Such an assessment, however, has been a serious mistake, underestimating one of the most important insects in cool, running waters. Not just among caddisflies, but among the entire fauna in many trout rivers the larvae, pupae, and adults of *Glossosoma* create more selective feeding situations than any other organism at certain times of the year.

The larvae, with their distinctive turtle-shell-like cases, inhabit a specialized area in streams. The portable shelter provides the protection that allows them to feed on the exposed upper surfaces of rocks. Crawling slowly over a stone, the insects scrape diatoms and fine organic particles off of it. They can feed while entirely underneath the case, silk skirts along the sides forming a tight seal against the current. There are two identical openings on the bottom with a strap of silk across the middle. The larvae easily reverse position inside the case, feeding or moving with head in either direction.

This case, adhering so strongly to the stone, should apparently eliminate the insect as a drift item. However, the unique feature of the case is that it is unsuitable for enlargement. Periodically, the larva simply abandons the old one and builds a new shelter.

These stages of abandonment are approximately synchronized for an entire brood class. The larvae crawl free of the case, frequently washing into the drift. This apparent total waste of a case-making effort occurs a number of times during the life cycle. Who carries size 16 imitations of these larvae? Virtually nobody; but these insects can be the predominant organism drifting in the current. The caseless larvae, with no swimming ability, are completely helpless until they regain the bottom.

In a Minnesota stream, the species *G. intermedium* reached drift rates of 350 per hour per foot of stream width, an incredible influx of available prey—certainly enough to capture the complete attention of any feeding trout.[4]

From May to July, when the larvae are reaching full growth, this genus, with its caseless drift, creates a unique situation. The dominant species in an area can completely control the dawn and dusk activity of a stream. The larvae form a food supply in the current that concentrates both forage fish and gamefish in or below riffles that have high populations of the insect.

Check the typical fly fisherman's nymph selection, however, and he seldom has even an adequate substitute to press into duty, and even if he did he would have no inkling of where and when to use it because the larva has never been described in angling literature, only the case, and neither has its habit of free drift.

It is always wise to check a stomach sample or spread a drift net to determine the presence of caseless larvae, but actually it is such a common occurrence that a *Glossosoma* imitation, with the peculiar pinkish coloration of the natural, is a fine choice anytime during early summer. A weighted pattern, needed to work the levels where the insects collect, can serve as a general searching fly as well as an imitation of an abundant food item.

Trout also feed on the emerging pupae and egg-laying adults. The population of a single species of *Glossosoma* can be very high in a stream, but usually in western waters there are a number of species sharing the habitat. When their activity overlaps they can be collectively important. The various species are enough alike in habit, size, and coloration to constitute a uniform and abundant food source.

The imitations listed for the pupa and adult are useful for foraging trout. The small flies attract even decent fish if they are presented with active twitch techniques. The slight motions of a fly controls the selective response for these trout as much as the appearance of the pattern because both the natural pupae and adults are vigorous swimmers.

Important Species

Primitive genera adapted only for cool, running water often have many closely related species, and this is certainly the situation with *Glossosoma*. The reason for this diversity is that every warm belt of flatland forms a geologic barrier to the dispersal of primitive insects. When dispersal is cut off long enough between mountain ranges the resident populations evolve into a slightly different insect (a new species).

G. intermedium E, M, W
This is the only species of the genus that can survive, although only marginally, in cold springs as well as in rivers. As a result it has been able to spread across the continent and settle from Labrador to British Columbia. It is common in many streams of the upper Midwest. The emergence period is very extended, ranging from March to August.

G. nigrior E, M
In their 1949 survey, Justin and Fannie Leonard wrote, "This is probably the most abundant and widely distributed species of caddis fly in the gravel-bottomed trout streams of Michigan." That assessment holds true for most cold-water areas in the East and Midwest. Emergence begins as early as the beginning of May, but the bulk of the population remains available for drift incidence through to June.

G. lividium E
(=*G. americanum*)
This is a locally common species in the East, emerging throughout the summer.

G. traviatum W
Both this species and *G. alascense* evolved originally on the western side of the continental divide. They are the main representatives of their family in the medium-size rivers along the mountain spine, abundant in Montana, Idaho, and Wyoming. *G. traviatum* emerges earlier than *G. alascense*, the bulk of the activity occurring in June for the former and in July for the latter.

G. alascense W
In my first course in aquatic entomology my assignment was to study the distribution of *G. alascense*. The work also included observations on the drift phenomenon of the larvae.

I tended my drift nets in Flathead Creek every half-hour, collecting over 800 uncased larvae during one peak period. I calculated that a trout with a three-foot feeding territory was seeing an amazing 1,600 free insects every hour. In between emptying the nets I fished, using a pinkish nymph along the undercuts, and caught trout that were stuffed with the larvae.

G. velona W
This is a common and widespread Northwestern species, prospering in the larger rivers of Oregon and Washington. Its range also extends east to Montana and south to Utah. The mating flights and emergence periods occur twice during the year, the species split into March-to-June and August-to-November groups. Especially during the late fall period, when it is often the largest insect available to the fish, it can be very important.

G. penitum W
This species' range extends over much of the mountain region. It is found in

smaller creeks than other members of the genus. The bulk of emergence is in late July and early August.

G. *califica* W

G. *califica* is an important species along the Sierra slope, common to abundant in large streams and small rivers as far north as southern Oregon. Emergence times occur around June in California, peaks coming earlier at lower elevations than at higher elevations.

I encountered the heaviest hatch I have ever seen of the *Glossosoma* genus in the Nature Conservancy water on the McCloud River. There were some other species besides G. *califica* mixed into the activity, but it was the main one. Trout fed on the pupae very selectively during the frenzy.

General imitations for *Glossosoma*:

LARVA: Pink Caddis Larva (sizes 14, 16, 18)
PUPA: Tan and Pale Green Deep Sparkle Pupa, Tan and Pale Green Emergent Sparkle Pupa (sizes 14, 16, 18)
ADULT DRY: Tan and Pale Green Dancing Caddis (sizes 14, 16)
ADULT WET: Tan and Pale Green Diving Caddis (sizes 14, 16, 18) (For darker colored species the Brown and Bright Green series of pupal and adult imitations can be substituted.)

ADULT KEYS: Ross, H. H. 1956. *Evolution and Classification of the Mountain Caddisflies*. Urbana: University of Illinois Press.

Family Helicopsychidae (tube-case maker)
(represented by 1 genus in North America)

Shelter type: the larvae construct a very distinctive case of sand grains, shaping their shelter like a coil.

Typical feeding habits of the larvae: the larvae are typical scrapers, moving over and under the stream rocks and feeding on the scummy layer of algae, detritus, and animal matter.

Typical method of emergence: the pupae swim to the surface and emerge in open water.

Typical egg-laying habits: the females deposit eggs in or near the water (to quote H. H. Ross, " . . . apparently as frequently one way as the other.")

There is only one genus in this family in North America, and within that genus there is only one common and widespread species. The distinctive larval case makes this one of the best-known caddisflies in our trout streams. The larva builds its curious case of sand grains, fashioning a coil-like structure that resembles the shell of a snail.

It is not known for certain what advantages such a case offers the insect, but there have been theories about it. Possibly it is the coil shape that, by dissipating heat, allows the larvae to survive in warmer water than most other caddisflies. Or maybe the compact nature of the case, by making it easier for the larvae to slip in between and under stones, lets it feed in under-utilized areas of the stream bottom. Whatever the reason for the snail-shell configuration, the ability of the larvae to survive, often under stressing conditions, in a wide range of habitats attests to the success of this adaptation. These caddisflies are abundant and widespread.

genus *Helicopsyche* (Speckled Peter)
(4 known species in North America north of Mexico)

Generalized description of the adult:
adult length up to 7mm

WING:	light-brown background, with a heavy speckling of darker brown
BODY:	varies from pale to straw yellow
LEGS:	straw yellow

Larva

Helicopsyche

Adult

The major species of the genus in this country and Canada is *H. borealis*. Since the other three species are very localized in the South or Southwest, and generally not important to fly fishermen, all the comments here in the generic description apply to *H. borealis*.

The range of this insect is very wide. It has been collected from Texas to northern Saskatchewan and from New Hampshire to Oregon. The larvae usually live in running-water environments, more abundantly in the moderate currents of spring creeks and medium-size or larger rivers than in fast streams, but they can also survive along the wave-washed edges of lakes. Some of the warm springs that the larvae thrive in have temperatures of nearly 110 degrees Fahrenheit.

Records indicate that this species has a very spread-out emergence period and flight period, but scattered collections can be deceptive. In some environments the adults may emerge during any month of the year. In trout rivers as different as the Henrys Fork (Idaho) and the White River (Arkansas), however, the emergence and egg laying are fairly concentrated, the entire adult stage lasting a few weeks. There is a definite peak period on most trout streams; early May to June in the East or Pacific West and mid-June to early July in the Rocky Mountain West.

Important species

H. borealis E, M, W
(= *H. californica*)

Both emergence and egg laying occurs mainly in the evening. The adult appears different in flight from other caddisflies because the top set of wings is attached to the bottom by a row of hooks, so the four wings beat together, not as two spread-out sets. The females, egg masses extruded and hanging off the tip of the abdomen, flop aimlessly on the water or even near the edge of it and attach the ball to some solid object.

General imitations for *Helicopsyche*:

LARVA:	none
PUPA:	Brown and Yellow Deep Sparkle Pupa; Brown and Yellow Emergent Sparkle Pupa (sizes 14, 16, 18)
ADULT DRY:	Brown and Yellow Dancing Caddis, Lawson Spent Partridge Caddis (sizes 16, 18, 20)
ADULT WET:	Brown and Yellow Diving Caddis (sizes 16, 18, 20)
ADULT KEYS:	Ross, H. H. 1944. "The caddis flies, or Trichoptera, of Illinois," *Bull. Ill. Nat. Hist. Surv.*, 23(1).

Family Hydropsychidae (net spinner)
(represented by 11 genera in North America)[5]

Shelter type: the larvae do not build cases, but they do build retreats beside their nets on the rock surfaces.

Typical feeding habits of the larvae: the net-making larvae filter drifting particles from the current.

Typical method of emergence: the pupa swim to the surface and emerge in open water.

Typical egg-laying habits: the females dive under the surface and lay their eggs on the bottom.

The genera of this family mirror the changes in a river system. Studies of larval populations show that there is usually a predictable sequence in which each genus appears in the watershed.[6]

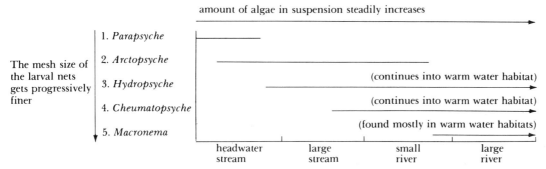

What factors control this habitat preference? *Parapsyche* weaves a net with the most open mesh of any genus in the family. This specialization helps the larvae utilize the large particles carried by the fast currents of headwater streams. At the other extreme, *Macronema* larvae weave a net with the tightest mesh of any hydropsychid. They collect bacteria and algae from the current. With this ability to feed efficiently on such small particles the genus thrives in large, rich rivers.

The correlation between the mesh size of the net and food preference is consistent in this family. As the mesh size decreases with each genus—from *Parapsyche* to *Arctopsyche* to *Hydropsyche* to *Cheumatopsyche* to *Macronema*—the insects feed on smaller particles and inhabit increasingly rich streams and rivers.

Other factors besides the food resources of a stream effect where each genus can survive and prosper—water temperature and current speed probably playing a role in separating them—but a fly fisherman can check the algae in a stream by simply scraping his fingernail over a rock on the bottom, or by counting the number of times he slips while wading. The richness of a stream makes a good indicator for the distribution of this family.

Parapsyche is not covered in this section, mainly because it occurs in such small waters that its value to anglers is limited. It can be common in high-altitude streams, however, so backpacking fly fishermen might look for *P. apicalis* and *P. cardis* in the East and *P. almota* and *P. elsis* in the West.

genus *Arctopsyche* (Great Gray Spotted Sedge)
(4 known species in North America)

Generalized description of the adult:
adult length up to 20mm

WING: predominantly dark gray with light spotting
BODY: greenish brown
LEGS: dark brown

Larva

Arctopsyche

Adult

What fly fisherman would turn down the chance to catch thirty or forty trout between eight and sixteen inches in a day? The best fishing in the West is not always in the famous waters. The smaller rivers receive much less angling pressure and produce much more consistently than the big ones. They might not hide many monster fish, although this remains a possibility, but they hold surprising numbers of decent trout.

The upper Big Hole River is basically a small-fish stream. The water is cold and pure and supports typical mountain caddisflies. In July, when the western species *Arctopsyche grandis* emerges, all the fish in this section—mainly grayling, brook trout, and rainbow trout—concentrate on this big, lumbering caddisfly.

Many fly fishermen miss this hatch completely on the Big Hole. They work the larger water below Wise River for big brown trout and rainbow trout. Sometimes they go home dissapointed because the lower river can be fickle. They are unaware of or uninterested in *Arctopsyche grandis*, and they end up turning down the chance to catch thirty or forty trout a day.

"Nursery water," one of my guiding clients called the upper river. "There's nothing up there but eight- and nine-inchers."

"Try it," I insisted.

That afternoon he put on a Gray and Green Diving Caddis and after some practice mastered the appropriate wet-fly methods. He waded the river and cast the imitation into the banks. He started catching fish, which was no surprise—but they were the big fish in this section, fourteen inches average, and he even nailed the twenty-one-inch, trophy rainbow he had not been able to get on the lower river during the stonefly hatch (*Pteronarcys californica*).

An angler can spend all of July in Montana synchronizing his fishing with the appearance of *A. grandis* at various altitudes. On many watersheds this caddisfly begins emerging just as the *Pteronarcys* hatch peters out, and it becomes abundant at the upstream limit of *Pteronarcys* distribution. The peak of the activity moves a little higher up the river each day, good fishing lasting three or four weeks.

Important Species

A grandis W
(= *A. inermis*)

This is the most abundant and widely distributed western species in the genus. It is a mountain caddisfly, associated mainly with pristine rivers and streams over 1,500 feet in elevation. It is common in the Cascade range throughout Oregon, Washington, and British Columbia; in both the Siskiyou and Sierra Nevada ranges of California; in the Rocky Mountains, down the continental spine, through Montana, Colorado, and Wyoming; and in the Sangre de Cristo, Park, and San Juan mountains of Colorado and New Mexico. *A. grandis* is one of those special insects that is worth making the focus of a fishing trip because it gets the best trout in a river interested in feeding.

A. irrorata E

This species is found in headwater streams of the Appalachian mountains in the Southeast.

General imitations for *Arctopsyche*:

LARVA: Olive Brown Caddis Larva (sizes 2, 4, 6, 8)

PUPA: Gray and Green Deep Sparkle Pupa; Gray and Green Emergent Sparkle Pupa (sizes 6, 8, 10)

ADULT DRY: Gray and Green Dancing Caddis (size 10), Parkany Deer Hair Caddis in appropriate colors (sizes 6, 8, 10)

ADULT WET: Gray and Green Diving Caddis (sizes 6, 8, 10)

Arctopsyche larvae, which feed mainly on insects, live in a river for two years. They apparently drift at a higher rate than other members of the family, demonstrating a nocturnal pattern with dawn and dusk peaks. They are available enough and distinctive enough to serve as good models during general nymphing tactics.

ADULT KEYS: Schmid, F. 1968. "La famille des Arctopsychides (Trichoptera)." *Mem. Ent. Soc. Quebec.* (This paper mentions one record of *A. grandis* from Quebec.)
Milne, L. J., and M. J. Milne. 1938. "The Arctopsychidae of continental America north of Mexico (Trichoptera)." *Brooklyn Entomol. Soc. Bull.,* 33(3): 97-110.

The source for much of my informatin on this genus has been *A synopsis of the Western Arctopsychinae* by Donald R. Givens, which contains specific records on the distribution of both *Parapsyche* and *Arctopsyche* in many streams and rivers throughout the West.

genus *Cheumatopsyche* (Little Sister Sedge)
(approximately 39 known species in North America)

Generalized description of the adult:
adult length up to 10mm

WING: light brown to dark brown, generally with a faint mottled effect

BODY: green to greenish brown

LEGS: light brown to dark brown

Larva

Cheumatopsyche

The common name, Little Sister Sedge, refers to the relationship between *Cheumatopsyche* and its closely related genus, *Hydropsyche* (Spotted Sedge). *Cheumatopsyche* is the smaller of the two, and overall slightly less important, but it must still be considered for what it is—one of the most abundant and valuable caddisflies in North American trout streams. The fact that it is second in many areas of the continent only to *Hydropsyche*, the number-one caddisfly, puts its importance in proper perspective.

This genus generally begins taking over for *Hydropsyche* at the downstream end of a trout river, but both occur abundantly in large, fertile waters, overlapping considerably in distribution. With increases in organic enrichment the populations

Adult

of *Cheumatopsyche* gradually become dominant. They also thrive beyond the trout habitat of a watershed, even prospering in areas where nutrient pollution is such a problem that few other caddisfly species can survive.

A series of collections by Arnie Gidlow on the Big Hole River showed how dramatically the populations of the genera in the Hydropsychidae family can shift from *Arctopsyche* to *Hydropsyche* to *Cheumatopsyche* in a drainage. Above the Wise River area *Arctopsyche* was the dominant genus. Just below Wise River, with the influx of many enriching springs, the larvae of all three genera were well represented in his samplings, a mixture reflecting the radical transformation of the Big Hole from a relatively sterile to a very fertile trout stream. *Cheumatopsyche* adults were so abundant that summer from late June through mid-August that they filled a light trap that Arnie was operating to overflowing every evening.[7]

Important Species

(In older taxonomies this entire genus was considered under the name *Hydropsychodes*; in even older taxonomies all the species were included in the genus *Hydropsyche*.)

C. etrona E

On the foothill streams of the southern Appalachian states it is not uncommon to catch a pleasant mix of trout and redeye bass on surface flies during April and May, both of these fish rising to the pupae and adults of *C. etrona* at these times.

C. miniscula E

In spite of its scientific name this species is not that small in comparison to other species in the genus; the males average 6 to 8mm in length. The name is a carry-over from 1907, before *Cheumatopsyche* was separated from *Hydropsyche*, and when compared to species from its sister genus it is small.

This is a common species primarily in the eastern states and provinces. Pupation and emergence can be as early as April in the southern portions of its range and as late as July in the northern reaches.

C. gracilus E, M, W

In my logs there are over seventy entries for *C. gracilus*, records of times that this species has created good fly-fishing opportunites. They are based on collections by my friends and me, mostly in the East and the Midwest, the earliest a 1964 notation about a June 20 egg-laying flight on the Farmington River in Connecticut and the latest a 1979 notation about a June 3 emergence on the Esopus River in New York (the latter from a collection loaned to me by Fred Arbona).

This species is transcontinental in distribution, absent only from the Southwest. It is found most abundantly in very rich rivers, often in watersheds suffering from too much organic pollution. It is also important in streams too warm to support trout, but in these waters it incites some fine rises of small bass and panfish.

C. harwoodi E

In small eastern rivers from Georgia to Maine this is frequently the most abundant species of *Cheumatopsyche*. The incredible numbers of emerging and egg-laying individuals during May and June also make *C. harwoodi* a very important species for anglers.

C. pasella E, M. W

Widespread across the continent, with a north/south distribution from Maine to Florida, this species can be common to abundant in rapid rivers. In most of my records its peak emergence in eastern and midwestern trout streams begins slightly earlier in May than the emergence periods of other species.

C. lasia M, W

This species is widespread in the Midwest and West. It is important in the tailwater rivers of Oklahoma and Texas, the July hatches on the Brazos River in the latter state a major happening for fly fishermen on that trout stream.

C. campyla E, M, W

During the salmon-fly hatch (*Pteronarcys californica*), the giant stonefly of western rivers, there is also a small, dark brown caddisfly on the water. The adults become active early in the afternoon, just as the cooler temperatures of the day retard the egg-laying flights of *Pteronarcys*. They can fool fly fishermen because trout begin feeding on the smaller but more numerous forms and begin ignoring the larger stoneflies.[8]

This caddisfly, *C. campyla,* has been a key element in many of my most successful days of guiding. Floating a river, the common method of fishing the major western waters, takes me and my clients through an area where the stoneflies are active, but after passing the prime salmon-fly section I ask my fishermen to switch to caddisfly imitations. The change to smaller flies frequently produces the fastest action of the day, giving people some huge trout on big, stonefly dry patterns and many decent trout on caddisfly dry patterns.

The peak for *C. campyla* occurs from April through to July, depending on which region of the country it is in, but the populations of this net maker are so tremendous that even the stragglers, popping out all summer, are numerous enough to constitute a major food item for trout. As the season progresses, the flights form later each day and individuals become lighter in color.

This species is important not only in western waters but also in almost every large trout river in this country or southern Canada. From the Penobscot in Maine to the Colorado in Arizona the emergence and egg-laying activities constitute a major event for fly fishermen who are aware of these caddisflies.

C. sordida E, M

This species is well distributed in states east of the Mississippi River, ranging as far south as Georgia. *C. sordida* is an important midsummer caddisfly on many trout rivers.

C. speciosa E, M

(also found rarely in North Dakota and Montana)

In larger rivers of the East and Midwest this species is frequently common. Its emergence and egg-laying periods extend throughout the summer.

C. pettiti E, M, W

(= *C. analis*)

This species is found virtually everywhere in this country, even in Hawaii, and rates second only to *C. campyla* in its value to fly fishermen. It is most abundant in streams and small rivers; whereas *C. campyla* seems to prefer larger habitats.

The emergence period for *C. pettiti* is very extended, dark-colored forms hatching earlier and light-colored forms hatching later in the season. The hours for emergence and egg laying also vary with the date; during late spring the activity begins in the afternoon and during midsummer it begins in the evening. The peak abundance for this species usually occurs during May on Eastern trout streams and during June or July on western ones. Like *C. campyla* it can also coincide with the *Pteronarcys* stonefly hatch.

General imitations for *Cheumatopsyche*:

LARVA: Olive Brown Caddis Larva (sizes 12, 14, 16)
PUPA: Brown and Bright Green Deep Sparkle Pupa; Brown and Bright
            Green Emergent Sparkle Pupa (sizes 14, 16, 18, 20)
ADULT DRY: Brown and Green Dancing Caddis (sizes 14, 16); Lawson Spent
            Partridge Caddis (sizes 16, 18, 20)
ADULT WET: Brown and Bright Green Diving Caddis (sizes 14, 16, 18, 20)

With the variable coloration and size even within species of *Cheumatopsyche*, it is absolutely necessary to check specimens at streamside.

ADULT KEYS: Gordon, A. E. 1974. "A synopsis and phylogenetic outline of the Nearctic members of *Cheumatopsyche.*" *Proc. Acad. Nat. Sci. Philad.* 126 (9): 117-160.

genus *Hydropsyche* (Spotted Sedge)
(approximately 70 known species in North America north of Mexico)

Generalized description of the adult:
adult length up to 14mm
WING: brown, with a mottled pattern of light and dark areas
BODY: brownish yellow
LEGS: vary from straw yellow to dark brown

Larva

Hydropsyche

Adult

This genus is so widespread and so abundant in running-water habitats that knowing something about it can do nothing but help a fly fisherman; on the other hand, not knowing about it can spoil many days on the stream. These insects are there; dangling in the current as larvae, swimming to the surface as pupae, and diving toward the bottom as egg-laying adults—and trout feed on all stages selectively.

My interest in the larvae began in earnest during my studies of behavioral drift on Flathead Creek in Montana. The *Hydropsyche* larvae were an important part of the caddisfly fauna in this rich, little spring creek, but they were not riding freely in the current and were not getting caught in my net while the larvae of other genera were. Their absence in the drift samplings was even more notable because of their overall abundance.

In a series of general observations in the stream itself I found out that *Hydropsyche* larvae were using a silk anchor line in two ways: one, the line, fastened near the retreat, served as protection against accidental dislodgment; and two, the line functioned as a rapelling rope, allowing the insect to migrate down to a new area, where after gripping a rock it would bite itself free of the line.

My observations on this silk anchor line were not the first ones. Entomologist C. E. Sleight noted it in his 1913 paper, "Relations of Trichoptera to their environment," and angler Sid Gordon, in *How to Fish From Top to Bottom* (1955), mentioned this habit for *Hydropsyche* larvae. It was a phenomenon, however, that was just waiting to be purposely mimicked with a fly-fishing technique. The trick of whitening the last eighteen inches of a leader, the "magic act" mentioned in Chapter 4, significantly improved the effectiveness of the larval patterns.

The development of a technique that could take advantage of the abundant *Hydropsyche* larvae in streams and rivers ended my angling frustrations with this stage, eliminating those fishless days in the presence of greedily feeding trout. It made the larvae almost as worthwhile as the pupae and adults; and, by adding to the overall angling value of this genus, the new fly-fishing method left little doubt that for me this was the most important trout-stream caddisfly in America (a position it probably held securely anyway on the strength of emergence and egg-laying activities).

The larvae pupate in or near their normal habitat, the riffles and runs of the stream, and the pupae emerge from these areas. They drift with the bottom currents immediately after escaping from the pupal cocoon and, once gasses are generated inside the skin, swim swiftly to the surface. To this point the emergence is fairly typical for caddisflies, but the pupae require a notoriously long time to shed the skin and fly away. The pupae take from minutes to hours to escape the water, most of this time spent drifting helplessly just under the surface film. It is not only their overwhelming numbers that make *Hydropsyche* pupae so important: it is this complete availability to the trout.

The adult females, returning to the stream to oviposit, also act like a well-coordinated horde. They dive underwater, swim to the bottom, and paste strings of eggs on solid objects. They do not swim back to the surface when this is done, however. They simply release their grip on the substrate and drift slowly upward. When they reach the meniscus they wiggle and push to break through, and once they are on the surface they ride along in an apparent state of exhaustion, some flopping feebly and some sprawling inert. These egg-laying females are excellent dry-fly models, one of the finest caddisflies in this regard, but when they are on the water in great numbers, and when individual trout feed selectively on either the active or inactive forms, they have to be imitated with a Dancing Caddis pattern for best angling results.

Total up the plus factors for this genus: it is abundant almost everywhere in rich trout flows; it is available to fish during every stage; and it is generally active during the pleasant hours of morning or evening. In the East the major early-summer species—*H. sparna, H. morosa, H. bronta,* and *H. betteni*—follow the *Brachycentrus* (Grannom) and *Psilotreta* (Dark Blue Sedge) flights of May and June, representing a third wave of caddisflies. In the upper Midwest the two most important species—*H. slossonae* and *H. sparna*—usually monopolize the evening action in May and June. In the West the early-summer emergers—*H. occidentalis* and *H. oslari*—and the autumn species—*H. cockerelli*—are fed on by trout almost exclusively during their peaks of abundance. They even increase in importance when there are two or three species in a stream because, with overlapping emergence and flight periods, the selectivity trout develop for each one carries over to the group.

Important Species

H. simulans E, M (range extends into the West, but it is generally rare in this area)

I collected many pupae and adults of this species during my survey of Nebraska waters. In a number of fine little trout streams in the panhandle region—Sowbelly, Tub Springs, Chadron, Niobrara, Soldiers, and Nine Mile—there were good hatches of this species and appreciative rainbows in late May. I took many of my insect specimens from trout with a stomach pump, one fourteen-inch rainbow yielding over a hundred pupae of *H. simulans*.

H. recurvata E, M
(= *H. codona*)

This species reaches its greatest abundance in swift, well-aerated streams and rivers of the upper Midwest, emerging from late May to August. Dr. Donald Denning, in his paper *The Hydropsychidae of Minnesota*, notes, "*Hydropsyche recurvata* is one of the most common species in Minnesota." He also includes records of good populations along the wave-washed shores of Lake Superior.

H. vexa E, M, W

This is an important May and June species in the medium-size rivers of the Midwest. My collections of *H. vexa* from the Henrys Fork in Idaho represent a considerable westward extension of its known range, but if the numbers taken on this river are any indication it is not that rare in the region.

Ken Thompson sent my samples of this species to two authorities for verification. He wrote a follow-up note to me, "Oliver Flint and Donald Denning were both surprised to see specimens of *Hydropsyche vexa* from Idaho. Denning, in fact, doubted if he was correct, but Flint feels certain that this is what it is. He kept a specimen of *H. vexa* for the Smithsonian."

H. oslari W

This is the most important species of the genus in the small and medium-size rivers of the mountain West. Two other species, *H. occidentalis* and *H. cockerelli*, take over for it in larger rivers, but in the Rocky Mountains, from British Columbia to Utah, it predominates in cold, swift habitats. Peak emergence occurs in June and July.

H. morosa E, M
(= *H. chlorotica*)

Eastern fly fishermen should learn to recognize and anticipate *H. morosa*. On rivers ranging in size from the small Mount Hope (Connecticut) to the large Delaware (New York) this is a major summer emerger. The twilight activity is so dependable that proper imitations for the prehatch and main hatch periods are indispensable. A canny angler could even sneak out at dawn the next morning and find trout in the backwaters sipping the drowned cripples of the previous evening's hatch.

H. betteni E, M

This important Eastern species is a large-stream and small-river form, emerging from late May through to August. The adults are significantly bigger than those of most other eastern species in the genus, 14 to 14.5 millimeters long, and imitations on

The large H. betteni *is an important species in streams and small rivers throughout the East.* Ken Thompson

a size 8 or size 10 hook are needed when trout are feeding selectively on them.

H. californica W

Dr. D. Denning has recorded this species as far east as Minnesota, but it is common mostly in Pacific Coast watersheds. In my collections the main emergence periods have occurred in June and July on rivers such as the Metolius (Oregon) and lower McCloud (California).

H. bronta E, M, W

Collections show that this stream and small-river species is common to abundant from Montana east to Connecticut. The peak of emergence seems to occur just as the weather begins to turn nice for the season in whatever region it is in.

H. sparna E, M

H. sparna and *H. slossonae* share the position as the top-rated species in the upper Midwest. They are both profuse in the gravel-bottomed trout streams of the region, where they emerge in late spring and early summer. This species is also common to abundant throughout the Northeast.

H. slossonae E, M, W

The range of *H. slossonae* extends from New Hampshire to Montana, and as far south as North Carolina, but it is not quite as abundant anywhere else as it is in the upper Midwest. In such states as Michigan and Wisconsin it is a major insect that excites even big fish—once during the June egg-laying flights a Diving Caddis wet fly fooled a beautiful 4½-pound brown for my good friend, Howard Bresson, on the Pigeon River in Michigan.

H. bifida E, M, W

This species has a wide range, records available from New York to Wyoming, but it is apparently most abundant in the rapid rivers of the northcentral states. Emergence is continuous from May to September, with a distinct early-season peak.

H. occidentalis W

This early-summer caddisfly often appears on rich streams and rivers in concert with a famous mayfly, the Western Green Drake (*Ephemerella grandis*); on the Henrys Fork, for example, June 20 is the date to expect both of them. This species achieves incredibly high populations on major trout rivers throughout the mountain West.

H. bidens E, M

H. bidens appears to be most abundant in a ring of states surrounding the central plains, populations especially high in Ozark tail-water rivers (see July and August records for the White River in Arkansas in Chapter 9).

H. alternans E

This has been one of the most highly tauted species in angling literature. Charles Wetzel first discussed it in *Practical Fly Fishing* (1943), and other writers followed his example. Few accounts of eastern caddisflies have failed to mention the profuse populations of *H. alternans*.

How important is it really? Wetzel made an honest mistake. He more than likely based his recommendation of this species on information from Dr. Cornelius Betten's *The caddis flies or Trichoptera of New York State,* but later entomologists revised Dr. Betten's description of *H. alternans*, noting that it had not only included this species but also, under the same name, data on *H. morosa* and *H. slossonae.* This resulted in an inflated view of its importance.

References to *H. alternans* in angling works are actually about a group of three caddisflies. The other two in the trio, *H. morosa* and *H. slossonae*, are both more widespread and abundant than *H. alternans*. The reputation of *H. alternans* as a major eastern caddisfly is open to doubt.

H. cockerelli W

H. cockerelli, like many members of the genus, produces split generations. In the West there is a June period and a late-summer to late-autumn period. The early emergence is very sparse, however, and of little importance to fly fishermen. The heavy flights begin building in the last week of August and reach peak abundance in October. At first the emergence takes place at dawn, but it starts later each day with the cooling weather.

This species has been reported as far east as New Hampshire, but it is rare outside of the West. In the Rocky Mountain region and along the West Coast it is one of the most important members of the genus in larger rivers, its range extending to Utah.

General imitations for *Hydropsyche*:

LARVA:	Olive Brown Caddis Larvae (sizes 6, 8, 10, 12)
PUPA:	Brown and Yellow Deep Sparkle Pupa; Brown and Yellow Emergent Sparkle Pupa (sizes 8, 10, 12, 14)
ADULT DRY:	Brown and Yellow Dancing Caddis (sizes 10, 12, 14, 16); Parkany Deer Hair Caddis (sizes 10, 12)
ADULT WET:	Brown and Yellow Diving Caddis (sizes 8, 10, 12, 14, 16)

ADULT KEYS:

The drawings and descriptions for identifying male adults to species level are divided into many papers. Good basic works which, if used together, give an overview of the most important species are:

Ross, H. H. 1944. "The caddis flies, or Trichoptera, of Illinois." *Bull. Ill., Nat. Hist. Surv.*, No. 23. (Midwestern and Eastern species)

Denning, D. G. 1956. "Trichoptera." Pages 237-270, in *Aquatic Insects of California*, R. L. Usinger, ed. Univ. of California Press, Berkeley. (Western species)

genus *Macronema* (Glossy Wing Sedge)
(3 known species in North America)

Generalized description of the adult:
adult length up to 18mm

WING:	brown with yellow markings (the wings have a shiny, polished appearance)
BODY:	metallic bluish brown
LEGS:	yellow

In temperate regions most adult caddisflies are fairly drab, shades of brown, gray, and green predominating, but there are exceptions, the most spectacular of which is *Macronema*. Its wings, conspicuously patterned brown and yellow, have a glossy sheen. Its head and thorax shine with a dark, metallic bluish brown color. Its exceptionally long antennae sweep back far behind the wing tips. The large size of the insect adds to its regal appearance.

Larva

Macronema

Adult

Macronema is not only beautiful and abundant, but the pupae and adults are both quite available to the fish. The pupae emerge from the same areas they inhabit as larvae (the swifter riffles), drifting under the surface as they attempt to extricate themselves from their skin. The adult females return to the river in late afternoon and evening to lay their eggs in the water. The adults fly with great agility, this genus one of the few caddisflies strong enough to breast even moderate winds, but they do not swim quite as well. Underwater their bulk makes them slow and clumsy, any turbulence washing them downstream. The egg-laying females suffer a high mortality rate.

Important Species

M. zebratum E, M

This is basically an eastern caddisfly, but there is one isolated record from Utah. It has a wide range throughout the Northeast and Midwest, where it is common to abundant in larger rivers. The peak of emergence and egg-laying occurs during June and early July in the North, but adults can be collected as late as September.

M. zebratum has been the main insect during many of my best fishing days on tail-water trout streams, but forget trout for a moment—this caddisfly is even more important on midwestern smallmouth-bass streams. It is possible during big hatches on clear, swift rivers to catch fifty smallmouths a day on surface imitations.

One July on the St. Croix in Minnesota, I hit heavy egg-laying activity, but I did not have any trout flies with me (the last time I ever made that mistake). I found an old, balsa-wood-bodied Bunyan Bug, a stonefly imitation, that adequately matched the silhouette of *M. zebratum*; or least the bass thought so. I never caught so many smallmouth bass on a fly rod before in my life—and the nice part is that I have often been able to catch as many or more since then by anticipating the appearance of this caddisfly.

M. carolina E, M

This species, slightly smaller than *M. zebratum*, is more common in the mid-South than anywhere else. It is an important summer caddisfly on many of the larger rivers in the area.

General imitations for *Macronema*:

LARVA:	Olive Brown Caddis Larva (sizes 4, 6, 8)
PUPA:	Brown and Blue Deep Sparkle Pupa; Brown and Blue Emergent Sparkle Pupa (sizes 6, 8, 10)
ADULT DRY:	Brown and Blue Dancing Caddis (size 10); Parkany Deer Hair Caddis in appropriate colors (sizes 6, 8)
ADULT WET:	Brown and Blue Diving Caddis (sizes 6, 8, 10)
ADULT KEYS:	Ross, H. H. 1944. "The caddis flies, or Trichoptera, of Illinois." *Bull, Illinois Nat. Hist. Surv.*, No. 23.

Family Hydroptilidae (purse-case maker)
(represented by 14 genera in North America)

Shelter type: the larvae of this family do not build a case until the final instar.

Case-making material for the various genera can be plant, stone, or just silken excretion.

Typical feeding habits of the larvae: the larvae feed mostly on algae. Some genera graze on diatoms, a type of algae, but others can pierce the cell wall of filamentous algae and suck out the contents.

Typical method of emergence: the pupae swim or crawl to the surface.

Typical egg-laying habits: the females crawl or dive under the surface and paste eggs to bottom objects.

Fly fishermen sometimes apply the term "microcaddis" to all small caddisflies, but the name actually refers only to the family Hydropilidae. Some of the genera in this family do have very small larvae and adults, insects with a maximum length of 2 millimeters. Other genera have species that are 6 millimeters long, and in this size range they are as large as some species in other families. Most microcaddis are not so miniscule that trout can afford to ignore them.

In general, how important a species is as a forage item is not only a function of size. A large number of insects concentrated in an area where they can be easily gathered by fish raises the value of any species as a food source. In spring creeks, slow-moving sections of rivers, or lakes and ponds, important species of microcaddis, matched with a size 18 to 22 imitation, create many challenging situations for fishermen.

Ernest Schwiebert included a significant chapter in *Nymphs* (1973), focusing attention on some of the smaller caddisflies of our trout streams for the first time in angling literature. He commented on two net-spinning genera, *Wormaldia* and *Dolophilodes*, and one Limnephilidae case-making genus, *Oligophlebodes*, as well as three true microcaddis genera, *Agraylea*, *Hydroptila*, and *Oxyethira*. He emphasized the importance of the emerging pupae, recommending small, sparse, soft-hackle imitations.

Hydroptilidae larvae are unique among caddisflies. During the early instars they do not construct any type of case, roaming freely over the bottom. They develop rapidly, however, passing through the first four instars within two weeks, and in the fifth instar they build a case of vegetation, stone, or simply silken excretion, the shape of the shelter for most genera in the family resembling a flat purse (and hence the name purse-case maker). Also during this fifth and final instar the abdomen of these insects swell to enormous proportions.

The emerging pupae are responsible for much of the "smutting" surface-feeding behavior of trout that anglers blame on midge pupae. On the long flats of big, weedy rivers, or on the gentle surfaces of spring creeks, microcaddis drift and struggle in the meniscus for long distances. In such slow currents, where fish can hold just under the surface and sip insects with great efficiency, they are consumed avidly by trout.

The egg-laying activity of the females is even more predictable and noteworthy than the emergence. When they crawl or dive below the surface these adult insects often manage to return safely, but there is a substantial mortality rate. They get swept away by the currents or caught in the surface film in enough numbers to attract the attention of very decent trout. These concentrations in turn inspire long and leisurely feeding periods.

genus *Agraylea* (Salt and Pepper Microcaddis)
(3 known species in North America)

Generalized description of the adult:
adult length up to 5mm
WING: speckled gray and white
BODY: green; very bright in freshly emerged specimens
LEGS: dark brown to black

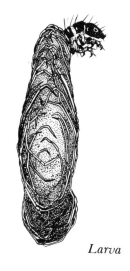

Larva

Agraylea

Of the three species in North America only one, *A. multipunctata*, is widespread. *A. costello* in the Northeast and *A. saltesea* in the West have more localized populations even within their range. *A. multipunctata* is abundant in lakes, quiet rivers, and spring creeks from coast to coast and as far south as Tennessee.

Important Species

A. multipunctata E, M, W
No other species in the family Hydroptilidae has produced such consistenly fine fishing for me as this one. In weedy spring creeks, from Hat Creek in California to the Letort Spring Run in Pennsylvania, the crippled adults and pupae from the nighttime activity, plus a few fresh stragglers, are nearly always on the water at dawn during June and July. The trout lay at the edges of the weeds and sip these caddisflies steadily and quite selectively for the first hour of daylight (see also Chapter 7 on lakes).

Adult

General imitations for *Agraylea*:
LARVA: none
PUPA: Gray and Green Deep Sparkle Pupa; Gray and Green Emergent Sparkle Pupa (sizes 20, 22, 24)
ADULT DRY: Lawson Spent Partridge Caddis in appropriate colors (sizes 20, 22, 24)
ADULT WET: Gray and Green Diving Caddis (sizes 20, 22, 24)

genus *Hydroptila* (Vari-Colored Microcaddis)
(approximately 60 known species in North America)

Generalized description of the adult:
adult length up to 4mm
WING: varies from gray to brown, colors can be solid or spotted
BODY: can be bright yellow, orange, brown, or any shade in between
LEGS: color varies from straw yellow to black
(There can be tremendous variations in size and color even within a single species in this genus.)

Larva

Hydroptila

This genus is so diversified that it is impossible to make generalizations. They are found throughout North America in nearly every kind of running-water habitat, from spring seeps to large rivers. Many species are important in lakes and ponds. The only safe statement about them is that they are usually common to abundant in most trout waters.

The larvae are an especially interesting stage with some exciting ramifications for even the most practical fly fisherman. The larvae, with their five-millimeter case of silk and sand grains, drift freely in the current. Dr. Norman Anderson, in his paper

Adult

"Biology and downtream drift of some Oregon Trichoptera," reported, "In the Metolius River, the larvae of *H. rono* were abundant on *Ranunculus* (rooted plants) and diatom-encrusted stones. Drift rates of larvae were surprisingly high considering that the sand-grained cases were relatively heavy."

Why is the Brassie, the nymph pattern with the copper body, becoming a popular fly in very small sizes—18, 20, and 22—on spring creeks across the country? This Colorado creation is spreading all over as a result of its successes, but many fly fishermen refuse to use it because occasionally it flops so completely. It is my belief that the effectiveness of this fly in small sizes is linked with the drifting of *Hydroptila* larvae in their yellowish sand cases. Possibly if fly fishermen make the effort to learn when fifth instar larvae are most abundant in a stream, they can figure out the best times to use a Brassie.

In the Metolius River the pupae of *H. rono* emerge mainly from June to mid-July. In this particular section of the country the larvae probably spend the whole winter in the fifth instar. If this is true the cased larvae are going to be most abundant and most likely to drift from April to June. It might be possible to construct similar drift profiles for other areas of the country, but the microcaddis are still a new mystery for fly fishermen. My studies of trout feeding habits on the Missouri River indicate that, at least in spring creeks and spring rivers, the drifting larvae of *Hydroptila* are worth investigating.

Anglers cannot overlook the pupae and adults of *Hydroptila* either. Both stages have moments when a lot of insects are in very vulnerable positions. In lakes as well as in streams and rivers the fish take advantage of any concentrations of these insects, especially if emergers and egg layers are gathering in the surface film.

Important Species

H. arctia W
(= *H. acoma*)
This gray and yellow western species is common in slow-moving rivers. It becomes important during its autumn emergence and egg laying. The bodies of the females, packed with eggs, are a much brighter yellow than the bodies of the males.
    H. rono W
The range of this species extends into the mountainous regions of the West, but it seems to be more abundant in the coastal states. The peak of emergence is in early summer.
    H. argosa W
This is one of the most common species in the genus in the big rivers of Montana and Idaho. It emerges throughout the summer.
    H. ajax E, M, W
H. H. Ross, in "The caddis flies, or Trichoptera, of Illinois," suggests that Illinois is the center of greatest abundance for this transcontinental species. This indicates that it is probably important in the streams and small rivers of nearby midwestern states such as Wisconsin and Michigan.

My own collections show that there was a heavy emergence on June 16, 1979, from the Clark Fork River at Deer Lodge, Montana. During this hatch in 1979, a year of low snow fall and little runoff, the brown trout fed heavily in the clear water on the pupae.

H. hamata E, M, W

The growing availability of trout fishing throughout the middle South has made this an important caddisfly to fly fishermen. This is the species that causes the porpoising feeding in many tail-water rivers and cold-water lakes each spring and summer in those states. It is also abundant in small and large rivers farther north (see the Mount Hope species list in Chapter 9).

H. jackmanni E, M

This is one of the predominant microcaddis in Maine, where it has a flight period from early July to early August.

H. consimilis E, M, W

This is one of the most widespread species in the genus, ranging throughout forested regions in clean streams from British Columbia to Texas to New York. The peak of emergence is generally in early summer.

H. albicornis E, M

During early July *H. albicornis* gave me a full week of fine, early-morning fly-fishing on the beautiful Namekagon in Wisconsin, the trout taking a size 20 brown and yellow Sparkle imitation of the emerging pupae.

H. waubesiana E, M (also recorded from the flatland areas of North Dakota and eastern Montana)

The larvae of *H. waubesiana* thrive in both rivers and lakes, but this species is probably more valuable to fly fishermen in stillwater environments. Early in the fall it is frequently important in pupae and adult stages in cold-water ponds and lakes.

General imitations for *Hydroptila*:

LARVA: Brassie (sizes 18, 20, 22)
PUPA: the Gray and Yellow, Brown and Orange, or Brown series of Deep and Emergent Sparkle patterns (sizes 20, 22, 24)
ADULT DRY: Lawson Spent Partridge Caddis in appropriate colors (sizes 20, 22, 24)
ADULT WET: the Gray and Yellow, Brown and Orange, or Brown pattern of the Diving Caddis (sizes 20, 22, 24)

genus *Leucotrichia* (Ring Horn Microcaddis)
(3 known species in North America)

Generalized description of the adult:
adult length   up to 4.5mm
WING: dark brown to black with a few scattered light spots
BODY: brown
LEGS: very dark brown

Larva

Only one of the three species of this genus, *L. pictipes*, is important in trout waters, but it is common to abundant throughout roughly the northern half of the United States. The larvae live in the fastest currents of streams and rivers, cementing their flat silken cases to rocks. The common name, Ring Horn Microcaddis, refers to the white bands around the antennae of the adults.

Leucotrichia

Adult

Important Species

L. pictipes E, M, W

In my conversations with Dr. George Roemhild, he estimated the population density of this species at 5,000 per square foot in some fast sections of the Madison River. The large boulders in the middle of the stream are so encrusted with the silk cases below the water line that they appear to have a rash of scabs. The pupae emerge in late June on this river.

In late June and early July on the Madison River, when the females return to lay their eggs and crawl down the backside of the rocks, so many slip into the currents that trout stack up behind midstream obstructions. A small, dark wet imitation, fished upstream dead drift in the slack water behind the boulders, is often a deadly pattern during midday at these times.

General imitations:

LARVA:	none
PUPA:	Black Deep Sparkle Pupa and Black Emergent Sparkle Pupa (sizes 20, 22, 24)
ADULT DRY:	Solomon's Delta Wing Caddis, Lawson Spent Partridge Caddis, both in appropriately dark colors (sizes 20, 22, 24)
ADULT WET:	Black Diving Caddis (sizes 20, 22, 24)

genus *Oxyethira* (Cream and Brown Mottled Microcaddis)
(30 known species in North America)

generalized description of the adult:
adult length up to 3mm

WING:	mottled cream and brown
BODY:	pale greenish yellow
LEGS:	straw yellow

(Some species are darker overall than this prototypical description.)

This genus is widespread on the continent. The preferred habitat is stillwater or very slow-moving water. The larvae are often abundant around plant beds in lakes and rivers. In spite of their small size the adults, pupae, and possibly even the larvae are worth imitating.

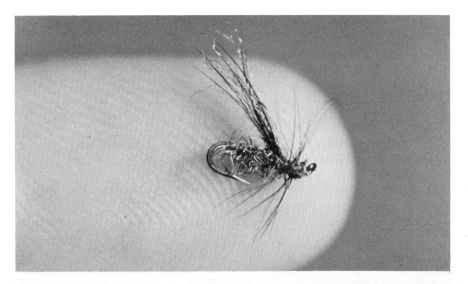

A size 22 Black-Diving-Caddis wet fly, fished dead drift behind midstream rocks, gave the author a banner day last summer on the Madison River. Gary LaFontaine

Dr. R. L. Blickle commented on the distribution of this genus in "Hydroptilidae (Trichoptera) of America north of Mexico," " . . . there does seem to be a general pattern in that the species are more numerous east of the Mississippi River and in the more northern regions of the area under consideration."

Larva

Important Species

Oxyethira

O. serrata E, M, W
This microcaddis is often very abundant in northern lakes and rivers, emerging in early summer. It is widespread, with records from British Columbia to New York.
O. pallida E, M, W
(= *O. cibola*)

The adults emerge throughout the warmer months (June to October). This species is common to abundant both in lakes and slow-moving streams. H. H. Ross, in "The caddis flies or Trichoptera of Illinois," includes an interesting comment in the section on *O. pallida,* "This is very likely the species taken in large numbers as larvae by various fish in certain experimental lakes investigated by the Natural History Survey."

Adult

O. michiganensis E, M, W
(= *O. sodalis*)
O. michiganensis is a widespread species, but in my collections and angling experiences it is most important in the upper New England states. In Maine the pupae and adults frequently are the reason the brook trout of the ponds and quiet rivers of the Allagash region rise on midsummer evenings.

General imitations for *Oxyethira*:

LARVA: none (I have no larval imitation at the moment for this genus, never having personally found trout feeding on this stage, but it might be needed in some lake situations.)

PUPA: Brown and Yellow Deep Sparkle Pupa; Brown and Yellow Emergent Sparkle Pupa (sizes 24, 26, 28)

ADULT DRY: Lawson Spent Partridge Caddis in appropriate colors (sizes 24, 26, 28)

ADULT WET: Brown and Yellow Diving Caddis (sizes 24, 26, 28)

Note on identifying members of the Hydroptilidae family:
The adults of this family are easy to distinguish from most other caddisflies. It is not just their size, six millimeters or less, that is unique; their wings are covered with disproportionately long and thick hairs. Even an eight- or ten-power eye glass magnifies the wing enough to make a fairly accurate identification possible.

ADULT KEYS: Blickle, R. L. 1979. "Hydroptilidae (Trichoptera) of America north of Mexico." *New Hampshire Agric. Expt. Stat. Bull.,* 509. (This bulletin contains keys and illustrations for the described species in all genera in this country and Canada.)

Family Lepidostomatidae (tube-case maker)
(represented by 2 genera in North America)

Shelter type: there is a great deal of variation in case-making habits even within the same genera. Sand or plant material may be used; the case may be circular or four-sided.

Typical feeding habits of the larvae: the larvae mainly consume plant material.
Typical method of emergence: the pupae swim to the surface in open water.
Typical egg-laying habits: the females lay their eggs in or near the water.

There are two genera recognized in this family, *Theliopsyche* and *Lepidostoma*. *Theliopsyche* is found in small streams in the East, the colonies very localized and never abundant. *Lepidostoma* is the important genus in this family for fly fishermen, good populations occurring in trout streams across the continent.

The larvae of these case-makers are generally found near accumulations of leaves or pine needles, their main food resource, in streams, rivers, and even in lakes. They are important processors of decaying detrital materials in woodland waters, but species of *Lepidostoma* have also been observed feeding on dead fish.

genus *Lepidostoma* (Little Plain Brown Sedge)
(65 known species in North America north of Mexico)

Generalized description of the adult:
adult length up to 10mm

WING: varying shades of brown
BODY: varying shades of brown (so light in some species as to appear tawny yellow)
LEGS: brown

Larva

Lepidostoma

I know many fly fishermen, some in the East and some in the Midwest, who have fallen in love with a certain type of trout stream. The big brawling rivers are not for them; no, they stalk the overgrown tributaries of these heavily fished waters instead. I can find some of these friends just by going to certain hidden brooks on a weekday evening because they always stop by their secret haunts after work. For these fly-fishing cronies I once had a picture postcard custom made showing an adult of *Lepidostoma*.

The larvae of this genus have three types of cases. Some species build a four-sided case with square pieces of bark or leaf material. Less frequently, others use sand grains

Adult

Not all species of Lepidostoma *construct four-sided cases. Some of them build tubular cases of plant fragments, sand grains, or a combination of the two materials. Shown above, left to right, are a larva, a sand-grain and plant-fragment case, and a plant-fragment case with larva inside.*
Ken Thompson

to construct a tubular case or twigs to construct a rough, log-cabin case. A particular species can have a different type of case during early instars than it has in later ones.

Lepidostoma larvae tend to drift with their cases at very high rates during June, a period just prior to pupation for many species, in western streams. In some studies the peak occurrence has been during daylight hours; in others there has been no discernible peak either day or night. Since only western species have been involved in these observations, and since there have not been any comprehensive drift studies done on eastern or midwestern species, it is not possible to generalize about the entire genus, but at least some *Lepidostoma* larvae are very available to nymphing trout.[9]

For pupation, the cases are fastened under stones and logs along gentler edges of a stream or river, usually fairly close to the larval habitat. The emergents rise to the surface, drifting and struggling, and any swimming motions by the pupae seem meant not so much for reaching the shore as for keeping themselves from being pulled out into faster currents. My observations of at least one western species, *L. pluviale*, indicate that it normally sheds the pupal skin on the surface.

The females lay a small ball of thirty to forty eggs either in or near the water. The egg masses have been found under the damp stones of a gravel bar and loose among debris in two feet of water in pools. It has been noted by Dr. N. H. Anderson that these disparate sites are both used by one species, *L. unicolor*. The general egg-laying habits for the entire genus are not known for certain.

Species of this genus are so abundant in woodland streams and in quieter backwaters of larger western rivers that a good set of imitations often proves indispensable, both as hatch makers and as searchers. The larval, pupal, and adult patterns all have their best times, depending on when a particular species emerges. It is important for fly fishermen who specialize in tributary waters to know the periods of availability for local species.

Important Species
(Some of the species appear in older entomological texts under the generic name *Mormomyia*.)

L. costalis E, M
On many midwestern streams there is a steady procession of *Lepidostoma* species, beginning with *L. bryanti* in June, shifting to *L. costalis* in late July, and ending with *L. togatum* in August and September. There is considerable overlap in the emergence periods of the three species, and in woodland habitats, where this genus is so important, the trout become accustomed to feeding on the roughly similar size, shape, and color of all three caddisflies. The value of these species is magnified by their similarity because trout get locked into a continuing, day-to-day selectivity to them.

L. quercina W
This is a common spring species in the Northwest, where it inhabits streams and small rivers.

L. veleda W
Records for this early-summer caddisfly are available from some swift mountain streams in Idaho, Colorado, Wyoming, and Montana. It is frequently common in these states.

The larvae of the midwestern species, Lepidostoma togatum, *inhabit quieter areas of overgrown trout streams such as the Straight River in Minnesota.* Bill Goegel (courtesy of Minnesota Department of Conservation)

L. togatum E, M

The larvae of *L. togatum* are a major component of the eastern and midwestern caddisfly fauna, a three-star species on my Species Lists (Chapter 9). In Michigan streams such as Silver and Cherry creeks (tributaries of the Chocolay River) and Syphon and East creeks (tributaries of the Upper Tahquamenon River) or in Wisconsin streams such as Bear Creek, Otter Creek, and of course Woods Creek, these insects are thick in the decaying leaf packs.

This was the most abundant species of the genus in my Quebec collections. In the cool, woodland streams of that Canadian province the pupae were developing during late August, and when they emerged in the evening hours the brook trout (or *omble de la fontaine* as our eastern char is called in Quebec) fed greedily in the pools and along the edges on the drifting pupae.

L. knowltoni W

This western species is common only in Rocky Mountain states, records for Montana, Colorado, and Utah indicating heavy summer emergences.

L. pluviale W

This is the dominant species of the genus in the western mountain region. In Montana, Wyoming, Colorado, Utah, and Idaho it emerges during June and July, the heavy daytime hatches a major event for fly fishermen who understand their significance.

The larvae build circular cases of sand grains. Unlike many other species in the genus, they are not restricted to streams. They establish large populations in the slow backwaters of many large western rivers, such as the Yellowstone, and when they emerge they draw trout into these areas.

L. rayneri W

L. rayneri is closely related to *L. pluviale* and replaces that species in the Coastal and Cascade mountain ranges. It also emerges in June and July.

L. roafi W

This species is most common in the Northwest. It is the main representative of the genus on Vancouver Island, where the September emergence prompts heavy feeding by trout in streams and small rivers such as the Cowichan and Little Qualicum.

L. bryanti M

In upper Midwestern streams this caddisfly rivals *L. togatum* and *L. costalis* in importance. It emerges mainly from mid-May to late June, earlier than its two sister species.

L. unicolor M, W

L. unicolor is distributed in a northerly band as far east as Minnesota, but it is most common in the Northwest. Emergence and egg-laying activity is concentrated in August and September. Dr. Norman Anderson, in *The distribution and biology of the Oregon Trichoptera*, notes that the larvae are primarily responsible for processing decaying pine needles in some western streams: "Laboratory studies indicated that final-instar larvae would ingest more than their body weight per day of conifer needles, but growth did not occur unless the needles were well colonized with a microbial flora."[10]

L. strophis E, M, W

This species is transcontinental in distribution. It emerges primarily in the summer months, but adults have a long flight period. Egg laying continues through October.

L. vernalis E

This species is very common in the spring-fed, woodland streams of the East. It is an early emerger, peaks occurring during April and May. Mating flights begin forming in the afternoon and serious egg-laying activity starts soon afterwards.

L. vernalis has produced fine fly-fishing opportunities for me on many streams, but the most memorable action has been on the beautiful spring creeks of Long Island, especially the Nissequogue and Carmans. A size 16 Brown Deep Sparkle Pupa, worked tight against the banks and fallen trees, has done well during the hatches, taking trout on four consecutive casts twice one afternoon on the Nissequogue River.

L. griseum E, M

The range of this small-stream species extends from Michigan to Ontario, with good populations in the Appalachian region as far south as Georgia. It is active in late summer and early autumn.

L. cascadense W

The larvae of this species, found in small, rapid streams, build a round case of sand grains rather than the typical four-sided bark case of the genus. *L. cascadense* ranges from California north to the Yukon Territory, and inland into the Rocky Mountain region. It is most common in coastal states and provinces, emergence beginning in July and continuing through the summer.

General imitations for *Lepidostoma*:

LARVA: Dark Cased Caddis Larva (sizes 8, 10, 12; case part clipped into a four-sided shape)

PUPA: Brown Deep Sparkle Pupa; Brown Emergent Sparkle Pupa (sizes 14, 16, 18)

ADULT DRY: Brown Dancing Caddis (sizes 14, 16); Thompson Foam Caddis (size 18)

ADULT WET: Brown Diving Caddis (sizes 14, 16, 18)

(The Brown and Yellow series of imitations is useful for some species in this genus.)

ADULT KEYS:

The information for identifying adult specimens is not all in one source. Three different scientific works are needed to key out males of this genus.

Ross, H. H. 1946. "A review of the Nearctic Lepidostomatidae (Trichoptera)." *Ann. Ent. Soc. Am.*, 39(2): 265-291.

Denning, D. G. 1956. "Trichoptera." in *Aquatic Insects of California*, ed. by R. L. Usinger, pp. 237-270. Berkeley and Los Angeles: University of California Press.

Flint, O. S., and G. B. Wiggins. 1961. "Records and description of North American species in the genus *Lepidostoma*, with a revision of the *vernalis* group (Trichoptera: Lepidostomatidae)." *Can. Ent.*, 93: 279-297.

Family Leptoceridae (tube-case maker)
(represented by 7 genera in North America)

Shelter type: larvae in different genera build cases of various materials—rocks, plant fragments, or even pure silk.

Typical feeding habits of the larvae: the larvae in some genera feed in a very specialized way, preying on other insects or on freshwater sponges, but others forage in a more general fashion on plant material.

Typical method of emergence: the pupae swim or crawl to the surface.

Typical egg-laying habits: the females dive under or sprawl on the surface to deposit eggs.

Leptocerus larvae, case and all, swim over and among the weed beds of eastern ponds.

This is one of the most advanced families of caddisflies. It has been suggested that it is not on the same evolutionary track as other tube-case makers, the speculation being that the leptocerid line branched off from fixed-retreat-making ancestors, net-spinning caddisflies, rather than from the free-moving ancestors of other case makers. There are definitely oddities about Leptoceridae that separate it from all other families; for example, these are the only caddisflies where the males of a species are larger than the females.[11]

Four genera are included in this section. *Ceraclea*, the most primitive North American genus in the family, and *Mystacides* are adapted to cool waters. *Oecetis* and *Nectopsyche* are able to thrive in a remarkably wide variety of environments. These genera live in both stillwater and running-water habitats.

Eastern and Midwestern fly fishermen might take note of a genus, *Leptocerus*, that is not covered here because it is only found in ponds and lakes. In the single North

American species, *L. americanus*, the larvae swim with hair-fringed legs, carrying their silk case, among the weed tops. The emerging pupae have been especially important for me in New England trout ponds, from Big Brook Bog in New Hampshire to Ball Pond in Connecticut, during the June and July hatches.

It is very easy for fly fishermen to recognize the adults of this family because the antennae are two and a half times as long as the body. Only one other caddisfly, *Macronema* (family Hydropsychidae), has antennae anywhere near as long, and that genus is so distinctive in its own right, with its metallic blue body, that it can be quickly distinguished from the Leptoceridae.

genus *Ceraclea* (Scaly Wing Sedge)
(approximately 34 known species in North America)

Generalized description of the adult:
adult length up to 13mm

WING: color varies considerably, ranging from light brown to dark brown, or from light gray to almost black. On many species the wings have patches of white hairs and/or pockets of white scales

BODY: varies from straw yellow to green to almost black

LEGS: vary from straw yellow to almost black

The larvae of some species in this genus burrow into and feed on freshwater sponges; other species feed in a more regular fashion on detritus. The burrowers, of course, are almost completely unavailable to trout, and even the crawlers seem to be rather reclusive insects, huddling under rocks or in thick vegetation. These larvae have never been significant in my stomach samplings of trout, even in waters where they have been very abundant, indicating that imitations of them would be of dubious value.

The pupae and adults, however, are very important as models for imitations. In many species emergence and egg laying peaks in early summer, after the flush of major eastern and midwestern caddisflies, and yet these insects are abundant enough to almost be a major caddisfly themselves in these regions. They are active in late afternoon and evening, and based on my personal experience not quite as sensitive to light as other midsummer caddisflies. They tend to begin flying before other warm-weather forms do, and sometimes trout are already feeding selectively on *Ceraclea* species when the general evening blitz of caddisflies begins.

This genus is restricted to cool waters, but it can live in both running and still-water environments. In trout lakes and in trout streams, especially in larger rivers of the mid-South, the major species initiate very predictable sprees of surface feeding by

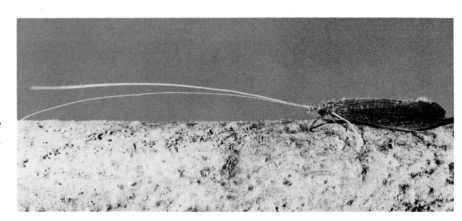

The long antennae on the adults of the Oecetis inconspicua *are very distinctive.* Ken Thompson

trout each season. None of the species are singularly important in the West, although some that are transcontinental in distribution contribute significantly to the overall caddisfly presence on Pacific Coast waters.

Larva

Ceraclea

Adult

Important Species

(Species were previously listed under the generic name *Athripsodes*.)

C. wetzeli E

Angling author Charles Wetzel first collected this northeastern species while researching the important cold-water insects of Pennsylvania. He sent specimens to Dr. H. H. Ross, who named this caddisfly after him. Wetzel wrote in his 1955 book *Trout Flies*: "It appears in great numbers on Kettle Creek around the end of June, at which time the artificial is most successful. One of the most conspicuous features of this insect is its white banded antennae, whence its name Silverhorns."

C. maculata E, M, W

(= *A. transversus*)

With the recent changes in nomenclature this genus can be very confusing for any angler searching old entomological records. For example, in "The caddis flies, or Trichoptera, of Illinois" (1944) by H. H. Ross, *Ceraclea maculata* is described under the name *Athripsodes transversus*, which might seem like a simple enough synonym; but there is also a modern *Ceraclea transversa*, which in older texts is listed as *Athripsodes angustus*. There is no link between the older *Athripsodes transversus* (now *Ceraclea maculata*) and the modern *Ceraclea transversa*.

C. maculata is widespread and common in the Midwest, ranging from Wisconsin south to Texas, with possibly its greatest value to fly fishermen being in the Ozark tail-water rivers. There are records from Georgia to California also. Emergence and egg laying may take place from May through September, but in the White River (Arkansas) the peak activity is in June.

C. transversa E, M

(= *A. angustus*)

This species is especially important for fly fishermen in the Northeast. It appears in great numbers along slower streams and rivers on summer evenings.

The larvae of some Ceraclea *species burrow into and feed on freshwater sponges. Large populations of these species occur where sponges are found. Shown above, left to right, are a clump of freshwater sponges, a sponge encrusted* Ceraclea *larva case, and the larva.* Ken Thompson

C. resurgens E, M, W

This is one of the species in the genus that feeds on freshwater sponges by burrowing into the colonies. The larvae build their cases entirely of silk excretions. In the spring, or in some instances in the fall, they pupate right in the sponge mats. Emergence occurs mainly in late spring or early summer, depending on the region, and it is frequently concentrated enough to make trout feed selectively on this species.

C. tarsipunctata E, M, W

H. H. Ross, in "The caddis flies, or Trichoptera, of Illinois," wrote about *C. tarsipunctata*, "The larvae live in lakes and streams. They are abundant in many of the glacial lakes in northeastern Illinois; the streams they frequent are generally fairly clear, rapid and cool. There is usually only one generation a year, the large wave of adults occurring during May and June."

This species is not only abundant in Illinois, which is not a hot-spot for trout, but throughout the eastern and midwestern states. The adults become so numerous around lights that this species is considered one of the "nuisance" caddisflies (although they have not been a nuisance to me on the evenings when I have found trout feasting on them).

General imitations for *Ceraclea*:

LARVA:	none
PUPA:	Brown Deep Sparkle Pupa, Brown Emergent Sparkle Pupa (sizes 12, 14, 16)
ADULT DRY:	Brown Dancing Caddis (sizes 12, 14, 16)
ADULT WET:	Brown Diving Caddis (sizes 12, 14, 16)
	(The quite variable coloration among species in this genus means that fly fishermen must also be prepared with a Gray and Brown series and a Brown and Green series of imitations when fishing specific hatches.)
ADULT KEYS:	Morse, J. C. 1975. "A phylogeny and revision of the caddisfly genus *Ceraclea* (Trichoptera: Leptoceridae)." *Contr. Amer. Ent. Inst.*, 11 (2).

Genus *Nectopsyche* (White Miller)
(approximately 12 known species in North America north of Mexico)

Generalized description of the adult:
adult length up to 17 mm

WING:	varies from white to pale brown to gray
BODY:	varies from white to pale green
LEGS:	vary from white to cream

Larva

Nectopsyche

These caddisflies, or millers, as they are commonly known, are nocturnal insects. The mating clouds start dancing at twilight, rising and falling in unison, but they seldom touch the water. The egg laying of the adults and the emergence of the pupae both happen in full darkness during midsummer. A white dry fly at dusk or a white pupa fly at dawn might fool a few trout, but to really take advantage of these abundant caddisflies the angler must fly-fish at night.

Adult

Night fishing is not for everyone. Some people find no enjoyment at all in the tangled leaders, unseen snags, voracious mosquitoes, and strange noises in the dark—but then, there is no accounting for odd prejudices of people. It is sufficient to note that a few fly fishermen love the excitement of night angling and most do not.

A group of anglers can avoid many of the frustrations of night fishing by pitching a tent and building a fire near a promising hole on the river. In between the one or two hour stretches of casting they can sip coffee or play cards. With a place to go to untangle lines or tie on new flies, they can have the excitement of night fishing without the disasters.

These caddisflies thrive in perfect waters for night fishing. Most of them prefer slow, weedy streams—and these are easy spots to work wet or dry imitations of the egg-laying females or to fish Deep or Emergent imitations of the struggling pupae. The fact that a white fly is highly visible to both fish and fishermen is a nice bonus.

Important Species

(The species of this genus all used to be considered under the generic name *Leptocella*.)

N. exquisita E, M

This species has a widespread north-to-south distribution, from Quebec to Florida, and is important not only in midwestern waters but also in Ozark trout streams and lakes.

N. diarina E, M, W

The preferred habitat of *N. diarina* is swift, clear streams, where the larvae stay under stones along the edges. None of the species in this genus are very abundant in the Rocky Mountain states, but this one can be common in some localities in the region. In the East and the Midwest it is an important trout-stream insect during the midsummer emergence period.

N. albida E, M, W

The range of this species, which probably served as inspiration for the name white miller, extends across the northern tier of states from Oregon to New York. It can be very abundant in the slow sections of streams and rivers.

Craig Mathews, now the police chief of West Yellowstone but formerly a resident of Michigan, described the great night fishing this species causes on rivers such as the Rogue and the White, and on their tributaries, from late July to mid-August. He recommended that anglers try the same method used for the *Hexagenia limbata* (a big mayfly) hatch: "It's best to get a position on a pool at dusk, but wait for the splashes of feeding fish. The hard part is not to flog the water. A fly fisherman should save his casts, and work steadily only over the biggest sounding trout."

General imitations for *Nectopsyche*:

LARVA:	Light Cased Caddis Larva for those species that make a case of stones; Dark Cased Caddis Larva for those species that make a case of plant material (sizes 2, 4)
PUPA:	White Deep Sparkle Pupa; White Emergent Sparkle Pupa (sizes 8, 10, 12, 14)
ADULT DRY:	White Dancing Caddis (sizes 10, 12, 14); Parkany Deer Hair Caddis, an all-white version (sizes 8, 10)

ADULT WET: White Diving Caddis (sizes 8, 10, 12, 14)
             (In some species the abdomen of the females, filled with eggs, can be bright green, and for these millers there is a White and Bright Green series in the pattern listing.)

ADULT KEYS: Ross, H. H. 1944. "The caddis flies, or Trichoptera, of Illinois." *Bull. Ill. Nat. Hist. Surv. No. 23.* (The insects will be listed under the name *Leptocella*.)

The adults of this genus must be preserved dry, not in alcohol, because the patterns of the wing hairs are important in the identification process.

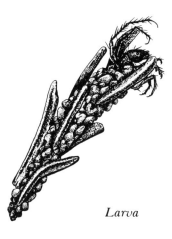

Larva

Mystacides

genus *Mystacides* (Black Dancer)
(3 known species in North America)

Generalized description of the adult:
adult length up to 9mm
WING: varies from metallic black to dark brown
BODY: varies from yellow to dark brown
LEGS: straw yellow

Adult

The common name, Black Dancer, comes from a description in entomologist Annie Hill-Griffin's 1912 survey of Oregon caddisflies, in which she notes how the mating swarms of the adults rise and fall "with dizzying pertinacity."

This genus is often abundant in lakes and slow-moving streams. Its value to fly fishermen is high because the adults are strictly a daytime insect, emergence and egg-laying flights occurring during the morning and evening hours. The pupae crawl out of the water, either on a shoreline rock or a protruding object, in the first hours after dawn. The females dive and lay their eggs underwater at dusk. The emergence and flight periods for all species are spread out over the warmer months of the summer.

The larvae crawl freely over the bottom, with little or no effort at concealment. They build relatively long, thin cases of plant, rock, or mollusk-shell fragments, a ten-millimeter insect carrying around a thirty-millimeter case. When they are ready to pupate the larvae attach these cases to the surface of submerged objects.

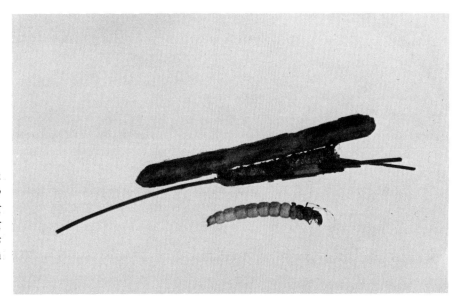

The larva of Mystacides *lay a long stick lengthwise on the case, possibly to keep other insects or small fish from swallowing the case whole. The fly tier can put a long stripped hackle quill lengthwise on his imitation to match this feature.* Ken Thompson

Important Species

M. interjecta **E, M, W**
(= *M. longicornis*)
This species has a wide range, records available from coast to coast. It is especially abundant in the Midwest. The dull gray-black or brownish black coloration of the wings, instead of a metallic black coloration, is a diagnostic characteristic used in some entomological keys to separate it from the other species in the genus, but this may not be a totally reliable feature.

M. sepulchralis **E, M, W**
This shiny black species is transcontinental in distribution. It is an important caddisfly in the trout ponds of the East, as well as in slow-moving sections of rivers.

M. alafimbriata **W**
This is the predominant member of the genus in the mountain and coastal regions of the West. It inhabits lakes, ponds, and reservoirs at a wide range of altitudes, but it also becomes very common in slow, weedy rivers. Peak emergence and egg-laying times for *M. alafimbriata* are in late June and early July.

My specimens from the Henrys Fork were of two varieties, the expected type with shiny black wings and another type with dull, dark gray wings. The bodies of both varieties were yellow, but those of the females were much brighter. These samples were identified to species level by Ken Thompson, and his findings were verified by Dr. Oliver Flint, so there was no doubt that both color types were *M. alafimbriata*.

General imitations for *Mystacides*:

LARVA:	Light Cased Caddis Larva, tied with a very slender body (sizes 4, 6, 8, 10)
PUPA:	Black Deep Sparkle Pupa; Black Emergent Sparkle Pupa (sizes 14, 16)
ADULT DRY:	Black Dancing Caddis (sizes 14, 16)
ADULT WET:	Black Diving Caddis (sizes 14, 16)
	(In the West the Black and Yellow series of imitations might be needed for *M. alafimbriata*.)
ADULT KEYS:	Yamamota, T., and G. B. Wiggins. 1964. "A comparative study of the North American species in the caddisfly genus *Mystacides*." *Can. J. Zool.*, 42: 1105-1126.

genus *Oecetis* (Long-Horn Sedge)
(20 known species in North America north of Mexico)

Generalized description of the adult:
adult length up to 12mm

WING:	varies from straw yellow to brown
BODY:	varies from yellow to brown
LEGS:	vary from yellow to brown

Larva

Oecetis

Adult

Even in my earliest caddisfly collections a pattern became apparent with *Oecetis;* both emergence and egg-laying periods were very spread out. Specimens of each species kept turning up in my samplings for months. Professional collections usually listed May to October records for this genus also.

These extended emergence and egg-laying periods have a great influence on trout. There is usually a two- to three-week peak in the activity, and if a particular species is abundant in a stream it can easily make fish feed selectively. After the peak time there may still be enough stragglers for fish to concentrate on that one species.

Stomach samplings of trout often confirm a strong selectivity to *Oecetis* even after the peak appearance of this caddisfly. The selective response would not normally carry over so long, but it does with this genus for two reasons: one, the populations of an *Oecetis* species can be so tremendous in certain habitats that even the stragglers create major concentrations; and two, the stragglers are popping during midsummer, a time when other caddisflies are not particularly prevalent. The pupal and adult imitations for the main species of this genus continue to work effectively all summer on some rivers.

The larvae of *Oecetis* prefer either stillwater or slow-water habitats. They are free-moving predators, crawling over sand or rubble patches of bottom. Especially during their final instar the larvae become an important item in the trout's diet. During May, June, and July, imitations of them are good searching patterns.

Important Species

The species of this genus are abundant in lakes and ponds as well as in streams. *O. immobilis*, *O. persimilis*, *O. osteni*, and *O. cinerascens* may show up in the angler's collections, but they are usually not common in trout streams. The stillwater fly fisherman should be aware of them because they are important food items for fish both in cold- and warm-water habitats.

O. inconspicua E, M, W
O. inconspicua probably has a distribution as widespread as any other caddisfly species. It is found almost everywhere in North America, ranging from Nova Scotia to Mexico. This broad geographic availability, coupled with the fact that it occurs in immense numbers in lakes and streams in most regions of the country, make it a very important midsummer insect for both fish and fishermen.

Most of my experiences with *O. inconspicua* have been on trout waters in the East, mainly on slow-moving rivers and ponds. When the pupae emerge or the females return to lay their eggs the trout cruise the shallow margins, actively searching for victims instead of letting the currents bring them. An imitation of either stage of *O. inconspicua*, worked with a subtle twitch, often attracts these prowling fish.

O. ochracea E, M, W
This species is widely distributed across the northern half of this country and the southern half of Canada. It is mainly a midsummer caddisfly.

O. avara E, M, W
The larvae of *O. avara* have the ability to inhabit fairly swift streams and rivers. These insects, with their horn-shaped cases of large sand grains, still prefer the quieter current areas, but they are not restricted to generally slower rivers as are many species in the genus.

Throughout the northern portion of its range this species is definitely a fair-weather caddisfly. In milder climates as in the East or far West it emerges mainly in

June; in the mountain West the activity does not begin in earnest until mid-July.

This is one of the lighter-colored species in the genus, the wings, body, and legs of the adults varying from a straw yellow to a rich amber. It has to be matched with the Ginger series of pupal and adult imitations rather than with the Brown series that is used for most species.

O. disjuncta W

In the past there has been some disagreement among entomologists about *O. disjuncta*. Is this a separate species or is it just a darker color phase of *O. avara*? It is generally considered a different species by modern caddisfly specialists.

On the Henrys Fork the peak emergence and egg-laying periods for *O. disjuncta* occur in late June (two to three weeks before the peak for *O. avara*). The morning and afternoon activities are heavy enough to get rainbows feeding on the flats, the fish rolling and occasionally jumping as they pursue either pupae or female adults. There is normally a two-hour lull in both the insect and the fish movement between noon and 2 P.M.

General imitations for *Oecetis*:

LARVA:	Light Cased Caddis Larva for those species that make cases of stone; Dark Cased Caddis Larva for those species that make cases of vegetation (sizes 10, 12, 14)
PUPA:	Brown Deep Sparkle Pupa; Brown Emergent Sparkle Pupa (sizes 12, 14, 16)
ADULT DRY:	Brown Dancing Caddis (sizes 12, 14, 16)
ADULT WET:	Brown Diving Caddis (sizes 12, 14, 16) (The coloration can vary widely within this genus. The Ginger Series better matches *O. avara* and the Brown and Yellow series better matches *O. disjuncta*.)
ADULT KEYS:	Ross, H. H. 1944. "The caddis flies, or Trichoptera, of Illinois." *Bull. Illinois Nat. Hist. Surv. No. 23.*

Why don't mayfly species emerge over a long period of time? Usually a mayfly hatch is finished in a matter of days, or at most a few weeks, on a particular section of river. It generally has to be concentrated because mayfly adults lead such brief existences. Any stray emergers, coming out either before or after the main hatch, might not find any mating partners from their species. To insure successful fertilization the hatching time is normally very well coordinated for a brood class.

Many caddisfly species emerge for weeks or months from a particular area. Unlike mayflies the adult caddisfly can ingest liquids, which prevents dehydration, and it can live a long time compared to mayflies. The stray emerger, even when it develops months earlier or later than the main group, is going to have a good chance of finding a mating partner still around.

Even when the emergence period for a caddisfly species is spread out there is usually a peak. In my records the main hatch occurs from one to three weeks after the start for spring and early-summer species, the stragglers continuing to emerge throughout the warmer months; for late-summer and fall species the stragglers appear early, a month or two before the main hatch, and the big burst of emergers occurs one to three weeks before the end of the activity period.

Family Limnephilidae (tube-case maker)
(represented by 52 genera in North America)

Shelter type: the larvae construct a true tube case, with an inner matrix of silk and an outer covering of plant or mineral material.

Typical feeding habits of the larvae: the larvae of most genera feed on algae or on decaying leaves and woody materials, but animal matter is consumed by some genera in the course of general foraging.

Typical method of emergence: in some genera the pupae swim and in some genera they crawl to emerge.

Typical egg-laying habits: in genera of the advanced subfamily Limnephilinae, with roughly half the species in the family, the females lay their eggs on rocks or vegetation near the water. The females of most species in the remaining genera dive or crawl beneath the surface and cement their eggs to objects on the stream bottom.

It is almost impossible to make general statements about this very diverse family. There are fifty-two genera with over three hundred species in North America. In physical features they vary in size from the 5.3-millimeter larvae of *Lepania*, as small as some microcaddis, to the 35-millimeter larval giants of genera such as *Hydatophylax* and *Dicosmoecus*. Coloration varies from the drab, dark wings of genera such as *Oligophlebodes* to the spectacularly patterned wings of *Hesperophylax*.

There certainly is no uniformity among the different genera in habitat preference. This family has adapted to life in most aquatic environments—spring seeps, fast streams, quiet rivers, lakes, swamps, and even damp soils. It is well represented in all types of trout water throughout North America. In most regional surveys of caddisflies the largest number of species and the greatest percentage of individual insects collected are usually from this family.[12]

Even the habits of the larvae, pupae, and adults in the fifty-two genera vary considerably. The larvae feed mainly as shredders on leaves or as grazers on algae, but there are types that scavenge dead fish or strain organic muck. The pupae emerge by swimming or crawling, but within those parameters there are all combinations and gradations. Adult females lay their eggs near, on, or in the water.

All-encompassing principles, even the kind of extensive inferences usually allowable in fly-fishing entomologies, are too risky with this family. Many of the misconceptions anglers have about the limnephilids are traceable to past attemps at generalization.

The fact that fly fishermen need broad principles of biology, not a collection of exceptions, makes it difficult to handle this family. It might be possible to clarify it somewhat by dividing it into two groups: the primitive and the highly advanced genera. Each group exhibits certain characteristics with fair—if not complete—consistency. (In Chapter 8, The Biology of Caddisflies, the discussion on evolution presented the entomologist's theory that the more primitive genera are restricted to cool, running-water habitats, and that more advanced genera, reacting to selective pressures, have adapted to fill a greater variety of ecological niches.)

Advanced genera. The next step down the taxonomic ladder below family is subfamily. Among the six subfamilies in Limnephilidae the most advanced is Limnephilinae. Not surprisingly it is the most diverse and most successful, containing nearly one-half of all species in the entire family.

The evolutionary adaptations that have allowed the genera of Limnephilinae to gain such dominance also tend to make some of them less important to trout fishermen. Many genera either live in habitats too warm for trout, or in marginal areas of trout waters where they are unavailable to fish. Even genera found in trout streams have often evolved habits that lessen their value as a food resource.

This subfamily is responsible for the misconception that all adult females in the Limnephilidae family lay their eggs near the water, either in overhead bushes or on streamside rocks, rather than in the water. If totally true, this would be very unfortunate, eliminating both feeding opportunities for trout and great angling situations for fly fishermen.

But it is not. For many primitive genera in other subfamilies underwater egg-laying is the rule, observations by entomologists confirming this habit for important trout-stream groups such as *Oligophlebodes* (W. D. Pearson and R. H. Kramer), *Onocosmoecus* (M. J. Winterbourn), and *Dicosmoecus* (G. B. Wiggins).

Dr. Wiggins has suggested that for the subfamily Limnephilinae, whose females do lay their eggs out of water, the habit is an adaptation that separates it from the more primitive subfamilies. One advantage this gives these caddisflies is that it helps them to populate streams and ponds that dry up in midsummer. The eggs do not hatch

5mm

Not all adult caddisflies are drab. The wings of Hesperophylax *(Silver Stripe Sedge) for example, are distinctly patterned.* Jon Speir

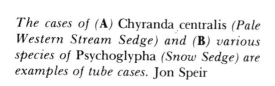

The cases of (A) Chyranda centralis *(Pale Western Stream Sedge) and (B) various species of* Psychoglypha *(Snow Sedge) are examples of tube cases.* Jon Speir

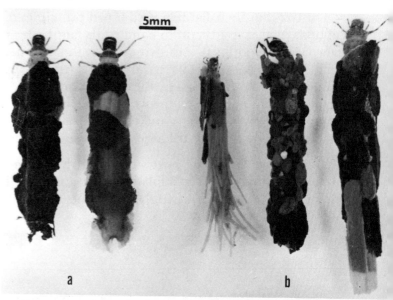

5mm

a   b

until the fall rains wash them into the streambed—the same rains filling these streams with water.

Some genera in the subfamily Limnephilinae are restricted to cool, running water (*Chyranda, Hydatophylax, Pycnopsyche, Frenesia, Psychoglypha*); others survive in a wide range of habitats but are also abundant in trout streams (*Hesperophylax, Limnephilus, Platycentropus*). These genera are included here because they can be important to trout as larvae, emerging pupae, and even as adults.

More primitive genera. It has not been proven that all genera in the advanced subfamily Limnephilinae lay their eggs out of water; nor has it been proven that all genera in the more primitive subfamilies lay their eggs in the water. Observations made so far by entomologists show that these habits seem to be the tendencies, but there will have to be many more biological studies on individual genera before statements can be made for all with any certainty.

The Limnephilidae genera in this second category, regardless of their egg-laying habits, are among the most important caddisflies in our gravel-bottomed trout streams and rivers. The larvae crawl freely over the bottom, a constant target for rooting fish, and in some instances drift quite heavily. This last habit is especially endearing in such genera as *Oligophlebodes* and *Dicosmoecus* because the peak rates of drift occur during the day.

Every one of the genera included here in this primitive category—*Dicosmoecus, Ecclisomyia, Neophylax, Oligophlebodes, Onocosmoecus, Apatania, Ironoquia,* and *Goera*—has a well-coordinated emergence period. Most of the pupae in the yearly brood hatch within a two-to three-week time span, creating good concentrations of a species even if the population figures are only moderately high. This is in contrast to other types of caddisflies that might hatch sporadically over a period of months.

Some of these Limnephilidae pupae, in both primitive and advanced categories, are supposed to emerge by crawling to the shallows and climbing out on rocks, but in my observations they have done more than just crawl. During their hasty migration the pupae half swim and half clamber toward the shore, bouncing up into the water column with every aberrant swirl of current. They become exposed to trout repeatedly while moving.

Dr. Walter Balduf, in *The Bionomics of Entomophagous Insects*, describes a rather odd behavior that emphasizes the importance of the adults regardless of how they later lay their eggs: "On hot days, where pools were shaded by old beech trees, he [Wesenberg-Lund, a Swedish entomologist] saw the large . . . Limnophilodae, often in large numbers, running and flying over the water surface. While being pursued by the males, the females circled and spiralled nicely over the mirror-like water. When hundreds tumble thus over the water they present an attractive insect picture. But these dances are only preliminary to copulation, which takes place in the woods along the shore. Here one sees the insects with caudal ends joined and the bodies lying in linear fashion, the smaller male partly concealed beneath the wings of the females. If disturbed the united individuals are unable to fly, but fall head foremost upon the water and seek to escape by running."

Sometimes it is large numbers or great size or unusual vulnerability that makes a particular genus valuable to trout and fly fishermen. For one limnephilid, *Dicosmoecus*, all three things work together to create a "dream insect." Many other genera have species that rate almost as high.

genus *Pycnopsyche* (Great Brown Autumn Sedge)
(16 known species in North America)

Generalized description of the adult:
adult length up to 22mm
WING: yellow background with brown shading
BODY: ginger
LEGS: straw yellow

Larva

Pycnopsyche

Adult

Pycnopsyche larvae, with their cases of lengthwise sticks, are one of the most important converters of leaf material in the woodland brooks and rivers of the East and Midwest. Their life cycle is completely synchronized with this food source—the eggs hatch in the fall, just as the deciduous trees are shedding their foliage; the larvae feed and grow throughout the winter and spring, until early summer when the high water flushes away the accumulations of decaying leaves; the larvae enter diapause, a quiescent period, sealing off their cases, once their food source is diminished; they remain in this inactive state until they pupate in late summer; emergence, mating, and egg laying occur in early fall, producing a new generation in time for the next input of leaves.

The pupae emerge and the adults fly mostly at night, but there is an evening and morning spill-over of both activities. Pupal imitations, swung in tight against a deep bank with the stutter-drift technique, have proven themselves very deadly at dawn. Big dry-fly imitations, twitched and skittered, provide exciting moments in the dark.

This genus is in the advanced Limnephilinae subfamily, but Dr. K. W. Cummins observed underwater egg laying with *Pycnopsyche*. He wondered if this habit might be abnormal because it conflicted with older, general statements on the terrestrial egg laying of limnephilid caddisflies, "No eggs were found in the field, but several gelatinous egg masses were discovered below the water surface and adult females were often seen submerged in laboratory cultures."[13]

One summer J. Marshall Edmonds and I, while preparing to write a pamphlet abut fly-fishing in Quebec's Laurentides Park, hiked through that beautiful preserve. We collected insect samples from every stream and river; and could have packed pint bottles full of *Pycnopsyche* larvae from any pool. We concluded that in these wild, tree-shaded waters populated with brook trout the pupae had to be the most important food item in the fall, and as such would dictate the cycle of good fly-fishing and poor fly-fishing hours then.

Important Species
(The old generic *Stenophylax* was a very broad term, encompassing what includes several modern genera, one of which is now *Pycnopsyche*.)

P. guttifer E, M
Adults have been collected as far West as Wyoming and Montana, but the species is very rare in these regions. It is the major member of the genus in eastern woodland streams.

P. lepida E, M
The ranges of *P. lepida* and *P. guttifer* overlap considerably, both species often sharing the same streams, but *P. lepida* seems to be the more abundant of the two in the upper Midwest, with *P. guttifer* predominating in the Northeast. The larvae of *P.*

lepida move into slightly faster currents than those inhabited by its sister species, and the pupae also emerge two to three weeks earlier.

In Michigan this species is very common, not only in major trout streams such as the AuSable and the Pere Marquette but also in those small Upper Peninsula flowages characterized by their dark, tannic-stained water and bright brook trout.

P. scabripennis E, M

In *A Book of Trout Flies*, the first American angling entomology to use scientific terminology, Preston Jennings introduced the genus to fly fishermen under the older name, *Stenophylax*. He noted the large populations of *P. scabripennis* on the upper Neversink River (New York).

General imitations for *Pycnopsyche*:

LARVA:	Strawman Nymph (sizes 4, 6)
PUPA:	Ginger Deep Sparkle Pupa; Ginger Emergent Sparkle Pupa (sizes 4, 6, 8)
ADULT DRY:	Light Bucktail Caddis (sizes 4, 6, 8)
ADULT WET:	Ginger Diving Caddis (sizes 4, 6, 8)
ADULT KEYS:	Betten, C. 1950. "The genus *Pycnopsyche* (Trichoptera)." *Ann. Ent. Soc. Am.*, 43 (4): 508-522.

genus *Chyranda* (Pale Western Stream Sedge)
(1 known species in North America)

Generalized description of the adult:
adult length up to 14mm

WING:	light mottled brown
BODY:	straw yellow
LEGS:	light brown

The larvae of *C. centralis*, the only species in the genus, are a characteristic part of spring-brook and small-stream fauna in the mountain West. They are common to abundant from Montana to Oregon and as far south as Utah. They pupate and emerge from mid-July to October, with a peak generally in the middle of that span. Most of the activity occurs in the evening.

Larva

Important Species

C. centralis W

This species is also distributed over much of northern Canada, but it is generally common only in the western mountain region.

Chyranda

General imitations for *Chyranda*:

LARVA:	Dark Cased Caddis Larva (sizes 2, 4, 6)
PUPA:	Brown and Yellow Deep Sparkle Pupa; Brown and Yellow Emergent Sparkle Pupa (sizes 10, 12)
ADULT DRY:	Brown and Yellow Dancing Caddis, Thompson Foam Caddis (sizes 10, 12)
ADULT WET:	Brown and Yellow Diving Caddis (sizes 10, 12)

Adult

A size 6 Ginger Deep Sparkle Pupa, shown above, might seem large for a caddisfly imitation, but it is on the small side of the recommended range for the giant Hydato-phylax emergers. Gary LaFontaine

ADULT KEYS: not needed; the angler can use any comprehensive key to identify the specimen to generic level.

genus *Hydatophylax* (Giant Cream Pattern-Wing Sedge)
(4 known species in North America)

generalized description of the adult:
adult length up to 34mm
WING: light brown background with cream, nearly transparent patterns
BODY: light ginger
LEGS: straw yellow

Larva

Hydatophylax

Adult

The larvae attain a length of thirty-five millimeters, but they build stick cases that are even larger, up to a huge seventy-five millimeters. These big crawlers live on the edges and in the backwater areas of midsize to large streams, where they feed on the woody debris that settles in these quieter areas.

Stomach samplings of eastern trout indicate that they feed heavily on *Hydatophylax argus* emergers early in the morning. An imitation of these stout-bodied pupae, as large as size 2, inched slowly across the bottom, often works well in June and July on small streams.

Important Species

(*Astenophylax* is an older scientific name for this species)

H. argus E, M
H. argus has a Z design on its wings. It is a common species in brooks from Maine to Wisconsin. Emergence periods range from midsummer to fall.
H. hesperus W
The distribution of this western species extends from British Columbia to California. It is common in small streams along the western slopes of the Pacific mountain ranges, emerging from August to October.

General imitations:

LARVA: none (The larvae build such large cases that they are outside the range of practical imitation during most of this stage.)

PUPA: Ginger Deep Sparkle Pupa; Ginger Emergent Sparkle Pupa (sizes 1/0, 1, 2, 4, 6)

ADULT DRY: Light Bucktail Caddis (sizes 2, 4, 6, 8)

ADULT WET: Ginger Diving Caddis (sizes 2, 4, 6, 8)

ADULT KEYS: Schmid, F. 1950. "Le genre *Hydatophylax*." *Mitt. Schweiz. Ent. Ges.* 23 (3): 265-295.

genus *Frenesia* (Dot Wing Winter Sedge)
(2 known species in North America)

Generalized description of adult:
adult length up to 15.5mm

WING: background a medium shade of brown uniformly covered with translucent dots

BODY: very dark brown

LEGS: yellowish brown

Many eastern and midwestern states have begun keeping their trout seasons open either longer or year-round, giving fly fishermen the chance to get out to their favorite places during the late-autumn and early-winter months. As a result some very late-season caddisflies such as *Frenesia* have assumed new importance for anglers.

The larvae of this genus are common in cold spring streams and rivers. They crawl freely over the bottom, feeding on decaying leaves and sticks. Often in late summer, just before pupation, they are one of the largest food items left in the streams. Because they also become more active and more available to trout at these times, the larvae and their rock and wood cases are worth imitating with the Cased Caddis pattern.

Emergence begins in late September and continues through the early-winter months, but the peak is usually in November. The dark pupae crawl and swim to the shallows, sometimes slipping away into the currents. As the weather turns colder the hours of emergence become more synchronized with the nicest period of the day.

The adults of this genus survive into the winter and are commonly seen on snowdrifts even in January. There are no reports of their being a significant food item during egg laying, but as more fly fishermen take advantage of late-season fishing and learn more about these caddisflies, there should be new information about their availability during this stage.

Larva

Frenesia

Adult

Important Species

(formerly part of the genus *Chilostigma*)

F. difficilis E

The range of this species does not extend into the midwestern states. It is the larger of the two, adults measuring from 14.5 to 15.5 millimeters (compared to 11.5 to 13.5 millimeters for *F. missa*).

F. missa E, M
This seems to be the more abundant of the two species in the genus, even though they often share the same streams. It is common throughout the East and as far west as Minnesota.

General imitations for *Frenesia*:

LARVA: Medium Cased Caddis Larva (sizes 2, 4, 6)
PUPA: Brown Deep Sparkle Pupa; Brown Emergent Sparkle Pupa (sizes 10, 12, 14)
ADULT DRY: Brown Dancing Caddis (sizes 12, 14, 16)
ADULT WET: Brown Diving Caddis (sizes 12, 14, 16)

ADULT KEYS: Schmid, F. 1952. "Le groupe de *Chilostigma.*" *Arch. Hydrobiol.* 47(1): 75-163.

genus *Platycentropus* (Chocolate and Cream Sedge)
(3 known species in North America)

Generalized description of the adult:
adult length up to 23mm

WING: various shades of brown; the distinct color pattern of the wings, blending shades of brown ranging from cream to chocolate, resemble an ice cream mix
BODY: varies from dark yellow to brown
LEGS: dark yellow

Larva

Platycentropus

Adult

Which caddisfly was the inspiration for Paul Young's Strawman Nymph? It could have been patterned after any one of several limnephilid genera that use sticks in a crisscross fashion for their cases, but there is a good chance that the main model for this fly was the larva of *Platycentropus radiatus*. In those upper Midwestern trout rivers where Paul Young fished this is the species he would have seen crawling like so many bristling hedgehogs in the quiet backwaters.

When high water stirs up the debris in the slacker areas of a stream it kicks these larvae into the current. They evidently drift for many miles, and while they are traveling helplessly with the flow fish pick them off with obvious relish.[14]

My stomach samplings of trout from rivers such as the Straight in Minnesota reveal that fish also prey heavily on the pupae. Most of this midsummer feeding takes

The rough case of Platycentropus *might have been the inspiration for the Strawman Nymph. Shown above, left to right, are a case with larva, an empty case, an uncased larva, and a case with larva.* Ken Thompson

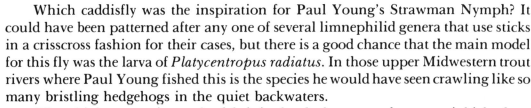

place at night, but at dawn there are generally a few trout still prowling the shallows searching for one last emerger.

Important Species

P. radiatus E, M
P. radiatus is able to thrive in a wide variety of habitats, including stillwaters and warm waters, but it is also common in medium-size streams and large rivers in the East, from Newfoundland to Georgia, as well as in the Midwest.

General imitations for *Platycentropus*:

LARVA:	Strawman Nymph (sizes 2, 4, 6, 8)
PUPA:	Brown and Yellow Deep Sparkle Pupa; Brown and Yellow Emergent Sparkle Pupa (sizes 4, 6, 8)
ADULT DRY:	Dark Bucktail Caddis (sizes 6, 8, 10); Brown and Yellow Dancing Caddis (size 10)
ADULT WET:	Brown and Yellow Diving Caddis (sizes 6, 8, 10)
ADULT KEYS:	*Platycentropus radiatus*, the most important trout stream species, is described and illustrated in the following text: Ross, H. H. 1944. The Caddis Flies, or Trichoptera, of Illinois. *Bull. Ill, Nat. Hist. Surv.* 23.

Larva

Limnephilus

genus Limnephilus (Summer Flier Sedge)
(approximately 95 known species in North America)

Generalized description of the adult:
adult length up to 20mm (but 13mm to 15mm is average)

WING:	varies from ginger to a rich, reddish brown
BODY:	varies from ginger to brown
LEGS:	vary from ginger to brown

The larvae in different species of Limnephilus build a variety of cases. The cases may be made of either mineral or vegetable matter, or a combination of the two. The stick case of Limnephilus submonilifer is shown above.

The English entomologist R. McLachlan, writing in 1874, described this genus as "most unruly," and the scientific confusion over it has not diminished much since then. There have been proposals to break up this single genus into as many as fifteen new ones. Some revision is likely in the near future.

Most species in this genus are stillwater forms, and as such they can be very important to fly fishermen who work the lakes, but they inhabit only the peripheral regions of trout streams, the cut-off oxbows and stagnant backwaters. There are a few species that live in running-water environments, ranging from free-stone streams to spring creeks, and some of these do become abundant enough to be valuable to trout.

One of the oddities of this genus is that when the adults of some species emerge in late spring or early summer they are not sexually mature. They remain near the stream or pond all summer. In the fall, with the delayed development of the reproductive capacity, they mate and the females lay eggs near the water.

Important Species
(In older taxonomies this genus used to be broken up into many smaller genera.

Adult

One of these genera that sometimes shows up in angling literature is *Arctoecia*.)

L. sericeus E, M, W

This transcontinental species lives in a wide range of habitats, including stillwaters (sloughs, ponds, and lakes) and running waters (small brooks, midsize streams, and full-size rivers). They can be abundant in spring-creek environments. J. Leonard and F. Leonard note in *An Annotated List of Michigan Trichoptera*: "This was the most prevalent species of *Limnephilus* seen along the AuSable River during the 1948 season. Adults occurred in large numbers throughout the summer."

L. indivisus E, M (rare in the Northwest)

The different species in the *Limnephilus* genus construct many different types of cases as larvae. Some of them use sand grains or pebbles; others use wood, leaves, or bark. *L. indivisus* builds a case of woody materials, laying flat pieces of bark and wood in a criss cross jumble (these cases look somewhat like the rough hedgehog cases of *Platycentropus*).

This species is most abundant in the Northeast. The larvae inhabit the pools, flats, and quiet edges of streams and small rivers, as well as a variety of stillwater environments. The adults become prominent in the late summer and the early fall months.

L. submonilifer E, M

This species, widely distributed throughout the East and Midwest, is frequently common in the slower areas of streams, but in my mind it is forever linked with a series of spring-fed beaver ponds in New Hampshire. The larvae are so plentiful there that they cover the bottom. In the latter part of May the brook trout move into the shallows in the evening to intercept the migrating pupae.

L. spinatus W

This species, a slow-water form, is to Rocky Mountain fly fishermen what *L. submonilifer* is to eastern fly fishermen. The larvae can be common in the gentler streams, but it is in spring-fed ponds that it becomes really important.

A basic knowledge of the emergence habits of this species once paid off beautifully for me on some beaver ponds above Deer Lodge, Montana—at dawn in late June, prepared with a perfectly matching Ginger Deep Sparkle Pupa, I caught two brook trout, 4½ pounds and 5½ pounds, and broke off one that was larger. These fish were gorging on the straggling emergers from the previous night.

General imitations for *Limnephilus*:
LARVA: Dark Cased Caddis Larva (sizes 2, 4, 6, 8)
PUPA: Ginger Deep Sparkle Pupa; Ginger Emergent Sparkle Pupa (sizes 4, 6, 8, 10)

The species Limnephilus submonilifer *is important not only in slower streams and rivers, but also in cold-water ponds and lakes.* Ken Thompson

ADULT DRY: Light Bucktail Caddis (sizes 4, 6, 8, 10); Ginger Dancing Caddis (size 10)

ADULT WET: Ginger Diving Caddis (sizes 4, 6, 8, 10)
(A darker set of imitations, basically brown, might be needed for some species.)

ADULT KEYS: Ross, H. H., and D. R. Merkley, 1952. "An annotated key to the Nearctic males of *Limnephilus*." *Am. Midl. Nat.* 47(2): 435-455.

genus *Hesperophylax* (Silver Stripe Sedge)
(6 known species in North America)

Generalized description of the adult:
adult length up to 34mm

WING: cream and light brown pattern, with a long, silver stripe along it
BODY: varies from yellow to amber
LEGS: straw yellow

Dr. Richard Baumann, Bruce Solomon, and I went out to the Provo River in Utah in late July for some field collecting. We pulled a medium-size rock, about the diamater of a man's head, out of a strong current from 2½ feet of water, and on this single rock there were at least a hundred pupae of *Hesperophylax*.

Larva

Hesperophylax

These giant caddisflies, up to thirty-four millimeters in length as adults, congregate on particular boulders during pupation. They emerge at night, but on a river such as the Provo this is going to coincide with the nocturnal feeding schedule of the resident brown trout anyway.

The adults remain close to the larval habitat all summer, returning frequently to drink. In many species the females do not lay their eggs until autumn. With such a long period of availability the adult insects are worth imitating, especially early in the morning when they are still very active. They can be models for a giant searching fly.

Adult

Important Species
(*Platyphylax* is an older name)

H. designatus E, M
This eastern and midwestern species is somewhat smaller than others in the genus, attaining a maximum adult size of twenty millimeters. It is generally found in smaller streams and rivers than is its western counterparts.

H. incisus W
This is probably the species that we collected from the Provo River. In records from its entire range, from Alaska to Utah, it is listed as common to abundant.

General imitations for *Hesperophylax*:

LARVA: Light Cased Caddis Larva (sizes 2, 4, 6); the larvae can be much larger than this, but beyond these sizes they are impossible to imitate realistically)

PUPA: Ginger Deep Sparkle Pupa; Ginger Emergent Sparkle Pupa (sizes 2/0, 1/0, 1, 2, 4, 6)

ADULT DRY:	Light Bucktail Caddis (sizes 2/0, 1/0, 1, 2, 4, 6)
ADULT WET:	Ginger Diving Caddis (sizes 2/0, 1/0, 1, 2, 4, 6)

ADULT KEYS: Ross, H. H. 1944. "The caddis flies, or Trichoptera, of Illinois." *Bull. Ill. Nat. Hist. Surv.*, No. 23.
(The diagnostic traits entomologists use to identify the adults of this genus to species level vary widely. The system of scientific names, including western species such as *H. incisus, H. consimilis,* and *H. occidentalis,* may be revised after more investigation into the larval forms.)

genus *Psychoglypha* (Snow Sedge)
(15 known species in North America)

Generalized description of the adult:
adult length up to 24mm

WING:	reddish brown with a long silver streak running down the center of the wing
BODY:	varies from light to dark brown
LEGS:	brown

Larva

Psychoglypha

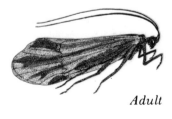

Adult

Dr. George Roemhild explained to me how he finds these winter caddisflies in February and March: "They crawl up on the snowbanks, but when the sun hits their dark wings they melt down out of sight. That's how I collect them, by walking along looking for holes in the snow."

The pupae can be worth imitating on warm winter days. In comparison to the Chironomidae midges and *Capnia* stoneflies that are around at this time, the emergers are a giant food item. When they scramble in toward the shallows they attract the attention of any trout that happen to be in there sunning themselves. The pupae are part of one of the secrets of winter fly-fishing; on sunny days the shallow flats warm up first—and so does the fishing there.

The greatest value of *Psychoglypha* is in the larval stage. Like many other caddisflies they drift readily, not only in high numbers but also during the day. It is this day-active pattern that separates them, and other day-active genera, from most of the other insect orders. This fortunate timing usually makes caddisfly larvae, in either cased or uncased condition, the most important organisms in the stream for nymph fishermen.

The larvae of *Psychoglypha* feed in a generally omnivorous manner, cleaning up leaf fragments and algae and even scavenging on dead fish. In their role as scavengers they locate their food very quickly—within hours fifty or more larvae may gather on a single dead fish—and rasp holes into the body cavity.[15]

Important Species

P. subborealis E, M, W
(= *P. alaskensis*)
Dr. Norman Anderson reported on the high drift activity of this species, with an April peak in Oregon. He also noted: "In the Metolius River, Jefferson County, *P. subborealis* larvae were abundant on Ranunculus beds as small larvae, whereas the

mature larvae occurred in backwater regions."[16]

P. subborealis has a transcontinental range, occurring from Alaska to Maine. It lives in a wide variety of habitats—small creeks, large rivers, ponds, and backwater sloughs—and can be common to abundant in any of them. Pupae emerge in both fall and winter throughout its range.

P. alascensis W

(= *P. ulla*)

This is a common western species, ranging from Alaska to California and east to Alberta and Montana. Adult collections indicate a later flight period, from winter into spring, than for *P. subborealis*.

General imitations for *Psychoglypha*:

LARVA:	Dark Cased Caddis Larva (sizes 2, 4, 6, 8)
PUPA:	Brown Deep Sparkle Pupa; Brown Emergent Pupa (sizes 4, 6, 8)
ADULT DRY:	Dark Bucktail Caddis (sizes 4, 6, 8)
ADULT WET:	Brown Diving Caddis (sizes 4, 6, 8)
ADULT KEYS:	Denning, D. G. 1970. "The genus *Psychoglypha* (Trichoptera: Limnephilidae)." *Can. Ent.*, 102: 15-30.

genus *Dicosmoecus* (Giant Orange Sedge)[17]

(5 known species in North America)

Generalized description of the adult:

adult length up to 30mm

WING:	mottled gray and brown (semitranslucent)
BODY:	reddish orange
LEGS:	brownish yellow

Larva

Dicosmoecus

Some fishermen specialize in catching large trout, five pounds or over, on a fly; others only hunt these big fish occasionally. Anglers who want to catch such a trout on a dry or semidry fly need to know which aquatic insects can make fish in this size range begin feeding on the surface.

Very large trout are not interested in most insects because they usually feed on crustaceans and small fish. Certain criteria must be met before these big predators will rise. There must be a heavy population of a very large insect, one that appears in a concentrated horde. Only in this way can an insect species make so much food available that five-pound fish can feed efficiently.

Adult

The question for fly fishermen seeking big trout is: "Which insects provide the best opportunity for catching such fish?" My list would be: Giant Orange Sedge (*Dicosmoecus* sp.), Salmon Fly (*Pteronarcys californica,* a stonefly), and the Michigan Mayfly (*Hexagenia limbata*). *Dicosmoecus* is the most important—and the contest is not even close.

I feel qualified to make this judgment because I get the chance to fish all over the country. I have fished the *Hexagenia limbata* hatches many times, and I am well aware of the spectacular potential of these giant mayflies. I have to know as much as possible about *Pteronarcys californica* because I guide during this hatch; it is my job to know the times and places of this occurrence on rivers such as the Madison and the Big Hole.

But there are many reasons why *Dicosmoecus* is more important than other aquatic insects. It is very large; not only is the adult nearly thirty millimeters long from its head to the tip of its wings, it is also a stout, full-bodied insect. The emergence and egg laying are usually very concentrated, the majority of the population in an area coming out in a two- to three-week span. It emerges in the fall; an advantage *Dicosmoecus* has over the Salmon Fly (*Pteronarcys*), which emerges during the high water of spring, because the rivers are low and clear in the fall. Also it is active in the afternoon and evening, not at night when the Michigan Mayfly *(Hexagenia)* is active. Finally, and possibly most important, it is abundant in rivers that have much larger trout than either of the other insects.

Dicosmoecus is most abundant in the Pacific Coast states of California, Oregon, Washington, and Alaska, and in the province of British Columbia. The habitats this insect frequents are usually great trout waters, the larger rivers that support the largest trout—and this is true in every area. The added bonus is that in many of these coastal streams the activity of *Dicosmoecus* coincides with the runs of summer stealhead, giving fly fishermen the chance to take trout of fifteen pounds or more on a dry fly. There are even rumours filtering out of British Columbia of fly fishermen catching various species of Pacific salmon on dry flies when these great fish are rising to adults of *Dicosmoecus*.

The larvae of *Dicosmoecus* are as important as the pupae and adults. During the early instars they use plant material to build their cases, and they stay in the slack areas at the sides of the stream. During later instars they shift abruptly to a gravel case, during the transition their cases often consisting partly of plant material and partly of mineral material. In these later stages the larvae move into the faster currents of the stream. Throughout their life cycle they are very indiscriminate feeders, consuming detritus, algae, and dead animal materials.

Even during the larval stage *Dicosmoecus* is a primary food form for big trout. In June and July they drift quite readily. Amazingly, this is one of those case makers that abandons its case, possibly to build another, and slips into the current. Unlike stonefly nymphs, mayfly nymphs, or free-living caddisfly larvae, which exhibit a higher rate of behavioral drift at night, the drift phenomenon for the uncased larvae happens in the daytime. The peak is connected with water temperature and occurs at approximately 4 P.M.[19]

These gigantic larvae, thirty-five millimeter chunks of yellow and brown food, drift freely at a time of day when most aquatic insects are hiding under rocks. Early each summer, on rivers from California to Alaska, they provide an incredible opportunity for trout. These caseless larvae are so unique, both in size and coloration, that they require a specific imitation.

Later in the summer, usually by early August, the larvae secure their cases to the underside of a rock and enter an inactive period (diapause) for several weeks. No bodily changes occur during this time, but the insects do not move around or feed at all.

When the giant larvae of Dicosmoecus *(35mm in length) abandon their cases and drift free in the current, they become a main food source for trout.*

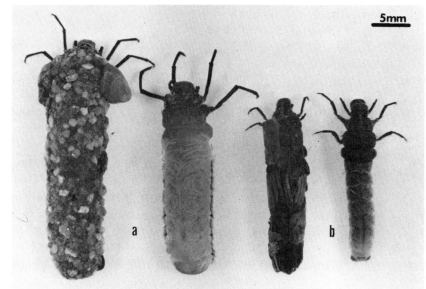

*The cased larvae and the uncased larvae of (**A**) Dicosmoecus are both eaten by trout. Due to their large size and yellow body coloration, the uncased larvae are especially conspicuous in the drift. The cased and uncased larvae of (**B**) Onocosmoecus, the next genus in the Insect Listing, are also shown.* Jon Speir

This period of inactivity happens in a number of Limnephilidae genera. One result is that it coordinates the emergence of the adults. In the fall the shorter days, or photoperiods, act as a controlling device for the development of the pupae. The population emerges in a very synchronized manner, most of the pupae in an area popping out in two or three weeks.

In my observations the emerging pupae both crawl and swim, using a clumsy combination of the two. They generally migrate into the shallows, but sometimes they rise in open water and escape on the surface. They are vigorous but slow swimmers. Emergence begins in late afternoon and continues until dark.

The adults mate and the females begin egg laying within forty-eight hours of emergence. They start flying late in the afternoon, but the activity becomes heaviest just before sunset. The females flop to the water and struggle for a long time, fluttering and drifting downstream on the surface.

Fly fishermen in Oregon and California are well aware of the *Dicosmoecus* hatches on their waters. In the inland states anglers know very little about this insect, but professional records show that there are populations in Nevada, Colorado, and New Mexico. More collections are needed from these areas to determine if it is important.

My efforts for the past four years, 1976 to 1980, have been largely concerned with this one genus. My obsession with it has merely reflected a steadily growing awareness of its importance to fly fishermen. The work with *Dicosmoecus* has included many trips throughout the western regions, my collections revealing where populations were high enough to create viable angling situations.

Idaho. It was Keith Stonebreaker, well known in Idaho for his ability to catch sea-run fish on a fly, who started my obsession with steelhead. We were at a banquet together when he offhandedly said, "Last year when the orange sedges were on the Clearwater something started rising to them. I thought at first that it might be whitefish working on them, but then I began taking steelhead on a Bucktail Caddis."

Rising steelhead? What more is needed to stir the blood of even the most jaded angler? Since that time I have been chasing these fish with a dry fly all over the West. I have found that some rivers, such as the Clearwater, are better than others because their holding runs tend to be shallower. In these streams the fish are susceptible to either fluttering naturals or imitations.

The main species of *Dicosmoecus* in Idaho, *D. gilvipes*, starts emerging as early as the first week of September in some of the higher-altitude rivers such as the St. Joe, but in the St. Mary, Salmon, Palouse, and Clearwater, all streams with good populations of this insect and resident trout, the hatch begins in late September or early October.

Oregon. It is easy to get hooked on the combination of *Dicosmoecus* and steelhead, but at the same time no fly fisherman should forget that the rivers where this insect is most numerous—cool and swift waters—usually support plenty of resident trout. These fish are what make the hatch such a dependable affair for the angler.

Such rivers as the Deschutes and its tributaries, the Metolius, Williamson, White, and Little Deschutes, offer tremendous fly-fishing for resident browns and rainbows in Oregon. These particular streams hold some big trout, six pounds or more, that never rise except during the *Dicosmoecus* activity of October.

Dicosmoecus occurs abundantly in major rivers throughout the state. Its emergence does coincide with the appearance of small steelhead, known as "half-pounders," in rivers such as the Rogue, McKensie, and Santiam, but whether the steelhead appear on time or not the pupae and adults create a great fly-fishing situation.

Utah. *Dicosmoecus* is listed as rare or uncommon in most Utah species lists, but there are good populations of this insect in some of the larger trout streams of the state. The hatches occur during the fall hunting season, which may explain why so few sporstmen in the area have discovered the fishing opportunities associated with these insects.

Dr. Richard Baumann wrote out a list of rivers where *Dicosmoecus* is common to abundant: Bear, Sevier, upper Weber, and Duchesne. He stressed that these are probably not the only streams in the state with good numbers of this genus.

My trip that year to Utah was in the summer. Since I could not return in the fall, I sent Brian Addot to look for the Giant Orange Sedge hatch. He found it in full swing on the Bear River in early October. He wrote in his notes, "It's spotty. The adults can be abundant in one place and missing in another, but it is easy enough to walk along the river in the late afternoon and find where they're flying."

Washington. Washington is one of those states where caddisflies have never been collected extensively. The distribution of species in many areas, especially along the coast, is still unknown. It is possible by using information from Oregon and British Columbia, where there are more complete records, to make an educated guess about the species in the state, but this still does not pinpoint what is available in specific rivers—or tell anything about the fishing opportunities particular caddisflies create.

My search for information on *Dicosmoecus* distribution was frustrating. Dr. Stamford Smith of Central Washington University sent me collection records on *Dicosmoecus* from two interior rivers, the Yakima and the Wenatchee, showing a September and October flight period for *D. gilvipes* and *D. atripes*, but there were no records for the steelhead rivers of the coast.

I had no other alternative but to make an October trip to that area to hunt down the elusive Giant Orange Sedge. I concentrated my efforts on those streams that carry good populations of summer-run steelhead, looking for rivers where the emerging or egg-laying activity or *Dicosmoecus* might coincide with the runs. I only had a day at most to sample each river, but I found substantial populations of larvae and developing pupae in all the important Columbia River tributaries, (the Grand Ronde, Kalama, Klickitat, Snake, Washougal, and Wind) and in the Puget Sound feeders (the Sol Duc and the North Fork of the Stillaguamish).

On the Sol Duc, my last stop of the journey, I found both adult insects and steelhead. I stayed a day and fished this stream, the combination of dry flies and sea-run rainbows offering a fly-fishing opportunity too good to pass by. I did not hook any of the larger fish, the ten- to twelve-pounders that were rolling, but with a number 6 Bucktail Caddis I caught some smaller steelhead, and these fish were definitely feeding on the natural Giant Orange Sedges.

California. California was the easiest place for me to find the *Dicosmoecus* hatches. Fly fishermen there, among the most entomologically aware anglers in the country, knew exactly where and when the emergence and egg laying would be taking place on most of the major rivers.

The activity on the rivers of the west slope occurs from mid-October to mid-November, earlier on the more northern waters. Major trout streams such as the Sacramento, McCloud, Klamath, Salmon, and Trinity have the heaviest hatches, but even the larger tributaries of these rivers produce good numbers of *Dicosmoecus.*

Ted Fay, resident expert on the upper Sacramento River, informed me that the larvae of *Dicosmoecus* are especially important there in late June and early July. These big insects get washed into the quieter backwaters, where trout feed heavily on them.

Alaska. In a recent fly-fishing article an author made one of the more amazing comments about the entomology of this state. He wrote, "There are no aquatic insects in Alaskan rivers."

Fortunately for fish and fisherman this is not true. Without insects to act as primary and secondary converters of plant material these rivers would be devoid of trout. Even the salmon that spawn in these streams would not exist because there would be no food for the immature fish before their return to the sea. There are great insect hatches—mayflies, stoneflies, caddisflies, and two-winged flies—all summer long in Alaska.

Tim Hansen, a graduate student at Idaho State University, spent a summer collecting insects from the inland streams of Alaska. He found a rich, diverse cold-water fauna. His records and specimens showed that dominant caddisflies include *Rhyacophila* (mainly *R. vao* and *R. vocala*), *Ecclisomyia,* and *Oligophlebodes.*

It is in coastal rivers that *Dicosmoecus* and such other genera of big limnephilids as *Onocosmoecus* and *Neophylax* are important. There are major populations of *D. gilvipes* and *D. jucundus,* the latter becoming the predominant species in these northern latitudes. The emergence dates are much earlier than they are in the Northwest, heavy hatching and subsequent egg laying beginning in July.

Bob Giannoni, a headmaster of Fenwick's fly-fishing schools, found four-pound and larger rainbow trout freely rising to *Dicosmoecus* adults on the American River in early August. These fish willingly accepted dry flies, proving the ability of *Dicosmoecus* to interest even the big trout of this particular stream, and indicating that similar situations probably occur in the other rivers of the famous Katmai National Monument region of southwest Alaska.

Montana. The *Dicosmoecus* hatch is important in a number of Montana streams along the West Slope of the Continental Divide—something well known by old-time fly fishermen in the area, but a fact somehow apparently lost to younger anglers. The activity of the Giant Orange Sedge passes unnoticed now, except by fly fishermen who might randomly encounter it, and the trout usually gorge undisturbed on the big caddisflies.

Fly tier Norman Means of Missoula, creator in the 1930s of the famous cork-bodied Bunyan Bug series, used to point out that one of his most popular flies was matched specifically to the *Dicosmoecus* adult. "Everyone thought that it was for the Willow Fly [a stonefly], but it wasn't. I tied it for that big orange caddis on Rock Creek."

Is there still a Giant Orange Sedge hatch on Rock Creek? I tried to pinpoint it for three years, but I kept missing it until Art Aylesworth indicated that it occurred in early September, not late in the month as I had supposed. In 1979 I hit it perfectly on September 7, fishing the lower ten miles of the stream successfully during a fine hatch.

Art listed other rivers where he has found important adult concentrations: mouth of the Jocko (first three miles of river), Flathead River (in the canyon area around the mouth of the Thompson River), lower Clark Fork (heaviest in Tarkio Canyon area, but extending as far upstream as Clinton).

Rivers on the East Slope of the Divide also have only scattered populations of *Dicosmoecus*, but there are still enough insects to create heavy hatches. In some situations even a sparse appearance of adults starts the fish hunting, making imitations good searching flies in the fall on streams such as the Big Hole.

British Columbia. British Columbia, with approximately 366,000 square miles of land area and 16,900 miles of coastline, has the finest accessible steelhead and salmon fishing in North America. Great forests of fir and spruce covering the mountain ranges hold the fall and winter water and release it into vast river systems. From an airplane the tributaries, too numerous to count, spread like lacework.

I collected larval samples from over forty trout and steelhead rivers in the province, from the Veddar on the lower mainland to the Brem and the Dean in the upper coastal region, and discovered abundant populations of *Dicosmoecus* in almost every one. I can only assume what this implies for fly fishermen, but with steelhead, Pacific Salmon, Dolly Varden, and both resident and sea-run cutthroat in most of these streams there has to be spectacular fishing during the hatch. I caught my best fish of the trip, a twenty-one-pound steelhead from the Brem on a dry fly imitation of *Dicosmoecus*.

My pilot, Ron Drolling, told me, "You can catch everything on the surface when that orange sedge comes on. Take Dolly Varden—we usually use sucker meat for them. But in the Fraser River you can take three- and four-pounders, and plenty of cutthroat, every few casts."

Important Species

D. atripes W

The ranges of the three major species—*D. atripes, D. gilvipes,* and *D. jucundus*—overlap considerably, but it is possible in a very general way to outline regions where each is dominant. *D. atripes* is the most abundant species in California and Utah rivers; and although it is found as far north as Alaska it seems to be more southern in its main distribution. *D. gilvipes* is the main species in Idaho, Oregon, Washington, and British Columbia. *D. jucundus* is the dominant species in Montana and Alaska, integrating with the others at higher altitudes and more northerly latitudes, possibly indicating a preference for colder streams.

D. gilvipes W

(= *D. grandis*)

This species tends to be slightly darker than *D. atripes,* the wings a deeper brown and the body a rustier orange. The larvae are often abundant in the faster sections of medium and large streams.

D. jucundus W

The geographical distribution of this species is from California to Alaska and from Oregon to Alberta. Specimens are often misidentified as *D. atripes* in older collection records, so the actual abundance and range of this species might be underestimated. Dr George Roemhild, in his paper, "The Trichoptera of Montana with distributional and ecological notes," lists it as the most common species of the genus in the state.

General imitations for *Dicosmoecus*:

LARVA:	Yellow Caddis Larva (sizes 1, 2, 4, 6); Medium Cased Caddis Larva (sizes 1, 2, 4, 6, 8)
PUPA:	Brown and Orange Deep Sparkle Pupa; Brown and Orange Emergent Sparkle Pupa (sizes 2, 4, 6)
ADULT DRY:	Orange Bucktail Caddis (sizes 2, 4, 6, 8)
ADULT WET:	Brown and Orange Diving Caddis (sizes 2, 4, 6, 8)

ADULT KEYS: Nimmo, A. P. 1971. "The adult Rhyacophilidae and Limnephilidae (Trichoptera) of Alberta and eastern British Columbia and their post-glacial origin." *Quaest. Ent.,* 7: 3-234.

genus *Onocosmoecus* (Great Late-Summer Sedge)

(approximately 6 known species in North America)

Generalized description of the adult:

adult length up to 28mm

WING:	varies from ginger to brown
BODY:	varies from ginger to brown
LEGS:	vary from straw yellow to brown

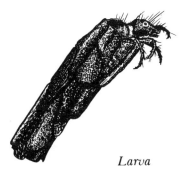

Larva

Onocosmoecus

This genus is closely related to *Dicosmoecus,* but there are differences between the two. Their habits vary slightly; *Onocosmoecus* larvae frequent quieter currents and they feed more as shredders of detrital material than as scrapers. The beginning of pupation and subsequent emergence are not quite as coordinated with *Onocosmoecus* as with *Dicosmoecus.* The flight period for the adults usually spans late summer and early fall for *Onocosmoecus,* the peak occurring a few weeks sooner than for *Dicosmoecus* in the same streams.

How important is *Onocosmoecus?*. It is not quite as valuable to stream fishermen as *Dicosmoecus,* but it is a large caddisfly that can control how and when trout feed wherever it is abundant. The single eastern species, *O. quadrinotatus,* is generally not common, but in the West the larvae of the major species can reach high densities in the proper habitats, cluttering the bottoms of pools and gentle flats. In lakes

Adult

Oncosmoecus is truly a major caddisfly (see Chapter 7, Stillwater Caddisflies).

Important Species
(Until 1955 all species of *Onocosmoecus* were considered part of the genus *Dicosmoecus,* and in older records they are listed in it.)

O. frontalis W
The larvae of this species, like most others in the genus, build their cases of wood fragments instead of stone. They are found in smaller streams, preferring the quieter side currents.

Its range includes British Columbia, Washington, and Oregon. In Oregon, where it emerges mainly in July, Dr. Norman Anderson lists records for streams such as the North Fork of Rock Creek, Chintimini Creek, and Woods Creek.

O. unicolor W
This species is well named—it is an even cinnamon shade all over, with virtually no patterning on the antennae, wings, body, or legs. It is a common caddisfly in small to large rivers as well as in lakes throughout the Northwest. Adults are on the wing from mid-August to late October.

General imitations for *Onocosmoecus:*

LARVA:	Dark Cased Caddis Larva (sizes 2, 4, 6, 8)
PUPA:	Ginger Deep Sparkle Pupa; Ginger Emergent Sparkle Pupa (sizes 6, 8, 10)
ADULT DRY:	Light Bucktail Caddis (sizes 6, 8, 10); Ginger Dancing Caddis (size 10)
ADULT WET:	Ginger Diving Caddis (sizes 6, 8, 10) (The darker Brown series might be needed to match some species in this genus.)
ADULT KEYS:	Schmid, F. 1955, "Contribution a l'etude des Limnophilidae (Trichoptera)." *Mitt. Schweiz. Ent. Ges.,* 28: 1-245. (This paper originally erected the genus *Onocosmoecus.* Dr. Schmid later shifted two additional species, *O. frontalis* and *O. schmidi,* from *Dicosmoecus* to *Onocosmoecus.*)

genus *Ironoquia* (Eastern Box Wing Sedge)
(4 known species in North America)

Generalized description of the adult:
adult length of some species in the genus is up to 20mm, but for *I. parvula,* the only species included here, the adult size is approximately 10mm.

WING:	golden brown (the common name refers to the curiously angled rear edge of the wings)
BODY:	golden brown
LEGS:	golden brown

These insects are typical plant processors in small to medium-size streams, where they feed on leaves and algae. For most species the larvae enter a period of inactivity

Larva

Ironoquia

Adult

(diapause) during the summer months and pupate in late summer or early fall. The adults fly in the evening on warm days, but begin their mating and egg laying increasingly earlier as the weather turns cooler.

Important Species
(species listed under generic name *Caborius* in older records)

I. parvula E, M
Monte Lodge sent samples of this species from the Wild Ammonoosuc River in New Hampshire, noting that brook trout were taking adults on the surface in late September.

General imitations for *Ironoquia*:

LARVA:	Light Cased Caddis Larva (sizes 8, 10, 12)
PUPA:	Brown Deep Sparkle Pupa; Brown Emergent Sparkle Pupa (sizes 14, 16)
ADULT DRY:	Brown Dancing Caddis (sizes 14, 16)
ADULT WET:	Brown Diving Caddis (sizes 14, 16)
ADULT KEYS:	Schmid, F. 1951. "Le genre *Ironoquia* Bks." *Mitt. Schweiz. Ent. Ges.* 23(3): 317-328.

genus *Goera* (Little Gray Sedge)
(6 known species in North America)

Generalized description of the adult:
adult length up to 10mm

WING:	gray
BODY:	pale yellow
LEGS:	speckled gray

Larva

Goera

The larvae of this genus build a very stout stone case, balancing it on each side with large stones. This added ballast helps the insect maintain its position in riffles, where it feeds by scraping algae and detrital matter off the rocks. It also pupates in and emerges from these fast-water areas.

Two species are covered here, *G. calcarata* and *G. stylata*, with a distribution from the Northeast down the mountain spine as far south as Georgia. Other species are found in the East and Midwest, and there is one, *G. archaon*, in Oregon, but in my collections only *G. calcarata* and *G. stylata* have been abundant enough to be important.

Adult

Important Species
(In older taxonomies this entire genus, along with two sister genera, were often placed in a separate family, Goeridae.)

G. calcarata E

Whenever considering the mid-South (the Appalachian region) it is necessary to split trout waters into tail-water rivers and cold, mountain streams. It is also necessary to look at these habitats separately. For example, Tennessee has over 500 miles of natural, gravel-bottomed trout streams and the caddisfly fauna in them is much different than the fauna in the dammed rivers.

Dr. S. W. Edwards noted about *G. calcarata*, "This species is common in Tennessee and may be collected from practically any cold, swift, clear stream."[18]

The same thing is true in the mountains of other mid-South states, especially in Virginia and West Virginia. *G. calcarata* emerges from May to June in these areas, the activity beginning suddenly about forty-five minutes before dark and probably continuing into the night. The swimming pupae can start trout boiling in the deeper riffles.

G. stylata M

In many small, gravel-bottomed trout streams of the upper Midwest this species is one of the dominant caddisflies. Emergence and egg laying takes place in late May and early June.

General imitations for *Goera*:

LARVA: Light Cased Caddis Larva; tied thick (sizes 10, 12, 14)
PUPA: Gray and Yellow Deep Sparkle Pupa; Gray and Yellow Emergent Sparkle Pupa (sizes 14, 16)
ADULT DRY: Gray and Yellow Dancing Caddis (sizes 14, 16)
ADULT WET: Gray and Yellow Diving Caddis (sizes 14, 16)

ADULT KEYS: Ross, H. H. 1947. "Descriptions and records of North American Trichoptera with synoptic notes." *Trans. Amer. Ent. Soc.*, 73: 125-160.

genus *Apatania* (Early Smoky Wing Sedge)
(15 known species in North America)

Generalized description of the adult:
adult length up to 8.5mm
WING: smoky gray
BODY: smoky gray brown
LEGS: grayish brown

Larva

Apatania

Most of the species in this genus have a very northerly distribution, ranging across Canada above the Arctic Circle, but a few of them have spread down the eastern and western mountain ranges as far south as Georgia and Arizona. At least one of these, *A. incerta*, rates as a very important caddisfly in southern New England trout streams—where it is a sleeper.

Fly fishermen come back after an early-season outing and ask, "What was that little dark caddisfly?"

"Grannom," someone guesses, naming one of the better-known caddisfly genera.

Along the eastern seaboard from Connecticut north to New Hampshire *A. incerta* emerges from mid-April to late May. On many small to moderate-size streams (the latter often called rivers in the East) it is one of the first caddisflies to appear

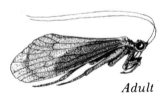

Adult

abundantly in the spring, the beginning of the emergence period often coinciding with Opening Day. The emergence and egg laying occur all day long.

Important Species
(this genus has been covered under the name *Radema* in older entomologies)

A. incerta E
The larvae of *A. incerta* in their stone cases become more restless just before pupation, exposing themselves to the trout. Their presence in great numbers make a heavily weighted Medium Cased Caddis Larva an excellent pattern for bottom-bumping tactics during early spring.

General imitations for *Apatania*:

LARVA:	Medium Cased Caddis Larva (sizes 12, 14)
PUPA:	Gray Deep Sparkle Pupa; Gray Emergent Sparkle Pupa (sizes 14, 16)
ADULT DRY:	Gray Dancing Caddis (sizes 14, 16)
ADULT WET:	Gray Diving Caddis (sizes 14, 16)
ADULT KEYS:	Schmid, F. "Contribution a l'etude de la sous-famille des Apataniinae (Trichoptera: Limnephilidae). I." *Tijdschr. Ent.*, 96(1-2): 109-167.
	Schmid, F. "Contribution a l'etude de la sous-famille des Apataniinae (Trichoptera: Limnephilidae). II." *Tijdschr. Ent.*, 97(1-2): 1-74.

(George Roemhild, in "The Trichoptera of Montana with distributional and ecological notes," lists three species, *A. chasica*, *A. cosmosa*, and *A. shoshone*, as common in the state.

Oddly enough I fish small streams in the East, probably because I grew up on those waters, much more than I do in Montana. So I have not personally found *Apatania* to be important in the mountain region, but I recommend that western fly fishermen look for this genus.)

genus *Ecclisomyia* (Early Western Mottled Sedge)
(3 known species in North America)

Larva

Ecclisomyia

Generalized description of the adult:
adult length up to 20mm

WING:	mottled brown
BODY:	green
LEGS:	dark brown

This caddisfly is common to abundant in cool mountain streams from Alaska to California and as far east as Montana. The larvae feed on diatoms and plant material, clambering freely over the rocky sections of the bottom. They are available to trout throughout the winter and are possibly an important food source then.

When the Montana fishing season opens in mid-May most of the larger rivers are swollen and muddy with snowmelt, but at higher elevations the smaller streams are

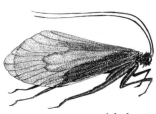

Adult

still running clear. The early emergence of *Ecclisomyia* often coincides with the best fishing on these waters, the big crawling pupa pulling trout into the shallows.

Rick Hafele made some comments on this genus for me, "I have collected the largest numbers from streams in southeastern Alaska, where they seem to be quite abundant."

Important Species

E. conspersa W
Both of the species covered here, *E. conspersa* and *E. maculosa*, inhabit similar riffle areas in the same streams. They emerge by crawling to the shallows.
E. maculosa W
(= *E. simulata*)
The emergence periods of the two species can overlap considerably, but *E. maculosa* usually pupates and emerges slightly later than *E. conspersa*.

General imitations for *Ecclisomyia*:
LARVA:	Light Cased Caddis Larva (sizes 4, 6, 8)
PUPA:	Brown and Bright Green Deep Sparkle Pupa; Brown and Bright Green Emergent Sparkle Pupa (sizes 6, 8, 10)
ADULT DRY:	Parkany Deer Hair Caddis in appropriate colors (sizes 6, 8, 10); Brown and Green Dancing Caddis (size 10)
ADULT WET:	Brown and Green Diving Caddis (sizes 6, 8, 10)
ADULT KEYS:	Ross, H. H. 1950. "Synoptic notes on some Nearctic limnephilid caddisflies." *Am. Midl. Nat.*, 43 (2): 410-429.

genus *Oligophlebodes* (Little Western Dark Sedge)
(7 known species; distribution restricted to the mountain west)

Generalized description of the adult:
adult length up to 8mm
WING:	varies from solid brown to black; no color pattern
BODY:	varies from yellow to dark brown
LEGS:	vary from yellowish brown to black

The larvae, pupae, and adults of this genus are among the smallest in the Limnephilidae family, adults ranging from six millimeters to eight millimeters, but they have some interesting habits that help compensate for their size. The larvae drift heavily during the day in June and July, stone case and all, reaching peak rates at noon. The pupae emerge at midday in August and September. Adult females lay their eggs in late afternoon, usually within a few days of emergence, falling onto the water surface and struggling mightily to break the meniscus. The high degree of availability at various points in the life cycle, all in daytime hours, makes this genus more important than usual for such a modestly sized insect.

Larva

Oligophlebodes

Adult

Important Species

O. *sigma* W
The larvae are common in gravel-bottomed streams in the southern region of the Rocky Mountains (Utah, New Mexico, and Arizona).
O. *minuta* W
This species can be abundant in the small streams of Wyoming, Utah, New Mexico, and Colorado.
O. *sierra* W
This is the most common species of the genus along the Pacific Coast, distribution extending from British Columbia to California

General imitations for *Oligophlebodes*:

LARVA:	Brassie; Light Cased Caddis Larva (sizes 16, 18)
PUPA:	Brown and Yellow Deep Sparkle Pupa; Brown and Yellow Emergent Sparkle Pupa (sizes 16, 18, 20)
ADULT DRY:	Brown and Yellow Dancing Caddis (size 16); Lawson Spent Partridge Caddis in appropriate colors (sizes 16, 18, 20)
ADULT WET:	Brown and Yellow Diving Caddis (sizes 16, 18, 20) (For darker pupae and adults the Black series can be used.)
ADULT KEYS:	Ross, H. H. 1944. "The caddis flies, or Trichoptera, of Illinois." *Bull. Illinois Nat. Hist. Surv.*, No. 23. (There is an excellent paper on the life cycle of *O. sigma:* Pearson, W. D., and Kramer, R. H. 1972. "Drift and production of two aquatic insects in a mountain stream." *Ecol. Monogr.*, 42(3): 365-385.)

genus *Neophylax* (Autumn Mottled Sedge)
(15 known species in North America)

Generalized description of the adult:
adult length up to 18mm

WING:	mottled brown
BODY:	brownish yellow
LEGS:	brownish yellow

In my ratings of the important caddisflies for each region of the country this genus ranks fourth in the Pacific Northwest. The larvae of *N. rickeri* and *N. splendens,* the two most common western species, thrive in the faster riffles of trout streams in British Columbia, California, Washington, and Oregon. In the streams of the inland states—Idaho, Montana, Nevada, and Wyoming—these species do not attain the same high populations, but they are common in localized areas.

Neophylax larvae build a short and thick case with heavier ballast stones along the sides that is ideally suited to fast currents. The insects move over the surfaces of midstream rocks and feed by scraping off diatoms and detritus, the added weight of

Larva

Neophylax

Adult

The short, thick case of a Neophylax *larva, lined along the sides with ballast stones, helps the insect navigate in areas of fast currents.* Ken Thompson

the case holding them down in the unpredictale turbulence of these areas.

This genus earns such a high rating because the larvae, like other autumn emergers among the Limnephilidae, enter a summer period of inactivity. This diapause synchronizes the development of the yearly brood. When the days grow shorter in the fall most of the insects begin pupation at the same time. The emergence is a well-coordinated affair, over ninety percent of the pupae hatching within a three-week period from a section of stream. They emerge from the faster riffles, swimming to the surface and flying off the water. [19]

The egg laying process has been described for some species. C. T. Vorhies observed females of *N. concinnus* pasting their eggs under overhanging banks and A. Patten observed females of the same species landing on sticks projecting from the stream and dropping their eggs into water. Neither method of egg laying exposed these insects to trout predation.

During one of my September collecting trips to the Box Canyon area of the Henrys Fork, the adults of *N. rickeri* exhibited a very strange behavior. The insects would fly twenty to thirty feet up in the air and hurtle downward. This in itself would not have been odd if all of these divers were hitting the water, but many were not; some were crashing on the ground. My first thought was that these were female egg layers that had somehow missed the river, but at least half of the specimens that I picked up from the dirt were males. There was no way to collect the insects that were falling on the water, but if there were males in this group it would only make the activity even more unexplainable. Whatever the reason for this strange afternoon ritual (possibly a clumsy attempt at midair copulation) the end result was that a lot of helpless adults were available on the surface of the river for the trout.

Important Species

N. concinnus E, M
(= *N. autumnus*)
This smaller species, the adult measuring nine to twelve millimeters long, is widespread throughout the Northeast and upper Midwest. Emergence usually occurs in the fall.

N. rickeri W
My name for this species is Brown Spot Sedge because of the prominent dark spot on the underside of the abdomen. It is also distinguishable by the ragged chunk that looks as though it's been accidently ripped off of the rear edge of each top wing.

The range of *N. rickeri* extends from British Columbia south to California and east to Montana. Emergence on the West Coast trout streams occurs in October and November.

N. splendens W

There is considerable overlap in the preferred habitat of this species and *N. rickeri*, the two often found in the same waters, but *N. splendens* tends to occur slightly farther upstream in a watershed than *N. rickeri*. The peak of its emergence also happens a few days before the peak of *N. rickeri*.

General imitations for *Neophylax*:

LARVA:	Light Cased Caddis Larva (sizes 8, 10, 12, 14)
PUPA:	Brown and Yellow Deep Sparkle Pupa; Brown and Yellow Emergent Sparkle Pupa (sizes 6, 8, 10, 12, 14)
ADULT DRY:	Brown and Yellow Dancing Caddis (sizes 10, 12, 14); Dark Bucktail Caddis (sizes 6, 8, 10)
ADULT WET:	Brown and Yellow Diving Caddis (sizes 6, 8, 10, 12, 14)
ADULT KEYS:	The adult keys for *Neophylax* are not collected in any single source. Two books used together illustrate the major trout stream species: Ross, H. H. 1944. "The caddis flies, or Trichoptera, of Illinois." *Bull. Ill. Nat. Hist. Surv.*, 23. (The eastern species, *Neophylax concinnus*, will be listed under its synonym, *Neophylax autumnus*.) Denning, D. G. 1956. in *Aquatic Insects of California*. pp. 237-270, ed. by R. L. Usinger. University of California Press, Berkeley.

Family Molannidae (tube-case maker)
(represented by 2 genera in North America)

Shelter type: the larval case, made with pieces of flat rock, has a hood that comes up behind the head of the larva.

Typical feeding habits of the larvae: the larvae are omnivorous, feeding on diatoms, smaller insects, and plant material.

Typical method of emergence: the pupae swim to the surface.

Typical egg-laying habits: the females crawl or dive underwater and paste their eggs to bottom objects.

Of the two genera in this family only one, *Molanna*, is found in the lower United States. The other, *Molannodes*, has a single species that is distributed across northern Europe and Asia, its range extending into Alaska and the Yukon. The larvae of both genera prefer lakes and quiet rivers for habitat.

genus *Molanna* (Gray Checkered Sedge)
(6 known species in North America)

Generalized description of the adult:
adult length up to 16mm

WING:	mottled gray, with a checkered pattern of light and dark areas
BODY:	brown
LEGS:	brown

This genus is better represented in lakes than in running-water environments, but it can occur in large populations in certain slow-moving rivers. One region where it can be particularly important is in the upper Midwest, an area blessed with spring-fed, sandy-bottomed streams.

The larvae, which prefer sand or mud substrates, crawl over the bottom and forage indiscriminately on plant material, diatoms, and smaller insects. They are protected from attack from above by a stone hood on their cases that extends over the insect, a mantle that resembles a cobra head in shape.

The pupae apparently require a very long time to discard their transparent skin and emerge as adults. In a series of timings in a home aquarium the pupae struggled in the surface film an average of nineteen minutes before freeing themselves completely. The length of the process was not due to a delay in the start of the shedding process, as it is with some other caddisflies, but in the actual escape from the clinging sheath, the unfolding of the wings an especially arduous task for the insect.

Larva

Molanna

Adult

Important Species

M. tryphena E, M
(= *M. cinerea*)
The range of this and the following species, *M. uniophila*, are restricted to the Midwest and the East. Adult records are available in Michigan for *M. tryphena* from mid-May through the end of August.

M. uniophila E, M
This is probably the most common species of the genus in the Midwest, both in some of the rivers and in the glacial lakes. It also begins emerging in mid-May in Michigan, but it has a flight period that lasts until early September.

M. ulmerina E
(= *M. musetta*)
This species is mainly found in the Northeast, but its range extends down through the Ozarks as far as Oklahoma. There are a few scattered records for the Midwest.

M. flavicornis E, M, W
M. flavicornis is transcontinental in distribution. There are scattered collection records from British Columbia and Colorado, but it is fairly rare in these areas. It starts to become common in the flatter areas of eastern Montana and North Dakota.

North Dakota, lacking any natural trout streams, has engaged in a vigorous program of cold-water pond construction. These artificial impoundments provide excellent fly-fishing. They also harbor excellent populations of *M. flavicornis*, the freshly emerged adults appearing in June.

General imitations for *Molanna*:

LARVA:	Light Cased Caddis Larva (sizes 4, 6, 8, 10)
PUPA:	Gray and Brown Deep Sparkle Pupa; Gray and Brown Emergent Sparkle Pupa (sizes 6, 8, 10)

ADULT DRY: Parkany Deer Hair Caddis (sizes 6, 8, 10); Gray and
                    Brown Dancing Caddis (size 10)

ADULT WET: Gray and Brown Diving Caddis (sizes 6, 8, 10)

ADULT KEYS: Ross, H. H. 1944. "The caddis flies, or Trichoptera, of Illinois."
                    Bull. Ill. Nat. Hist. Surv., 23.

Family Odontoceridae (tube-case maker)
(represented by 6 genera in North America)

Shelter type: the larvae build a curved, tapered case of sand grains or rocks.

Typical feeding habits of the larvae: the larvae, which burrow into the sand, silt, or gravel deposits in riffles, feed very indiscriminately. Gut contents of larvae from various genera include algae, detritus, and animal parts.

Typical method of emergence: the pupae swim or crawl to the surface.

Typical egg-laying habits: the females land on the water surface and extrude a mass of eggs.

In most of the genera there are only remnant populations left of what was once probably a widespread family. Many of the species in these genera now exist in small, isolated pockets, having become restricted over the ages in both geographical range and habitat. The eastern genus *Psilotreta* (Dark Blue Sedge) is the one exception to this pattern of shrinking distribution.

The larvae of this family have the unusual habit for caddisflies of burrowing in sand, silt, or gravel. Their cases are extremely resistant to crushing, probably to protect the insect against the grinding action of shifting bottom materials. The larvae feed in omnivorous fashion, ingesting algae, detritus, and animal matter indiscriminately. Most species in the six genera are indigenous to small, cool streams, and even in these limited habitats they are not common, but species in the genus *Psilotreta* attain great abundance in both small and large eastern trout rivers.

The case and larva of Psilotreta labida *are shown above. The larval cases of this family are extremely resistant to crushing.*

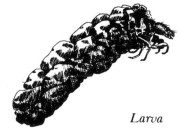

Larva

Psilotreta

Adult

genus *Psilotreta* (Dark Blue Sedge)
(7 known species in North America)

Generalized description of the adult:
adult length up to 15mm

WING:	dark grey
BODY:	green
LEGS:	brownish grey

Why can't *Psilotreta* be ignored, just like so many other caddisflies are ignored by American fly fishermen? To be ignored, an important caddisfly must either be "cooperative" or "invisible"—and *Psilotreta* is neither. Cooperative caddisflies are ones that ride the surface serenely, creating angling situations where standard techniques might work. The unobservant fly fisherman never even has to know that caddisflies are the center of the feeding activity to catch a few fish. The *Chimarra* (Little Black Sedge) genus of the Philopotamidae family is an example of a cooperative caddisfly.

Invisible caddisflies are ones that get trout rolling and jumping, but they are not on the surface. The pupae emerge from the underside of the meniscus directly into the air, without drifting for any appreciable distance on top of the water. The adult females lay their eggs by diving or crawling to the bottom. The concentrations of insects during these activities are not visible to anglers, and major feeding sprees by trout are usually not attributed to caddisflies. The *Rhyacophila* (Green Sedge) genus in the family Rhyacophilidae—and for that matter most other caddisflies—are examples of invisible types.

The egg-laying activities of *Psilotreta* cause problems that cannot be ignored. The females certainly are not invisible: they fall on the surface instead of going underneath it. The females certainly are not cooperative: they fuss, flop, and flutter all over the place. As if to add insult to injury, these caddisflies make their appearance at exactly the same time and on the same rivers as the Green Drake (*E. guttulata*). The trout frequently take the *Psilotreta* females in preference to the larger mayflies.

This insect played an important role in the modern reassessment of caddisfly lore by being so obviously important to the trout and yet so frustratingly useless to fishermen. It made people discard older techniques and patterns—Preston Jennings admitted his inability to cope with the *Psilotreta* hatches on his rivers; Ernest Schwiebert wrote about his experiences with *Psilotreta* in *Nymphs;* Leonard Wright credited *Psilotreta* with inspiring his experiments with twitch presentations and high-riding imitations; my own early failures with the *Psilotreta* hatches began my fascination with caddisflies.

My personal common name for *Psilotreta* was the Slap-in-the-Face Caddis. That is what it was—the caddisfly hatch that always seemed to interfere with my beloved

The author's personal name for Psilotreta labida, *shown left, is "Slap-in-the-Face" Caddis.*

green drake hatch. At first it was just a nuisance, but it became a burning challenge.

The larvae of *Psilotreta* have a two-year cycle. For most of their underwater lives they are safe from trout because they burrow into the silt or gravel of the stream bottom, but just before pupation the larvae migrate to specific rocks. When they are moving to these pupation sites they are likely to be exposed to fish.

Their habit of pupating in selected spots is an amazing affair. A hundred or more cases might be stacked in layers on the underside of a particular rock. When the emergence period begins the pupae pop continually from this area. They escape from the cocoon and wash out from under the rock, creating a food line for trout on the downstream side of the pupation site. During the peak evening hours the emerging pupae may create feeding situations in only a small part of the stream. They attract trout into these prime zones (which fly fishermen can find beforehand by searching for the clusters of pupae).

The adult females carry the eggs in a ball at the tip of the abdomen. They skid onto the water clumsily, skipping and hopping upstream, never really resting until the egg packet is dropped. Sometimes they manage to fly off and sometimes they do not, but no matter how many spent insects gather on the surface the trout show a strong preference for the active egg layers.

Like many evening caddisflies the emergence and egg laying of *Psilotreta* happens in a burst, the spectacular flurry generally lasting a few hours at most. It is not a hatch that an angler can easily take advantage of if he stumbles upon it. Fortunately it is such a predictable event that there is no reason a fly fisherman cannot be on the river a little early to select his imitations, stake out the prime water, and review his tactics.

Important Species

P. labida E

This is the most abundant species of *Psilotreta* in small and large trout rivers. It has a distribution from northern New England to the mid-South. Emergence periods occur in late April on the Tye River in Virginia, in mid-May on Penns Creek in Pennsylvania, and in late June on the Saco River in New Hampshire. The populations of this species are tremendous throughout its range, but it is best known for the June flights on the classic Catskill rivers of New York.

P. frontalis E

This species reaches its greatest abundance in smaller streams than *P. labida,* but there is a great overlap in their habitat and emergence times.

General imitations for *Psilotreta*:

LARVA:	Light Cased Caddis Larva (sizes 8, 10)
PUPA:	Gray and Green Deep Sparkle Pupa; Gray and Green Emergent Sparkle Pupa (sizes 12, 14, 16)
ADULT DRY:	Gray and Green Dancing Caddis (sizes 12, 14, 16)
ADULT WET:	Gray and Green Diving Caddis (sizes 12, 14, 16)
ADULT KEYS:	Ross, H. H. 1944. "The caddis flies, or Trichoptera, of Illinois." *Bull. Ill. Nat. Hist. Surv.,* 23.

Family Philopotamidae (net spinner)
(represented by 3 genera in North America)

Shelter type: the larvae do not build cases. They construct nets of very fine mesh on the undersides of rocks.

Typical feeding habits of the larvae: the larvae filter small particles from the current.

Typical method of emergence: the pupae swim or crawl to the banks or emerge on the surface.

Typical egg-laying habits: the females dive under the surface and lay their eggs on the bottom.

The larvae of this family generally build their finger-shaped nets under rocks rather than in the stronger currents on the tops or sides of these stones. They weave nets with the finest mesh of any net-spinning family, which allows the larvae to filter out the tiny particles carried by the slower currents in sheltered areas. They share a particular rock with net makers of other families; the Hydropsychidae larvae taking the exposed surface and the Philopotamidae larvae taking the protected pockets.

Two of the three genera—*Wormaldia* (Little Autumn Stream Sedge) and *Dolophilodes* (Medium Evening Sedge)—are classified as mountain caddisflies. Their distribution is restricted to smaller streams and rivers with cold and highly oxygenated water. Species of *Wormaldia* are definitely small-stream caddisflies. Species of *Dolophilodes* are found in a wider range of running-water habitats, but they are not abundant either in larger, warmer rivers.

The third genus, *Chimarra* (Little Black Sedge), is much more cosmopolitan. There are many species throughout the tropical regions as well as in more temperate climates, distribution often reflecting the original, South American dispersal point of this genus. *Chimarra* is important in a wide range of trout streams, from small rivers to giant tail-water rivers, in the eastern half of the continent, but apparently high altitude is a limiting factor for the genus. There are species in the West, even in the Rocky Mountain region, but they are all rare or uncommon.

genus *Chimarra* (Little Black Sedge)
(17 known species in North America north of Mexico)

Generalized description of the adult:
adult length up to 8mm

WING:	velvety black
BODY:	very dark brown
LEGS:	brown

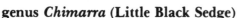

Larva

Chimarra

It is not hard to understand why some caddisflies have become well known in the fly-fishing world. The egg layers of certain genera fall to the water in the most obliging fashion and ride the surface serenely. They are perfect dry-fly models, creating fishing situations that may not be easy but that at least can be countered with standard tactics. In a fly-fishing society oriented toward the habits of mayflies, it has been the caddisflies whose actions conform to this image that have been recognized as valuable. Some of these caddisflies even have well-established common names; for example, *Brachycentrus* (Grannom) and *Chimarra* (Little Black Sedge).

The egg layers of *Chimarra* do everything a great dry-fly insect should do, and

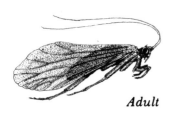

Adult

they justly deserve their fame. The returning females pepper the water in incredible numbers on some rivers, their importance magnified because the activity is concentrated into a few hours each day. Many of them drown, and even survivors drift quietly for long distances before flying off. They force trout into a very selective pattern of feeding, making fine leader tippets and small imitations, size 16, 18, or 20, mandatory.

The fame of the egg layers has not spilled over to other stages of this caddisfly. The emerging pupae are also important, especially since they come out at roughly midday, but they have been ignored because they cannot be matched with the standard tactics or flies. They have baffled anglers just as other caddisflies have done.

The habit the pupae have of crawling out on streamside rocks suggests possible shallow-water fishing tactics. At patches of bank shaded by trees or bushes, which usually hold more and better trout than sunlit areas, the wading fly fisherman can sneak upstream and cast a dry or semidry fly over visible fish using the stalker's method (see Chapter 6), or they can crawl a sunken fly through these same spots with the limbo method (see Chapter 5). Small, bright imitations, such as the Sparkle Pupa or the Thompson Foam Caddis, work most effectively for these *Chimarra* hatches.

Important Species

C. aterrima E, M
The hatches of *C. aterrima* on the Au Sable River in Michigan, and on other rich midwestern rivers, are legendary, but somehow this species has never become quite as well known anywhere else in the East. This is a mystery, especially in regions where fly fishermen are entomologically aware, because it is abundant over a wide range. In Pennsylvania all the limestone streams with good riffle bottoms, such as the Yellow Breeches, have great hatches. In New York the tail-water rivers, such as the Amawalk Outlet and the East Branch of the Delaware, support heavy populations. This filter-feeding caddisfly is most important in highly productive environments such as spring creeks and tail-water rivers, but even in the richer freestone streams it is a major insect.

Throughout its range *C. aterrima* often appears simultaneously with a famous mayfly, the Hendrickson (*E. subvaria*), in May. Trout feed heavily on both insects, but their attention shifts between them—at noon they concentrate on the emerging pupae of *C. aterrima*; between 2 P.M. and 4 P.M. they change over, working the peak of the *E. subvaria* hatch; when the mayfly duns taper off and the egg-laying *Chimarra* females begin arriving, the trout become selective to the caddisfly form and color; at dusk they shift preference once more to falling *E. subvaria* spinners. This constant switching on the part of the trout requires that fly fishermen remain alert to the insects, but meeting the challenge of this selective feeding produces exciting moments from midmorning until nightfall.

C. socia E
This species has been collected as far west as Illinois, but it is common mainly in the Northeastern region. It is important in both cold-water and warm-water fisheries in northern New England states and bordering Canadian provinces.

C. obscura E, M
(= *C. lucia*)
My caddisfly seminars on the Illinois River, below Lake Tenkiller in Oklahoma, are timed each year to coincide with the appearance of this species in April. These schools are especially gratifying because they introduce many people to fly-fishing for the first time as well as to caddisflies, and *C. obscura* gives them the chance for

incredible fishing during the daily floats. They cast a size 16 Black Emergent Sparkle Pupa against the banks and even beginners usually catch twenty or more rainbows a trip.

This is the most widely distributed species in the genus, extending from Maine as far west as Minnesota and as far south as Texas. It is frequently abundant in clear and rapid streams throughout its range, but it is an especially memorable caddisfly in southern tail-water rivers.

General imitations for *Chimarra*:

LARVA:	Yellow Caddis Larvae (sizes 14, 16, 18)
PUPA:	Black Deep Sparkle Pupa, Black Emergent Sparkle Pupa (sizes 16, 18, 20)
ADULT DRY:	Black Dancing Caddis (size 16); Thompson Foam Caddis (sizes 16, 18, 20)
ADULT WET:	Black Diving Caddis (sizes 16, 18, 20)
ADULT KEYS:	Ross, H. H. 1944, "The caddis flies, or Trichoptera, of Illinois." *Bull. Ill. Nat. Hist. Surv.*, 23.

genus *Dolophilodes* (Medium Evening Sedge)
(8 known species in North America north of Mexico)

Generalized description of the adult:
adult length up to 12mm

WING:	varies from gray to brown, with all gradations in between
BODY:	brown
LEGS:	brown

Larva

Dolophilodes

Adult

The eastern species, *D. distinctus,* is a notable oddity because it produces wingless females in the winter months, these adults running with great agility over the snowbanks. The same species also has a midsummer generation, either a second or an overlapping brood, but the adults of this later hatch all have normal, functioning wings.

The larvae of this genus are common in large streams and small rivers. They may show up on species lists from a wider selection of habitats, including headwater trickles and full-size rivers, but these extremes are not optimum environments. The larvae need cool, clear water flowing steadily over clean rubble.

The pupae and adults have both produced good fly-fishing for me on many streams and rivers; not so often in the big or famous waters as in the less heralded ones. The emergence and egg laying during midsummer occur in the evening and probably last into the night on these smaller waters, but it starts early enough to incite an hour or more of steady feeding by trout.

Important Species
(the old name for this genus is *Sortosa*)

D. pallides W
This species, known from Vancouver Island to Montana, is the last to emerge

among the western *Dolophilodes*. Most collections of adults show a September flight period.

D. novusamericana W

The distribution of this species is from British Columbia to Utah. The emergence period is very spread out, records available from February to August, but there is usually a peak of activity in June or early July in the mountain West.

D. aequalis W

This is the most important species of *Dolophilodes* in Montana, where it often attains great abundance in small streams and rivers. In Rock Creek, above the Hogback stretch, the emergence in early July creates very dependable evening fly-fishing.

Dr. Donald Denning made an interesting observation about this species. He noted that early emergers were larger and darker, their wings almost black, than later ones. Adult colors gradually shifted to a light brown.

D. distinctus E, M

(H. H. Ross treated this species under the name *Trentonius distinctus* prior to 1949.)

This species is common and widespread in eastern and midwestern North America, records showing a range as far south as North Carolina. During the summer emergence period the pupae and adults are part of a crowd of other caddisflies, their activity not concentrated enough to make them individually important, but during the winter period the emerging pupae are available to fish when little else is around.

General imitations for *Dolophilodes*:

LARVA: Yellow Caddis Larva (sizes 10, 12, 14)
PUPA: Brown Deep Sparkle Pupa; Brown Emergent Sparkle Pupa (sizes 12, 14, 16)
ADULT DRY: Brown Dancing Caddis (sizes 12, 14, 16)
ADULT WET: Brown Diving Caddis (sizes 12, 14, 16)
            (Color can vary widely in this genus. Fly fishermen should also be prepared with the Black series and the Gray and Brown series of pupal and adult imitations.)

ADULT KEYS: Ross, H. H. 1949. "A classification of the Nearctic species of *Wormaldia* and *Dolophilodes*." *Proc. Ent. Soc. Wash.*, 51: 154-160.

genus *Wormaldia* (Little Autumn Stream Sedge)
(13 known species in North America north of Mexico)

Generalized description of the adult:
adult length up to 10mm for most common trout-stream species

WING: uniformly gray in some species; mottled brown in others
BODY: varying shades of olive brown
LEGS: varying shades of brown

Larva

Wormaldia

The species of this genus are most common in small and big streams that have diverse caddisfly communities. Often, when the adults are on the wing, they are one of

Adult

many caddisfly species, but they can be the major representative for the order. Their colors and size are typical enough so they can serve as the main model for an imitation.

Two friends, Bob Damico and Paul Fling, came to Deer Lodge in late August to fish the Clark Fork River with me, but a week of steady rain had muddied up even this spring-fed river. We went to Warm Springs Creek instead, a stream small enough to jump over at any place, and fortunately we hit the peak appearance of *Wormaldia gabriella*.

Bob and Paul popped general, adult imitations on the tumbling runs and drummed up the fat, energetic rainbows of this creek. They caught fish up to fourteen inches long and, even if these were not the big brown trout from the Clark Fork they had been promised, neither of these fine fly fishermen seemed disappointed in the rainbows or the insects—or the inevitable surface activity that occurs when the two come together.

Important Species
(*Dolophilus* is an older name for this genus)

W. anilla W
This species has a split emergence period, April to June and September to November, indicating that there are two generations each year. It is a common element of the small-stream caddisfly fauna in the Northwest.
W. gabriella W
This is mainly an autumn species, records showing an August to October peak, but scattered specimens have been collected as early as May. It often inhabits the same systems as *W. anilla*, but it apparently takes over for that species downstream and is found in larger streams.
W. moesta E, M
Emergence for this species, widespread throughout the eastern half of the continent, occurs in March and April.

General imitations for *Wormaldia*:

LARVA:	Yellow Caddis Larva (sizes 10, 12, 14)
PUPA:	Brown and Green Deep Sparkle Pupa; Brown and Green Emergent Sparkle Pupa (sizes 14, 16)
ADULT DRY:	Brown and Green Dancing Caddis (sizes 14, 16)
ADULT WET:	Brown and Green Diving Caddis (sizes 14, 16) (The Gray and Green series of pupal and adult patterns can be substituted with some species.)
ADULT KEYS:	Ross, H. H. 1956. *Evolution and Classification of the Mountain Caddisflies*. Urbana: U. of Ill. Press.

Family Phryganeidae (tube-case maker)
(represented by 10 genera in North America)

Shelter type: the larvae usually build cases of leaf or bark, winding this material spirally or fastening it in rings.

Typical feeding habits of the larvae: the larvae in most genera are, during at least some part of this stage, predacious.

Typical method of emergence: the pupae crawl or swim to the bank and climb out.

Typical egg-laying habits: the females lay their eggs in the water, but when returning to land those of many genera run across the surface rather than fly off.

This family, considered the most primitive of the tube-case makers, is mainly indigenous to lakes and slower areas of streams and rivers across the northern tier of the continent. The two genera covered in this section, *Ptilostomis* and *Phryganea,* can be particularly abundant in gentle, weedy rivers, but even the others, such as *Banksiola* and *Agrypnia,* are important to fly fishermen because of the role they play in the diet of stillwater trout (see Chapter 7 on lake caddisflies).

The larvae of this family, unlike larvae of more advanced tube-case makers, readily abandon their cases if disturbed, scuttling quickly away over the bottom. The free larvae, without the camouflage coloration of their cases, make conspicuous targets for any trout in the vicinity. The tactic of crawling a big yellow-bodied caddisfly-larva imitation with a hand-twist retrieve through quiet backwaters is predicated on this odd behavior of the Phryganeidae.

The pupae and adults of this family are big enough to attract large trout. The pupae generally swim into the shallows and climb out on shoreline vegetation. The adults of some stream and lake genera run across the water rapidly, this habit earning certain species the nickname of Travellers or Caperers.

genus *Phryganea* (Rush Sedge)
(2 known species in North America)

Generalized description of the adult:
adult length up to 25mm

WING: a conspicuous pattern of gray, brown, and yellow
BODY: reddish brown
LEGS: vary from yellowish brown to dark brown

During the day the adults of this genus remain quietly along the water's edge, clinging to the rush stalks. Their folded wings, a pattern of gray, brown, and yellow, blend perfectly with the vegetation; hence, they are called Rush Sedges. In the evening they begin the mating and egg-laying activities, the females flying thirty to forty feet up in the air and dive-bombing the surface. The large insects hit the water with such force that they send up small splashes. During intense egg-laying activity they make a smooth surface look rain spattered.

Trout feed heavily on the different stages of this genus. They find larvae crawling in the quiet backwaters and indentations along the bank, especially during April and May; they take emerging pupae migrating into the shallows; and they gorge on adults. The impressive size of the insect in all stages is enough to make them interesting to even large fish.

The range of the two species in the genus overlaps, both sometimes inhabiting

Larva

Phryganea

Adult

the same waters. *P. cinerea* is transcontinental, records showing a distribution from California to Newfoundland. *P. sayi* is an eastern species, found from Maine to Wisconsin, but it is also reported from states in the middle South. Both species prefer lakes, *P. cinerea* living more than 300 feet deep in Lake Superior, and the very quiet areas of rivers.

Important Species

P. cinerea E, M, W

The emergence of this species occurs during the nice weather of late spring and early summer—in Ohio on the Mad, it takes place mainly at the end of June; in Michigan on the Muskegon it takes place mainly in July. In far northern streams or lakes the pupae develop and emerge more toward midsummer. This caddisfly does not like inclement conditions.

One of my favorite tactics on the Mad River is to creep along the bank, careful not to step too heavily, and drift a Deep Sparkle Pupa tight against the rush beds. In this marshy, meadow brook this close fishing with a fly matching *Phryganea* turns nice trout in water that seems too shallow to hold fish—such an approach once producing a two-pound hold-over brown from this stream.

P. sayi E, M

The emergence and flight period for this species begins a few weeks later than it does for *P. cinerea*. The adults also live longer, specimens still around the water in late August.

General imitations for *Phryganea*:

LARVA:	Yellow Caddisfly Larvae (sizes 2, 4, 6, 8)
PUPA:	Gray and Brown Deep Sparkle Pupa; Gray and Brown Emergent Sparkle Pupa (sizes 4, 6, 8, 10)
ADULT DRY:	Dark Bucktail Caddis (sizes 4, 6, 8, 10); Gray and Brown Dancing Caddis (size 10)
ADULT WET:	Gray and Brown Diving Caddis (sizes 4, 6, 8, 10)
ADULT KEYS:	Ross, H. H. 1944. ''The caddis flies, or Trichoptera, of Illinois.'' *Bull. Ill. Natur. Hist. Surv.*, 23.

genus *Ptilostomis* (Giant Rusty Sedge)
(4 known species in North America)

Generalized description of the adult:
adult length up to 25mm

WING:	light reddish brown (no patterning)
BODY:	yellowish brown
LEGS:	brown

When the larvae of this genus reach their final instar in the fall they become predators. They search the edges of streams and lakes throughout the winter and early spring for food, growing rapidly during the final months. While busily hunting they expose themselves to trout, which often move into the sun-warmed shallows in the

Larva

Ptilostomis

Adult

spring, and in many weedy ponds they are a major item in the trout's diet.

Most of my encounters with this caddisfly have been in lakes and ponds, not streams, so I wrote and asked midwestern fly fisherman Gary Borger about this genus. Gary, author of the books *Nymphing* and *Naturals*, replied, "The two common species here are *P. ocellifera* and *P. semifasciata* [these two are widespread across the United States also]. *P. ocellifera* is more generally distributed in terms of habitat preference—spring ponds, lakes, streams. Adults are large (twenty-one to twenty-four millimeters) and yellowish brown to light rusty brown. They emerge in June and July and have only one generation per year. They emerge at night (at least I've never seen them in the day); occasionally you can encounter them coming off in early morning (just at daybreak). The pupae swim to shore to emerge. Best fishing is in pools of streams or in ponds where there is vegetation. The pupae can get the big trout moving. Places like the 'lakes' on the upper Bois Brule River are good *Ptilostomis* habitat, and there are some really fine trout there.

"The pupa imitation is fished rather fast along the weed edges or cast out into the pool and allowed to swing down and across while working it with the rod. The adult imitation is fished dead drift, twitched along the surface or fished with action just below the surface."

Important Species
(This is one of the genera that in older taxonomies was part of the more encompassing genus *Neuronia*.)

P. ocellifera E, M, W
This hardy transcontinental species has been collected from streams and large rivers, from ponds and lakes, and even from temporary pools. It becomes very abundant in many types of trout habitat.

Craig Mathews tells me that there is great night fishing in the slow waters of the upper White in Michigan. Right after the big mayfly, *Hexagenia limbata*, makes its appearance and fades, the major species of *Ptilostomis* start dominating the fishing, but by this time most of the anglers have left the area. Even when the madness of *Hexagenia* is over the night action remains spectacular, with big wet flies taking large trout.

P. semifasciata E, M, W
This species, like *P. ocellifera*, is transcontinental in distribution. Both species are often found in the same waters.

P. postica E, M
This species is widespread throughout the Northeast, its range extending as far south as Georgia.

Ptilostomis occelifera *is becoming a famous caddisffly in the upper Midwest, where it creates exciting midsummer angling opportunities.*

General imitations for *Ptilostomis*:

LARVA: Yellow Caddis Larva (sizes 2, 4, 6, 8)

PUPA: Brown and Yellow Deep Sparkle Pupa; Brown and Yellow
           Emergent Sparkle Pupa (sizes 4, 6, 8, 10)

ADULT DRY: Dark Bucktail Caddis (sizes 4, 6, 8, 10)
           (The tier may choose to alter the colors of this pattern to more
           exactly match those of the natural.)

ADULT WET: Brown and Yellow Diving Caddis (sizes 4, 6, 8, 10)

ADULT KEYS: Ross, H. H. 1944. "The caddis flies, or Trichoptera, of Illinois."
            Bull. Ill. Natur. Hist. Surv., 23.

Family Polycentropodidae (net spinner)
(represented by 7 genera in North America

Shelter type: the larvae do not build cases. Some genera spin trumpet-shaped nets; some genera construct retreats on pieces of wood or rock; and one genus spins a tube in the soft bottom sediments.

Typical feeding habits of the larvae: the larvae of most genera are predacious. They either filter drifting insects from the current or come out of their retreat to attack them.

Typical method of emergence: the pupae swim or crawl to the surface.

Typical egg-laying habits: the females enter the water and lay a string of eggs on the bottom.

In some taxonomic systems the Polycentropodidae genera have been considered a subfamily of Psychomyiidae, but there are significant differences in both the habits and body structure of the respective larvae. For the most part the larvae of Polycentropidae are predators, using their silk-spinning ability in many diverse ways to capture smaller insects; the larvae of Psychomyiidae are basically vegetarians, feeding mainly on detritus.

No other family of net makers has exploited slow-water and stillwater environments as completely as Polycentropidae. One important trout-stream genus, *Neureclipsis* (Little Red Twilight Sedge), is restricted to running-water habitats, but even their larvae are found in the gentler currents. Two other genera, *Nyctiophylax* (Dinky Light Summer Sedge) and *Polycentropus* (Brown Checkered Summer Sedge), can be common to abundant in streams as well as in lakes.

The family as a whole is not well represented in the West; there are only a few species and even these are seldom common in trout streams. In the East, however, the ten- to twenty-five-millimeter larvae of the three important genera—*Nyctiophylax*, *Neureclipsis*, and *Polycentropus*—occur in great numbers in slow-moving spring creeks and freestone rivers.

Larva

Neureclipsis

genus *Neureclipsis* (Little Red Twilight Sedge)
(5 known species in North America)

Generalized description of the adult:
adult length up to 9mm

WING: reddish brown
BODY: straw yellow
LEGS: straw yellow

Adult

The carnivorous larvae string their trumpet-shaped nets on debris and rooted plants poking up from the bottom. They arrange them vertically on the object, each net filtering its victims from one little slice of the water column. Because of the general instability of both these nets and the sites they are attached to, the larvae usually inhabit only the slower portions of the stream.

The scientific name of the main species, *N. crepuscularis*, is a giveaway for the timing of the adult activities. They are twilight, or crepuscular, creatures, emerging and laying eggs in that last half-hour or so of lingering glow after sunset.

Important Species

N. crepuscularis E, M
(= *N. parvula*)
This species is common in streams and rivers throughout the East and Midwest. The emergence and egg-laying periods are very spread out, without a very pronounced peak, and this lessens the importance of these activities. Both pupae and adults add to the overall caddisfly impact, however, from May through September.

General imitations for *Neureclipsis*:

LARVA:	Yellow Caddis Larva (sizes 12, 14, 16)
PUPA:	Brown and Yellow Deep Sparkle Pupa; Brown and Yellow Emergent Sparkle Pupa (sizes 16, 18, 20)
ADULT DRY:	Brown and Yellow Dancing Caddis (size 16); Thompson Foam Caddis (sizes 16, 18, 20)
ADULT WET:	Brown and Yellow Diving Caddis (sizes 16, 18, 20)
ADULT KEYS:	Ross, H. H. 1944. "The caddis flies, or Trichoptera, of Illinois." *Bull. Ill. Nat. Hist. Surv.* 23

genus *Nyctiophylax* (Dinky Light Summer Sedge)
(8 known species in North America)

Generalized description of the adult:
adult length up to 9mm

WING:	brown
BODY:	yellowish brown
LEGS:	yellowish brown

The small, yellow-and-brown larva of this genus builds a chamberlike retreat, open at both ends, over a hollow in a stick or rock. It leaves loose threads over each opening and when a smaller animal touches the retreat, disturbing the threads, this eight- to ten-millimeter carnivore rushes out and seizes its prey.

When it is ready to pupate the larva simply closes off its silken retreat. Emergence takes place in the same quiet areas—the pools, slow runs, and stream edges—where the larva has spent its immature life. The pupa swims up and hits the extra-thick meniscus that forms on these flat waters, drifting and struggling on the underside. It inspires a quiet riseform from trout, a sip or a gentle roll, rather than the splashy riseform often associated with swimming emergents.

The adults become active at the same time the pupae begin hatching (late

Larva

Nyctiophylax

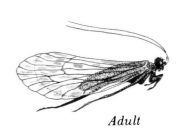

Adult

The larva of Nyctiophylax *uses silk to build a chamber-like retreat. The larva rushes out to attack if a smaller insect touches the loose threads over either end of the retreat.*

afternoon and evening) and they collect into swarms over land. In my notes there are records of the females laying their eggs both by diving underwater and by crawling down objects (during an observation of the latter behavior, trout held close to a wooden bridge abutment and rubbed their snouts raw picking off the adults).

Important Species

N. celta **E, M**
The area of greatest abundance for this species is in the Southeast, and it can be important in Appalachian trout streams. The peak emergence occurs in late May and early June in the southern states.

N. affinis **E, M, W**
This species is predominant in the upper Midwest. It also ranges in a northern band from Nova Scotia to British Columbia, inhabiting both lakes and rivers. It is mainly an early-summer emerger.

N. moestus **E, M, W**
Most of my experiences for the genus have been with *N. moestus* on eastern streams, from Penns Creek in Pennsylvania to the Wood River in Rhode Island. It is very common in a wide range of running-water habitats, but it is probably more important to fly fishermen in slow-moving streams and rivers. Despite their small size, five to seven millimeters (matched with a size 20 or 22 fly), the pupae and adults are so available to trout that on flat, gentle water the June activity is a major occurrence.

General imitations for *Nyctiophylax:*

LARVA:	Yellow Caddis Larva (sizes 16, 18)
PUPA:	Brown and Yellow Deep Sparkle Pupa; Brown and Yellow Emergent Sparkle Pupa (sizes 18, 20, 22)
ADULT DRY:	Thompson Foam Caddis (sizes 18, 20, 22)
ADULT WET:	Brown and Yellow Diving Caddis (sizes 18, 20, 22)
ADULT KEYS:	Morse, J. C. 1972. "The genus *Nyctiophylax* in North America." *J. Kansas Ent. Soc.*, 45: 172-181. (This genus was extensively revised by J. C. Morse. Many older records under the name *N. vestitus* were placed in a sort of a taxonomic limbo, and any angler searching older lists should ignore the references to this species.)

My friend Dick Batten, a professional fly tier, has been supplying the simplified version of the Sparkle Pupa to eastern fly shops ever since the dressing appeared in the Connecticut Fly Fishermen's Association newsletter, the *Lines and Leaders*, in February of 1974, and later in national magazines; and for nearly this long I have been trying to get him to tie the regular Sparkle Pupa (with the overbody construction) for commercial distribution instead. "The old style works fine." he kept insisting. "I don't think the 'sack' fly, or any other fly, can outfish it."

I have no personal bias for either the simplified or the regular Sparkle Pupa—they are both my creations. I have observed them enough underwater, however, to know that the overbody provides a small but significant advantage for the pattern. I still find it disconcerting to see someone so completely sold on my second-best effort (the simplified version).

An emergence of *Nyctiophylax moestus* on Big Flat Brook in New Jersey gave me the chance to demonstrate for Dick—one way or the other—the added effectiveness of the regular pattern. The hatching pupae were swimming up near the banks and drifting among the overhanging sticks, drawing the fish into these nightmarish tangles. The insects were numerous enough to get even the larger trout into a feeding mood.

Dick worked on one rolling brown trout for fifteen minutes with the Simplified Sparkle Pupa, but he could not get the fly back under the trees. The dangling branches hung in such a way that at best he could only drift it within eighteen inches of the fish's position. He covered the peripheral area very skillfully, but he finally gave up.

I took a gamble, "He'll come out for the regular Sparkle Pupa."

Dick snorted, "I'll buy the beer if he does."

"Will you start tying the damn flies right?"

On the third cast the fish spotted the fly way above his hold, sidled over and hung at the edge of the tangle, and as it drew abreast snuck out and grabbed it. When he felt the hook this old war-horse quickly broke me off in the sticks, but with his take he proved that the regular Sparkle Pupa had a greater attraction distance than the simplified version—and he convinced Dick to tie the overbody style for his customers.

genus *Polycentropus* (Brown Checkered Summer Sedge)
(40 known species in North America north of Mexico)

Generalized description of the adult:
adult length up to 11mm
WING: checkered in a light brown and a dark brown pattern
BODY: yellowish brown to brown
LEGS: brown

These mottled summer caddisflies are common in both running-water and stillwater habitats. They live in the quieter areas of streams and rivers, where the larvae either build a silk tube, from which they hurry out of to attack their prey, or a bag net in the current. The pupae, emerging on the surface, and the egg-laying females, swimming to the bottom, can be active in substantial numbers on summer evenings.

Important Species

P. cinereus E, M, W

Larva

Polycentropus

Adult

This species, with a decided preference for cool, clear water, is distributed across the continent from Nova Scotia to British Columbia and as far south as Oklahoma. Emergence occurs mostly in June and July in the northern states, but it can continue sporadically throughout the summer.

General imitations for *Polycentropus*:

LARVA:	Yellow Caddis Larva (sizes 14, 16, 18)
PUPA:	Brown and Yellow Deep Sparkle Pupa; Brown and Yellow Emergent Sparkle Pupa (sizes 16, 18, 20)
ADULT DRY:	Brown and Yellow Dancing Caddis (size 16); Thompson Foam Caddis (sizes 16, 18, 20)
ADULT WET:	Brown and Yellow Diving Caddis (sizes 16, 18, 20)
ADULT KEYS:	Ross, H. H. 1944. "The caddis flies, or Trichoptera, of Illinois." *Bull. Ill. Nat. Hist. Surv.*, 23.

Family Psychomyiidae (net spinner)
(represented by 5 genera in North America)

Shelter type: the larvae build a silken tube on rocks or sunken logs, covering it with fragments of stone or vegetation.

Typical feeding habits of the larvae: the larvae consume algae, fragments of leaf material, and animal matter.

Typical method of emergence: the pupae swim to the surface.

Typical egg-laying habits: the females dive under the surface and lay their eggs on the bottom.

Except for one western genus these small caddisflies live in cool, running-water environments. There are two important trout-stream genera: *Lype* (Dark Eastern Woodland Sedge), a common caddisfly in tree-lined streams; and *Psychomyia* (Dinky Purple-Breasted Sedge), often an abundant caddisfly in habitats ranging from streams to large rivers.

Larva

Lype

genus *Lype* (Dark Eastern Woodland Sedge)
(1 known species in North America)

Generalized description of the adult:
adult length up to 7mm

WING:	uniformly dark, almost black
BODY:	dark brown
LEGS:	dark brown

The single North American species of the genus, *L. diversa*, is common in cool woodland streams. The larva builds a retreat, or dwelling tube, by raising a simple roof over a groove in a sunken piece of wood. The tube is camouflaged with pieces of detritus and a layer of silk—so an angler sampling the larval populations of a trout stream might easily miss this species.

The adults are not so difficult to collect. The mating flights occur during

Adult

afternoon and evening from May to July, these little dark caddisflies flying upstream in determined fashion. They beat against anyone who happens to be in their way, getting in hair or down collars. The females start dropping to the water about 6 P.M. and trout quickly focus on the activity.

Important Species

L. diversa E, M
In my collecting, this species has been most common in the upper Midwest, but it is also found from Maine to Florida.

General imitations for *Lype*:

LARVA:	Olive Brown Caddis Larva (sizes 16, 18, 20)
PUPA:	Black Deep Sparkle Pupa; Black Emergent Sparkle Pupa (sizes 18, 20, 22)
ADULT DRY:	Solomon Delta Wing Caddis (sizes 18, 20, 22)
ADULT WET:	Black Diving Caddis (sizes 18, 20, 22)
ADULT KEYS:	Ross, H. H. 1944. "The caddis flies, or Trichoptera, of Illinois." *Bull. Ill. Nat. Hist. Surv.*, 23.
	(Since there is only one species in the genus, it is only necessary to key out a specimen to the generic level.)

genus *Psychomyia* (Dinky Purple-Breasted Sedge)
(3 known species in North America)

Generalized description of the adult:
adult length up to 6mm

WING:	varies from light to dark brown
BODY:	straw yellow base color but with a distinctive purplish tinge
LEGS:	straw yellow

On strength of numbers alone this genus should rate as a major caddisfly. In cold and swift rivers the populations of *Psychomyia flavida* frequently match or exceed that of any other species in the entire order. It does not, however; on the three-star rating system *P. flavida* usually merits two stars at best and sometimes only one star. The adults are small, four to six millimeters, and both emergence and egg laying generally take place at night, 10 to 11 P.M., the peak time from June until August. These factors lessen the angling importance of this caddisfly.

On summer evenings the adults are conspicuous enough. Usually the hordes are composed of ninety-nine percent females, which are able to produce fertile eggs without male insemination (the ability of the females to reproduce without male partners is known as parthenogenesis). The abundance of caddisflies can be aggravating to an angler on the river because they generally do not start returning to the water until after dark.

There are exceptions to this nighttime activity pattern, however, and it is the daylight flurries that make this caddisfly valuable to fly fishermen. On very overcast days the emergence and egg laying continues sporadically from morning to evening,

Larva

Psychomyia

Adult

stomach samples from trout often revealing steady feeding on both pupae and adults. In midsummer, when heavy thunderheads roll in at dusk, often a blitz of activity begins just before the storm hits, producing a half-hour or so of spectacular fly-fishing for someone who is ready for it.

The larvae of this genus are found in cold-water habitats ranging from small streams to large rivers, but they are most abundant in the rapid sections of the bigger environments. The pupae and adults are most likely to become important to fly fishermen on those rivers with a riffle-and-run structure. They can then drift and collect in the quieter areas of the river, where trout may sip these food items with unhurried ease.

Important Species

P. flavida E, M, W

For a long time I believed that only fly fishermen in the East and upper Midwest had to know about this species, and that populations in the West were scattered and uncommon, but I changed my opinion after collecting extensively on the Missouri River in Montana. I found heavy summer activity on this large river, and I would not be surprised to hear about good populations in other Rocky Mountain and Pacific Coast watersheds.

I know for certain that fly fishermen in the eastern half of the continent need to be aware of this species. I have been caught unprepared far too many times by cloudy day splurges on rivers such as the Housatonic in Connecticut and the upper Allegheny in Pennsylvania, the trout refusing my inadequate imitations. Finally, I began carrying pupal and adult patterns to approximate the small size and purplish coloration of this insect.

General imitations for *Psychomyia*:
LARVA: Olive Brown Caddis Larva (sizes 16, 18, 20)
PUPA: Brown and Dark Blue Deep Sparkle Pupa; Brown and Dark Blue Emergent Sparkle Pupa (sizes 18, 20, 22)
ADULT DRY: Thompson Foam Caddis in appropriate colors (sizes 18, 20, 22)
ADULT WET: Brown and Dark Blue Diving Caddis (sizes 18, 20, 22)

ADULT KEYS: Hagen, H. A. 1861. "Synopsis of the Neuroptera of North America, with a list of the South American species." *Smithson. Inst. Misc. Coll.*, No. 4
Ross, H. H. 1938a. Descriptions of Nearctic caddis flies (Trichoptera) with special reference to the Illinois species. *Bull. Illinois Nat. Hist. Surv.*, 21: 101-183

Family Rhyacophilidae (free living)
(represented by 3 genera in North America)

Shelter type: the larvae do not build any type of shelter before the pupal stage. They roam freely over the rocks, the larvae of some species leaving a silk line wherever they go.

Typical feeding habits of the larvae: most of the species in this family are predators, but a few feed on plant material.

Typical method of emergence: the pupae swim to the surface.

Typical egg-laying habits: the females dive under the surface and place a string of eggs on a bottom object.

The Rhyacophilidae are one of the most primitive families of caddisflies. The larvae are unique in their simple existence; they are the only ones in the order that do not build a case or a retreat sometime during this stage. They scramble freely over the rocks, feeding on other insects or, in a few species, on algae, detritus, moss, or fresh aquatic plant leaves.

H. H. Ross, in *Evolution and Classification of the Mountain Caddisflies*, postulated that this free-living insect was not an evolutionary forerunner of the net makers, which also do not build cases, but of the case-making families. The net makers sprang from another branch, their habit of building a retreat eliminating the need for a case. The case-making habit developed from the free living Rhyacophilidae because a portable shelter could provide many advantages for an insect that had to move over the stream bottom.

There are three North American genera in this family—*Atopsyche*, *Himalopsyche*, and *Rhyacophila*. Only *Rhyacophila*, with over one hundred species, is covered in this section. *Himalopsyche* is mainly an Asian genus, but the single species on this continent, *H. phryganea*, can be common in small streams in Washington, Oregon, and northern California. *Atopsyche* is mainly a South American genus that has migrated into the southwest portion of the United States.

Larva

genus *Rhyacophila* (Green Sedge)
(more than 100 known species in North America)

Rhyacophila

Generalized description of the adult:
adult length up to 16mm

WING: mottled with light and dark areas of gray and brown
BODY: olive green
LEGS: various shades of brown

The study of aquatic insects obviously has an effect on how an angler determines the flies and tactics he is going to use in a given situation. This is not enough, however; the knowledge he has gained from his research can also control how he "reads" water. He can adopt the leap-frog method of reading a stream.

Adult

Family Rhycophilidae, larvae and pupa: (a) Himalopsyche phryganea *larvae; all others,* Rhyacophila *sp.* (Green Sedge)

5mm

Most fly fishermen move along a stream at a steady pace, either up or down, hitting every good-looking spot. They pop casts in the backwaters, along the edges, and over the broken pockets in succession. The problem with such a straight-line method of reading water is that these anglers are probably using an imitation suited to one type—not all types—of water.

Will an imitation of a specific insect work best in only certain types of water? Bet on it. A good imitation of a *Rhyacophila* larva is going to catch a lot of trout in swift, bouncing stretches of stream. The same fly is going to do poorly in slow areas of the same stream.

In one of my experiments on the Wind River in Wyoming, the two best nymph fishermen in my group, Graham Marsh and Wayne Huft, moved upstream side by side. They cast to every prime piece of holding water. Graham used a fast-water fly (a size 12 Green Caddis Larva) and Wayne used a slow-water fly (a size 12 Dark Cased Caddis Larva). They covered a quarter-mile of river.

Their results were very different:

	Wayne	*Graham*
Slow-water areas:	19 fish	6 fish
Fast-water areas:	11 fish	22 fish

A fly fisherman can avoid wasting time in the wrong sections of a stream by working leap-frog fashion instead of in a straight line. If he is using an imitation of a fast-water insect he should fish only the swift, broken currents, skipping past the slower current areas. Likewise, if he is using an imitation of a slow-water insect he should cover only the quieter pools and flats.

The leap-frog method of reading a stream is especially valuable with *Rhyacophila* species. This genus is a double-edged dilemma for fly fishermen because the matching flies can either work so well or so poorly. Proper imitations of the larvae, pupae, and adults in this genus are too bright, and often too large, to look convincing if there are no natural insects around. The proper imitations, however, are critically needed where the natural insects are abundant.[20]

Fly fishermen must remember that *Rhyacophila* larvae are fast-water insects. The activities of the larvae, pupae, and adults begin and end in broken curents, and this is where anglers must use the imitations.

The larvae of most species in this genus are restricted to riffles or rapids in cool streams because they need a steady flow of oxygenated water passing over their bodies. Only a few species have highly developed, branched gills; most of them either have simple, spikelike gills or they lack gill structures entirely.

The larvae crawl freely over, under, and around the rocks. Most of them are predators. In many species they leave a strand of light brown silk on the bottom, a type of safety line, and if washed into the currents they break away with a short length of dangling silk. Their general habit of moving about audaciously makes them a good model for nymph patterns anytime, but they drift in the currents more at dawn and dusk than during the day.

Their practice of leaving an anchor line means that imitations of these larvae should be fished with a specially colored leader tippet. For this genus the coloring should not be white. A felt-tip marker can be used to stain the first eighteen inches of nylon a light brown.

The pupae usually emerge from the same swift areas where they lived as larvae. They are fast, strong swimmers, starting to rise after drifting along the bottom for only a few feet and breaking through the surface quickly. They usually escape into the air within forty feet of where they leave the pupal cocoon even in fast-flowing water.

The egg-laying females do not move as quickly as the pupae. They seem to have little concern about their own safety underwater. They crawl or dive to the bottom and lay a string of eggs on a solid object, but then they simply release their grip and drift away with the currents. They ride for long distances, making no effort to swim, and they rise very slowly to the surface. It also takes them quite a bit of time to push through the surface film.

Trout feed readily on both the pupae and adults. Their rhythm speeds up or slows down accordingly. In fast water trout strike with a violent haste that throws spray into the air, creating the classic pyramid riseform. They can feed efficiently because they do not hold up in the heavier currents near the surface. The trout lay in the dead water at the bottom and wait until they see a swimming insect before starting to rise.

Often the emergence of egg-laying periods of *Rhyacophila* begin very suddenly. It is easy for an angler to panic because of the frenzied nature of the rises in fast water— and if he does he fishes poorly. Anticipating the hatches helps with this genus if for no other reason than because the feeling of being prepared can keep the fisherman calm.

Important Species

R. fuscula E, M

Hundreds of specimens were gathered from the East to determine which caddisflies were or were not important. The larval, pupal, and adult collections left no doubt about the major *Rhyacophila* species; in the samplings from New Hampshire, Vermont, Massachusetts, Connecticut, Rhode Island, New York, and Pennsylvania the most abundant representative was *R. fuscula*. More extensive collecting might easily prove that it is also a dominant species in surrounding states and provinces.

All stages are important to trout in cold, swift streams and rivers. The larvae grow as long as eighteen millimeters and serve as a major underwater food source in the early spring. Pupation begins in late April, the event fairly well synchronized in any particular stretch of a stream. Emergence hits a peak in mid-May or June in the eastern states. The adult egg-laying flights are heavy throughout the early part of the summer.

A fly fisherman must be careful on May evenings on eastern trout streams. There can be a crowd of four or more major caddisflies emerging or laying their eggs, and *R. fuscula* can be one of them. Often *R. fuscula* controls the action in a fast riffle, but in another type of water a different caddisfly might be more abundant.

R. torva E, M

This is an important species in the East, mainly in upper New England and New York, but its range also extends as far west as Minnesota. My records show a peak emergence during the first two weeks of June in New Hampshire streams (an occurrence closely followed by the appearance of *R. glaberrima* in the same area).

R. glaberrima E, M

The main range for this small dark species is the mountainous band running up the eastern seaboard from Virginia to Nova Scotia. This is a late-summer emerger in the northern regions, the early harbingers popping out in late June.

R. fenestra E, M

This is one of the most primitive existing caddisflies in North America. Nevertheless it is fairly common in the Ozark region, especially in the cold, clear streams of Kentucky and Tennessee. In these states it emerges in April and May. In more northern states emergence occurs mainly in late May and June.

R. carolina E

This eastern caddisfly is most important in the Appalachian and northeastern states. The late-afternoon and evening hatches during May are the highlight of the season on many cold mountain streams.

R. lobifera E, M

Charles Wetzel, in *Trout Flies,* made a most interesting observation on the females of this species, "I have had them fasten their green egg sacks to the submerged portion of my waders while wading in swift water; these eggs are fastened with a glue-like substance and are difficult to remove. Now and then the flies would congregate in a ball about one inch in diameter, rise to the surface, then float down stream, when the ball would break up."

During the May and June flight periods fly fishermen might look for both these floating "balls" of caddisfly adults and for any feeding trout such an accumulation might attract. The states where this species is most common are Pennsylvania and New York.

R. manistee E, M

J. W. Leonard and F. A. Leonard wrote about Michigan, "Our collections indicate that *manistee* is by far the commonest species of *Rhyacophila* in Lower Peninsula trout streams."[22]

The same is true for much of the Midwest and East. In a band of northern states from Michigan to Connecticut this species is well represented in swift streams and small rivers. The pupae emerge in May and June in these regions.

R. acropedes E, M, W

This is one of the two species in the genus, along with *R. angelita,* that has managed to spread across the continent. There are records from New Hampshire to California. It is a common caddisfly in the mountainous regions of the West. The eastern populations are less abundant.

The larvae inhabit the riffles of small and large streams, but unlike most *Rhyacophila* species they are not predators. They feed mainly on decaying leaves. Pupation begins during April at lower altitudes and during July at higher ones. The adults fly in the afternoon, their activity stopping completely at dusk.

R. angelita W

(There are also isolated records of this species from the northern areas of the Appalachian Mountains in the East.)

R. angelita is widespread and common in clear, fast streams throughout the West. It is an autumn caddisfly, pupation beginning in July and August and emergence occurring mainly in September and early October. The adults start flying in the evening, but they stop with the arrival of complete darkness. Their short activity period creates a large concentration of insects.

In July collections sent to me by Bruce Solomon from Utah's Strawberry River the larvae of *R. angelita* were very numerous. It was not just coincidence that later in the year Bruce caught a twenty-four-inch brown trout from this fine little river using a

Brown and Bright Green Emergent Pupa, a fly designed to match the coloration of *Rhyacophila* caddisflies.

R. grandis W

The larvae of this giant species grow to thirty millimeters long. They are most abundant in small streams from California to British Columbia. They serve as great models for searching patterns because final instar forms are available all months of the year. The importance of the pupae and the adults is diminished somewhat by the very spread out, February-to-August emergence period.

R. basalis W

Entomological records for this species show a distribution in California, Utah, and Wyoming. It is found mainly in streams at higher elevations and emerges in midsummer.

R. narvae W
(= *R. vepulsa*)

This is a common species in small mountain streams, its range extending from British Columbia as far inland as Montana. Emergence and egg laying begins with the warmer summer months, from late June to July, the bulk of the activity occurring during the morning hours.

R. vao W

This species is able to tolerate slightly warmer and siltier stream conditions than most other members of the genus, occurring commonly in the lower reaches of coastal creeks and rivers. It is found at lower elevations and emerges a few weeks earlier than the closely related *R. acropedes*. In drainages where both are present there is a broad area of overlapping distribution in the middle.

R. vocala W
(= *R. hyalinata*)

This species is common in the mountain West. The preferred habitats are cold, tumbling streams with large boulders. Emergence occurs in early summer, with a July peak in Idaho.

R. pellisa W

This species has something in common with many other caddisflies mentioned in this book—it owes its inclusion here to my use of the stomach pump. My western samplings from stream trout frequently are dominated by the pupae and adults of this species, and the first time I noticed this domination was at Kelly Creek in Idaho on July 29.

The emergence and egg laying occur during the morning hours, mostly from 7 A.M. to 11 A.M. in my observations. Both activities are well received by trout, which often feed with some degree of selectivity on one form or the other.

R. vaccua W

This is one of the most common species of *Rhyacophila* on Vancouver Island. It is also widespread throughout the Northwest. Emergence and egg laying take place during the late summer and autumn in the afternoon.

R. verrula W

R. verrula is widespread throughout the West, reaching its greatest abundance in cold streams with some spring-water influences. The larvae feed on algae, fresh aquatic plant leaves, and mosses. The main emergence period occurs in the fall months.

R. coloradensis W

Dr. D. Denning wrote about *R. coloradensis*, "This species is widely distributed throughout Wyoming and Colorado. It is probably the most abundant *Rhyacophila* in Wyoming; the majority were taken from August 9 to September 7."[23]

It is also common to abundant in other mountain states such as Idaho and Montana, where the larvae inhabit the rapids of large rivers. They pupate in and emerge from these fast-water areas. Adults are active on warm afternoons in the fall.

R. bifila W

In the rapids on the Madison River below Quake Lake this species emerges in good numbers every evening during July. The pupae make trout feed steadily, but how fish react to them apparently depends on the current speed—in the very fast white water, the center of a chute, the trout rocket into the air; in the moderate currents along the sides, they roll on the surface; in the slow area of a pool they sip daintily.

These fish, a mix of rainbows and browns, are all feeding on the same caddisfly, but they rise to it differently. These variations in their behavior, or riseforms, correlate well with the different currents, indicating that it is not just how fast an emergent swims that controls how trout rise.

This species is abundant in the Northwest, records showing a range from British Columbia south to California and east to Wyoming and Montana. It inhabits streams and rivers, the larvae clinging to large boulders in fast water. It has a flight period from early summer to midsummer.

General imitations for *Rhyacophila*:

LARVA: Bright Green Caddis Larva (sizes 6, 8, 10, 12, 14, 16)

PUPA: Brown and Bright Green Deep Sparkle Pupa; Brown and Bright Green Emergent Sparkle Pupa (sizes 10, 12, 14, 16, 18)

ADULT DRY: Brown and Green Dancing Caddis (sizes 10, 12, 14, 16), Parkany Deer Hair Caddis in appropriate colors (sizes 8, 10)

ADULT WET: Brown and Green Diving Caddis (sizes 10, 12, 14, 16, 18)

ADULT KEYS: Ross, H. H. 1956. *Evolution and Classification of the Mountain Caddisflies*. Urbana: University of Illinois Press.

The species of this genus were especially easy to write about because there have been so many fine professional papers on the biological aspects—papers that fly fishermen might want to review also.

Smith, S. D. 1968. "The *Rhyacophila* of the Salmon River drainage of Idaho with special reference to larvae." *Ann. Ent. Soc. Amer.*, 61: 655-674.

Wold, J. 1972. "Systematics of the genus *Rhyacophila* (Trichoptera: *Rhyacophilidae*) in western North America with special reference to the immature stages." M. S. Thesis. Oregon State University, 229 pp.

Aquatic Moths (order Lepidoptera)

This group of insects could easily prove important to fly fishermen at certain times, but they are so closely related to caddisflies that an angler on the stream might not recognize them as a separate order. Although caddisfly imitations should suffice in these situations, knowing when hatching and egg-laying activities are at a peak might give anglers the chance to anticipate these moments.

W. H. Lange, in his chapter on aquatic Lepidoptera in *Aquatic Insects of California*, writes, "The rock-dwelling forms are well represented in the West. The larvae of a typical rock dweller construct silken tents under which they feed on algae and diatoms. Pupation occurs in dome-shaped, feltlike cocoons, which have openings at each end to allow the passage of water. The pupae are found in an inner waterproof silken lining, and just before pupating the larva cuts a semicircular escape slit for the adult to escape from the tough cocoon. The adult females enter the water (wings folded and covered with a silvery sheen of air bubbles), using the two hind pairs of legs as oars, and deposit the eggs in groups on rocks, often several feet under water in swift streams."

There are obvious similarities between the life cycle of aquatic moths and the life cycle of caddisflies. During at least two phases of their existence, emergence and egg laying, the adults are freely exposed to fish predation. Since they are common and widespread across the continent, inhabiting many good trout streams and lakes, they deserve the notice of angling entomologists. The task for the future is to discover where and when they attract significant trout feeding.

This species, Parargyractis truckeealis, *has a wingspan of up to 22mm. It is widespread in Northern California, Oregon, Washington, and Idaho, inhabiting the highly oxygenated sections of lakes and streams. It reaches population densities of thirty to forty larva per square foot of rock surface.*

12

Collecting and Identifying Caddisflies

Fly fishermen collect and study insect specimens in different ways. Some do it haphazardly, swatting down a "bug" on the stream and matching it on the spot from their fly box. Others systematically collect the important species from their area, setting up emergence tables for home waters.

Each angler must decide for himself how deeply he wants to become involved in entomology. Even the most casual study of aquatic insects, however, makes the investigator a better fly fisherman. The benefits are roughly proportional to the amount of work devoted to understanding the biological rhythms of the trout's habitat.

Methods for the Casual Collector

There are a number of quick methods for sampling larvae and nymphs. Spreading a screen and turning over rocks to let the dislodged insects drift down against the mesh is a simple way to check the general fauna. Even picking up a rock and studying the forms clinging to it reveals many important species in a stream. Unfortunately, while such samplings might tell which caddisfly larvae are on the bottom, they do not necessarily indicate which ones trout are feeding on at the moment, which is all the casual collector wants to know.

A stomach pump gently used on a fish twelve inches or bigger shows fly fishermen exactly what trout are eating, at least in that particular section of the stream, and roughly what the matching fly should look like. Dead specimens alone, however, do not tell someone how to use the imitation. Without knowing the habits of the living insect, information that is available only to the serious angling entomologist, the casual collector has to fish in a trial-and-error fashion until he stumbles upon the right tactic—which is how he will have to catch that first trout anyway.

The casual collector learns more from the adults than from the larvae because at least he can see how trout are taking food on or near the surface. He can observe the actions of the insects, and if he can capture a specimen he can match its color, size, and silhouette with a fly.

Many caddisfly adults are very strong fliers, darting and flitting continuously. In spite of the incredible numbers sometimes hovering near the stream, it is frequently difficult to grab one out of the air. It is not uncommon to see a fisherman clad in waders and weighed down with equipment futilely stumbling after a swarm.

Sometimes it is better for an angler to give up on the fliers, unless he has a butterfly net, and look for ones that are crawling around. He can search the crevices in the bark of trees, the undersides of bushes or streamside rocks, or the insides of road culverts, picking up the adults by gently pinching the rear edges of the wings together.

Nearly every mention in modern angling literature of adult caddisflies includes the solemn advice, "Always catch one because caddisflies appear lighter in flight than they actually are."

The most common reason caddisflies appear lighter in the air than they do in the hand is that the wings of most species are fairly translucent, and they allow a lot of sunlight to pass through them. When an angler holds an adult in his hand and looks down at it, the light does not affect the coloration. Maybe someone finds it valuable to view adults this way, but it has been my experience that it is difficult to get wild trout to take caddisflies from my hand. They usually suck adults off the surface, looking up at them, which is roughly the same way fly fishermen see them in the air.

Even considering that the wings are folded if the insect is at rest on the water, the top set of wings is still longer. There is an overlap that produces a bright edge around the body. There is a fly that can recreate that effect, the Thompson Foam Caddis, but with any imitation the angler can take the lighter edge into consideration and use a fly with an appropriately colored wing.

Some species of caddisflies appear lighter in the air than in the hand because the underside of the insect's wings are significantly lighter than the topside, and when the insect is in the air anglers see the underside. Of course, a trout also sees the underside of the insect's wings. So the lighter color is the correct one for the adult imitation.

Even the way fly fishermen look at an insect is warped by the "mayfly" obsession. It is fine to study a mayfly in the hand because the wings are upright, but certainly a caddisfly, with two sets of wings over the body, must be looked at against the natural background of the sky for a fish-eye view; and a matching artificial should be chosen the same way.

A casual collector usually does not care about the scientific name of the insect, so it is enough for him to check the color of the body, the color of the underside of the wings, and the size of the insect. He might also find it valuable to make notes on the time, place, and successful fishing tactics for the hatch.

Tools for the serious collector include a seine for gathering larval specimens and a butterfly net for capturing adult specimens.

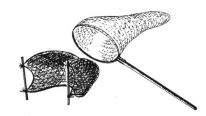

Methods for the Serious Collector

The serious collector needs to be more methodical in his studies. As soon as he attempts to make emergence charts and species lists for his local waters, he must become careful about how he collects, preserves, and identifies specimens. To insure validity he must also gather not only once in an area, but enough times to guarantee the inclusion of all the important species.

The fascination with entomology often begins when the angler becomes curious about a particular hatch, and this is exactly how I became involved with caddisflies. In my case it was the huge flights in late June on the Clark Fork River. My samples, sent to a university, were identified as the Spotted Sedge (*Hydropsyche occidentalis*). The Latin name, in turn, opened up a whole world of written material, all the scientific papers on the species, that yielded amazing details about the insect—how it lived as a larva, when it emerged, how it emerged, how it layed eggs—and made fishing the hatch much easier.

This initial step is usually not the last because it becomes obvious how much help the entomological information can be. The study of insects is addictive, and it can soon have the fly fisherman happily mumbling Latin names.

Next, the angler wants to know all the important aquatic insects in his area. This is when he begins to make a list of species and a calendar of emergence. These tasks can take a full season of collecting, or even two, but they provide information that usually does not change. These are facts that will make him a better fly fisherman for the rest of his angling life.

To make an accurate species list he should collect adult insects from a stream at least once every three days. There are a number of techniques, beginning with the same simple choose-and-pick method the casual collector uses. Another method, requiring a butterfly net, involves beating the bushes and capturing the insects that fly off. A third, equally simple method means driving a car to the stream at dusk, turning on the headlights, and gathering the adults attracted to the lamps.

The drawback of all three of these procedures is that the collector has to be there, spending time each visit chasing the adults. If he is getting samples from three or four spots spaced along the stream, which he should be, the task of collecting can take an entire evening.

Entomologists use light traps, electrically powered devices that attract adults at night, but a portable unit is an expensive piece of equipment. Besides, it still requires monitoring every day unless there is a photocell to turn it on and off, and a light trap usually does not capture all the species found in a stream because some are not drawn to lights.

Robert Newell, a professional entomologist, outlined in a letter two simple and inexpensive methods of capturing adult caddisflies even when the collector is not present. They are ingenious, and perfect for the amateur, "I have used two methods that collect insects when you are not on the stream and they work twenty-four hours a day. I suspend a three-foot by three-foot piece of window screen above the water perpendicular to the stream and facing up and downstream. Spray this screen with a product called 'Sticky Tanglefoot.' Adult insects that fly along the stream and hit the net become stuck to the screen. A few drops of xylene will dissolve the material enough to remove the insect. This works best on small streams.

"A second technique works very well on any stream. I call it a formalin/oil trap. You can use any size container, but I prefer a cake pan of about two by twelve by twelve inches. Pour one-half inch of formaldehyde into the pan and over this pour a very thin layer of vegetable oil. Place the pan in any dark recess (under tree roots, undercut banks, bridges) and check the pan every few days. Caddisflies appear to be quite active in these dark areas and when they come in contact with the oil they are trapped and they sink into the formaldehyde where they are preserved. Pick the adults out, blot off the oil, and place in alcohol. It is a very effective way to collect many streams continually with a minimum amount of travel."

Preserving Specimens

Obtain the small, glass bottles that are designed for holding specimens. Place the insects, either adults or larvae, in a mixture of eighty percent ethyl alcohol and twenty percent distilled water, changing this fluid a couple of times in the first few days so that the water in the tissue of the specimen is replaced. Do not use formalin for long-term preservation, not on insects that will be continually examined, because it is a known cancer-causing agent (as is xylene) and poses a danger to the collector.

Write any pertinent data—date and place collected—in pencil on a slip of paper and put it inside the bottle. Always fill the bottle to the top with preservative, inserting a small cotton wad at the top, or else the air bubble in the closed jar allows the specimen to slosh and break apart.

The exceptions to liquid preservation are the adults of the genus *Nectopsyche*, the common White Miller. These slim, pale specimens are stored dry in a closed container or pinned to a board. The color pattern of the scales on the wings are used for identifying them.

Following are the addresses of a firm that sells the entomological supplies fly fishermen will need:

Western outlet:
BioQuip Products
P.O. Box 61
Santa Monica, California 90406

Eastern outlet:
BioQuip Products
1115 Rolling Road
Baltimore, Maryland 21228

Identifying Specimens

The fly fisherman, once he has all these wonderful specimens, still has the problem of identification. Professional entomologists usually are not interested in looking at the scattered samples of the amateur collector. Sometimes a fellow angler who has the expertise, or a graduate student at a university, is willing to identify well-preserved male adults to the species level.

Until my entomology courses and practice sessions with a microscope gave me the skill to identify my own specimens, I used to help graduate students with the studies they were conducting. In exchange for manual labor and other work, the easy but time-consuming tasks that these types of research are always filled with, they would check my collections. As an added benefit, I would learn about insects by helping with the various studies.

Often, once the fisherman has his local caddisflies identified, there is no need to go beyond this step. He will usually be able to recognize the important hatches when he sees them again. The features of the adults are distinctive enough so that once he has worked with them he will know them.

The final stage in the entomological education of a fly fisherman is learning how to identify his own specimens with a microscope. This involves the use of keys, couplets containing descriptions of the body parts of an insect, and the angler must know what the names of the structures refer to and what the structures look like.

With practice these keys are not difficult to follow. In each couplet there are two descriptions: one that fits a specimen and one that does not. Each couplet narrows the possibilities, until the species is finally determined.

For example, the first couplet for the adult keys either places a specimen in or out of the family Hydroptilidae:

1. Small insects, usually 5mm or less in length; mesoscutum lacking setal warts, mesocutellar setal warts transverse and meeting mesally to form an angulate ridge (Fig. 14.92); hind wings narrow and apically acute (Fig. 14.93), often with posterior fringe of long hairs........Hydroptilidae

1'. Insects usually more than 5mm long; mesoscutum frequently with setal warts (Fig. 14.98), mesocutellar setal warts usually rounded or elongate (Figs. 14.96, 14.98); hind wings usually broader and rounded apically (Fig. 14.30), posterior fringe when present of relatively shorter hairs........2
(The number 2 directs the examiner to the second couplet)[1]

Keys to the generic level for the larvae, with illustrations of the body parts, are found in *Larvae of the North American Caddisfly Genera* by Glenn B. Wiggins. Keys to genera and many species for the adults are found in "The caddis flies, or Trichoptera, of Illinois" by H. H. Ross. Other keys to the species level for adults, usually requiring a male specimen, are available in papers dealing with a specific family or genus.

This might seem like an extreme level for an angler, but during a recent visit to California I was surprised at the numbers of devotees who spoke the technical language. The high degree of sophistication on the West Coast was due, in part, to special courses in entomology offered to fly fishermen by universities. There, at least, the trend was obvious, and it seemed to represent the growing closeness all over the country between anglers and professional entomologists.

CHECKLIST OF NORTH AMERICAN CADDISFLY GENERA

	Important in running water habitats; covered in this book.	Not covered in this book but future research might show instances where the genus is important to trout.	Not covered in this book; probably not important as a food resource for trout	Discussed as a stillwater genus.
Family Beraeidae *Beraea*			X	
Family Brachycentridae *Adicrophleps*			X	
Amiocentrus	X			

CHECKLIST OF NORTH AMERICAN CADDISFLY GENERA

	Important in running water habitats; covered in this book.	Not covered in this book but future research might show instances where the genus is important to trout.	Not covered in this book; probably not important as a food resource for trout	Discussed as a stillwater genus.
Brachycentrus	X			
Eobrachycentrus			X	
Micrasema		X		
Oligoplectrum			X	
Family Calamoceratidae				
Anisocentropus			X	
Heteroplectron		X		
Phylloicus			X	
Family Glossosomatidae				
Agapetus		X		
Anagapetus		X		
Culoptila			X	
Glossosoma	X			
Matrioptila			X	
Protoptila		X		
Family Helicopsychidae				
Helicopsyche	X			
Family Hydropsychidae				
Aphropsyche			X	
Arctopsyche	X			
Cheumatopsyche	X			
Diplectrona		X		
Homoplectra			X	
Hydropsyche	X			
Leptonema			X	
Macronema	X			
Oropsyche			X	
Parapsyche		X		
Potamyia		X		
Smicridea		X		
Family Hydroptilidae				
Agraylea	X			
Alisotrichia			X	
Dibusa			X	
Hydroptila	X			
Ithytrichia			X	
Leucotrichia	X			
Mayatrichia			X	
Neotrichia			X	
Ochrotrichia			X	
Orthotrichia			X	
Oxyethira	X			
Family Lepidostomatidae				
Lepidostoma	X			
Theliopsyche			X	

CHECKLIST OF NORTH AMERICAN CADDISFLY GENERA

	Important in running water habitats; covered in this book.	Not covered in this book but future research might show instances where the genus is important to trout.	Not covered in this book; probably not important as a food resource for trout	Discussed as a stillwater genus.
Family Leptoceridae				
Ceraclea	X			
Leptocerus				X
Mystacides	X			
Nectopsyche	X			
Oecetis	X			
Setodes		X		
Triaenodes				X
Family Limnephilidae				
Allocosmoecus			X	
Amphicosmoecus			X	
Anabolia		X		
Apatania	X			
Arctopora			X	
Asynarchus		X		
Chilostigma			X	
Chilostigmodes			X	
Chyranda	X			
Clistoronia				X
Clostoeca			X	
Cryptochia			X	
Desmona			X	
Dicosmoecus	X			
Ecclisocosmoecus			X	
Ecclisomyia	X			
Farula			X	
Frenesia	X			
Glyphopsyche			X	
Goera	X			
Goeracea			X	
Goereilla			X	
Goerita			X	
Grammotaulius		X		
Grensia			X	
Halesochila		X		
Hesperophylax	X			
Homophylax			X	
Hydatophylax	X			
Imania			X	
Ironoquia	X			
Lenarchus				X
Lepania			X	
Leptophylax			X	
Limnephilus	X			
Manophylax			X	
Moselyana			X	
Nemotaulius		X		
Neophylax	X			
Neothremma		X		
Oligophlebodes	X			
Onocosmoecus	X			
Pedomoecus			X	
Phanocelia			X	
Philarctus			X	
Philocasca			X	

CHECKLIST OF NORTH AMERICAN CADDISFLY GENERA

	Important in running water habitats; covered in this book.	Not covered in this book but future research might show instances where the genus is important to trout.	Not covered in this book; probably not important as a food resource for trout	Discussed as a stillwater genus.
Platycentropus	X			
Pseudostenophylax		X		
Psychoglypha	X			
Psychoronia			X	
Pycnopsyche	X			
Rossiana			X	
Family Molannidae				
Molanna	X			
Molannodes			X	
Family Odontoceridae				
Marilia			X	
Namamyia			X	
Nerophilus			X	
Parthina			X	
Pseudogoera			X	
Psilotreta	X			
Family Philopotamidae				
Chimarra	X			
Dolophilodes	X			
Wormaldia	X			
Family Phryganeidae				
Agrypnia				X
Banksiola				X
Fabria			X	
Hagenella			X	
Oligostomis			X	
Oligotricha			X	
Phryganea	X			
Ptilostomis	X			
Yphria			X	
Family Polycentropodidae				
Cernotina			X	
Cyrnellus		X		
Neureclipsis	X			
Nyctiophylax	X			
Phylocentropus		X		
Polycentropus	X			
Polyplectropus			X	
Family Psychomyiidae				
Lype	X			
Paduniella			X	
Psychomyia	X			
Tinodes		X		
Xiphocentron			X	
Family Rhyacophilidae				
Atopsyche			X	
Himalopsyche		X		
Rhyacophila	X			
Family Sericostomatidae				
Agarodes		X		
Fattigia			X	
Gumaga			X	

Postscript

A book on fly-fishing, even one concerned with entomology, is not a scientific text. At best it can pay homage to science, depending on and crediting articles and books by professionals, and any experiments specifically done for it can adhere as closely as possible to scientific methodology.

This is not meant to diminish angling writing—very few endeavors have inspired such a rich and intense body of literature as fly-fishing. A fly-fishing book by necessity contains more generalizations and opinions than a professional treatise, but these are in part a happy admission that angling is an art, not a science, and cannot ever be boiled down completely to measurable facts. R. L. Usinger, writing in *Aquatic Insects of California*, possibly summed up the way professional entomologists feel about anglers' work in their field, "... [in fly-fishing books] we find an astonishing amount of fact and fiction, of novelty and tradition, of superficiality and meticulous care."

Caddisflies was greatly influenced by a conversation with Dr. George F. Edmunds, a talk that could have been titled, "What Do Entomologists Expect from a Fly-Fishing Book?" The gist of his answer was that if the writer separates the science from the art by citing entomological facts, these statements should be as accurate and complete as possible. The scientific sections in a book of fly-fishing entomology should be accountable by the same standards applied to a professional treatise.

Dr. Edmunds, one of the most knowledgeable mayfly authorities in the world, wrote a paper that specifically analyzed one fly-fishing entomology. He thought that this mayfly book was well done for an angling work, but he pointed out over fifty major errors in it. "I didn't write the article as criticism," Dr. Edmunds said, "I wrote it because the color photographs in the book were beautiful, and I wanted college students to be able to use it in classes."

He pointed out two ways an angling writer could make his work more valid for both fly fishermen and entomolgists:

One, use a uniform system of scientific names. Most fly-fishing entomologies explain the reason for using Latin names: so that a fisherman from one region will be able to communicate with someone from another. The common names for insects vary from region to region, even from person to person, but the Latin names do not.

It is a nice explanation. The truth is, however, that some fly-fishing books jumble up the Latin names so badly that even entomologists have a difficult time understanding the terminology, and the average fly fisherman is lost even more easily. How does this happen? Latin names do change. Entomology is still an expanding field of knowledge. As new facts are discovered, the families and genera are revised. A specific caddisfly can be moved from one genus to another, and then the name changes.

The problems begin when an angling writer picks the names of insect species out of both old and new entomological texts. There is no uniformity. Is a caddis *Hydropsyche analis*, or is it *Cheumatopsyche pettiti*? Both names, old and new, refer to the same species. Taking names at random from different texts frustrates the reason for using the Latin terminology because it only creates chaos.

The solution is for the writer to pick the best modern entomology book on the insect order and use the system of Latin names that it uses. Then he should identify the source. *Caddisflies* follows the nomenclature of *Larvae of the North American Caddisfly Genera (Trichoptera)* by Glenn B. Wiggins. This provides a reference point for present as well as future readers.

322

This book uses the system from Wiggins' entomology because it has been a major source of information for me. *Caddisflies* also draws on many other professional books and papers, including older ones, and in those instances the names of caddisfly species have been updated to the modern equivalents. The previous names are shown in parentheses, allowing the reader to trace Latin references in other angling books.

Two, have the book proofread by an entomologist before publication. When an entomologist writes a book or an article, it is read by other experts in the field before publication. The work is submitted for comments and corrections, not because the author doubts his own knowledge or research but because whenever a subject is as complex as entomology it is easy for mistakes to go unnoticed.

Many angling books and articles, however, are never proofread by an expert. For any work presenting scientific information such an omission is very dangerous, but the fact that publishers seldom require proof of accuracy for fly-fishing entomologies almost constitutes a license to spread mistakes. An error in a fishing book can snowball, other writers repeating it over and over until it grows into a commonly accepted statement. Most of these inaccuracies, however, are unnecessary because they would be discovered even in a cursory reading by an expert on the subject.

Six readers carefully went through the manuscript of *Caddisflies*. Some of these men were fly fishermen and some of them were not; none were chosen strictly because of their fly fishing background. All of the readers had particular areas of scientific expertise.

1. Dr. David Engerbretson—professor at Washington State Universty; an expert on animal anatomy.

2. Dr. Robert Newell—an aquatic entomologist for the Anaconda Mining Company who has done many professional studies on stream ecosystems.

3. Kenneth Parkany—an engineer for United Technologies; a specialist on the physical properties of materials.

4. Dr. George Roemhild—professor of entomology at Montana State University; author of many scientific papers on aquatic insects.

5. A.C.S.W. John Richard Rosenleaf—psychologist at Warm Springs State Mental Hospital; reviewer here of the theories on behavioral psychology (the stimulus/response feeding pattern of trout).

6. Kenneth Thompson—Masters graduate at the University of Connecticut; a student who is quickly becoming a caddisfly expert (and the main worker on many of the original studies done for this book).

This book has been written with accuracy as a goal. The research has been extensive. The original experiments and observations have been checked and rechecked. Opinions from other fly-fishing books have not been merely parroted, they have been poked, prodded, and examined—and such scrutiny makes this work run counter many times to accepted ideas. As a work of angling entomology, *Caddisflies* must rise or fall on its accuracy.

To anglers and other angling writers I still must say this: do not blindly accept any of the statements in this book. Check everything yourself—careful research and experimentation will confirm many of the theories here but future scientific discoveries will certainly provide fresh insights into the problems and dictate periodic reassessments of caddisfly lore. Skepticism is not only healthy—it is the only way new ideas can find room to stand.

Gary LaFontaine
Deer Lodge, Montana
August, 1980

Footnotes

Preface

1. These figures, from the Saluda River in South Carolina, are based on sixty-eight trout collected from April through September. This is unpublished research by John Galloway and Ralph Stropes, graduate students in fisheries biology.

Chapter 2

1. This was an artificially controlled experiment. Trout confined in a caged area of a stream were fed the different types of nymphs and larvae, the insects dropped into the current above their position.

2. This basic color recipe matches the spotted sedge (*Hydropsyche*)larva. There is another trait for *Hydropsyche* larvae that must also be imitated in a natural situation besides the insect itself—this net maker spins a white silk anchor line and dangles from it in the current. Simulating this line is even more important than matching the color, size, shape, and body position of the larva (see Chapter 4).

3. The Swedish Dry Fly Hooks are available from George Uptegrove's Angling Specialities, Ancaster, Ontario, L9G3L3, Canada. They come in sizes 10, 12, 14, 16, 18.

4. A hackle from a Cree neck is brown, black, and white. Not only is this a fine color combination for a fly, a single hackle duplicating the effect achieved by wrapping a brown hackle and a grizzly hackle together, but quality necks are common and inexpensive.

Chapter 4

1. Still-water methods are discussed in the chapter on lakes. A river can also have some placid areas, and in these places lake tactics are applicable. A patient hand-twist retrieve, for example, can imitate slow-moving caddisfly larvae in pools or backwaters.

Chapter 5

1. H. E. Hinton, in his paper, "On the function, origin, and classification of pupae," pointed out these theories. In that paper he also speculated that the extra dun stage (subimago) of the mayfly might be considered a very primitive form of pupation.

2. Creslan, the American Cyanamid product, was listed under the common brand name of the yarn, Dazzle (seventy percent Creslan).

3. Original source of information; Corbet, P. S. 1966. "Diel Periodicities of emergence and oviposition in riverine Trichoptera. *Can. Ent.*, 98: 1025-1034.

Chapter 6

1. Occasionally a tactic or fly pattern is developed in England and America at roughly the same time unbeknownst to creators on either side of the ocean. These cases of parallel evolution are due to a lag in communications between the fly fisherman of the two areas; as a result, in the realm of tactics the Americans have their Leisenring Lift, a method of teasing life into a wet fly, and the English have their Induced Take, a nearly identical idea introduced by Oliver Kite.

Robert Ince, my correspondent from England, pointed out that a similar situation of separate development exists with flies: "Richard Walker is a well-known English angling author who in the late sixties popularised a pattern which is virtually identical to Leonard M. Wright's Fluttering Caddis with the exception that Walker's pattern has a butt of orange 'd.f.' wool."

2. The term "tick cast" is used here for its descriptive quality, but this technique was introduced by George LaBranche in *The Dry Fly and Fast Water* under the names "bounce cast" and "fluttering cast."

Chapter 7

1. These insects are an important food source by themselves, but they also serve as an intermediate step in the food chain. They attract small forage fish that can in turn attract even the largest trout in a lake.

2. Sometimes in British Columbia the common name, Traveller Sedge, is used for any large caddisfly running across the surface, but it is generally applied to just one species, *Banksiola crotchi*.

Chapter 8

1. In his reading of the first draft of this chapter, Dr. Glenn Wiggins corrected both the terms "caddis" and "caddis fly." He noted "The general standard is to separate 'fly' if the insect is in the order Diptera, hence black flies, deer flies; but combined if not—mayflies, dragonflies, caddisflies, etc."

This modern entomological usage has been adopted throughout the book. The term "caddis" is used only in the names of artificial flies, or in the name "microcaddis" (the professional designation for one family, the Hydroptilidae). The order Trichoptera is referred to by the accepted term, "caddisflies."

2. This is a partial list of case-making advantages included by Dr. Glenn B. Wiggins in *Larvae of the North American Caddisfly Genera (Trichoptera)*.

3. This book sets up a system that allows the fly fishermen to determine the important caddisflies of his home waters: the macrohabitat (the type of environment a species can live in) and the microhabitat (the areas within a particular environment a species can live in), each narrowing the choices. The genera and species covered in the Insect Listing, fit into this distributional framework.

4. This description, written by the author, appeared originally in a French language pamphlet about fishing in Laurentides Park, Quebec.

Chapter 9

1. Source for data: Spindler, John C. "The Clean-Up of Silver Bow Creek." Mining Congress Journal, June 1977.

2. Rabeni, C. F., and G. W. Minshall. 1977. "Factors affecting microdistribution of stream benthic insects." *Oikos.*, 29: 33-43.

3. The study of various caddisfly species as biologic indicators is still very new. There are a few known quantities; for example, *Helicopsyche borealis* is able to survive higher water temperature than most other caddisflies. It is important to realize that even with this species the ability to withstand extreme conditions evolved in special, but natural environments; *H. borealis*, with a spiral case that can possibly dissipate heat, is also able to withstand high temperatures and mineral concentrations of hot springs.

4. That broke that myth. No one is touting the "hardiness" of caddisflies in angling literature anymore. There is still a problem because the statement was made so often in older books that fishermen who are unaware of the new information are still reading about and believing in the generally invincible caddisfly.

5. Fisher, S. G., and G. E. Likens. 1973. "Energy flow in Bear Brook, New Hampshire: An integrative approach to stream ecosystem metabolism." *Ecol. Monog.*, 43: 421-439.

6. Ken did the initial identifications of caddisfly adults for both his collection on the Mount Hope (Connecticut) and mine on the Henrys Fork (Idaho). Once it became obvious that our samplings were discovering many species that had not been previously reported from these states, he decided to send the specimens to Dr. Oliver Flint of the Smithsonian Institute for verification so that our lists could be used as official records by entomologists.

Dr. Flint kindly checked the adults from these two lists. Dr. D. Denning and Dr. R. L. Blickle also provided advice and confirmations on the identifications. The efforts of these entomologists, all outstanding caddisfly specialists, insured the accuracy of our findings.

7. My supplementary collections included *Nectopsyche diarina* and *Ceraclea annulicornis*. Neither species occurs in any great numbers in the Yellowstone, but both of them are fairly common in other Montana rivers.

8. Muttkowski, R. A. 1929. "The ecology of trout streams in Yellowstone National Park." *Bull. N. Y. St. Coll. for. Roosevelt Wild Life Annals*, Vol. 2, No. 2, pp. 151-240.

9. Five species that had not been previously collected from the state, and not listed in the fine general survey, *An Annotated List of the Aquatic Insects of Southeastern Idaho, Part II: Trichoptera* by Robert L. Newell and G. Wayne Minshall, were taken from the Henrys Fork: *Hydropsyche vexa* (Hydropsychidae), *Oecetis avara* Leptoceridae), *Oecetis disjuncta* (Leptoceridae), *Hydroptila arctia* (Hydroptilidae), and *Neophylax rickeri* (Limnephilidae). One genus, *Molanna* (Molannidae), not previously recorded from the state was also collected. (All specimens were verified by Dr. Oliver Flint.)

10. All of my adult specimens of this genus from the Henrys Fork were *L. pluviale*, but in the Montana State University caddisfly collection there are records of *L. veleda* adults (gathered in late June from the Railroad Ranch area by Tom Young).

11. The same enrichment process occurs below natural lakes. As long as the outlet stream is normally cold and clear the effects are similar on its trout fishery.

12. If the reader checks the Species Lists in this book for the White River, Yellowstone River, or Woods Creek against the original papers he will notice discrepancies in the scientific names. For example, in my list for the White

River there is no species named *Athripsodes angustus*, but that name appears in the original paper.

Some scientific names change; old names are updated by later entomologists. Thus in my list for the White River there is a species named *Ceraclea transversa*, the modern equivalent of *Athripsodes angustus*. The translations from older to modern names in the Species Lists are my work, and of course their accuracy is my responsibility.

Chapter 10

1. Neill, R. M. 1938. "The food and feeding of the brown trout in relation to the organic environment." *Trans. Roy. Soc. Edin.*, 59: 481-520.

It would be hard to find a trout stream in North America where the insect fauna is only five percent caddisflies. Are caddisflies as an order less well represented in the waters of the British Isles? Does this explain the fly-fishing heritage and its emphasis on mayflies that we have inherited from Ireland, Scotland, and England?

2. Hess, A. D. and A. Swartz. 1941. "The forage ratio and its use in determining the food grade of streams." *Trans. 5th N. Am Wildlife Conf.*, 1940: 162-164.

3. A stomach pump is a completely acceptable tool for gathering food samples. It does not recover the entire contents in the stomach, only items recently eaten, but this limiting factor actually has certain advantages over the analysis of a complete gut. A sampling of everything in the gut can be inaccurate because organisms with soft bodies, such as black-fly larvae or caddisfly pupae, are digested and passed more rapidly than hard-bodied forms such as stonefly nymphs. Source for information: Hess, A. D. and J. H. Rainwater. 1939. "A method for measuring the food preferences of trout." *Copeia*, No. 3, pp. 154-157.

4. Surface organisms include those aquatic insects that were probably captured from the underside of the meniscus, such as caddisfly pupae and midge pupae, as well as those taken on top of it.

5. Source: Corbet, P. S., and A. Tjonneland. 1955. "The flight activity of twelve species of East African Trichoptera." *Univ. Bergen Arb. Naturv. R.*, 9: 1-49.

6. Source: Brindle, A. 1957. "The effect of temperature and humidity on the flight of Trichoptera." *Ent. Mon. Mag.*, 93: 63-66.

Chapter 11

1. See the illustration on Page 158 for an example of how tube-case makers ventilate.

2. Anderson, N. H. 1967 a. "Biology and downstream drift of some Oregon Trichoptera." *Can. Ent.*, 99: 507-521.

3. This specimen was keyed out by Ken Thompson and his identification was verified by Dr. Oliver Flint.

4. Waters, T. F. 1962. "Diurnal periodicity in the drift of stream invertebrates." *Ecology*, 43 (2): 316-320.

5. It has been proposed that some of the species now in the genus *Hydropsyche* be removed and placed into a new genus: *Symphitopsyche*. Whether or not this new classification will be completely accepted by entomologists remains to be seen, but *Symphitopsyche*, which includes important trout-stream species such as *H. cockerelli*, *H. oslari*, *H. bifida*, *H. bronta*, and *H. slossonae*, is already beginning to appear in the professional literature. See: Ross, H. H., and J. D. Unzicker. 1977. "The relationships of the genera of American Hydropsychinae as indicated by phallic structure (Trichoptera: Hydropsychidae)." *J. Georgia Entomol. Soc.*, 12: 298-312.

6. Sources for information: Gordon, A. E., and J. B. Wallace. 1975. "Distribution of the family Hydropsychidae (Trichoptera) in the Savannah River basin of North Carolina, South Carolina, and Georgia." *Hydrobiologia*, 46: 405-423; Alstad, D. N. 1979. "Comparative biology of common Utah Hydropsychidae (Trichoptera). Unpublished. University of Utah.

7. Don Alstad, an expert on the Hydropsychidae family, visited us at our streamside cabin that summer and with a microscope tentatively indentified the light-trap specimens as *C. campyla*.

8. *Cheumatopsyche* species are not the only caddisflies that can undermine the *Pteronarcys* hatch. Other fast-water species, including *Glossosoma velona* (Little Tan Short-Horn Sedge), are found in the same types of rivers and emerge at the same time. Also, in a few spring-fed rivers with a mix of slow and fast sections, slow-water forms such as *Oecetis disjuncta* (Long-Horn Sedge) and *Amiocentrus aspilus* (Little Western Weedy-Water Sedge) can spill over into adjacent areas and create similar situations.

9. Sources for information: Brusven, M. A. 1970. "Drift periodicity and upstream dispersion of stream insects." *J. Entomol. Soc. Brit. Columbia*, 67; Anderson, N. H. 1967. "Biology and downstream drift of some Oregon Trichoptera. *Can. Entomol.* 99: 507-521.

10. Original study: Anderson, N. H., and E. Grafius. 1975. "Utilization and processing of allochthonous material by stream Trichoptera." *Verh. int. Ver. Limnol.*, 19: 3083-3088.

11. Riek, E. F. 1970. "Trichoptera." *The Insects of Australia*, pp. 741-764. Melbourne: C.S.I.R.O. and Melbourne University Press.

12. Regional surveys of course include stillwater species. If this statement was limited to running-water species then the Hydropsychidae, at least in the percentage of individual insects collected, would probably be the dominant family.

13. Cummins, K. W. 1964. "Factors limiting the microdistribution of larvae of the caddisflies *Pycnopsyche lepida* (Hagen) and *Pycnopsyche guttifer* (Walker) in a Michigan stream (Trichoptera: Limnephilidae)." *Ecol. Monogr.*, 34 (3): 271-295.

14. H. H. Ross, in "The caddis flies, or Trichoptera, of Illinois" noted that *P. radiatus* larvae were carried from a neighboring state into Illinois, far downstream from their normal habitat.

15. In a talk that Dave Engerbretson and I had with Dr. Merlyn Brusven, who reported this scavenging activity for larvae of *Psychoglypha*, *Dicosmoecus*, and *Lepidostoma* in his paper, "Sarcophagous habits of Trichoptera larvae on

dead fish," he stated unequivocally that these larvae were feeding on the flesh of these freshly killed fish for its own food value, and not for the microorganisms that would be present with advanced decay.

16. This quote is from Dr. Anderson's *The Distribution and Biology of Oregon Trichoptera*.

17. Dr. Stanley Jewett, in his section on caddisflies in *McClane's Standard Fishing Encyclopedia*, used the common name Autumn Phantom for one species, *D. atripes*, in this genus.

18. Edwards, S. W. 1966. "An annotated list of the Trichoptera of middle and west Tennessee." *J. Tenn. Acad. Sci.*, 13(4): 116-128.

19. Anderson, N. H., and Wold, J. L. 1972. "Emegence trap collections of Trichoptera from an Oregon stream." *Can. Ent.*, 104(2): 189-201.

20. The special need for great flies, not just generally good ones, to match *Rhyacophila* can be explained by one of my primary laws of selectivity: *the more distinctive the natural insect the greater the need for a proper imitation.*

21. Leonard, J. W., and F. A. Leonard. 1949. "An annotated list of Michigan Trichoptera." *Occ. Pap. Univ. Mich. Mus. Zool.*, 522.

22. Denning, D. G. 1948. "A review of Rhyacophilidae (Trichoptera)." *Can. Ent.*, 80: 97-117.

Chapter 12

1. This key is from *An Introduction to the Aquatic Insects of North America* by R. W. Merritt and K. W. Cummins.

Bibliography

The scientific papers and books listed below were used as references for *Caddisflies*. Four of the entries in the bibliography served an additional important function as general resource material. In order of importance to the author they were: *The Larvae of the North American Caddisfly Genera* by G. B. Wiggins, a complete work on the biology of caddisfly larvae; "The Caddis Flies, or Trichoptera, of Illinois" by H. H. Ross, the classic work on caddisflies; "The Distribution and Biology of the Oregon Trichoptera" by N. H. Anderson, an indispensable source of information for the West-Coast angler; and *Evolution and Classification of the Mountain Caddisflies* by H. H. Ross, the source of information on the evolution of this insect order.

ANDERSON, N. H. 1967b. Biology and downstream drift of some Oregon Trichoptera. *Can. Ent.* 99(5):507-21.

———— 1976. The distribution and biology of the Oregon Trichoptera. *Ore. Agric. Exp. Sta. Tech. Bull.* 134:1-160.

ANDERSON, N. H., and BOURNE, J. R. 1974. Bionomics of three species of glossosomatid caddis flies (Trichoptera: Glossosomatidae) in Oregon. *Can. J. Zool.* 52(3):405-11.

ANDERSON, N. H., and GRAFIUS, E. 1975. Utilization and processing of allochthonous material by stream Trichoptera. *Verh. Int. Ver. Limnol.* 19:3083-88.

ANDERSON, N. H., and WOLD, J. L. 1972. Emergence trap collections of Trichoptera from an Oregon stream. *Can. Ent.* 104(2):189-201.

BALDUF, W. V. 1939. *The Bionomics of Entomophagous Insects*, pt. II. St. Louis: John S. Swift.

BETTEN, C. 1902. The larva of the caddis fly, *Molanna cinerea* Hagen. *J. N. Y. Ent. Soc.* 10:147-54.

———— 1934. The caddis flies or Trichoptera of New York State. *Bull. N. Y. St. Mus.* 292.

———— 1950. The genus *Pycnopsyche* (Trichoptera). *Ann. Ent. Soc. Am.* 43(4):508-22.

BJARNOV, N., and THORUP, J. 1970. A simple method of rearing running-water insects, with some preliminary results. *Arch. Hydrobiol.* 67(2):201-9.

BLICKLE, R. L. 1979. Hydroptilidae (Trichoptera) of America North of Mexico. *New Hampshire Agricultural Experiment Station Bull.* 509.

BLICKLE, R. L., and MORSE, W. J. 1966. The caddis flies (Trichoptera) of Maine, excepting the family Hydroptilidae. *Maine Agric. Exp. Sta. Tech. Bull.* T-24:1-12.

BRUSVEN, M. A. 1970. Drift periodicity and upstream dispersion of stream insects. *J. Entomol. Soc. Brit. Col.* 67.

BRUSVEN, M. A., and SCOGGAN, A. C. 1969. Sarcophagous habits of Trichoptera larvae on dead fish. *Ent. News* 80:103-5.

CHAPMAN, D. W., and DEMORY, R. L. 1963. Seasonal changes in the food ingested by aquatic insect larvae and nymphs in two Oregon streams. *Ecology* 44(1):140-46.

CLOUD, T. J., and STEWART, K. W. 1974. Seasonal fluctuations and periodicity in the drift of caddisfly larvae (Trichoptera) in the Brazos River, Texas. *Ann. Ent. Soc. Am.* 67(5):805-11.

COFFMAN, W. P., and CUMMINS, K. W., and WUYCHECK, J. C. 1971. Energy flow in a woodland stream ecosystem: I. Tissue support trophic structure of the autumnal community. *Arch. Hydrobiol.* 68(2):232-76.

CORBET, P. S. 1966. Diel periodicities of emergence and oviposition in riverine Trichoptera. *Can. Ent.* 98:1025-34.

—— 1966. Parthenogenesis in caddisflies (Trichoptera). *Can. J. Zool.* 44(5):981-82.

CUMMINS, K. W. 1964. Factors limiting the microdistribution of larvae of the caddisflies *Pycnopsyche lepida* (Hagen) and *Pycnopsyche guttifer* (Walker) in a Michigan stream (Trichoptera: Limnephilidae). *Ecol. Monogr.* 34(3):271-95.

—— 1973. Trophic relations of aquatic insects. *A Rev. Ent.* 18:183-206.

DENNING, D. G. 1937. The biology of some Minnesota Trichoptera. *Trans. Am. Ent. Soc.* 63:17-43.

—— 1943. The Hydropsychidae of Minnesota (Trichoptera). *Entomologica Am.* 23:101-71.

—— 1948a. A review of Rhyacophilidae (Trichoptera). *Can. Ent.* 80:97-117.

—— 1950. Order Trichoptera, the caddisflies, pp. 12-23 in *The Insects of North Carolina* (2nd suppl.), D. L. Wray, ed. N. Carolina Dept. Agric.

—— 1956. Trichoptera. pp. 237-70, in *Aquatic Insects of California*, R. L. Usinger, ed. Berkeley and Los Angeles: Univ. of California Press.

—— 1970. The genus *Psychoglypha* (Trichoptera: Limnephilidae). *Can. Ent.* 102(1):15-30.

DODDS, G. S., and HISAW, F. L. 1925. Ecological studies on aquatic insects. III. Adaptations of caddisfly larvae to swift streams. *Ecology* 6(2):123-37.

EDWARDS, S. W., 1966. An annotated list of the Trichoptera of middle and west Tennessee. *J. Tenn. Acad. Sci.* 41:(4):116-28.

—— 1973. Texas caddis flies. *Texas J. Sci.* 24:491-516.

EDWARDS, S. W., and ARNOLD, C. R. 1961. The caddis flies of the San Marcos River. *Tex. J. Sci.* 13(4):398-415.

ELKINS, W. A. 1936. The immature stages of some Minnesota Trichoptera. *Ann. Ent. Soc. Am.* 29(4):656-81.

ELLIOT, J. M. 1970. The diel activity patterns of caddis larvae (Trichoptera). *J. Zool. Lond.* 160(3):279-90.

ETNIER, D. A. 1965. An annotated list of the Trichoptera of Minnesota with a description of new species. *Ent. News* 76:141-52.

FELDMETH, C. R. 1970. The respiratory energetics of two species of stream caddis fly larvae in relation to water flow. *Comp. Biochem. Physiol.* 32:193-202.

FISHER, S. G., and LIKENS, G. E. 1973. Energy Flow in Bear Brook, New Hampshire: An integrative approach to stream ecosystem metabolism. *Ecol. Monog.* 43:421-39.

FLINT, O. S. 1956. The life history and biology of the genus *Frenesia* (Trichoptera: Limnephilidae). *Bull. Brooklyn Ent. Soc.* 51(4, 5):93-108.

—— 1958. The larva and terrestrial pupa of *Ironoquia parvula* (Trichoptera, Limnephilidae). *J. N. Y. Ent. Soc.* 66:59-62.

—— 1959. The immature stages of *Lype diversa* (Banks) (Trichoptera, Psychomyiidae). *Bull. Brooklyn Ent. Soc.* 54(2):44-47.

—— 1960. Taxonomy and biology of Nearctic limnephilid larvae (Trichoptera), with special reference to species in eastern United States. *Entomologica Am.*, n. s. 40:1-117.

—— 1961a. The immature stages of the Arctopsychinae occurring in eastern North America (Trichoptera: Hydropsychidae). *Ann. Ent. Soc. Am.* 54(1):5-11.

—— 1962c. Larvae of the caddis fly genus *Rhyacophila* in eastern North America (Trichoptera: Rhyacophilidae). *Proc. U. S. Nat. Mus.* 113(3464):465-93.

——1964a. Notes on some Nearctic Psychomyiidae with special reference to their larvae (Trichoptera). *Proc U. S. Nat. Mus.* 115(3491):467-81.

FLINT, O. S., and WIGGINS, G. B. 1961. Records and descriptions of North American species in the genus *Lepidostoma*, with a revision of the *Vernalis* group (Trichoptera: Lepidostomatidae). *Can. Ent.* 93(4):279-97.

FOX, H. M., and SIDNEY, J. 1953. The influence of dissolved oxygen on the respiratory movements of caddis larvae. *J. Exp. Biol.* 30(2):235-37.

FREMLING, C. R. 1960. Biology and possible control of nuisance caddisflies of the upper Mississippi River. *Iowa State Univ. Sci. Tech., Res. Bull.* 483:856-79.

GALLEPP, G. W. 1974a. Diel periodicity in the behaviour of the caddisfly *Brachycentrus americanus* (Banks). *Freshwat. Biol.* 4(2):193-204.

—— 1974b. Behavioral ecology of *Brachycentrus occidentalis* Banks during the pupation period. *Ecology* 55(6):1283-94.

GIVENS, D. R. 1976. Synopsis of western Arctopsychinae (Trichoptera: Hydropsychidae). Unpubl. Master's Thesis, Central Washington St. College, Ellensburg.

GORDON, A. E. 1974. A synopsis and phylogenetic outline of the Nearctic members of *Cheumatopsyche. Proc. Acad. Nat. Sci. Philad.* 126(9):117-60.

HICKIN, N. E. 1967. *Caddis Larvae*. London. Hutchinson.

HILL-GRIFFIN, A. L. 1912. New Oregon Trichoptera. *Ent. News* 23:12-21.

HILSENHOFF, W. L. 1975a. Aquatic insects of Wisconsin, with generic keys and notes on biology, ecology and distribution. *Tech. Bull. Wisc. Dept. Nat. Res.* 89-1-52.

HINTON, H. E. 1949. On the function, origin, and classification of pupae. *Proc. Trans. S. Lond. Ent. Nat. Hist. Soc.* 1947-48:111-54.

—— 1971. Some neglected phases in metamorphosis. *Proc. Roy. Ent. Soc. Lond.* (C)35:55-64.

HODKINSON, I. D. 1975. A community analysis of the benthic insect fauna of an abandoned beaver pond. *J. Anim. Ecol.*

44(2):533-51.

HYLAND, K., JR. 1948. New records of Pennsylvania caddis flies (Trichoptera). *Ent. News* 59:38-40.

HYNES, H. B. N. 1970. *The Ecology of Running Waters.* Toronto: Univ. of Toronto Press.

JUDD, W. W. 1953. A study of the population of insects emerging as adults from the Dundas Marsh, Hamilton, Ontario, during 1948. *Am. Midl. Nat.* 49:801-24.

KNOWLTON, G. F., and HARMSTON, F. C. 1938. Notes on Utah Plecoptera and Trichoptera. *Ent. News* 49:284-86.

KRIVDA, W. V. 1961. Notes on the distribution and habitat of *Chilostigma areolatum* (Walker) in Manitoba (Trichoptera: Limnephilidae). *J. N. Y. Ent. Soc.* 69:68-70.

LEONARD, J. W., and LEONARD, F. A. 1949. An annotated list of Michigan Trichoptera. *Occ. Papers of the Mus. of Zoo.* 522.

LLOYD, J. T. 1915a. Notes on *Astenophylax argus* Harris (Trichoptera). *J. N. Y. Ent. Soc.* 23(1):57-60.

——— 1921. The biology of North American caddis fly larvae. *Bull. Lloyd Libr.* 21.

MACKAY, R. J. 1968. Seasonal variation in the structure of stream insect communities. M. Sc. thesis, McGill University.

——— 1969. Aquatic insect communities of a small stream on Mont St. Hilaire, Quebec. *J. Fish. Res. Bd. Can.* 26(5):1157-83.

——— 1972. Temporal patterns in life history and flight behaviour of *Pycnopsyche gentilis, P. luculenta,* and *P. scabripennis* (Trichoptera: Limnephilidae). *Can. Ent.* 104(11):1819-35.

MACKAY, R. J., and KALFF, J. 1973. Ecology of two related species of caddis fly larvae in the organic substrates of a woodland stream. *Ecology* 54(3):499-511.

MACKAY, R. J., and WIGGINS, G. B. 1979. Ecological diversity in Trichoptera. *Ann. Rev. Entomol.* 24:185-208.

MECOM, J. O. 1972a. Feeding habits of Trichoptera in a mountain stream. *Oikos* 23:401-7.

——— 1972b. Productivity and distribution of Trichoptera larvae in a Colorado mountain stream. *Hydrobiologia* 40:151-76.

MECOM, J. O., and CUMMINS, K. W. 1964. A preliminary study of the trophic relationships of the larvae of *Brachycentrus americanus* (Banks) (Trichoptera: Brachycentridae). *Trans. Am. Microsc. Soc.* 83(2):233-43.

MERRILL, D. 1965. The stimulus for case-building activity in caddis-worms (Trichoptera). *J. Exp. Zool.* 158(1):123-30.

MILNE, L. J. 1934. Studies in North American Trichoptera, 1. Cambridge, Mass.

MINCKLEY, W. L. 1963. The ecology of a spring stream, Doe Run, Meade County, Kentucky. *Wildl. Monogr.* 11.

MORSE, J. C. 1972. The genus *Nyctiophylax* in North America. *J. Kans. Ent. Soc.* 45(2):172-81.

——— 1975. A phylogeny and revision of the caddisfly genus *Ceraclea* (Trichoptera, Leptoceridae). *Cont. Am. Ent. Inst.* 11(2).

MORSE, W. J., and BLICKLE, R. L. 1953. A check list of the Trichoptera (caddisflies) of New Hampshire. *Ent. News* 64:68-73, 97-102.

MURPHY, H. E. 1919. Observations on the egg laying of the caddice-fly *Brachycentrus nigrisoma* Banks, and on the habits of the young larvae. *J. N. Y. Ent. Soc.* 27:154-59.

MUTTKOWSKI, R. A., and SMITH, G. M. 1929. The food of trout-stream insects in Yellowstone National Park. *Roosevelt Wild Life Ann.* 2(2):241-63.

NEWELL, R. L. 1976. Yellowstone River study. *Montana Fish and Game Report.*

NEWELL, R. L., and MINSHALL, G. W. 1977. An annotated list of the aquatic insects of southeastern Idaho, Part II: Trichoptera. *Great Basin Naturalist* 37(2):353-57.

NEWELL, R. L., and POTTER, D. S. 1973. Distribution of some Montana caddisflies (Trichoptera). *Proc. Mont. Acad. Sci.* 33:12-21.

NIELSEN, A. 1948. Postembryonic development and biology of the Hydroptilidae. *Kgl. Danske Vidensk. Selsk. Biol. Skr.* 5(1).

NIMMO, A. P. 1965. A new series of *Psychoglypha* Ross from western Canada, with notes on several other species of Limnephilidae (Trichoptera). *Can. J. Zool.* 43(5):781-87.

——— 1966. A list of Trichoptera taken at Montreal and Chambly, Quebec, with descriptions of three new species. *Can. Ent.* 98(7):688-93.

——— 1971. The adult Rhyacophilidae and Limnephilidae (Trichoptera) of Alberta and eastern British Columbia and their post-glacial origin. *Quaest. Ent.* 7:3-234.

——— 1974. The adult Trichoptera (Insecta) of Alberta and eastern British Columbia, and their post-glacial origin. II. The families Glossosomatidae and Philopotamidae. *Quaest. Ent.* 10:315-49.

NOVAK, K., and SEHNAL, F. 1963. The development cycle of some species of the genus Limnephilus (Trichoptera). *Cas. Cs. Spol. Ent.* 60(1-2):68-80.

NOYES, A. A. 1914. The biology of the net-spinning Trichoptera of Cascadilla Creek. *Ann. Ent. Soc. Am.* 7(4):251-72.

PEARSON, W. D., and KRAMER, R. H. 1972. Drift and production of two aquatic insects in a mountain stream. *Ecol. Monogr.* 42(3):365-85.

PERCIVAL, E., and WHITEHEAD, H. 1929. A quantitative study of the fauna of some types of streambed. *J. Ecol.* 17:282-314.

PHILIPSON, G. N. 1953a. A method of rearing trichopterous larvae collected from swift-flowing waters. *Proc. Roy. Ent. Soc. Lond.* (A)28(1-3):15-16.

RABENI, C. F., and MINSHALL, G. W. 1977. Factors affecting microdistribution of stream enthic insects. *Oikos* 29:33-43.

RESH, V. H. 1976. The biology and immature stages of the caddisfly genus *Ceraclea* in eastern North America (Trichoptera: Leptoceridae). *Ann. Ent. Soc. Am.* 69(6):1039-61.

——— 1975. A distributional study of the caddisflies of Kentucky. *Trans. Ky. Acad. Sci.* 36:6-16.

RESH, V. H., MORSE, J. C., and WALLACE, I. D. 1976. The evolution of the sponge-feeding habit in the caddisfly genus *Ceraclea* (Trichoptera: Leptoceridae). *Ann. Ent. Soc. Am.* 69(5):937-41.

RESH, V. H., and UNZICKER, J. D. 1975. Water quality monitoring and aquatic organisms: the importance of species identification. *J. Wat. Pollut. Control Fed.* 47(1):9-19.

RIEK, E. F. 1970. Trichoptera, pp. 741-64, in *The Insects of Australia.* Melbourne: C.S.I.R.O. and Melbourne Univ. Press.

ROEMHILD, G. 1980. Pheromone glands of microcaddisflies, (Trichoptera: Hydroptilidae). *Jour. of Morphology* 163:9-12.

ROSS, H. H. 1938. Descriptions of Nearctic caddis flies (Trichoptera) with special reference to the Illinois species. *Bull. Ill. Nat. Hist. Surv.* 21(4):101-83.

——— 1944. The caddis flies, or Trichoptera, of Illinois. *Bull. Ill. Nat. Hist. Surv.* 23(1).

——— 1946. A review of the Neartic Lepidostomatidae (Trichoptera). *Ann. Ent. Soc. Am.* 39(2):265-91.

——— 1947. Descriptions and records of North American Trichoptera, with synoptic notes. *Trans. Am. Ent. Soc.* 73:125-68.

——— 1950. Synoptic notes on some Nearctic limnephilid caddisflies (Trichoptera, Limnephilidae). *Am. Midl. Nat.* 43(2):410-29.

——— 1956. *Evolution and Classification of the Mountain Caddisflies.* Urbana: Univ. of Illinois Press.

——— 1964. Evolution of caddisworm cases and nets. *Am. Zoologist* 4:209-20.

——— 1967. The evolution and past dispersal of the Trichoptera. *A. Rev. Ent. 12:169-206.*

ROSS, H. H., and GIBBS, D. G. 1973. The subfamily relationships of the Dipseudopsinae (Trichoptera, Polycentropodidae). *J. Georgia Ent. Soc.* 8(4):312-16.

ROSS, H. H., and MERKLEY, D. R. 1952. An annotated key to the Nearctic males of *Limnephilus* (Trichoptera, Limnephilidae). *Am. Midl. Nat.* 47(2):435-55.

ROSS, H. H., and SPENCER, G. J. 1952. A preliminary list of the Trichoptera of British Columbia. *Proc. Ent. Soc. British Columbia (1951)* 48:43-51.

ROSS, H. H., and UNZICKER, J. D. 1977. The relationships of the genera of American Hydropsychinae as indicated by phallic structures (Trichoptera, Hydropsychidae). *J. Georgia Entomol. Soc.* 12(4):298-312.

ROY, D., and HARPER, P. P. 1975. Nouvelles mentions de trichopteres du Quebec et description de *Limnephilus nimmoi* sp. nov. (Limnephilidae). *Can. J. Zool.* 53:1080-88.

SCHMID, F. 1950d. Le genre *Hydatophylax* Wall (Trichopt. Limnophilidae). *Mitt. Schweiz. Ent. Ges.* 23(3):265-96.

——— 1951. Le genre *Ironoquia* Bks. (Trichopt. Limnophilid.) *Mitt. Schweiz. Ent. Ges.* 24(3):317-28.

——— 1952c. Le groupe de *Chilostigma. Arch. Hydrobiol.* 47(1):75-163.

——— 1953. Contribution a l'etude de la sous-famille des Apataniinae (Trichoptera, Limnophilidae). II. *Tijdschr. Ent.* 97(1-2):1-74.

——— 1968a. La famille des Arctopsychides (Trichoptera). *Mem. Ent. Soc. Quebec* 1.

——— 1970. Le genre *Rhyacophila* et la famille des Rhyacophilidae (Trichoptera). *Mem. Ent. Soc. Can.* 66.

SCHMID, F., and GUPPY, R. 1952. An annotated list of Trichoptera collected on southern Vancouver Island. *Proc. Ent. Soc. British Columbia (1951)* 48:41-42.

SHERBERGER, F. F., and WALLACE, J. B. 1971. Larvae of southeastern species of *Molanna. J. Kans. Ent. Soc.* 44(2):217-24.

SLEIGHT, C. E. 1913. Relations of Trichoptera to their environment. *Jour. N. Y. Ent. Soc.* 21:4-8.

SMITH, S. D. 1965. Distributional and biological records of Idaho caddisflies (Trichoptera). *Ent. News* 76:242-45.

——— 1968a. The Arctopsychinae of Idaho (Trichoptera: Hydropsychidae). *Pan-Pacif. Ent.* 44(2):102-12.

——— 1968b. The *Rhyacophila* of the Salmon River drainage of Idaho with special reference to larvae. *Ann. Ent. Soc. Am.* 61(3):655-74.

——— 1969. Two new species of Idaho Trichoptera with distributional and taxonomic notes on other species. *J. Kans. Ent. Soc.* 42(1):46-53.

SNODGRASS, R. E. 1954. Insect metamorphosis. *Smithson. Misc. Coll.* 122(9).

SOLEM, J. O. 1970. Contributions to the knowledge of the larvae of the family Molannidae (Trichoptera). *Norsk. Ent. Tidsskr.* 17(2):97-102.

THUT, R. N. 1969. Feeding habits of larvae of seven *Rhyacophila* (Trichoptera: Rhyacophilidae) species with notes on other life-history features. *Ann. Ent. Soc. Am.* 62(4):894-98.

UNZICKER, J. D., AGGUS, L., and WARREN, L. O. A preliminary list of the Arkansas Trichoptera. *J. Georgia Ent. Soc.* 5:167-74.

VORHIES, C. T. 1905. Habits and anatomy of the larva of the caddis-fly, *Platyphylax designatus*, Walker. *Trans. Wis Acad. Arts Lett.* 15:108-23.

——— 1909. Studies on the Trichoptera of Wisconsin. *Trans. Wis. Acad. Sci. Arts Lett.* 16:647-738.

WALLACE, J. B. 1975a. The larval retreat and food of *Arctopsyche*; with phylogenetic notes on feeding adaptations in Hydropsychidae larvae (Trichoptera). *Ann. Ent. Soc. Am.* 68(1):167-73.

——— 1975b. Food partitioning in net-spinning Trichoptera larvae: *Hydropsyche venularis, Cheumatopsyche etrona*, and *Macronema zebratum* (Hydropsychidae). *Ann. Ent. Soc. Am.* 68(3):463-72.

WALLACE, J. B., and MALAS, D. 1976. The fine structure of capture nets of larval Philopotamidae (Trichoptera), with special emphasis on *Dolophilodes distinctus. Can. J. Zool.* 54(10):1788-1802.

WALLACE, J. B., and SHERBERGER, F. F. 1974. The larval retreat and feeding net of *Macronema carolina* Banks (Trichoptera: Hydropsychidae). *Hydrobiologia* 45(2-3):177-84.

WATERS, T. F. 1962. Diurnal periodicity in the drift of stream invertebrates. *Ecology* 43(2): 316-20.

——— 1968. Diurnal periodicity in the drift of a day-active stream invertebrate. *Ecology* 49(1):152-53.

WIGGINS, G. B. 1960b. A preliminary systematic study of the North American larvae of the caddisfly family Phryganeidae (Trichoptera). *Can. J. Zool.* 38(6):1153-70.

——— 1965. Additions and revisions to the genera of North American caddisflies of the family Brachycentridae with special reference to the larval stages (Trichoptera). *Can. Ent.* 97(10):1089-1106.

——— 1973c. Contributions to the systematics of the caddisfly family Limnephilidae (Trichoptera). *I. Life Sci. Cont., Roy. Ont. Mus.* 94.

——— 1975. Contributions to the systematics of the caddisfly family Limnephilidae (Trichoptera). *II. Can. Ent.* 107(3):325-36.

——— 1976. Contributions to the systematics of the caddis-fly family Limnephilidae (Trichoptera). III: The genus *Goereilla*, pp. 7-19, in *Proc. of the First Int. Symp. on Trichoptera, Dunz am See (Austria), 1974*, H. Malicky, ed. The Hague: Junk.

——— 1977. *Larvae of the North American Caddisfly Genera.* Toronto: Univ. Toronto Press.

WILLIAMS, D. D., and WILLIAMS, N. E. 1975. A contribution to the biology of *Ironoquia punctatissima* (Trichoptera: Limnephilidae). *Can. Ent.* 107(8):829-32.

WILLIAMS, N. E., and HYNES, H. B. N. 1973. Microdistribution and feeding of the net-spinning caddisflies (Trichoptera) of a Canadian stream. *Oikos* 24:73-84.

WINTERBOURN, M. J. 1971a. The life histories and trophic relationships of the Trichoptera of Marion Lake, British Columbia. *Can. J. Zool.* 49(5):623-35.

——— 1971b. An ecological study of *Banksiola crotchi* Banks (Trichoptera, Phryganeidae) in Marion Lake, British Columbia. *Can. J. Zool.* 49(5):637-45.

WOLD, J. 1974. Systematics of the genus *Rhyacophila* (Trichoptera: Rhyacophilidae) in western North America with special reference to the immature stages. Unpubl. Master's Thesis, Oregon St. Univ., Corvallis.

YAMAMOTO, T., and ROSS, H. H. 1966. A phylogenetic outline of the caddisfly genus *Mystacides* (Trichoptera: Leptoceridae). *Can. Ent.* 98(6):627-32.

YAMAMOTO, T., and WIGGINS, G. B. 1964. A comparative study of the North American species in the caddisfly genus *Mystacides* (Trichoptera: Leptoceridae). *Can. J. Zool.* 42(6):1105-26.

Index

Italicized numbers indicate illustrations